A JACOBEAN JOURNAL
1603–1606

G. B. HARRISON

Author of:—

Elizabethan Plays and Players—1940—Routledge.
Shakespeare at Work—1933—Routledge.
An Elizabethan Journal 1591-4—1928.
A Second Elizabethan Journal 1595-8—1931.
A Last Elizabethan Journal 1599-1603—1933.
    Reprinted in one vol. as:
The Elizabethan Journals—1938—*Routledge.*
Shakespeare—1927—Benn's Sixpenny Library, 9th edition, 1938.
John Bunyan: a study in personality—1928—Dent.
Elizabethan England—1930—Benn's Sixpenny Library.
The Life and Death of Robert Devereux, Earl of Essex—1937—Cassell.
The Day Before Yesterday: a Journal of 1936-1938—Cobden-Sanderson.

                                         etc.

Editor of:—

The Bodley Head Quartos, 15 vols., 1922-6—Lane.
The Pilgrim's Progress, 1928—Nonesuch Press.
The Church Book of Bunyan Meeting, 1928—Dent.
The Diary of Agnes Beaumont, 1928—Constable.
Breton's Melancholic Humours, 1929—Scholartis.
The Trial of the Lancaster Witches, 1929—Peter Davies.
De Maisse's Journal, 1931 (with R. A. Jones)—Nonesuch.
Guilpin's Skialethia, 1931—Shakespeare Association Facsimiles.
The Letters of Queen Elizabeth, 1935—Cassell.
Day's Isle of Dogs, 1936—Shakespeare Association Facsimiles.
The Penguin Shakespeares, 1937-8—Penguin Books.

                                   etc., etc.

General Editor of:—

The Shakespeare Association Facsimiles, 1931-8.
A Companion to Shakespeare Studies, 1934 (with Harley Granville-Barker)—
    Cambridge.

A
JACOBEAN JOURNAL

BEING A RECORD
OF THOSE THINGS MOST TALKED OF
DURING THE YEARS
1603–1606

By
G. B. HARRISON

LONDON
GEORGE ROUTLEDGE AND SONS, LTD.
Broadway House, Carter Lane, E.C.4

First published 1941
Revised and Reprinted 1946

PRINTED IN GREAT BRITAIN BY
LUND HUMPHRIES
LONDON · BRADFORD

CONTENTS OF A JACOBEAN JOURNAL

INTRODUCTION

THE *Jacobean Journal* is a sequel to the *Elizabethan Journals*, and its purpose the same: to record those things most talked of during four memorable years. There is a common misconception that the last forty years of the sixteenth century were wholly glorious, and the first forty of the seventeenth mainly regrettable; yet it is often forgotten that the greatest achievements of 'Elizabethan' literature and learning were written in the reign of King James. In the brief period covered by this *Journal* were begun, completed, or first published such works as *Hamlet, Macbeth, Lear, Volpone, The Advancement of Learning*, Florio's translation of the *Essays* of Montaigne, and the Authorized Version of the Bible.

Nor were events less interesting in these months than in the preceding years. The death of the old Queen had long been anticipated with dread as the moment when anarchy would again break over England. Thanks to the foresight, wisdom, and intrigue of Sir Robert Cecil, King James succeeded without opposition, to the amazed surprise and delirious joy of Englishmen (p. 3). After an astonishing welcome everywhere, the King reached London on 7th May (p. 24), nine days after the last progress of Queen Elizabeth (pp. 16–19).

The first impressions of Englishmen were favourable (pp. 39, 45). King James lacked the ceremonious dignity of Queen Elizabeth, and her love of cheering crowds; but there was no hint as yet that—as Macaulay put it in his florid style—'Nature and education had done their best to produce a finished specimen of all that a king ought not to be. His awkward figure, his rolling eye, his rickety walk, his nervous tremblings, his slobbering mouth, his broad Scotch accent, were imperfections which might have been found in the best and greatest men. Their effect, however, was to make James and his office objects of

vii

contempt, and to dissolve those associations which had been created by the noble bearing of preceding monarchs, and which were in themselves no inconsiderable force to royalty.'

Whatever may have been the King's physical deficiencies in later life, there is no trace of any contempt for his person. His failings were soon noted (pp. 39, 45). He lacked that instinct for understanding what his subjects were feeling which was one of the Queen's greatest gifts. This is not surprising; he was a foreigner, who failed moreover to realize that most of his English subjects were less intelligent than himself.

Elizabeth's England was an uneasy inheritance. The long war with Spain was as costly as ever, for the garrisons in the Low Countries were being maintained. In Ireland Tyrone had at last submitted; but both wars left the Crown heavily in debt, and the temper of the nation frayed and uneasy. Queen Elizabeth had magnificently soothed the discontents of her last Parliament but the general causes of irritation remained. Unfortunately too many malcontents had hoped that at the death of the Queen all troubles would cease in a new golden age; and James himself had been overgenerous with his promises. The easy optimism of the hopeful and the greedy was disappointed, and signs of a reaction soon appeared. The grievances were various and discordant; such matters, their origins and motives, belong rather to history than to a journal.

The first four years of the King's reign were full of incident, even if there were no heroic actions to be set alongside the defeat of the Armada or the sack of Cadiz. The King had no sooner reached London than the plague broke out (p. 33); and it spread so rapidly that by August the weekly death rate was over 2,000, reaching a climax at the end of the month with 3,035 deaths (p. 59). The plague interfered with the Coronation, and sent the Court on progress to the great disturbance of all public business.

Meanwhile new excitements were caused by the plots which immediately involved the priests Watson and Clarke, and soon implicated Sir Walter Ralegh and Lord Cobham and others.

The trials of the conspirators at Winchester in the autumn (pp. 73–82) were sensational even to a generation used to such spectacles, but certainly not prepared for the amazing reprieve on 9th December (pp. 86–90). By the end of the year 1603 the Court was again in the neighbourhood of London, and the first of the long series of Christmas masques was staged at Hampton Court (p. 90). Here also, early in 1604, was held the great Conference between the King and the Anglican and Puritan divines (pp. 95–104) which resulted incidentally in the Authorized Version of the Bible but immediately in each party being more convinced than ever of the wrongheadedness of the other.

Then came the first of the many scenes of elaborate pageantry and triumph when King and Court made royal progress through the City of London on 15th March (p. 110), as prelude to the meeting of the first Parliament of the reign, and attempts to grapple with some of the major political and social problems of the time. In the summer England and Spain were officially at peace (p. 156), and in the autumn the long siege of Ostend at last came to an end (pp. 159–160).

The peace had curious and unexpected results. Certain gentlemen who had hitherto lived by privateering were now out of employ, and thinking of some means of easy wealth devised the plantations of Guiana and Virginia. Both ventures failed dismally, but the sequels belong to a later year.

The year 1605 (afterwards named The Black Year) began appropriately with the Masque of Blackness at Court (p. 181). Prophecies, anxieties and confusions accumulated. In August the King paid his first state visit to the University of Oxford, where he made the best of opportunities to display his learning. Late in the autumn he returned to London, and to the discovery of the great Gunpowder Plot, which for some weeks overshadowed everything else. Few events have more profoundly stirred Englishmen. The hysterical scenes in the following March (pp. 286–7) when the King's death was falsely reported were some indication of the state of national nerves.

The year 1606 opened with renewed sensations over the Plot: the trials of the chief conspirators, the exciting arrests of others implicated, including Father Garnet, who was allowed to live until 3rd May, when he too was executed with the usual bloody ceremonial (pp. 299–302). The last of the public proceedings connected with the Plot concluded on 27th June, when the Earl of Northumberland was drastically, though unjustly, punished in the Star Chamber (p. 315). In the summer the Court welcomed the first foreign Sovereign to visit England for two generations. King Christian of Denmark came over to see his sister, Queen Anne. The notorious debauchery (p. 325) of this affair brought home to courtiers of an older generation the regrettable changes in high society, so different from the home life of Queen Elizabeth.

During these years there was the usual crop of scandals, crimes and mysteries. In Court circles, Sir Robert Dudley's unsuccessful attempt to establish himself as the Earl of Leicester's lawful heir excited many interested parties; whilst Lady Penelope Rich, having won general sympathy when divorced by her disagreeable husband, lost it a month later when she married her lover (pp. 251, 256). Others, such as the sleeping preacher, had their nine days of fame, and some of the cases of murder such as Sir John Fitz' bloody outburst or the horrible affair of the dumb wench (pp. 219–22, 330–1) were more shocking than usual.

Men of letters were less prominent than in former years. Except for plays and a very few outstanding works, the general level of the books printed in these years is dull and low. In the spring of 1603 there was a sudden spate of squinting panegyrics in all tongues wherein the poets, with one wet eye lowered, lamented the great dead, with the other sparkling and elevated gazed hopefully towards her successor. Many writers spent their energies in religious controversy, which was usually pedestrian and conventional, except for the rare forthright common sense of William Bradshaw (pp. 177, 259).

Players prospered. For some years at the end of the Queen's

reign their existence was precarious. The new King immediately adopted the Chamberlain's men as his own company
(p. 30), and they played frequently before him.

Shakespeare pleased his new Master, and several of his plays
were acted at Court, including the *Merchant of Venice* (p. 186),
Othello (p. 165), and *Lear*, which was chosen as suitable for a
Christmas entertainment (p. 349). Ben Jonson distinguished
himself in various ways. He was in trouble over *Sejanus* (p. 31)
and again over *Eastward Ho* (p. 231); but he was quickly
established as a writer of Court Masques (pp. 136, 262).
Dramatists, especially those who wrote for the Boys' companies,
were inclined to be saucy (pp. 172, 194, 230), though there
were dangers; and even the mild Daniel found himself, to his
horror and surprise, in a den of lions because the purposes of his
academical play *Philotas* were misunderstood (p. 179).

The method of compilation of these *Journals* has already
been explained in the Preface to the 1938 edition in one volume
and need not here be repeated. In the *Jacobean Journal* I have
again used the sub-title which offended some reviewers who
questioned (but without troubling to discover) how much of the
matter was indeed generally talked of. This charge can seldom
be made against the *Jacobean Journal*, for most of the entries
come either from personal letters or sources available to all; and
indeed anyone who reads through the correspondence of such
accomplished gossips as John Chamberlain or Dudley Carleton
will soon realize that King James's subjects in high places
were even less discreet than some of their modern descendants.
But, as I pointed out in the preface to the *Last Elizabethan
Journal*, such a book as this, collected from sources so diverse
and considerable, cannot be made by any mechanic rule or
rigid academic principle; it must be as much work of art as of
scholarship. As such it should be judged; by the Text, and not
by the references in the Notes.

There were certain difficulties in writing the *Jacobean
Journal* beyond my control. I had hoped that it would follow
closely upon the *Last Elizabethan Journal* which was originally

published in 1933; but slumps and disappointments, national and personal, intervened, and I was constantly interrupted. The *Journal*, however, was three parts finished by the summer of 1939. Then came the War, and with it a period of forced, irksome, and unexpected idleness. Though I now had the leisure, access to certain sources, which I had kept for the end, was denied, for most of the great manuscript collections were hidden away. Nevertheless, the available sources were so considerable—for the records for these four years have been well sifted by such enthusiasts as Nichols or Lodge—that there was enough and to spare. It seemed better to let the book go as it is than to wait for the end of these uncertain times. If, therefore, by the expert 'it shall be found that much is omitted, let it not be forgotten that much likewise is performed,' and that an author who scours all activity for his province perforce knows less of the particular parts than one who hoes in a narrower field of knowledge.

I wish to thank all who have helped me in this work, of whom I would particularly name Mr. R. L. Atkinson, Miss Margaret Dowling, and especially Dr. S. H. Atkins, who read the proofs and compiled the Index.

G. B. HARRISON.

A new edition of the *Jacobean Journal* being called for, certain minor misprints have been set right; other additions and corrections are noted on p. 352. I have again to thank my friend Dr. S. H. Atkins for re-reading text and notes.

G. B. H.

24*th March.* THE DEATH OF QUEEN ELIZÁBETH.

At about 2 of the clock in the morning died Queen Elizabeth at her Manor of Richmond in Surrey, being in her seventieth year, and having reigned 44 years, 5 months and odd days.

THE ACCESSION OF KING JAMES.

At about 10 of the clock, the Council and divers noblemen having been a while in consultation, proclaimed King James to be King of England, France and Ireland, beginning at White-hall upon the green, where Sir Robert Cecil, the Secretary, read the proclamation which he carried in his hand, and after read it again at Cheapside, in the presence of many noblemen, Lords Spiritual and temporal, knights, five trumpets and many heralds. The gates at Ludgate were shut and the portcullis down by the Lord Mayor's command. Whereupon the Lord Treasurer, Buckhurst, with the rest knocked at the gates. The Lord Mayor being there with the Aldermen and the City in arms asked them what they meant to do. The Lords desired the Lord Mayor to open the gates for that, their Queen being dead, they would proclaim the King. The Lord Mayor answered that he would know what King before they should come in, for, said he, 'If you will proclaim any King but he that is right, indeed you shall not come in.'

Then they said that they would proclaim James. Then said the Lord Mayor, 'I am very well contented, for he is my master, liege lord and King. But I will have a pledge to assure me of this; that you mean to do as you say.'

Hereupon the Lord Treasurer took off his collar of esses and put it under the gate, together with the proclamation. Then the Lord Mayor, being well guarded, let them come in, and with great joy they went to the broad place before Paul's and there proclaimed the King.

I

The proclamation, which is signed first (according to ancient custom) by my Lord Mayor and by thirty-seven others, noblemen and Lords of the Council, declareth that forasmuch as it hath pleased Almighty God to call to his mercy out of this transitory life our Sovereign Lady, the high and mighty Prince, Elizabeth, late Queen of England, France and Ireland, by whose death and dissolution, the Imperial Crown of these Realms aforesaid is now absolutely, wholly and solely come to the high and mighty Prince, JAMES, the Sixth, King of Scotland, who is lineally and lawfully descended from the body of Margaret, daughter to the high and renowned Prince, Henry the Seventh, King of England, France and Ireland, his great-grandfather, the said Lady Margaret being lawfully begotten of the body of Elizabeth, daughter to King Edward the Fourth (by which happy conjunction both the houses of York and Lancaster were united to the joy unspeakable of this Kingdom, formerly rent and torn by the long dissension of bloody and civil wars), the same Lady Margaret being also the eldest sister of Henry the Eighth, of famous memory, King of England aforesaid.

Therefore the Lords Spiritual and temporal of the Realm with one full voice and consent of tongue and heart proclaim that the high and mighty Prince James the Sixth, King of Scotland, is now become also our only, lawful, lineal and rightful liege Lord, James the First, King of England, to whom as to our only Prince, adorned (besides his undoubted right) with all the rarest gifts of mind and body, we do acknowledge all faith and constant obedience.

After the proclamation had been read, they went on till they came to the Cross in Cheap; where likewise they again proclaimed the King; and thence to Cornhill by the Exchange towards Tower Hill. The Lord Mayor and the Aldermen sent to the Lieutenant of the Tower, who had drawn up the drawbridge and made fast the outer gate, certifying to him that they were come to proclaim the King, and desired him to accompany them; who sent answer that they should not come there, for if they would proclaim any but the right indeed, he would set them further. Whereupon they came to the Tower Gate and certified him that they meant to proclaim James.

2

He answered that he was his King, Lord and Master, and he would join his best assistance thereto. So he came out and joined with them in the proclamation upon Tower Hill. He also caused the King to be proclaimed within the Tower.

The proclamation was heard with great expectation and silent joy, but no great shouting.   To the astonishment of all men there is no tumult, nor contradiction nor disorder in the City; every man going about his business as readily and securely as though there had been no change, nor any news ever heard of competitors, so that the people, finding the just fear of forty years for want of a known succession to be dissolved in a minute, do so rejoice as few wish the Queen alive again; and at night they showed it by bonfires and ringing of bells. The people are full of expectation and great with hope of the new King's worthiness and of our nation's future greatness; everyone promises himself a share in some famous action to be hereafter performed for his Prince and country.   They assure themselves of the continuance of our Church, Government and doctrine.   Their talk is of advancement of the nobility, of the subsidies and fifteenths taxed in the Queen's time, and how much she died indebted to the Commons, notwithstanding all the charges laid upon them; they half despair of the repayment of their privy seals, and of the loan.   One wishes the Earl of Southampton and others were pardoned and at liberty; others that some men of great place might pay the Queen's debts, for they gathered enough under her.   All long to see our new King.

Nevertheless, it was much observed at the time of the proclamation that the ancient Councillors for the most part showed their sorrow by their countenances, apprehending the greatness of their loss by calling to mind the manifold benefits which they had received during the Queen's life, and doubting perhaps their continuance.   Others tempered their grief with joy, seeming neither glad for the death of the old Prince, nor discontented with the entrance of the new.   But some, that for many favours had been specially bound to the Queen, made semblance above the rest of excessive joy by loud shouts and acclamations, which is imputed in them a kind of levity and unseasonable flattery. Such is the condition of great Princes, more unhappy in this

3

respect than their own subjects, that while they live they are followed by all men and at their death lamented of none.

There were thirty-seven earls and barons that dined this day with Master James Pemberton, one of the Sheriffs of London, and with the others of the Privy Council they sat in Council all that afternoon.

26th March. THE CORPSE OF QUEEN ELIZABETH.

The corpse of the late Queen for some time after her death was in a manner left alone and very mean persons had access to it. This night it was conveyed with multitudes of torches burning from Richmond to Whitehall. The barge, wherein it lay, was covered with black, accompanied by divers Ladies-of-Honour, and some Privy Councillors, with the pensioners and officers of the household following after in other barges. The body is now laid upon a bed of state in the withdrawing chamber, and certain ladies continually attend it till the day of the funerals.

The body was not opened but wrapped in cereclothes and other preservatives. There was some whispering that her brain was somewhat distempered, but there was no such matter; only she held an obstinate silence for the most part, and because she had a persuasion that if she once lay down she should never rise, could not be gotten to bed in a whole week till three days before her death. She made no will, nor gave anything away, so that they which come after shall find a well-furnished house, a rich wardrobe of more than 2,000 gowns with all things else answerable.

THE QUEEN'S DEATH.

There are strange tales of the Queen's death, especially put about by the Papists and some of the Ladies-in-Waiting. It is said that two of them found the Queen of Hearts with a nail of iron knocked through the forehead and thus fastened to the bottom of her chair. Another of the Maids absenting herself for a while from the Queen's Chamber met her, as it seemed, three or four chambers off. Others say that when she was near her end the Archbishop came to see her with other Bishops, but at their sight she was much offended, and

4

bade them be packing, for she was no atheist but she knew full well they were but hedge priests.

Sir Robert Carey was the first to carry the news of her death into Scotland, which he did of his own motion. Yesterday Master George Carew, a Master of the Chancery, and Master Thomas Lake were despatched about other business. There is much posting that way and many run thither of their own errand as if it were nothing else but first come first served. The Lords have sent to know whether the King will come by land or sea, for which purpose there be eight or ten ships ready that were to have gone for the coast of Spain.

During the Queen's sickness some principal Papists were made sure and dangerous companions clapped up among whom Sir Edmund Baynham was committed to the Marshalsea but is now at liberty again.

27th March. THE PAUL'S CROSS SERMON.

The Sermon at Paul's Cross was preached by Master John Hayward from Psalm xxiv, ver. 1, 'The Earth is the Lord's and the fullness thereof,' wherein he spake of the Queen's death, showing how when her Almoner rehearsing to her the Grounds of the Christian Faith, and requiring her assent unto them by some sign, she readily gave it both with hand and eye.

THE CORPSE OF QUEEN ELIZABETH.

Last night whilst the ladies were in their places watching about the Queen's corpse which was fast nailed up in a board coffin, with leaves of lead covered with velvet, her body burst with such a crack that it splitted the wood, lead and cerecloth, so that to-day she was fain to be new trimmed up.

28th March. THE NEW KING WELL RECEIVED.

From all sides come reports that King James is well received in the counties. In Cambridge the accession was proclaimed by the Vice-Chancellor and the Heads of all the Colleges in the open market-place, with great applause. In the north there is general satisfaction, the people being very well content, for they all expected that their houses would have been spoiled and sacked.

30th March. BERWICK HANDED OVER.

The Lord Abbot of Holyrood took possession of Berwick to the King's use on the 28th. He was given the keys and the staff, and then, having administered the oath of allegiance to the Mayor and Governor, he re-delivered the keys and staff in the King's name, declaring that it was his Majesty's good pleasure that they should enjoy all their ancient privileges, charters, and liberties, and not only they, but all other his loving and well-affected subjects.

31st March. SIR ROBERT CAREY'S RIDE.

Sir Robert Carey was the first to tell the King of the Queen's death. He took horse between 9 and 10 o'clock on the morning of the 24th, and that night he reached Doncaster. The next night he came to his own house at Witherington and there took order with his deputies to see the Borders kept in quiet. Very early on the next morning (26th) he took horse for Edinburgh, and came to Norham about noon, but he got a great fall by the way, and his horse with one of his heels struck him a blow on the head that made him shed much blood so that he was forced to ride a soft pace. The King was newly gone to bed when he knocked at the Palace gate, but he was quickly let in, and carried up to the King's chamber. Sir Robert knelt by the King and saluted him by his title of King of England, Scotland, France and Ireland. The King gave him his hand to kiss, and bade him welcome. When Sir Robert had discussed of the manner of the Queen's sickness and death, the King asked him what letters he bore from the Council. He answered that he had none, for they would have stayed him had he not got away by favour of the Marshal. But, said Sir Robert, he had brought the King a blue ring from a fair lady. The King took it, and looked upon it, and said, 'It is enough: I know by this that you are a true messenger.'

Soon afterwards came Master Lewis Pickering, who first brought the King news that he had been proclaimed King of England.

HESITATIONS AT YORK.

The certain news of the Queen's death did not reach the city of York until Sunday, 27th March. Neither did the Lord

Mayor and Aldermen give full credit to it at that time, though they had received it from my Lord Burghley, the Lord President of the Council in the North. The Lord Mayor and the Aldermen had prepared themselves to make proclamation, but such was their doubt of the truth of the Queen's death that they stayed the proceedings and sent their Recorder and two Aldermen to the Lord President to know what certainty his Lordship had. He answered that he had no other intelligence but only by a secret friend whom he believed; but whilst they were in his house there arrived a gentleman of his with a packet of letters from the nobility and late Privy Councillors wherein was related the death of the Queen, and how King James had been proclaimed King in London. The Lord Mayor of York by this time had received the proclamation in print, and forthwith proclaimed it with joyful acclamations.

THE KING'S LETTER TO THE LORD MAYOR.

The King hath written a letter to the Lord Mayor, Aldermen and Commons of the City of London, which is set in print, giving them gracious thanks for their great forwardness in proclaiming his Majesty as our Sovereign and withal assurance that they cannot crave anything fit for the maintenance of all in general and everyone in particular, but it shall be most willingly performed by him whose special care shall ever be to provide for the increase of their present happiness.

1st *April*. THE GENTLEMEN PENSIONERS.

Lord Hunsdon, as Captain of the Gentlemen Pensioners, has written to the King desiring his direction concerning that office, and informing his Majesty of the nature, quality and service of that honourable band. They are in all fifty gentlemen, besides the Captain, the Lieutenant, the Clerk of the Cheque and Gentleman Harbinger, including some of the best and ancientest families in England, and some of the sons of earls and barons, knights and esquires, all thereunto specially recommended by their fitness in office, without any stain or taint of dishonour or disparagement. Both the late Queen and her predecessors have had great use of the service, in the guard and defence of their royal persons, as also in other employment, as well civil as military, at home and abroad; insomuch that it has served them always as a nursery for the breeding up of Deputies of Ireland, Ambassadors into foreign parts, Councillors of State, Captains of the Guard, Governors of places, and Commanders in the wars, both by land and sea. The Guard still remain about the Court to attend the body of the Queen, but are eager to wait upon the King at his entry into the Kingdom.

2nd April. THE DEAD QUEEN.

The Queen's body lies still in Whitehall Palace, which is hung all with black. The Council wait on her continuously with all the accustomed ceremonies down to the very table service as if she were still alive, and so will it continue according to ancient custom until the King gives order for her funeral.

3rd April. THE KING'S BOOKS PRINTED IN ENGLAND.

Three of the King's books are now printing in London, viz., *ΒΑΣΙΛΙΚΟΝ ΔΩΡΟΝ*, or the book of instructions written for the Prince and first printed in Scotland in 1599; *Dæmonology*, a dialogue concerning witches and witchcraft which his Majesty wrote in 1597; and *The True Law of Free Monarchies* or the reciprock and mutual duty betwixt a free King and his natural subjects, printed in 1598 under the name of *C. Φιλόπατρις.*

5th April. A PROCLAMATION CONCERNING OFFICERS OF THE STATE.

Because of the doubts concerning the authority of those officers which derived from the person of the Queen, a proclamation is now made by letters from the King that all persons who at the Queen's decease were lawfully possessed of any office of authority shall continue to hold and execute their places till his Majesty's pleasure be further known. It is moreover commanded that, since the overmuch resort of people to those parts where his Majesty as yet remaineth is inconvenient and may prove dangerous, such concourse shall be forborne, and, above all others, of those persons that have any place of charge either on the sea coast or inland.

6th April. TROUBLES ON THE BORDERS.

Certain of the West Marches to the number of two or three

hundred assembled themselves and committed great robberies
and spoils. Sir William Selby had 200 footmen and 50 horse
out of Berwick garrison, and at his request Master Henry
Wooderington and Master William Fenrick were joined in
commission with him to command all officers and others, as
well Scots as English borderers, to assist them. They marched
along the border with 1,000 horse and the footmen. When they
came to the habitation of those disordered men they found them
fled from their houses, whereof they blew up and razed to the
ground many. In the pursuit some of the offenders were
apprehended, and committed to the castle of Carlisle where
they were executed according to law.

7th April. A JAR AT COURT.

It is said that there hath been a foul jar betwixt Sir Robert
Cecil and the Lord Cobham because, on the death of the Queen,
the Council thought good to appoint another Captain of the
Guard, since Sir Walter Ralegh was then absent; which the
Lord Cobham took in foul dudgeon as if it had been a device of
Sir Robert, and would have been himself deputy to Sir Walter
rather than have any other. Lord Cobham is now gone to the
King.

A BELATED ANSWER TO DOLEMAN'S 'CONFERENCE.'

Sir John Hayward hath now sent to the press an *Answer* to the
first part of that book called *A Conference concerning Succession*,
published under the name of R. Doleman, that caused such stirs
about eight years ago, which is dedicated to his Majesty.
Herein it is maintained that the people have no lawful power to
remove the present authority of Princes or to deny the succession
according to proximity of blood. He declareth further that his
book of the deposition of King Richard the Second and usurpa-
tion of King Henry the Fourth (that occasioned so much
suspicion in my Lord of Essex's time) was undertaken with
particular respect to his Majesty's just title of succession in this
realm.

8th April. THE WAR IN THE LOW COUNTRIES.

The Council are at a stand concerning the action proposed to
be taken towards the war in the Low Countries, for news is come

from Zealand that the Archduke has taken three special works without Ostend which have much interrupted his attack on the town hitherto, but is now like to fall very soon.

Some weeks ago men were promised from England. The States have long since sent captains, imprest, and transportation for volunteers to fill up the English companies, but since the alteration volunteers come in so slowly that even with the taking up of loose vagabonds, but 500 of 3,000 promised have been assembled. Without our help the Dutch can hardly go on with their purposed diversion into the enemies' country, unless greater help be sent. Moreover, it is not yet known how the King will declare himself in this point. As King of Scotland he hath amity with Spain and the Archduke, but in the succession to the throne of England he hath a confederacy with the United Provinces, and an interest in the great sums of money due from them.

10*th April*. COURT NEWS.

To-day my Lord of Southampton and Sir Henry Neville, by warrant of the King, were delivered out of the Tower where they have lain since Essex's rebellion. These bountiful beginnings raise all men's spirits and put them in great hopes, insomuch that not only Protestants, but Papists and Puritans, and the very poets with their idle pamphlets, promise themselves such great part in his favour, that to justify and please all would be more than a man's work. There is no certainty where the King is; they that come last say he appointed to be at Berwick on the 7th of this month. The King uses all very graciously and has made Sir Robert Carey of his bedchamber and groom of his stool. There have come divers from the King, who think that he is now on his way to York.

There is a common bruit that the Earl of Clanrickard hath married the Lady of Essex wherewith many that wished her well are nothing pleased: and the speech goes that the King hath taken order and sent her word that her son shall be brought up with the young Prince.

A FOOLISH RHYME.

There is a foolish rhyme runs up and down in the Court of Sir Henry Bromley, Lord Thomas Howard, Lord Cobham, and

Dr. Neville, the Dean of Canterbury, that each has gone to
move the King for what they like—
    Neville for the Protestant,
    Lord Thomas for the Papist,
    Bromley for the Puritan,
    Lord Cobham for the Atheist.

A VOYAGE SET OUT FROM THE CITY OF BRISTOL.

Certain of the chief merchants of the city of Bristol induced
thereto by the inducements of Master Richard Hakluyt, resolve
to set forth a voyage for the further discovery of the northern
parts of Virginia. Having obtained permission of Sir Walter
Ralegh, who had the patent of those parts from Queen Elizabeth, they prepared a small ship called the *Speedwell*, of about
50 tons, manned with thirty men and boys, and a bark called the
Discoverer of 26 tons with thirteen men and a boy, victualled for
eight months, and furnished with certain merchandise to trade
with the people of the country; as hats of divers colours, apparel
of coarse kersey and canvas, ready-made, stockings, shoes, saws,
pickaxes, hooks, knives, scissors, bells, beads, looking-glasses,
thimbles, needles, thread, and such-like. They set sail from
Milford Haven on the 10th April.

11*th April*. THE KING'S JOURNEY BEGUN.

On the 5th April the King departed from Edinburgh,
gallantly accompanied with multitudes of his nobility and gentlemen of Scotland, as the Duke of Lennox, the Earls of Argyle,
Murray, Cassilis, and Mar, the Lord Howe, the Lord Oliphant
and many others, and some French, as the French Ambassador,
whose wife is carried in a chair with slings by eight porters, one
four to relieve the other four by turns. That day he came to
Dunglass; and on the 7th drew near to Berwick where, when his
Highness was half a mile off, the whole town was suddenly concealed in a mantle of smoke from the discharge of all the
ordnance. At the gates he was received by the Gentleman
Porter and sundry gentlemen; whence passing through he was
received by the Captain of the Ward and so passed through a
double guard of soldiers to the Market Cross where the mayor
and his brethren received him with great signs of joy, and the
common people also, kneeling, shouting, and crying 'Welcome'

and 'God save King James' till they were entreated to keep silent. Here the Recorder made a brief speech to his Majesty, who, the customary ceremonies being ended, passed to the church, where the Dr. Toby Matthew, the Bishop of Durham, made a learned sermon. Afterwards the King ascended the walls, where the cannoneers stood, everyone in his place; and here his Majesty was pleased to make a shot himself out of a cannon. He departed on the 8th, having spent the morning in bestowing upon the officers and soldiers a plentiful reward. That afternoon he rode so fast upon the spur that in less than four hours he came near 37 miles and attained Witherington, where Sir Robert Carey and his lady received him. Here, after reposing himself a little, he suddenly beheld a number of deer near the place. So he could not forbear, but after his wonted manner he went forth and slew two of them. Which done he returned with good appetite to the house. Here he knighted three gentlemen.

12th April. THE SUBMISSION OF TYRONE.

A few days before the death of the Queen, the Lord Deputy having received from Tyrone a new offer of submission, replied that if he desired to obtain her Majesty's mercy he must beg the same on his knees in such a place as should be directed. These conditions, though hard and dangerous for one whose head was set to sale by a public Act not yet reversed, were by him accepted. Tyrone therefore came to Mellyfant with a very small train, and there in a great presence offered himself on his knees to the Lord Deputy. Thence he attended my Lord to Tredagh and to Dublin, where he was the only Irish nobleman present at the proclaiming of his Majesty. On the 8th April he made his submission in the Castle of Dublin upon his knees, in the presence of the Lord Deputy and Council, solemnly swearing upon a book to perform every part thereof as much as lies in his power; and if he could not perform any part thereof he vowed to put his body into the King's hands to be disposed at his pleasure. Moreover, he renounced all kinds of dependency on any foreign power, and especially the King of Spain, and will serve the King against all invaders, divulging any practices he shall know of against the King's person or crowns. He will be conformable and assistant to the King's magistrates for the advancement of his service and the peaceable government of his Kingdom, especially for the abolishing of all barbarous customs contrary to the laws.

14th April. A Sermon Against Women.

Of late Mr. Hemmings, sometime of Trinity College in Cambridge, in his sermon at Paul's Cross, speaking of women, said that if a man would marry, it were a thousand to one but he should light upon a bad one, there were so many naught; and if he should chance to find a good one, yet he were not sure to hold her so; for women are like a cowl full of snakes amongst which there is one eel, and a thousand to one if a man happen upon the eel; and if he get it with his hand, all he has gotten is a wet eel by the tail.

16th April. The Secretary Goes to See the King.

Master Secretary is now at Huntingdon on his way to see the King, and to impart to him certain matters from the Council, as the date of the Queen's funeral and his coronation. Further, there is the matter of the Irish coin which will not easily be settled in this present scarcity in the Exchequer, as well as the extraordinary disbursements to come for the funeral and coronation.

20th April. The States want Volunteers.

The United States have written to the King begging that they may continue to recruit in England for the English companies, and in Scotland for the Scottish companies, for their service and particularly for the preservation of Ostend; and further, seeing that the urgent necessity of this affair, that the soldiers may be levied and transported without delay.

21st April. Sir Robert Cecil at York.

Master Secretary reached York on the 17th April at midnight, and next day had access to the King and speech for about an hour. His Majesty has resolved to hold the coronation on the 25th July, and that the Queen shall be crowned jointly with him.

22nd April. The Order of the Garter.

This afternoon being Good Friday divers Knights of the

Garter called a chapter in the King's Closet next the Chapel at Whitehall and chose into the Order the King of Denmark and the young Prince Henry Frederick, adjourning the solemnity of the Feast until the 2nd July which is made the eve of St. George's Feast.

23rd April. THE KING'S JOURNEY.

The King and his train reached Newcastle upon the 9th of this month and lay there the next day, being Sunday; and on the 13th came to Durham where he was entertained by the Bishop, taking great delight at his Lordship's merry and well-seasoned jests. At his departure his Majesty greatly commended the Bishop, promising to restore divers things taken from the bishopric.

He came to York on the 16th April where he was very royally received by the Lord Burghley, the Lord President, and many knights and gentlemen. In the city he was met by the Lord Mayor, who delivered to his Majesty the keys and a cup filled all with gold, which he very graciously received, delivering the keys again; but about the bearing of the Sword there was some contention, the Lord President taking it for his place, and the Lord Mayor for his. But to decide the doubt the King merrily demanded if, the Sword being his, they would not be pleased he should have the disposing of it; so he delivered it to one that knew well how to use it, my Lord of Cumberland, who bore it before his Majesty, riding in great state from the gate to the Minster; in which there was a conduit that all day long ran white and red claret wine, every man to drink as much as he wished. The next day, being Sunday, the King heard the sermon in the Minster, but he would not ride in a coach that was offered, for, quoth he, 'I will have no coach; for the people are desirous to see a King, and so they shall, for they shall as well see his body as his face.' This Sunday there was a seminary priest apprehended who before (under the title of a gentleman) had delivered a petition to his Majesty in the name of the English Catholics. When he was taken his Majesty had some conference with him, but by reason of other great affairs, he referred him to be examined by the Bishop of Limerick, which priest was the next day committed. Dinner being ended, the King walked into

14

the garden of the palace, and there he knighted twenty-three. This same day he also received from the Mayor and Alderman of Kingston-upon-Hull a petition that they might be relieved and succoured against the daily spoils done by the Dunkirkers. His Majesty showed great pity for their wrongs, and comforted them with these words, that he would defend them, and no Dunkirker should after dare to do any of his subjects wrong. Next day, after dinner, following the custom that he hath begun, he commanded all the prisoners to be set at liberty, except Papists and wilful murderers.

25th April. NEW COUNCILLORS.

This day letters were received from his Majesty directing that the Earls of Northumberland and Cumberland, the Lord Mountjoy and the Lord Thomas Howard should be admitted and sworn of the Privy Council. Whereupon my Lord Northumberland and Lord Thomas Howard were sworn, but the other two being absent their oath shall be taken at another time. Nevertheless the Lord Mountjoy, by his Majesty's express order, shall be reported as one of the Council, and be qualified accordingly in the despatches that are made unto him.

THE KING HANGETH A THIEF.

The King came to Worksop, my Lord of Shrewsbury's house, on the 20th April, being met on the way by a number of huntsmen, all in green, who invited him to see some game.   So he hunted a space very much delighted; and at last went into the house, where he was so nobly received that each entertainment seemed to exceed others. The next morning before his departure his Majesty knighted nineteen. Thence the train proceeded to Newark, and here in the Court was taken a cutpurse doing the deed, who though a base pilfering fellow yet was gentleman-like in the outside. Good store of coin was found about him, and upon examination he confessed that he had come from Berwick to this place and played the cutpurse. When the King heard of it, he directed a warrant to the Recorder of Newark to have him hanged, which was accordingly executed; but he commanded all the prisoners in the Castle to be set free. Here nine were knighted, and the next day at Belvoir Castle, where his Majesty was entertained by my Lord of Rutland, forty-eight.

26th April. THE MAUNDY.

The Maundy was kept at Westminster, and performed by the Lord Bishop of Chichester, when thirty-six poor men received their ancient allowance.

THE KING'S JOURNEY.

The King came to Stamford on the 23rd of this month, and at his coming there appeared upon a heath near the town about a hundred high men, huge long fellows of twelve or fourteen feet high, that seemed like those Patagones who are reported to dwell near the Straits of Magellan. The King at first sight wondered what they were, for they overlooked both horse and man, but at their coming they proved to be a company of poor honest suitors, all going upon stilts, preferring a petition against the Lady Hatton, which his Majesty referred till his coming to London.

27th April. GOWRY'S BROTHERS SOUGHT.

Proclamation is made for the apprehension of William and Patrick Ruthven, brethren to the Earl of Gowry. They are said to have left Scotland with the desperate intention of following and murdering the King in revenge for the death of their brother, whom some very secretly whisper was put to death because he was in love with the Queen.

28th April. THE FUNERALS OF QUEEN ELIZABETH.

This day were the funerals of Queen Elizabeth celebrated with great pomp and magnificence. First went 260 poor women, four in a rank, apparelled in black, with linen kerchiefs over their heads: the inferior officers of the household and gentlemen of mean quality following after them. The standards of the Dragon, of the Greyhound and the Lion (the supporter of the arms of England) were carried in convenient distance and intermingled with the train; among which also there were led along by certain querries of the Stable, two great horses, the one covered with black cloth, the other with velvet, whereto the scutcheons of the arms of England and France were fastened. Then came the gentlemen and children of the Chapel in copes and surplices, singing in a mournful tune. The Ensigns of the Earldoms of Chester, of the Duchy of Cornwall, of the Principality of Wales, and of the Kingdom of Ireland were severally borne by some of the nobility. Between them were placed the Aldermen of the City of London, the Justices of the Benches, and the Gentlemen Pensioners, whose poleaxes were covered with black, and the heads of them carried downwards. Then followed the Lord Mayor, the Privy Councillors, the Lords Spiritual and temporal, and the principal officers of the Kingdom. The Agent for the States of the United Provinces in the Low Countries was accompanied by the first Secretary of the Estate. The French ambassador (representing the person of the King's Majesty) went alone by himself, having the train of his robe carried up behind him. The Agent for the State of Venice (who was sent hither but recently to demand restitution of Venetian goods taken at sea by the English) was expected to have been there, but he excused his absence upon pretence lest by assisting at the ceremony in the church he might incur the Pope's excommunication. The banner of England, richly embroidered, was borne by one of the chief Peers of the Realm. The Coat of Arms, the Sword, Target, Helm and Crest were carried by the Officers of Arms.

Then was there an open chariot, drawn by four horses, trapped with black velvet, beset with the arms of England and France, wherein lay the body of the dead Queen, embalmed, and enclosed in lead; and over that her image in her Parliament robes with a crown on her head and a sceptre in her hand, all very exquisitely framed to resemble the life. At the sight thereof divers of the beholders fell aweeping, especially women, who naturally are tender of heart and have tears at command-ment.

Then the people began to talk diversely; many seeming to marvel even at vain and ordinary things, as that living and dying a virgin, she was born on the vigil of that Feast, which was yearly kept in remembrance of the birth of our Lady the Virgin and that she died on the vigil of the Feast of the Annunciation of Our Lady; that she departed the world at Richmond, where her grandfather, whom she much resembled, ended his life, and upon the same day of the week; that she had reigned so many years as the greater part then living had never known other Prince. Some also spoke fondly of the predictions going before her death, and amongst others it was given out that an old lion in the Tower bearing her name, during the time of her sickness, pined away and died.

But among men of better understanding the actions of her life and the manner of her government were called to mind and censured. Some recounted the long and peaceable time of her reign, her clemency and other virtues, wishing that things may continue in no worse state than they have done, alleging the old proverb 'That seldom cometh the better.' Others again complained that they cannot lightly be in worse state than they are, considering that the people generally are much impoverished by continual subsidies and taxes, besides other exactions of contributions extorted by corrupt officers; that little or no equality is observed in these impositions so that the meaner sort commonly sustain the greater burdens and the wealthier no more than they themselves list to bear; that wrongs now and then are either bolstered out by authority or winked at for private respects; that many privileges have passed under her name for the benefit of some particular men to the detriment of the commonwealth; albeit it could not be denied that of herself naturally she was well-disposed, if she had not been misled by overmuch credulity and secret informations of persons about her, an inconvenience which even the best Princes ofttimes can very hardly avoid.

These, or the like matters, were diversely argued, as it falleth out commonly upon like occasions, while the mourners passed along attending the corpse, which was assisted by six Earls, certain Knights holding a canopy over the chariot, and six Barons on each side carrying bannerols with the arms of her predecessors, Kings and Queens of England; and the Master of Horse leading behind it the palfrey of honour covered over with black.

The chief mourner was the Lady Marchioness of Northampton, who was assisted by the Lord Treasurer and the Lord Admiral; and they also had two Earls assigned to them as assistants. The Lady Arabella Stuart, being of the royal blood, was specially required to have honoured the funerals with her presence; which she refused, saying that since her access to the Queen in her lifetime might not be permitted, she would not after her death be brought upon the stage for a public spectacle.

After the chief mourner there followed fourteen Countesses and divers Baronesses and maids of honour. Lastly came Sir Walter Ralegh, Captain of the Guard, with his company, five in a rank holding their halberds downwards. In this manner the corpse was conveyed to the Church at Westminster where it was placed under a sumptuous hearse.

The whole ceremonies of the funerals of Queen Elizabeth held for some six hours with the sermon, which was preached by the Bishop of Chichester.

29th April. A POETICAL FLOOD.

There hath been a great outpouring of poetry these last days. All our poets almost, promising themselves great part in the King's favour, vie with each other to lament the old Queen and welcome the new King. Both the Universities come forth with their Latin, Samuel Daniel is forward with *A panegyric congratulatory*. Drayton also has a congratulatory poem, with the tree of the King's descent. Chettle has *England's Mourning Garment*, a thing in the pastoral manner. And many others, not hitherto (nor hereafter) famous as poets hasten to the press in number more than thirty.

30th April. THE KING'S JOURNEY.

On the 27th April, the King came from Burleigh towards Master Oliver Cromwell's; and in the way he dined at the house of Sir Anthony Mildmay, where both dinner and banquet was most sumptuously served and by art made beauteous to the eye, for Sir Anthony's lady is one of the most expert confectioners in England. At his departure thence, Sir Anthony presented his Highness with a gallant Barbary horse and a very rich saddle and furniture. Thence at his remove, great companies met him, beseeching his Majesty that the commons may be laid open again for the poor inhabiters thereof (which they complain Sir John Spencer of London hath very uncharitably molested). This his Majesty very graciously promised should be performed according to their hearts' desire.

At Master Cromwell's there attended the Heads of the University of Cambridge in scarlet gowns and corner caps, who welcomed his Majesty and entreated the confirmation of their charter and privileges, which was most freely granted. They also presented his Majesty with sundry books in commendation of the late Queen.

Upon his departure on the 29th the King took kind and gracious leave of Master Cromwell and his lady (late widow to that opulent knight Sir Horatio Palavicino), whose entertainment is said to have been the greatest feast that hath been given by a subject, there was such plenty and variety of meats, and drink with the cellars open at any man's pleasure, with open beer houses wherein was no want of beer and beef for the poor.

The King hath made very many knights, though of late he hath held his hand, for he repents him of many he hath made, and is very angry with some Scots for he hath heard that they took money for making of them.

A Scot's Saying.

A certain blunt Scotsman, seeing the obsequious applause of the people towards the new King said, 'This people will spoil a gud King.'

An Explosion of Powder.

From Redriffe it is reported that three days ago thirteen persons were slain and blown in pieces with gunpowder by misfortune at the gunpowder mill, which did much hurt in divers places.

1st May. The Humble Petition of the Thousand Ministers.

Of late a long petition was presented on behalf of the Puritans, which they call 'The humble petition of the thousand ministers,' or 'The Millenary Petition,' because it was said to be subscribed by a 1,000 ministers, though indeed the number was some 750, but these collected only out of five and twenty counties. This business is chiefly entrusted to Mr. Arthur Hildersham and Mr. Stephen Egerton. In this petition they ask that of the offences in the Church some might be removed, some amended, some qualified, which they gather under four heads.

In the Church Service, they would have the cross in baptism, interrogations administered to infants, and confirmation, as superfluous, to be taken away; that baptism be not ministered by women; the cap and surplice not to be urged; that examination might go before the communion which shall be ministered with a sermon; that divers terms, viz. of *priests* and *absolution* altered, and the ring in marriage corrected; the longsomeness of service abridged; that the Lord's Day be not profaned; the rest upon holy days not so strictly urged; that there may be a uniformity of doctrine prescribed; no popish opinions be any more taught or defended; no ministers charged to teach their .people to bow at the name of Jesus; that the Canonical Scriptures only be read in the Church.

Concerning Church ministers, they pray that none hereafter be admitted into the ministry but able and sufficient men, and those to preach diligently, and especially upon the Lord's Day; and that such as be already entered and cannot preach, either be removed and some desirable course taken with them for their relief, or else be forced, according to the value of their livings, to maintain preachers; that non-residence be not permitted; that the Statute for the lawfulness of ministers' marriages be revived; that ministers be not required, but according to the law, to subscribe to the Articles of Religion and the King's Supremacy only.

For Church livings and maintenance, that bishops should leave their *commendams*, some holding prebends, some parsonages, some vicarages with their bishoprics; double beneficed men not to be suffered to hold some two, three or four benefices with cures, and some two, three or four dignities besides; that impropriations annexed to bishoprics and colleges be demised only to the preachers incumbents.

In matters of Church discipline, that discipline and ex-communication be administered according to Christ's own institution, or at least that enormities be redressed, as, that excommunication come not forth under the name of lay persons, chancellors, officials, etc.; that men be not excommunicated for trifles and twelve penny matters; that none be excommuni-cated without consent of his pastor; that the officers be not suffered to extort unreasonable fees; that none having jurisdic-tion or register's places put out the same to farm; that divers popish canons (as for the restraint of marriage at certain times) be reversed; that the longsomeness of suits of Ecclesiastical Courts (hanging sometime so long as seven years) be restrained;

that the oath *ex officio*, whereby men are forced to accuse themselves, be more sparingly used; that licence for marriage without
banns be more cautiously granted.

These, with other such abuses yet remaining and practised
in the Church of England, they can show not to be agreeable
to the Scriptures if it shall please the King to hear them, or more
at large to be informed by writing, or by conference among the
learned to be resolved. And at the end of the petition they subscribe themselves his Majesty's 'most humble subjects, the
ministers of the Gospel, that desire not a disorderly innovation,
but a due and godly reformation.'

2nd *May*. THE QUEEN'S JOURNEY.

There are sent to attend the Queen from Scotland the Earl
of Sussex, the Earl of Lincoln, the Lord Compton, the Lord
Norris, Sir George Carew (Lord President of Munster), Sir
John Buc, the Countess of Worcester, the Countess of Kildare,
and the Ladies Anne Herbert, Scroop, Rich, and Walsingham.
They are directed to remain at Berwick until her Majesty's
coming thither. Other Ladies have voluntarily gone thither, as
the Countess of Bedford, also sundry gentlemen of good quality.

3rd *May*. THE KING AT THEOBALDS.

Yesterday the King was at Broxbourne, and to-day is come
to Theobalds, where have met him the Lord Keeper, the Lord
Treasurer, the Lord Admiral, with most of the nobility and of
the Council, together with most part of the old officers in the
household of the late Queen, and with the Guard. His Majesty
dined at Broxbourne with Sir Henry Cocks, and about half an
hour after 1 o'clock proceeded forward to Theobalds, accompanied with Sir Edward Denny, Sheriff of Essex, who had
followers 150 in parti-coloured hats, red and yellow bands,
round rolled, with a feather of the same colour in every one.
As his Highness was espied coming towards Theobalds, many
ran from their carts leaving their horses; and the concourse of
people was so frequent that it were incredible to tell of. So the
King came riding up the walk with the whole nobility of
England and Scotland around him. At the entrance into the
court Sir Robert Cecil met him and conducted him towards the
house with great applause of the people, hearty prayers and

throwing up of hats; and so great a multitude thronged into the upper court to see the King, that he showed himself openly out of his chamber window by the space of half an hour together.

4th May. THE KING.

To-day the King rode very early in the morning into Enfield Chace, accompanied by many noblemen, riding for the most part between the Earl of Northumberland and the Earl of Nottingham, but returned early by reason that the morning seemed to promise a shower.

THE KING AND THE PRIVY COUNCIL.

This day the King came and sat in Council, the Court being at Theobalds, when all the Councillors to the late Queen took the oath both of Supremacy and of Privy Councillors. There were also sworn of the Council the Lord Henry Howard, Lodovice Stuart, Duke of Lennox; John Erskine, Earl of Mar; Sir George Hume, Treasurer of Scotland; Sir James Elphinston who also is sworn one of his Majesty's Principal Secretaries of State for all affairs concerning the Kingdom of Scotland, and Edward Bruce, Lord of Kinloss. There are also appointed special commissioners to meet and settle a course for order to be taken in the King's House. Also special commissioners to consider all monopolies and grants that are offensive to the subjects of his land, and to inform his Majesty of the same that order may be taken. The King hath declared, sitting in council, that from henceforth he would not have the Council exceed the number of twenty-four persons.

5th May. THE STATE OF IRELAND.

From Ireland comes news that in Ulster, where at the coming of the Lord Deputy there was not one man in subjugation there is now not one in rebellion. In Connaught and Leinster likewise there is but little or no rebellion. Only in Munster those in the towns (and especially in Cork), with Kilkenny and Wexford, have, with some insolence, set up the public exercise of the Mass. Unto them the Lord Deputy has written commanding them on their allegiance to desist, and purposeth to go against them with 2,000 men, fearing lest in the miseries and ill disposition the towns may cast themselves into the protection of Spain. The discontent at the new base coin is infinite; nor is there any way to make it acceptable save by the cannon. The companies are found exceeding weak of English, for the miseries of the war are so intolerable, specially by the new coin, that all the best men forsake them, and no providence can prevent it. As for the Lord Deputy himself, he is tired of wrestling with this generation of vipers, and cannot hope to bring things to better pass but with a long time that must polish what he has rough-hewed, which he hopes that the King will appoint to be the work of some other man.

7th May. THE KING COMES TO LONDON.

This day his Majesty removed from Theobalds towards London, riding through the meadows; and as he went was made a train with a tame deer with such twinings and doublings that the hounds could not take it faster than his Majesty proceeded, yet still by the industry of the huntsman and the subtlety of him that made the train the hounds were in a full-mouthed cry all the way, never more than one close from the highway so that the King and the whole company had the lee wind from the hounds that they might the better perceive the uniformity in the cries. At Stamford Hill the Lord Mayor of London presented him with the Sword and Keys of the City, with whom were the Knights and Aldermen in scarlet gowns and great chains of gold about their necks, with all the chief officers of the City, besides 500 citizens, all very well mounted, clad in velvet coats and chains of gold. There also met his Majesty all his chief officers of Estate, the Sergeants-at-Arms with their rich maces, the Heralds with their coats of arms, and trumpeters, the Duke of Lennox bearing the Sword; and so the King passed on in royal and imperial manner. At this time old Sir Henry Lee, that was Champion to Queen Elizabeth, met him, attended by sixty gallant men, all mounted; to whom his Majesty spoke very lovingly, and so paced through his troop very well pleased. The multitudes of the people in the highways, fields, meadows, closes, and on trees was so great that they covered the beauty of the fields; and so greedy were they to behold the King that they injured and hurt one another; but they received his Majesty as he passed with shouts and cries, and casting up of hats, of which many never returned to the owners' hands. At length the King entered the Charterhouse Garden by a way that was cut of purpose through a bank. Here also a great multitude awaited his coming, amongst whom were the Children of the Hospital singing, orderly placed for his Majesty's coming along through them, but all displaced through the rudeness of such a multitude, who cried out so loudly that one could scarce hear another speak.

THE KING'S PROCLAMATION.

There is a proclamation by the King declaring his Majesty to be so greatly moved by the zeal and affection expressed towards him by all sorts of people that he hath considered ways that might make manifest how willing he is now, and will be hereafter, to be as forward in requiting their love as they have been to express it. Wherefore he hath commanded that from henceforth none shall execute any charter or grant made by the late Queen of any kind of monopolies (except such grants as have been made to any Corporation or Company of any art or mystery) until the charter or grant shall be examined and allowed. Further, his Majesty straitly chargeth all lawyers, attorneys, officers and clerks in any court of Justice, ecclesiastical or temporal, not to extort any undue or excessive fees, but only such as are allowed. The people, moreover, are admonished that if they shall find cause to seek anything at his hands, they shall forbear all assembling and flocking together in multitudes, but shall in lawful and decent manner without numbers, without clamour, or any other kind of disorder, resort by way of petition, and they shall receive favourable answer if their complaints be just. But on the other side, if their petitions savour of humour, and tend only to slander and calumniation (as often happeneth in vulgar people) under pretence of seeking public redresses to utter private malice then shall they understand that it is no less the office of a Prince to protect his magistrates and officers than to give redress to the vulgar sorts. Finally to avoid all impious profanation of the Sabbath day, no bear-baiting, bull-baiting, interludes, common plays or other like disordered pastimes shall be used upon any Sabbath day.

HUNTING NEAR LONDON.

Sir Thomas Fleming, the Solicitor-General, is ordered to draw a proclamation forbidding all persons of what degree and quality soever to hunt within four miles of the cities of London and Westminster, except the King, the Queen and the young Prince.

8th May. SIR WALTER RALEGH DISMISSED FROM HIS POST.

This day Sir Walter Ralegh was called before the Council and the King's pleasure signified to him that in the office of Captain of the Guard the King would henceforth use the service of Sir Thomas Erskine, whereunto Sir Walter in very humble manner submitted himself.

11th May. THE KING COMES TO THE TOWER.

Whilst he was at Theobalds the King made twenty-nine knights and to-day at his departure from the Charterhouse one hundred and thirty-three. His Majesty set forth quietly by foot to Whitehall where he took barge. Having shot the Bridge his landing was expected at the Tower stairs, but it pleased his Highness to pass the Tower stairs towards St. Katherine's, and there stayed on the water to see the ordnance on the White Tower (commonly called Julius Cæsar's Tower), being 20 pieces, and the great ordnance on Tower Wharf 100 pieces, and chambers to the number of 130 discharged and shot off. Then he came to the stairs with the Lord Admiral, the Earls of Northumberland and Worcester, the Lord Thomas Howard and other noblemen. At his coming up the Sword was presented by Sir Thomas Coningsby, Gentleman usher of the Privy Chamber, and by the King delivered to the Duke of Lennox who bore it before him into the Tower. All the prisoners of what quality soever, even Jesuits, have been set at liberty.

13th May. MR. SECRETARY PROMOTED.

This day the King made these Lords and Knights: viz., in the Presence Chamber before dinner: Sir Robert Cecil, Lord Cecil of Essenden; Sir Robert Sidney, Lord Sidney of Penshurst; Sir Edward Wotton, Lord Wotton of Morley; Sir William Knollys, Lord Knollys of Grays; and at the same time Mr. William Dethick, Garter King-at-Arms, was made knight.

In the afternoon Mr. Thomas Smith, that was Sheriff of London at the time of the Earl of Essex's troubles and for a while lay in the Tower, was knighted, with nine others.

The number of knights made since the King entered Berwick is nigh on 240.

The assembly at Court is so great that it is reckoned to be more than 40,000 persons, and for certain there will be 100,000 more mouths in London.

15th May. THE TROUBLES IN IRELAND.

On 27th April the Lord Deputy departed from Dublin to make his journey to the seditious towns in the south. On the 29th the Sovereign and four principal citizens of Kilkenny were brought before him, and charged with allowing the erection of the Mass, and public breach of the laws of the Realm. They humbly besought pardon, confessing that they had been seduced by one Dr. White and a friar named Edmund Barry, who came unto them from Waterford, hallowed their churches and enjoined them to celebrate Mass openly. This friar also at the same time submitted himself, and confessed his fault, alleging that he thought it agreeable to his Lordship's pleasure, but now understanding the contrary, promised to desist from further exercise of the Mass.

Two days afterwards, the Lord Deputy with his army encamped within five miles of Waterford, from which city is much disorder reported, for some have exclaimed openly, 'We will not have a Scot to be our King': and even after they had yielded, they erected the Mass in several churches, deferring the proclaiming of the King's title and right until their churches had first been hallowed.

From the city four agents came to request public toleration of the Mass and that the Lord Deputy would enter the city with no greater number than they themselves would allow, to which effect they showed a clause from the ancient charter granted by King John.

The next day, which was the 2nd May, learning that they were manning the walls of the city for resistance, the Lord Deputy encamped his army within a mile of the city, when the agents came again asking that only a certain number should

enter the city, and that Dr. White might come to the camp in
the name of the Commons, with a Dominican friar, as one
that had great power with the common people; to which the
Lord Deputy agreed. This Jesuit doctor hath caused them to
establish the further exercise of the Mass, contrary to law. He
hath, moreover, entered by force into churches, taking away
the keys and excluding the ministers, and torn and burnt the
service books: and beside this, he exacted an oath of all the
inhabitants that they should be true for the Pope, and maintain
the Romish religion with their goods and lives.

The Jesuit and the friar, apparelled after their orders (the
Doctor wearing a black gown and cornered cap, and the Friar
a white woollen frock), came therefore to the camp, attended by
divers of the town, carrying a crucifix which they showed
openly, so that the soldiers could hardly be kept from offering
them violence. When he came unto his Lordship's presence,
the Jesuit protested that he had ever been a loyal subject to the
Queen, and now to the King, whom he acknowledged to be
the lawful heir to the crowns of England, Scotland, France and
Ireland. It was true that he was a Catholic and a Jesuit: these
names he would not deny.

Hereupon the Lord Deputy, perceiving the Doctor to be a
scholar, began to enter into a learned discourse with him touching obedience, and by degrees did urge him to answer whether
a subject might take arms against his Prince for matters of
religion; to which the Jesuit would give no direct answer, but
seemed to answer that he might. At one point the Doctor
cited a passage in St. Augustine for his proof, whereat his
Lordship, having the book in his tent, showed all the company
that he had falsely cited the Father, for howsoever the very
words were found there, yet they were by way of an assertion
which St. Augustine confuted in the discourse following.

At length the Lord Deputy said, 'To deal plainly with you,
if your conscience will not let you answer negatively to this
question, you shall upon my honour return safely to the town,
but presently after I will proclaim you a traitor, and all that shall
relieve you. For my master is by right an absolute King, subject
to no Prince or Power upon the earth: and if it be lawful for
his subjects upon any cause to raise arms against him, and

28

deprive him of his royal authority, he is not then an absolute King, but hath only a *precarium imperium*. This is our opinion of the Church of England, and in this point many of your own great doctors agree with us.'

So the Jesuit and the rest withdrew; but after three hours he came again, renewing his protestation of loyalty, and disclaiming the principle that it is lawful for subjects upon any cause to bear arms against his Prince. Further he declared that the people would receive his Lordship and his army.

The next morning the Lord Deputy, leaving a sufficient guard in his camp, marched towards Waterford, which he entered in state. At the cross there was an oration in Latin, magnifying the King and justifying their courses, that what they had done was only for their consciences, and the further profession of their religion. After dinner, the Lord Deputy admonished the chief men, and administered to them an oath of fidelity to the King. Then he told them that because they had confessed that they were too weak-handed to keep in awe their unruly multitude, he would leave 150 English soldiers. Accordingly these men were placed in a strong castle, commanding one of the ports, and my Lord returned with the rest of his army to his camp, purposing within a day or two to make his journey to Cork.

In Cork the townsmen behave very seditiously; for after things had remained doubtful for some days upon the death of the Queen, they treated Lady Carew (the wife of the Lord President of Munster), with great insolency, so that she had to remove to Shandon Castle. When Sir Charles Wilmot and Sir George Thornton had received confirmation of their commissions, they came to Cork intending either to place some companies within the town or take thence some victuals and munitions. But the townsmen would not admit them, and made a tumult, sending forth 800 men to pull down the Fort of Skiddir where the munition was, until Sir Charles drove them forth with 300 men and some loss on both sides. Hereupon the townsmen manned their walls and began to play upon the companies until Sir Charles manned all the alleys at both ends of the town, and beat them from the walls. Every day since then there is an action, the cannon sometimes playing

29   B*

upon Shandon, and sometimes upon the Bishop's house. Never-theless, Lady Carew is nothing daunted thereat, nor would she be persuaded to move to any other place for her safety, such is her disdain for the mayor of Cork. Moreover, as it seems, this trouble hath brought her to very good health, for before she was extremely sickly.

18th May. THE NEW QUEEN.

The Queen was formerly, it is said, a Protestant, but became a Catholic through the persuasion of three Jesuits, and although she goes publicly to service yet in private she hears Mass. In order that the young Prince Henry might be brought up a Protestant, the King has kept him from his mother, and when he set out for England he left him in the care of the Countess of Mar, intending later to bring him in state to London. The Queen desired to have him with her in Edinburgh but could not persuade any to carry him off, whereat she began to form a dis-like for him; and besides she was told that if he goes with her into England the Catholics will carry him off as a hostage. These crosses so greatly moved her to anger that though she is four months gone with child she beat her own belly and is in manifest danger of miscarriage if not of death.

A NEW CHANCELLOR OF THE EXCHEQUER.

The King has chosen Sir George Hume to be Chancellor of the Exchequer, whereby Sir John Fortescue is put out of his old place, but is to become Chancellor of the Duchy of Lan-caster.

19th May. THE KING'S NEW PLAYERS.

The players that were my Lord Chamberlain's servants are now by letters patent made the King's servants, of whom the chief are Lawrence Fletcher, William Shakespeare, Richard Burbage, Augustine Phillips, John Hemmings, Henry Condell, William Sly, Robert Armin, and Richard Cowley.

20th May. DIFFICULTIES ABOUT THE CORONATION.

Churchmen are in some difficulty about the Coronation, for the sacring has always been done by a Catholic bishop and with the Catholic rite, even with King Edward VI and Queen Elizabeth, though she first gave public sign of her turning from the Church of Rome when she hid her face in her handkerchief at the elevation of the Host. As anointing is a function ordained of God to mark the pre-eminence of kings it cannot well be omitted, and yet many dislike the sign of the Cross in oil or in water. The King thinks likewise, and that neither he nor any other King can in truth have power to heal the disease called the Evil, the age of miracles being past. Nevertheless he will have the full ceremony lest he lose that prerogative which belongs to him as King of France.

22nd May. THE LORD DEPUTY AT CORK.

The Lord Deputy came into Cork on the 10th May, and the day following he admitted the townsmen to speak on their own behalf of any offences which they had received or justly suspected before they were called in question for their own disorders. They endeavoured to divert their public offences by a colourable excuse of private spleen, and some grudges against one of the commissioners. The next day his Lordship heard the towns-men's answers in justification of their own actions. It was objected against them that they had publicly set up the Romish religion, against the laws, and maintained these actions by force and armed men; they had attempted to demolish the King's fort at the south gate of the city; they had stayed the issue of the King's munitions and victual, seizing them into their own hands, and imprisoning the King's officers and munitions; lastly, they had borne arms and done acts of hostility against the King's forces, wherein their insolency was so far followed that they had killed a grave and learned preacher walking upon the hills adjoining to their walls, and had battered Shandon Castle where the wife of the Lord President lay. After due examination of these accusations, his Lordship resolved to leave the censure to his Majesty's pleasure. Only he took notice of some few of the principal offenders and ringleaders, whom he commanded to be hanged for example and terror to the rest. Others are left in prison, principally Master Meade, the Recorder, to be tried by course of law.

25th May. 'SEJANUS.'

Of late the King's Players enacted at the Globe a new tragedy by Ben Jonson called *Sejanus, his fall,* very learnedly written and

31

setting forth the rise and fall of that Sejanus who was favourite
to the Roman Emperor Tiberius; but though the gentle wits
applauded, the people would none of it and in almost beastly
rage hissed it away. Moreover, my Lord of Northampton, who
is no friend to Jonson, hath caused him to be called before the
Council to answer for the play, suspecting it of treason.

A Speech of Macro, that supplanted Sejanus as the Emperor's Favourite.

It is the bliss
Of courts to be employ'd, no matter how;
A Prince's power makes all his actions virtue.
We, whom he works by, are dumb instruments,
To do, but not enquire: his great intents
Are to be serv'd, not search'd. Yet, as that bow
Is most in hand, whose owner best doth know
T'affect his aims, so let that statesman hope
Most use, most price, can hit his Prince's scope.
Nor must he look at what, or whom to strike,
But loose at all; each mark must be alike.
Were it to plot against the fame, the life
Of one, with whom I twinn'd; remove a wife
From my warm side, as lov'd as is the air;
Practise away each parent; draw mine heir
In compass, though but one; work all my kin
To swift perdition; leave no untrain'd engin,
For friendship, or for innocence; nay, make
The gods all guilty; I would undertake
This, being impos'd me, both with gain and ease:
The way to rise, is to obey, and please.
He that will thrive in state, he must neglect
The trodden paths, that truth and right respect;
And prove new, wilder ways: for virtue, there,
Is not that narrow thing, she is elsewhere;
Men's fortune there is virtue; reason, their will;
Their licence, law; and their observance, skill.
Occasion, is their foil; conscience, their stain;
Profit, their lustre; and what else is, vain.

26th May. THE PLAGUE IN LONDON.

Of late the plague increaseth in London and this last week it is reported that thirty-two are dead of it.

30th May. A DEFENCE OF RHYME.

Master Daniel has composed *A panegyric congratulatory* to his Majesty, whereto is added *A Defence of Rhyme,* answering certain *Observations in the Art of English Poesy* set out by Doctor Campion last year wherein he declared rhyme to be a vulgar and unartificial custom that hath deterred many excellent wits from the exercise of English poesy, and would have all our writers follow the examples of Greece and Rome, except in the hexameter. To which Mr. Daniel's answer is that we should not so soon yield our consents captive to the authority of Antiquity unless we see more reason; all our reasons are not to be built by the square of Greece and Italy. We are the children of nature as well as they; we are not so placed out of the way of judgment, but that the same sun of Discretion shineth upon us; we have the same portion of the same virtues as well as of the same vices; *Et Catalinam Quocunque in populo videas, quocunque sub axe.*

31st May. A MASTER OF CEREMONIES APPOINTED.

Because of the great repair of foreign princes and the ambassadors who are already here or on their way to congratulate his Majesty, the King has created an office of Master of Ceremonies to receive and entertain them worthily. Sir Lewis Lewkenor is appointed to this office, and his fee is £200 a year.

2nd June. THE KING.

The King now begins to change the habits of his life. In his Scottish days he lived so modestly that he was hardly even like a private gentleman, let alone a Prince, for many sat at table with him. He was waited on by rough servants who did not even remove their hats, but treated all with French familiarity, reserving all pomp for the service of the Queen. But now the Council bring back the ancient majesty of the English Court, and almost adore his Majesty. Last Sunday he dined in state, waited on by the great Lords. Yet our courtiers note great change between the fashion of the Court as it now is and in the Queen's time;

and certain great ladies having sat awhile in the chamber of Sir Thomas Erskine came hence all lousy.

6th June. VALENTINE THOMAS EXECUTED.

Two days ago Valentine Thomas was arraigned at the King's Bench Bar at Westminster. Some five years since this Thomas declared that he had been sent by the King of Scots (his present Majesty) to murder Queen Elizabeth, who caused him to be imprisoned in the Tower where he hath lain ever since. He was condemned of treason for conspiring against the late Queen and some of her Council. This evening, some time after six of the clock, he was drawn from the King's Bench at Southwark to St. Thomas Watering's and there hanged, bowelled and quartered.

THE LORD MOUNTJOY'S RETURN.

The Lord Mountjoy, Lord Lieutenant of Ireland, is now come to London, bringing in his company Hugh O'Neil, Earl of Tyrone, who abides private at Wansted. Before his departure his Lordship gave authority to Sir George Carew to be the King's Deputy during his absence. Moreover, because at the first settling of peace so many petitions were exhibited against the late rebels for restitution of goods which cannot now be restored, that the exacting thereof is like to produce new troubles, his Lordship caused an Act of Oblivion (for all like grievances) to be published.

On their way thither, the Lord Lieutenant and his company were in great danger, for sailing towards the coast of England in the King's pinnace called the *Tramontana*, they encountered a sudden fog, and, bearing all sails, fell suddenly upon the Sherries, a hideous black rock off the Isle of Anglesey. Here they had all been cast away, had not the gulls, seeing the ship ready to rush upon their desert habitation, rose calling and fluttering about them. Whereat the governors of the pinnace cried out to the steersmen, 'Aloof for life!' which the steersmen effected and brought the ship suddenly about, but so near to the rock that the boat hanging to the stern was dashed against it. Having landed at Beaumaris, the Lord Lieutenant, with the Earl of Tyrone and his company rode to London, and on the way, howsoever his Lordship's happy victory against the traitor made him gracious in the eyes of the people, yet no respect for him could contain many women in those parts, who have lost husbands and children in these Irish wars, from throwing dust and stones at the Earl of Tyrone as he passed, and reviling him with bitter words.

The Lord Mountjoy has requested that the King shall make some public declaration to avoid violence or disgrace in speech to the Earl of Tyrone, as he sees the people much inclined to it, and it would give him great discontent that might exceedingly prejudice the King's service.

The Charges of the Irish Wars.

At the departure from Ireland of the Lord Mountjoy, the list of the army stood at 1,000 horse and 11,150 foot. During the last year, ending 31st March, the charges of the Irish wars, besides concordatums, munition and other extraordinaries, amount to £290,733 8s. 9⅞d.; and from the 1st October 1598, being four years and a half, besides extraordinaries, to £1,198,717 19s. 1d. For the year now coming, if the horse stand at 1,000, and the foot be reduced to 8,000, the cost to his Majesty will be £163,315 18s. 3¾d.

6th June. The French Ambassador.

The Marquis de Rosny, the French Ambassador, embarked at Calais on an English warship which the King had sent for him. M. de Vic, the Governor of Calais, accompanied him with two light French ships as far as Dover, the Ambassador's train being divided amongst the three ships. As the ships set sail, the English Admiral signalled to the Frenchman to break his ensign, of which he took no heed, and one of the French ships even took the lead of the English ship. Whereupon without more ado the English ship fired three shots at the French ship, of which one cut the shrouds and put the ship in some peril. Thereupon the Frenchman hoisted his ensign and fell into his place.

7th June. Sir Walter Ralegh and Durham House.

Some days ago the King granted to the Bishop of Durham to have possession of Durham House from Sir Walter Ralegh, who is commanded to deliver up the house by the 24th of this month, and that the stables and garden should be surrendered forthwith. To which Sir Walter greatly complaineth that the poorest artificer in London hath a quarter's warning given him by his landlord. He hath made provision for forty persons in the spring, and for almost twenty horses; to cast out his hay and oats into the streets at an hour's warning, and to remove his family and staff within fourteen days after is such a severe expulsion as hath not been offered to any man before. To which the Bishop answereth that Sir Walter goes about but to gain time to deface the house by removing the wainscot, or else to shuffle in some nobleman (if not more than one), whom to remove may be harder for him that he would willingly assay.

8th June. A PROCLAMATION FOR THE EARL OF TYRONE.

It is proclaimed that, since the Earl of Tyrone did obtain pardon of Queen Elizabeth, and hath sithence been confirmed in his state and condition of a good subject and in the rank and dignity of an Earl, he is received into his Majesty's grace and favour. Wherefore if any man shall by words or deed abuse the Earl of Tyrone, or misbehave towards him, and not yield him such respect and usage as belongeth to the person of his sort, it shall be esteemed an offence, deserving such punishment as contempt of his Majesty's pleasure expressly signified doth deserve.

THE AMBASSADOR FROM FRANCE IN LONDON.

Monsieur de Rosny, with a large train of noblemen and gallant gentlemen has arrived in London, as Ambassador Extraordinary from the French King. He landed at Dover two days ago. At night they rode in thirty coaches to the Barbican by Red Cross Street to the house of the French Ambassador Legier and there supped with him, and afterwards returned to Crosby Place (Sir John Spencer's house) in Bishop's Gate Street where the principal of them lodge.

ESSEX'S 'APOLOGY' TO BE PRINTED.

Essex's *Apology*, which caused such stirs five years ago, is now to be printed; as also that notorious sermon made before Queen Elizabeth in 1596 by Dr. Anthony Rudd, Bishop of St. David's, wherein he spoke of the Queen's grand climacterial year and of her old age, which moved her to great indignation.

36

9th June. THE ARREST OF PATRICK RUTHVEN.

A man has been arrested in the night, and is supposed to be
Patrick Ruthven, brother to the late Earl of Gowry. At first he
denied it, but it is now said that the Scottish man by whom he
was discovered declares that he is Ruthven, and he himself has
since confessed it. The arrest was after this manner. Certain
Scottish men being at supper, one said that he knew where the
arrantest traitor was, that was in all England or Scotland.
Another challenged him upon it, and brought him to the constable. Whereupon being urged on pain of imprisonment to discover where the party was he brought them to an alley in Tower
Street, where in a chamber of the house they found him asleep.
When he was awaked he was much dismayed, and declared that
he had been banished three years, but that the King had forgiven
him his offence.

10th June. A BOOK CALLED 'THE AMBASSADOR.'

That little book called *The Ambassador*, written by M. Jean
Hotman, is now translated into English from a private copy dispersed amongst the author's friends. Of ambassadors noteth that
there be two sorts; the first being extraordinary for one office
only, as for renewing some alliance, or to congratulate, condole
or to do the like office in the beheld of their masters; the other
ordinary or liegier, without having any time limited but at the
pleasure of the Prince which sendeth them. Ambassadors
should have knowledge of many things, especially of philosophy,
moral and politic, and before all other Roman Civil Law; and
moreover a knowledge of histories will greatly help him, which
besides the pleasure of it will increase in him wisdom and
judgment in the affairs of his charges, and will make him not
to be astonished at anything.

11th June. THE UNIVERSITY OF CAMBRIDGE AND THE
    PURITAN DOCTRINES.

Two days since at a public congregation in Cambridge it was
agreed that whosoever in the University should in any way
oppose the doctrine and discipline of the Church of England,
or any part thereof, should be suspended from any degree taken
or to be taken. This is an answer to the recent petition of the
Puritans which they call the 'Millenary Petition.'

12th June. THE FRENCH AMBASSADOR RECEIVED IN AUDIENCE.

This day (being Sunday) M. de Rosny was received in audience by the King at Greenwich, whither he was carried with his following of 120 gentlemen in the King's barges. It had been his firm intention that all his following should appear in mourning for the late Queen, though he had been told on all sides that no one, be he ambassador, Englishman or stranger, is admitted into the King's presence in black; for indeed neither the memory nor the name of Queen Elizabeth is nowadays mentioned in Court. Nor would M. de Rosny consent to wear other garments than black until last night he was informed that the whole Court consider his intention to be a direct affront which would greatly prejudice his business. He therefore ordered his following to change their apparel. Upon his landing, he was met by the Earl of Northumberland by whom he was conducted into the presence through great crowds of courtiers.

14th June. IRISH NEWS.

In Ireland there is general expectation that the new base moneys will shortly be called in. Whereupon all the King's tenants and farmers hasten to bring their rents and debts into the receipt, but those that have any fees or pensions forbear to ask for them. Hereby the whole loss is like to fall upon the King.

15th June. COURT NEWS.

The Count of Aremberg, that is Ambassador from the Archduke, was appointed to have his audience the next day after the French Ambassador, but he desired to have it deferred for some days, by reason of some pretended indisposition.

The King is said to be very ill-satisfied with the Duke of Lennox for not having more effectively dissuaded the Queen from some courses which greatly displease his Majesty, for conferring the place of her Chamberlain (to which Sir George Carew was recommended) on one Mr. Kennedy, a Scottish gentleman of whom the King hath a very ill conceit, saying that if she do bring him hither to attend her, he will break the staff of his Chamberlainship on his head and so dismiss him. It is said also that she hath hitherto refused to admit my Lady Kildare and the Lady Walsingham to be of her privy chamber, and hath only as yet sworn my Lady of Bedford.

18*th June*. A CITIZEN SLAIN BY THE FRENCHMEN.

Certain of the company of M. de Rosny, the Ambassador of the French King, going to entertain themselves at a bawdy house encountered some citizens, and falling out with them they fought, and one of the citizens is slain. Hereupon the citizens assembled to the number of 3,000 and began to threaten the Frenchmen, who fled for protection to the house of the Ambassador. M. de Rosny, being much put out that his coming to London should be marred by so fatal an accident, caused all his household (being in number about a hundred) to range themselves round the walls, hoping by this means to discover the murderer, which he did by reason of the man's manifest signs of fear. So he held a council forthwith and pronounced sentence of death upon the gentleman whose name is Combaut. Then he sent to the Lord Mayor desiring him to send the officers the next day to conduct the condemned to the place of execution; nor would M. de Rosny revoke his sentence but sent the prisoner to the Lord Mayor to be punished according to the laws of the Realm. He is now set at liberty.

22*nd June*. COURT NEWS.

Affairs go on with a smooth pace and a smiling countenance, the King making the hopes of all to swell, his actions being suitable to the time and his natural disposition. Sometimes he comes to Councils but most time he spends in the fields, parks and chases, chasing away idleness by violent exercise and early rising, wherein the sun seldom prevents him. The people approve his actions and words save that they desire some more of the generous affability which the good old Queen did afford them. The King is now at Windsor, having viewed all his houses and all that he purposeth to entertain the Queen and the Prince who are expected there about fourteen days hence.

THE GALLANTRY OF LORD CECIL'S LITTLE SON.

On the King's birthday (20th June) the Queen, who is now at Worksop Manor, showed herself to the sight of many most honourable persons. She took Lord Cecil's little son in her arms, and kissed him twice, and bestowed a jewel on him, tying it herself in his ear. After the Prince had danced, the Queen commanded that all of his age who attended him should dance, but no one taking it on them, Lord Cecil's son stepped forth in a comely and lowly manner, and took the young Princess and danced his galliard.

23rd June. PIRACY TO BE REPRESSED.

Now that the war with the King of Spain is ceased at his Majesty's entrance into this Kingdom, many, that had commission from the Queen to set out and furnish to sea for the surprising of the King of Spain's subjects and goods, might be utterly undone if they be not suffered to enjoy such goods as they have taken not knowing of the discontinuance of the war. It is therefore proclaimed that ships and goods taken before the 24th April last shall be quietly enjoyed; but any taken thereafter shall be sequestered to the use of the true proprietors. Further, all such men of war as are now at sea without sufficient commission, or shall hereafter take the ships or goods of any subject of Princes in amity with his Majesty, shall be reputed pirates, and they and their accessories shall suffer death as pirates with confiscation of all their lands and goods.

25th June. THE FRENCH AMBASSADOR'S DEPARTURE.

M. de Rosny during his stay hath made many presents. To his Majesty six fine horses richly caparisoned, to which the French King added that he sent a gentleman called Saint Anthony considered to be the best and most accomplished of this age. To the Queen he gave a fair Venetian glass, whereof the golden frame was covered with diamonds; to the Prince a golden lance and helmet, a fencing master and a vaulter; to the Duke of Lennox, the Earl of Northumberland, and other noblemen, boxes, rings and chains of gold and diamonds; and to certain ladies also rings and pearl necklaces. All these presents are valued at more than 60,000 crowns; whereby some at Court shall not be the less inclined to the cause of his master, the French King.

THE QUEEN AT ALTHORP.

On their journey southward the Queen and the Prince were

entertained by Sir Robert Spencer at Althorp, where a particular entertainment was fashioned against their coming by Ben Jonson. As they approached the house from a spinney there appeared a satyr who leapt out, and having spoken sundry verses ran away into the wood again, when to the sound of soft music there came tripping up the lawn a bevy of Fairies, attending on Mab their Queen. After sundry songs and dances in which the satyr hopped amongst the Fairies and was chased away again, he came out of the wood again leading Sir Robert's son before the Queen. Hereat the whole wood and place resounded with the noise of cornets, horns and other hunting music, and a brace of deer were put forth which were killed, as they were meant to be, even in the sight of her Majesty.

27th June. The King Meets the Queen.

The Queen left Althorp and went on to Sir George Fermor's at Euston Neston, where the King met her, with an infinite company of Lords and Ladies and other people. There were 250 carriages, and 5,000 horses. The Prince comes with her. Before her departure there was a speech suddenly thought on to present a morrice of the clowns hereabouts who most officiously presented themselves; but by reason of the throng of the country that came in, their speaker could not be heard, who was in the person of Nobody, attired in a pair of breeches which were made to come up to his neck, with his arms out at the pockets, and a cap drowning his face.

28th June. The Earl of Mar.

The King has now released the Earl of Mar from his charge as guardian to the young Prince, in whose safe keeping he has remained since he was an infant, very handsomely acknowledging the care taken by my Lord in that service.

Troubles at Plymouth.

There are great complaints from Plymouth that since the Queen's death there daily resort thither a great number of sailors, mariners and other masterless men that heretofore have been at sea in men of war, but now being restrained from that course they pester the town, which is already overcharged with many poor people. Some of them commit intolerable outrages, for they steal and take away boats in the night out of the harbour and rob both English and French.

AN EMBASSAGE TO DENMARK.

The Earl of Rutland departed from Gravesend on his journey to Denmark to King Christian the Fourth, to solemnize on his Majesty's behalf the baptism of the King's son, and to present him with the Order of the Garter.

30th June. M. DE ROSNY'S SPLEEN.

M. de Rosny sailed on the 28th but in great discontent, for as he was standing upon the pier at Dover with Sir Lewis Lewkenor a packet of letters was delivered to him, wherein amongst others was one of the King's own hand to the French superscribed '*A mon trescher Frere le Roi trechretien,*' which put him into a great and sudden passion because his master the French King had addressed his letter '*A Monsieur mon Frere &c.*' He was so greatly moved that he requested Sir Lewis with all secrecy and speed to despatch a messenger to Court that his Majesty might alter the style, for he cannot (saith he) deliver it as it is without great scandal to his master and imputation to himself.

THE PLAGUE.

The plague now continually increaseth. This last week 158 are dead of it.

1st July. THE EARL OF SOUTHAMPTON AND THE LORD GREY.

The Earl of Southampton and the Lord Grey have renewed their old quarrels and last night fell out flatly before the Queen. She was in discourse with my Lord Southampton touching the Earl of Essex's action, and wondered, as she said, that so many great men did so little for themselves; to which my Lord answered that the Queen being made a party against them they were forced to yield; but if that course had not been taken, there was none of their private enemies, with whom their only quarrel was, that durst have opposed themselves. This being overheard by Lord Grey, he would have maintained the contrary part, upon which he had the lie given him. The Queen bade them remember where they were, and soon after sent them to their lodgings, to which they were committed with guard over them. To-day they were brought before the Council and condemned to be sent back to the Tower; but soon after the King sent for them, and taking the quarrel upon him, and seeing that the wrong and disgrace had been done to her Majesty and not exchanged between them, he forgave it to make them friends; which is accordingly effected and they set at liberty.

2nd July. THE FEAST OF ST. GEORGE.

The Feast of St. George was held this day at Windsor, where the young Prince was installed Knight of the Most Noble Order of the Garter, and after, in his robes, presented to the Queen. He is much commended for his quick witty answers, princely carriage, and reverend performing his obeisance at the altar. Likewise there were installed the Duke of Lennox, and the Earls of Southampton, Mar, and Pembroke, and elected the King of Denmark and the Duke of Wirtenburg. At the same time the great ladies of England came to the Court to discharge their homage to her Majesty, who kissed her hand, kneeling one by one.

3rd July. A CONSPIRACY SUSPECTED.

A proclamation has been signed and sent out for the apprehension of Anthony Copley, a busy-headed fellow, and a writer of late in these controversies between the seminaries and the Jesuits. He is suspected of some practice against the King's person, of which he would not only be the undertaker of the attempt himself but has excited divers others to do the like.

5th July. A GREAT DROUGHT.

This spring there has been such an exceeding great drought in all parts of England that everywhere the grass, even in the best meadows by the sides of rivers, was all burnt up, so that it seemed impossible any grass should grow before next spring, for even the roots of the grass were withered and dry. Nevertheless, at the end of June there was an after spring, and grass in good plenty.

7th July. SIR JOHN FORTESCUE'S COMPLAINT.

Sir John Fortescue greatly complaineth that he is ordered to yield the house which all the Chancellors of the Duchy of Lancaster have held to Sir George Hume. He complaineth that it will be a great touch to his reputation to become an under-servant, and dwell in the Wardrobe, whereof for forty-five years he has been Master. He prays that the King will not insist on a matter of such inconvenience to himself and to his service, and especially since in the house of the Wardrobe are kept the stores and provisions and stuffs, which causes a continual repair of all artificers belonging to that service. It will but add to the offences and disagreements which may arise from the mingling of Sir George's servants and his own.

10th July. A Secret Press Taken.

Yesterday a seminary priest being taken in Westminster, the lodgings of his kinswoman in Ely House rents were this day searched, when there were found sundry conveyances by doors out of one chamber into another, with passages into the leads for escaping, all very convenient for persons of evil affection to the State. There were discovered also divers great chests and coffers, full of printed books of that seminary faction; and, upon further search, the press itself with all things appertaining to printing, with letters ready set upon the press, and paper for proceeding in the business.

11th July. The Coronation Curtailed.

By reason of the daily increase of the infection in the City, there is great fear lest by the great assembling of the people at the Coronation the infection be dispersed into all places of the Realm. It is now proclaimed that all parts of that solemnity which are not essential to it are forborne, together with his Majesty's solemn entry and passage through the City of London which is put off till the winter. Those that have necessary employment in the solemnity shall bring with them no greater train of servants than of necessity they must each use in his degree about their persons, which is limited to Earls sixteen, to Bishops and Barons ten, to Knights six, and to Gentlemen four. Moreover the Feast of St. James that is commonly held at Westminster at this time is to be put off for eight or ten days.

12th July. The State of Ireland.

Since the departure of the Lord Lieutenant from Ireland a great swarm of Jesuits, seminaries, friars and priests frequent the towns in the English Pale and borders more boldly than before, and few of the best houses in the Pale but relieve and receive them. These priests would persuade the people that there will

44

be a toleration of religion, and for procuring of it they will send agents to the Court, wherein they are strongly supported by some lawyers and some of the King's officers. William Meade, the Recorder of Cork, is still in prison in Dublin, for such is his popularity that the commissioners have much ado even to bring in an indictment against him for his treasons.

14th July. SIR WALTER RALEGH AND OTHERS ARRESTED.

Lord Cobham, Master George Brooke his brother, Sir Walter Ralegh and Lord Grey have been arrested. The cause as yet is unknown.

THE KING'S DELIVERANCE TO BE REMEMBERED.

Upon the motion of the Council, the Archbishop of Canterbury hath instructed the Bishops that the day of the King's delivery from the conspiracy of Gowry, being the 5th August, shall be yearly solemnized by public assembly, prayer and thanksgiving to God in all parish churches throughout the realm and by cessation from work and labour, as is done in the Kingdom of Scotland. Until some other is devised, the same order shall be used as was used on the 17th November in the late Queen's time, with special charge that in every particular church there shall be a sermon and service with a declaration of the great blessing of God for his Majesty's deliverance.

UNRULY NEGLECT OF PLAGUE ORDERS.

In the City of Westminster there is much neglect of the orders concerning the plague. Near St. Clement's Church in the Fields the people are very unruly, so that the townsmen are constrained to watch their houses and force them back into their houses which are infected. The bills that are set up upon the doors are constantly pulled down, whereby the infected houses cannot be known but to very few. Moreover many persons of good ability, who are chargeable to contribute towards the relief of these poor infected people, refuse to pay any reasonable taxation.

15th July. THE CHARACTERS OF KING JAMES AND QUEEN ELIZABETH COMPARED.

Now that Queen Elizabeth is passed beyond flatterers, and the King has been three months in his Kingdom of England their true natures can more clearly be discerned. The King hath a magnanimous spirit, venturous to hazard his body in hunting especially, and most patient of labour, cold and heat. So was the old Queen, far above all other of her sex and years. Both of them most merciful in disposition, soon angry yet without bitterness or stinging revenge. In prudence, justice and temperance, both are the admiration to Princes. The King is most bountiful, seldom denying any suit: the Queen was strict in giving, which age and her sex inclined her unto. The one often complained of for sparing; the other so benign that his people fear his overreadiness in giving. The Queen slow to resolution, seldom to be retracted; his Majesty quick in concluding and more variable in subsisting. The Queen solemn and ceremonious, and requiring decent and disparent order to be kept convenient in each degree; and though she bore a greater majesty, yet would she labour to entertain strangers and suitors and her people with more courtly courtesy and favourable speeches than the King useth, who, although he be indeed of a more true benignity and ingenuous nature, yet the neglect of these ordinary ceremonies which his variable and quick wit cannot attend makes common people judge otherwise of him. The Queen took delight and made profit in simulation and dissimulation, and thereby discovered fashions and pretences and the true meaning of her several Councillors in matters of importance: the King seems to neglect that as baseness, thinking his own wit sufficient to exploit things pertinent by ordinary means, without such labour and insinuation.

The Queen was quick of apprehension, wise in counsel by reason of her great reading and overreaching experience, of an admirable felicity of memory, and albeit of great constancy; yet by continual labour her benign nature was changed and in part depraved by years and jealousies about her, which she could hardly eschew, being in age as a recluse cloistered to hear only such tones as her keepers sounded unto her. The King is of the sharpest wit and invention, ready and pithy speech, an exceeding good memory, of very sweet and pleasant nature. God forbid that his most gracious disposition and heroic mind be not depraved with ill counsel, and that neither the wealth and peace of England make him forget God nor the painted flattery of the Court cause him to forget himself.

16*th July.* CONSPIRATORS TO BE APPREHENDED.

It is given out that Copley in his confessions hath discovered a conspiracy of a great number of others to have made an attempt not only dangerous to the King's person but to the whole State. Proclamation is now made for the apprehending of Sir Griffin Markham, and the two priests Watson and Clarke, that were such busy stirrers on behalf of the secular Catholics against the Jesuits.

THE DESCRIPTION OF THE PERSONS

Sir Griffin Markham hath a large broad face, of a bleak complexion, a big nose, one of his hands is maimed by an hurt in his arm received by the shot of a bullet; he hath thin and little hair upon his beard. All his brethren are tall of stature, young, and without any hair of their faces, of exceeding swarthy and bad complexions, and all have very great noses.

William Watson, priest, is a man of the lowest order, about 36 years of age, his hair betwixt abram and flaxen. He looketh asquint, and is very purblind, so as if he read anything he pulleth the paper near to his eyes. He did wear his beard at length, of the same coloured hair as his head; but information is given that now his beard is cut.

William Clarke, priest, is a man of middle stature, inclining to the lower sort, about the age of 36 years; his hair is betwixt red and yellow. He keepeth his beard close cut; he is not lean nor corpulent, but betwixt both, rather lean.

17*th July.* FORTY POUND LANDHOLDERS TO BE KNIGHTED.

It is now commanded by the King that all who hold land, tenements or hereditaments to the value of £40 annually shall come to receive the honour of knighthood, or shall compound with the commissioners in sums of money to be determined. The commissioners herewith appointed are the Lords Zouch, Mountjoy and Knollys, Sir John Popham, Lord Edward Bruce and Sir John Herbert.

19*th July.* A NEW GREAT SEAL.

To-day the Lord Keeper brought in a new Great Seal and had the old defaced and cut in pieces by the King himself, which was done in the presence of most of the Council called thereto

into the Privy Chamber; after which the King made delivery of
the new Seal to the Lord Keeper and allowed him the old Seal
as a perquisite. The King hath also signed bills, which my Lord
Cecil brought him, for the creation of eight Barons and two
Earls; but he signed them all at one time confusedly, not
respecting who should have antiquity.

20th July. SIR WALTER RALEGH TRIES TO KILL HIMSELF.

While the Lord Cecil and some Councillors were in their
Tower examining the prisoners, Sir Walter Ralegh tried to
murder himself by stabbing himself with a knife under the right
pap, but the blow struck one of his ribs and so saved his life, and
his jailors prevented him from striking again. When the Councillors heard of the attempt they went to him and found him in
some agony, as one unable to endure his misfortunes and careless
of life, albeit protesting his innocence.

The causes of this conspiracy are now said to be mainly two.
Firstly, because most of the accused having always been of the
King's party expected large rewards at his coming, instead of
which he has never regarded them with a favourable eye; the
other, that the coming of the new King would bring about the
downfall of certain of the Council whom they hated. But now
these Councillors are in greater authority than ever, for they
very soon won over the Scottish Councillors who were principally
in want of money. Some say that the King is now so entirely in
the hands of his Council that he seems almost to have forgotten
that he is a King, except in his kingly pursuit of the deer, and
leaves his Councillors with such absolute authority that they are
more powerful even than before.

21st July. NEW PEERS CREATED.

The King this day in the Great Hall at Hampton Court,
in the presence of the Queen, created these peers following:
the Earl of Southampton restored and newly created; Thomas,
Lord Howard of Walden, created Earl of Suffolk; Charles
Blount, Lord Mountjoy, created Earl of Devonshire; Sir
Thomas Egerton, Lord Chancellor, created Baron Ellesmere;
Sir William Russel, Lord Russel of Thornhaugh; Sir Henry
Grey, Lord Grey of Groby; Sir John Petre, Lord Petre of
Writtle; Sir John Harington, Lord Harington of Exton; Sir

Henry Danvers, Lord Danvers of Dauntsy; Sir Thomas Gerard, Lord Gerard of Gerard's Bromley; and Sir Robert Spencer, Lord Spencer of Wormleighton.

THE PLAGUE.

They begin now to reckon the out parishes in the weekly returns of death and christenings; of the plague 917 persons are dead in one week.

22nd July. THE BASE MONEY IN IRELAND.

The Lord Deputy and the Council in Ireland declare that there is great scarcity of all things, and excessive prices of provisions, for the people fear to sell unless they be paid in silver, crying that they will keep their wares in their shops rather than rent them for this base money, seeing they can make no use of it. Wherefore the sooner the coin is altered, the better for the King.

24th July. MORE KNIGHTS MADE.

Yesterday not less than 300 Gentlemen were knighted by his Majesty in the garden at Whitehall. To-day was performed the solemnity of Knights of the Bath who, riding honourably from St. James to the Court, made show with their squires and pages about the Tiltyard; and after went up into the Park of St. James and there lighted from their horses, and went up to his Majesty in the Gallery, where they received the Order of Knighthood of the Bath, being in number sixty.

25th July (St. James's Day). THE CORONATION OF THE KING AND QUEEN.

This day was King James crowned at Westminster, the first King of England and Ireland of this name, and the sixth of Scotland; but the pomp was diminished and the customary banquet forborne by reason of the pestilence. The Lord Mayor, Sir Robert Lee, in a gown of crimson velvet, and his brethren the aldermen in gowns of scarlet came by water from the City, and twelve principal citizens were admitted to attend on them, but all other citizens were stayed from passing to Westminster by water or by land as much as might be. Nevertheless the presence of the nobility, the bishops, the sixty Knights of the Bath newly made, and the officers about the King made a great assembly

The coronation was performed after the ancient manner. The King and Queen were led up to the throne of estate, which was spread with cloth of gold and silver. Then Garter King of Arms proclaimed in each of the four angles and quarters of the church in the King's hearing, demanding whether they would have King James their King; and the people assented with applause, shouting, and throwing up their hats.

Then the sermon was preached by the Bishop of Winchester upon Romans xiii, ver. 1, 'The powers that are, are ordained of God.' And after the sermon the King took the oath. Then was sung 'Come, Holy Ghost' and the Litany was sung by the Bishop. Then was performed the ceremony of the anointing (for which purpose the King's undergarments were so made that the places to be anointed might, by the undoing certain loops, be made open); and, after other prayers had been said, the King was invested with the Robes of King Edward the Confessor by the Abbot of Westminster. Then was he crowned with the crown of King Edward the Confessor, and enthroned in the Throne Royal and there received the homage of all the peers.

Then the Lord Keeper published to the people in the four several quarters of the theatre that the King had granted to his people a most ample and general pardon as ever Prince did, at which the people with shouts again prayed for the King.

Then the Queen was likewise anointed and crowned. Then was the Communion made, and after the King and the Queen received the Holy Sacrament. When the Communion was ended, they withdrew themselves into the traverse and the King put off the robes of King Edward and was arrayed in his own robes by the Great Chamberlain of England. Then coming forth, the Archbishop put upon the heads of the King and the Queen the imperial crowns which they are to wear. So the King, taking his sceptre in his hand and the Queen hers, the train was set in order and they returned the same way they came.

A SCOTS PROPHECY FULFILLED.

It is much noted by the superstitious that in the coronation is fulfilled an ancient Scots prophecy, for the King was crowned upon the Throne of Edward the First that holds the venerable stone which he brought from Scotland, called *Saxum Jacobi*, and which some old saws declare to be the same that Jacob rested his head upon. Concerning this stone (so the Scots declare) there is this saying:

> *Ni fallat Fatum*
> *Scoti hunc quocunque locatum,*
> *Invenient lapidem*
> *Regnare tenentur ibidem.*

Englished thus:

> Fate hath designed
> That wheresoe'er this stone
> The Scots shall find
> There shall they hold the throne.

26th July. THE RECORDER OF CORK ACQUITTED.

Notwithstanding extraordinary courses taken against at his trial William Meade, the Recorder of Cork, is of late acquitted by an Irish jury. So eager were his judges for his conviction, that upon the indictment the grand jury were dealt with severely, every man by himself giving his own verdict not knowing the mind of his fellows, and at the arraignment the evidence against him was enforced *viva voce* in open court of them that were his judges. But all would not serve, for such is the disposition of an Irish jury, that a traitor is acquitted against all the evidence that can be brought. There is an intention to indict these same jurors because they acquitted Meade falsely and contrary to their evidence, which was indeed very sufficient on all heads of the indictment.

27th July. SIR WALTER RALEGH.

The King's will is now that Sir Walter Ralegh shall be well examined, and that at the examination some good preacher shall be present to make him known that it is his soul he must wound not his body.

28th July. THE PLAGUE.

This week 1,396 are reported dead of the plague.

31st July. DR. THOMAS LODGE.

In these days many set up their bills professing such miracles against the plague as if they held the rein of Destiny in their hands, and amongst them one near to the house of Dr. Thomas Lodge in Warwick Lane. But as he omitted to underwrite his name, everyone that read came flocking to Dr. Lodge, conjuring him by large proffers and persuasions to store them with the promised preservatives; whereat he is much annoyed because it would seem that he makes himself vendible (which is unworthy a liberal mind and a physician and philosopher who ought not to prostitute so sacred a profession so abjectly), and amazed that the multitude dare trust themselves to such persons. Wherefore he now goes about to write a book of the plague which he will freely and charitably offer to all who want means to relieve their estates in this time of visitation.

1st August. SUITORS ORDERED TO AVOID THE COURT.

There is a new proclamation that no suitors shall repair to the Court till the winter, and that all men not ordinarily employed there shall return to their dwellings until they are recalled.

4th August. THE LATE CONSPIRACY.

The truth of the late discovered plot is now given out to have been of this nature. Sir Griffin Markham and Master George Brooke, brother to the Lord Cobham, having dealt with the King in former time, finding their hopes somewhat deceived, fell into discontent against the King and most of the nobility that are Councillors; and observing in the Lord Grey a like discontented humour they began to project an alteration of the State, hoping that if they could with some convenient number possess the person of the King, they might by his authority raise themselves to what places they would. They planned further that Lord Grey should be Earl Marshal, Markham be Secretary, Brooke Lord Treasurer of England, and Watson the priest Lord Chancellor. And to further their designs one of them undertook by Watson and Clarke, the two priests (who were very forward in that controversy between the Jesuits and the Seculars two years ago), to draw in some Catholics to assent to deliver a petition to the King for the toleration of religion, but

52

so well provided as the King should not have thought himself in safety to deny them. But being in a state of great irresolution nothing was attempted and the day put off, for new fears distracted them, which arrived not only from the difficulty to surprise the Court where there never sleepeth under 300 gentlemen that carry arms, but because the Council having some secret notice began to set better order of doors and passages. Nevertheless they gave not over their designs until Copley, the principal conspirator, was taken; and since then the others also have been apprehended, since when all have confessed under their hands.

The Lord Cobham was no particular actor or contriver of this conspiracy, yet he had another iron in the fire, which he let fall to his brother and some others. He purposed to go over to Spa, thereby to have access to the Archduke to whom he meant to have intimated big discontentment, and the general disposition of others in the country on whom he would have pretended that good sums of money would have taken great hold. Thence he would have gone into Spain and there seen what the King would have embraced; and at his return he would have passed to Jersey, where Sir Walter Ralegh would have met him and so have conferred together what course to take for advancement of those intentions which his overtures should have begot.

Sir Walter Ralegh is committed for divers reasons. First, he hath been discontented in the sight of all ever since the King came in, although for those offices which are taken from him, the King gave him £300 a year during his life and forgave him a good arrearage of debt. Secondly, his inwardness, or rather his governing the Lord Cobham's spirit, made great suspicion that he had part in these treasons; which were increased by a letter that he wrote before he was sent to prison secretly advising Lord Cobham if he were examined of anything to stand peremptory and not to be afraid, for one witness could not condemn him. After which Lord Cobham, being called in question, did first confess these treasons, and then before eleven councillors accused Sir Walter to be privy to his Spanish course, and that he would never have dealt therein but by his own incessant provocation.

THE PLAGUE.

The plague still increaseth, and there died of it last week
1,922 persons.

5th August. A DAY OF THANKSGIVING.

This day was kept holy day, with morning prayers, sermons,
and evening prayers, and at night bonfires, in thanksgiving for
the King's escape from being murdered by the Earl of Gowry
three years since.

TROUBLE IN THE LOW COUNTRIES.

There was lately a great quarrel in the camp of the Count
Maurice at Gertrudenberg between the English and the French
regiments, and some fifteen men slain and thirty hurt on either
side. A Colonel who tried to thrust himself between was hurt
in the belly with a pike and is dead, and if Sir Horace Vere
had not come, there had been the last of the French regiment
for the soldiers had beaten the French to their ships and were
entering. All our men were killed with musket shots from the
ship, but the French with pikes and swords, for our men had
no powder having shot it all away in honour of the King's
Coronation. There has been a discontent between our men
and the French for some time.

Not long since forty or fifty houses were burned in Breda
which was caused by a Frenchman who came to a house where
a whore was lodged, and would have come in to lie with her,
but she refused to open the door, whereupon he fetched a
bundle of straw and fired the house and many more.

6th August. THE EARL OF RUTLAND'S EMBASSAGE.

The Earl of Rutland has landed at Scarborough on his way
back from Denmark, having had a stormy passage, for he set
sail for England on the 19th July and afterwards by contrary
winds was delayed fourteen days at sea. My Lord was present
as Lord Ambassador on his Majesty's behalf at the baptism of
the son of the King of Denmark on the 10th of July, which
was performed according to the Lutheran Church at Copen-
hagen, where the Bishop with one deacon in rich vestments
read prayers both in the Latin and the Danish tongues, and then
descended to the font which stood in the body of the choir.

Here the Queen, the King's mother, being led by the Lord Ambassador and the Duke Ulric, the King's brother, bore the child in her arms, and then delivered it to be held by the Ambassador whilst she slipped back the head-attire for the baptism. The same day the King made a solemn feast for the Ambassador and other deputies of gossips, placing the English Ambassador upon the right hand of the Queen Mother. For eight days the King entertained the Ambassador with divers princely pastimes, such as the viewing of his ships, his strange devices of water-works for the forging of ordnance, his store-houses of munitions, his stables and other things of state. On the 14th of July the King received the Order of the Garter in the Castle of Elsinore at the hands of the Earl of Rutland, who was assisted by William Segar, Norroy King-at-Arms.

A DEPUTATION FROM IRELAND.

Two knights and two lawyers from Ireland have petitioned the King for the redress of three grievances; that there shall be a change in the officers of justice, that the Irish money may be restored to what it was before the war, and that they may have liberty to worship as Catholics. To the first and second the King showed some inclination, but to the third he replied that if he had to wade in blood and had but ten followers, and on such conditions might he recover his kingdom, he would lose all rather than grant this request. And with that he commanded them to the Tower.

7th August. THE NEW KNIGHTS.

There is much talk at Court of the many new Knights, some of them being yeomen's sons, and divers pedlars' sons of London, amongst the rest one Thimblethorpe, an attorney of Norfolk, that is called 'Nimblechaps,' full of the pox, who hath his knighthood for £7 10s. One knight from Suffolk followed the Court so long for a knighthood as, whether for want of good lodging or shift of raiment, he and his men were most wonderfully lousy; and yet (paying well for it) in the end he is made a lousy knight. Of these kind of knights there are many jests bred; as that a knight coming to a door very straitly kept by the usher, he earnestly requested to come in. The usher asked him what he was. He told him a knight. The usher answered he must stay without, for there were so many new knights would come in as they should have no room for the Squires. Another jest was that two walking espied one far off, the one demanded what he should be. The other answered he seemed to be a gentleman. 'No, I warrant you,' says the other, 'I think he is but a knight.'

8th August. FAIRS PUT OFF.

Because of the infection still increasing it is forbidden to hold either Bartholomew Fair or Stourbridge Fair. Nor shall any fair be held within fifty miles of London.

9th August. A STRANGE COACH.

This day it is said that a coach passed through London strangely and wonderfully dressed, for it was all hung with rue from the top to the toe of the boot to keep the very leather and nails from the infection, even the very nostrils of the horses being stopped with herb grace; and thus it ran through Cornhill just in the middle of the street with such a violent trample as if the devil had been coachman.

10th August. MASTER RALPH WINWOOD SENT TO THE STATES.

Master Ralph Winwood, that was formerly the Queen's agent in the French Court, is now sent to the States. He is to inform them that, howsoever the King may reason to settle all things between his Kingdoms and the King of Spain and the Archduke, nevertheless nothing shall be concluded to their prejudice, nor any treaty made to which they may not become parties if they shall find it convenient for their affairs.

PRAYERS FOR THE PLAGUE.

This day is appointed to be kept a holy day with fasting, with frequent prayers to God and sermons of repentance to the people, and charity to the poor to be collected and distributed; and the like is commanded to be done weekly every Wednesday so long as the heavy hand of God by the plague of pestilence shall continue among us.

THE LADY ARABELLA.

The Lady Arabella has now been summoned to Court and

placed near the King and Queen as a Princess of the Blood Royal; and in her appointments, table and rank she takes precedence of all other ladies in Court. She has already begun to bear the Queen's train when she goes to the chapel. For the rest she lives very retired, concerning which there are many rumours.

12th August. THE CITY MARSHAL RESISTED.

The Lord Mayor hath of late sent out precepts that not above six persons shall accompany the corpse of any dying of the plague to their burials; but it is very generally disobeyed, the people of the meaner sort, for the most part women, continuing still in accompanying the dead. Hereupon order is given to the ministers of parishes to admonish their parishioners; but they neglect it, both preaching at funeral sermons and accompanying the corpses, alleging that burial is a spiritual jurisdiction belonging to the Bishops. To-day at Moorgate, being the way going to the new churchyard, there was a great multitude accompanying the corpse of one dead of the plague, and when the City Marshal put them back, many of them fell upon him and beat him and grievously hurt his men.

15th August. CLARKE ARRESTED.

Clarke, the priest, for whom proclamation was lately made, was arrested at Worcester two days since, lurking in these parts under the name of Francis.

17th August. A PALL FOR THE KING'S MOTHER.

On the 14th Sir William Dethick, Garter King-of-Arms, being sent to Peterborough, assisted by many knights and gentlemen, and much people at the time of divine service, laid a rich pall of velvet over the tomb of the Queen Mary of Scots, his Majesty's mother (who was beheaded on the 8th of February, 1587). Then the Bishop preached a sermon in that behalf in the morning and made a great feast at dinner, and the Dean preached of the same in the afternoon. Sir William it was who royally and sumptuously interred that Queen on the 1st of August 1587.

TYRONE'S FEARS.

The Earl of Tyrone, finding himself quite out of favour at Court, has asked leave to go back to Ireland. The King gave him a present of 2,000 angels and gave him leave, but he is alarmed because of the imprisonment of those from Ireland, fearing lest if he sets out now the King will have him slain on the road.

18th *August*. THE PLAGUE STILL INCREASING.
Last week there was some lessening of the infection, the dead being 1,745; but this week there are nigh on a thousand more dead, in all 2,713.

19th *August*. DR. LODGE'S 'TREATISE OF THE PLAGUE.'
Dr. Thomas Lodge hath now written a *Treatise of the Plague*, containing the nature, signs and accidents of the same, with the certain and absolute cure of the fevers, botches and carbuncles that reign in these times, and also many singular experiments and preservatives gathered of divers worthy travellers. As for the cause of the plague, they differ from the usual causes of private sicknesses (which are too great repletion, a general depravitation of the humours in the body, obstruction, or binding, or putrefaction) and are contagious and pestilent, arising from the attraction and breathing in of the air, infected and poisoned with a certain venomous vapour contrary to the nature of man. Writeth much of the policy that ought to be held in a city during the plague time, as that it should be kept clean and neat from all filth and dung-hills and stinking rubbish; and that the sick should be separated from the well in a hospital or pesthouse to be built without the city in some unfrequented place.

23rd *August*. COURT NEWS.
At Court they say that our great and gracious Ladies leave no gesture nor fault of the late Queen unremembered.

25th *August*. THE PLAGUE DEATHS.
This week 2,539 are dead of the plague.

31st *August*. DOGS KILLED.
As in former times of plague, there has been a great killing of dogs, which are very generally believed to be one cause of spreading the infection. In Westminster alone more than 500 have been slain this summer.

1st September. THE PLAGUE STILL INCREASING.

The plague still groweth, and now 3,035 are reported dead of it this last week.

5th September. A BOOK AGAINST THE RELIGION.

One Matthew Kellison, a Catholic priest, hath written a vast book called *A Survey of the new Religion, detecting many gross absurdities which it implieth,* which is printed at Doway, and dedicated in a very bold and presumptuous Epistle to His Majesty, wherein this author would have him by all manners of persuasions to admit the Catholic faith, alleging, amongst many others, that the Catholics are more in number than any sect in the Realm, and linked in religion to all Catholic Princes and countries who would be more loving neighbours if they see this favour granted.

6th September. THE ARRIVAL OF THE SPANISH AMBAS-
SADOR.

After many slow and tedious journeys the Spanish Ambassador reached Oxford on the 2nd of September. My Lord Danvers met him at Canterbury, and attended on him all the way with many great and noble courtesies, to him and the gentlemen of his train to their great satisfaction. My Lord of Devonshire met him at Henley, and came on with him, being by the way attended on by the Sheriff and sundry gentlemen of the county. He took my Lord of Devonshire's coming as an exceeding honour, being a man whose name and actions he had very favourable reports of in Spain, and was the one nobleman above all the rest he chiefly desired to see. Upon his entry into Oxford he was visited by the Vice-Chancellor and sundry Doctors of the University at his lodgings, and greeted with a short oration in Latin, and presented with certain gloves embroidered with gold. He is lodged in Christ Church, which he has already trimmed with his own hangings and furniture, and his hangings of estate equal in every way both in rank and pride those of the King. His plate and furniture are very honourable and sumptuous, but the rest of his expenses and liberalities hitherto are very mean, and in no way answerable to what was expected and bruited by his forerunners. Some gentlemen known to be recusants have repaired to him, and some even awaited his landing at Dover, and followed him the most part of the way.

10th September. BEN JONSON'S SON.

Ben Jonson's eldest son, a boy of seven years old, is dead of the plague, Ben himself being in the country at Sir Robert Cotton's house with Master Camden. He declareth that he saw in a vision his son with the mark of a bloody cross on his forehead, and in the morning he told Master Camden who would persuade him that it was but an apprehension of his fantasy; but anon came letters from his wife of the death of that boy. Upon whom Ben hath written an epigram wherein he calls him 'Ben Jonson, his best piece of poetry.'

11th September. COURT NEWS.

The judges of late met at Maidenhead to consider of the crime of the prisoners, and it is said they make no question of finding all culpable save only Sir Walter Ralegh, against whom the proofs are less pregnant. The Court is now at Woodstock, and hath been so continually haunted with the sickness by reason of the disorderly company following from place to place that they do infect all places whither they come. In a few days they go to Winchester to seek a purer air there. The Lord Admiral in his passage to Court hath recovered possession of Donnington from the Lady Elizabeth Russell, she being absent in Wales.

The Lord Treasurer is much disquieted how to find money to supply the King's necessities, and protested to some that he knoweth not how to procure money to pay for the King's diet, so that the penury is like more and more to increase, and small hope of relief to any of the suitors.

The Lord Hunsdon died five days ago, on the 6th.

THE RETURN OF THE SHIPS FROM THE EAST INDIA VOYAGE.

The ships sent forth by the company for the discovery of a trade in the East India are come home again, and anchored in the Downs on the 11th September, having left England in April, 1601. The ships were the *Dragon*, being the Admiral wherein went Captain James Lancaster, the General, of 600 tons with 202 men, the *Hector*, with Captain John Middleton,

300 tons with 108 men, the *Ascension*, 260 tons with 82 men, the *Susan* with 88 men, and the *Guest*, a victualler of 130 tons.

After leaving the Grand Canaria they were becalmed for a month, but near the Line they captured a Portugal ship from which they took much wine, oil and meal for their own uses. On the way down by the Africk coast the men were much afflicted with scurvy, except in the General's ship, because he had brought with him certain bottles of the juice of the lemon, of which he gave spoonfuls to each man fasting every morning. Also he would not allow his men to eat salt meat, which is a principal cause of the disease. They thereupon put into a certain place called Saldania, where they brought the sails ashore and of them made tents for the sick. Here they traded with the savages for oxen and sheep; and because there was no interpreter the General spoke to them in the cattle's language, which was never changed at the confusion of Babel, which is 'moath' for oxen and 'baa' for sheep. The people here are of a tawny colour, and their speech is wholly uttered in the throat, and they clock with their tongues in such a sort that not one of the company could discover a word of their language in all the seven weeks they stayed there. One hundred and five of the company were dead before they left this place.

They doubled the Cape of Buena Esperanza on the 1st November; but not long after this the men began again to fall sick of the scurvy, so that they sought land again, and bartered with savages for rice, hens, oranges and lemons, and a fruit called a plantain, which is much esteemed; but they took great care always to have some of the men with their pieces ready. At this time they lost several of the principal men, as the Master's mate, the Preacher and the Surgeon in the General's ship; and besides as they carried the Master's mate ashore to his burial, the gunner fired off three pieces in salute, but the bullets being in them, one struck the Captain and the boatswain's mate of the *Ascension* stark dead, so that they who went to see the burial of another were both buried themselves.

They reached the Islands of Nicobar in April. Here the people go naked, except for a girdle of linen cloth; but they were very fearful of our men. The General reports that he saw some of the priests in this place all apparelled, but so close to their bodies as if they had been sewn into it; and upon their heads a pair of horns, with their faces painted green, black and yellow, and behind them on their buttocks a tail hanging down like the Devil in a painted cloth. When he demanded why they go in that attire, they replied that the Devil appeared in this form at their sacrifices.

They reached the Road of Achin in the Island of Sumatra, which was the goal of their journey, on the 5th of June last year. Here at their landing they encountered two Holland merchants who had been left behind to learn the language. Then Captain John Middleton with four or five to attend him was sent to the King of Achin with a letter from Queen Elizabeth to deliver. He treated them with great honour, sending a special robe and a tuck of calico for the General. Here they stayed long whilst a treaty of trade was made, after many conferences between the General and the King's noblemen; after which the merchants began to buy in stores of pepper, but by reason of sterility the year before the price was high. Moreover, they were much hindered by the Portugal Ambassador, though the King did not favour him.

They remained at Sumatra until September; and then, leaving the merchants under the King's protection to buy up pepper while he was gone, the General took the ships, and accompanied by a Dutch ship which asked to sail in his company, went for the Moluccas; and here in the Straits they fell in with a Portugal carrack of 900 tons, which was first espied by the *Hector*. When the rest of the ships heard the noise of the cannon they closed in on her, and from the Admiral were discharged six pieces together from the prow, which brought down the main yard. So they lay round her all night without shooting lest they should sink her. At the break of day, the Captain of the carrack put off in his boat and came aboard the *Hector*, whence Captain John Middleton brought him to the General's ship, where they rendered their ship and goods. Captain Lancaster was careful to prevent any rifling or spoil of the ship, and after sending the principal officers to our ship, he allowed only four of his men to be put in charge of the prize, nor would he go on board himself lest the mariners or the merchants in London should charge him with helping himself. From this ship they unladed 950 packs of calicoes and pintados. She also had on board 600 persons, men, women and children.

Thus they came back to Achin towards the end of October, where the King greeted them kindly. Then the General willed the merchants to put aboard the *Ascension* all the pepper, cinnamon and cloves that they had bought, for he intended to go for Bantam in Java. Then they held their course along the coast of Sumatra, to see if they could encounter the *Susan*, which had been sent before to buy up pepper from other parts where it was cheaper. They met her at a port called Priaman, and found that already a great store of pepper and cloves had been brought together. So the General ordered the Captain of the *Susan* to take on board as much as he could and sail for England, whilst the rest of the ships went on to Bantam.

In this place also they were very well received by the King, who is a boy of 10 or 11 years, and his nobles, and had free leave to trade. By the 10th February of this year the ships were fully laden, but at this time Master Middleton, the Captain of the *Hector*, fell sick and died.

Then the General put all things in order, and left behind him a pinnace of 40 tons, with twelve men and some of the merchants to trade in the Moluccas, and to settle a factory there against the next shipping out of England. Besides, he hath left eight men and three factors in Bantam, of whom the chief is Mr. William Starkey, to sell such commodities as are left there against his next return.

The 20th February they sailed from Bantam, and on their return were in great danger from storms, especially near to the land of Madagascar, and again in May by the Cape of Buena Esperanza, for there is a contrary wind that drove them almost 40 degrees to the southward with the hail and snow, so that their case was very desperate, especially in the Admiral where the rudder was broken away. At this time they were in such danger that Captain Lancaster bade the Master of the *Hector* shift homewards and save himself; but he would not.

At last, after much buffeting by the sea, on the 5th June they had sighted the Island of St. Helena; and here they had much refreshing from the good water and the wild goats which they shot. They left this island on the 5th July, and neared Land's End on the 7th of this present month.

15th September. THE PLAGUE DEATHS.

The deaths from plague these two several weeks are 2,724 and 2,818.

16th September. FOREIGN AMBASSADORS.

The French and Spanish Ambassadors who are recently come to gratulate his Majesty have as yet no audience but continue both at Oxford, and it is thought they shall not be heard before the King's coming to Winchester. The King gave M. de Vitry, the French Ambassador, a house which the Ambassador disliked, saying that he had given the King, when he was poor King of Scotland, £20 better than that was, with other speeches of discontent, all of which came to the King's ear. The Spanish Ambassador hath brought great store of Spanish gloves, hawk's hoods, leather for jerkins, and a perfumer; these delicacies he bestoweth amongst the lords and ladies, and with such courtesies winneth their affections so that he is esteemed a far welcomer guest than M. de Rosny. At Oxford he took some distaste at his lodgings, and would needs lodge in an inn because he had not all Christ Church to himself, and was not received by the Vice-Chancellor *in pontificalibus* (which is never used save to the King or Queen or the Chancellor of the University). But these scruples were soon digested and he vouchsafeth to lodge in a piece of the College till his repair to Winchester.

17th September. COURT NEWS.

The inconveniences that have grown by the late profuse gifts of his Majesty have caused a restraint to be made of passing any new grants till there be a consideration how to settle things in some better state, and to improve some means for the raising of money for supplying of the King's necessities, about which some of the Lords that are selected Commissioners for that purpose have been all this week much busied, and all inventions strained to the uttermost; but notwithstanding some gifts are still being made; and the Queen's jointure also is now passing which amounteth in land to the value of £5,000 yearly, which is as much or more than hath been granted to any former king's wife, and yet it is meant to enlarge it.

The King is very passionately affected to a peace and hath already very far engaged himself therein. The King of Spain and the Archduke do shortly intend to send hither men of affairs to be employed in the treaty.

New Coin for Ireland.

It is now resolved to take away the base money current in Ireland and to establish a new standard of 9 ozs. fine, being the amount standard of the country. A large quantity of the new moneys have been coined and will shortly be sent over, each piece bearing the name of a shilling, and appointed to be current term for 12d., and containing 9d. of fine silver. At the publishing of the new standard, the base coin shall be called down, the piece of 12d. current to be current for 4d. of the new standard. The copper money, as pence, halfpence and farthings, shall remain for the use of the poor, but no man shall take in payment above 50s. in the £100.

The Increase of Vagabonds.

In the Parliament of 1597 a profitable law was made for the repressing of rogues and vagabonds by which much good ensued, but now of late by the remissness of some justices of the peace they swarm everywhere more frequently than in times past. In that law it was ordained that the Council might assign places whither such persons should be banished, by virtue of which power it is now thought expedient that the places of conveyance shall be the New-found Land, the East and West Indies, France, Germany, Spain and the Low Countries.

24th September. Court News.

The Spanish Ambassador hath been received by the King and Queen very graciously at Winchester. He delivered his message in Spanish and that ended he caused one of his people to deliver it in Italian to the King. The King delivered his pleasure to Sir Lewis Lewkenor in English who delivered it to the Ambassador in Spanish.

As for the Union of the two Kingdoms, the old Lord Admiral hath begun it, for a few days since when there was dancing before the Queen this gallant of 70 years fell into such liking of the Lady Mary Stuart that he married her, and the morning after came up to tell the King that he had wedded his cousin. He greatly boasted of his acts the first night, but the next day he was sick of the ague.

25th September. AN INHUMAN REPORT FROM HERTFORD.

It is reported that the country folks at Hertford very impiously and barbarously pray that the sickness may last till Christmas that the Term may be kept there, as was done in the last plague, to their great profit.

29th September. THE PLAGUE DECREASING.

The plague beginneth to diminish, for last week 2,195 died, and this week 1,732.

30th September. THE VOYAGE TO VIRGINIA.

On the 10th May last the *Elizabeth of London*, a bark of 50 tons, wherein Mr. Bartholomew Gilbert went as Master, set out to go for Virginia. At the island of Santa Lucia they traded with the people on the shore for tobacco, pine-apples, plantains and pompions, and thence to Nevis (or Nieves) where they went ashore to seek *lignum vitæ*, but, landing and beginning their search on a Sunday, they found none but one small tree, which they took to be a just plague for profaning the Sabbath, and travailing about their worldly business when there was no necessity. Nevertheless, that same evening, some of the men brought on board a tortoise, so big that four men could not get her into the boat, but tied her fast by one leg and so towed her to the ship. When they opened this tortoise, she had in her about 500 eggs, excellent sweet meat. The next day they searched another part of the wood for *lignum vitæ*, and found great quantities. So for a fortnight they continued every day sawing down the great trees, and cutting them into logs, which they carried down to the ship. In this manner in a fortnight they took on board 20 tons. As the island yielded no more of these trees they went for Virginia; but in a few days the wind began to blow constant from the west, and it was not until the 23rd July that they reached land. They had hoped to fetch the Bay of Chesepian to seek out the people that Sir Walter Ralegh left in those parts in the year 1587, but the wind was so contrary that they never made it. At length they did touch upon the land, and there Captain Gilbert and his mate and the surgeon and two others went on shore in the boat and marched up into the country, leaving two youths to keep the boat. But shortly after the Indians set upon them and killed them, and the two young men had much ado to save themselves. There were now but eleven men and boys left in the ship, and though their want of water and wood was great, yet they durst not venture the loss of any more of their small company in that place. Master Henry Sute, the Master, took his course home for England, by the Islands of the Azores, and is now come to anchor at Radcliffe.

2nd October. THE BRISTOL MERCHANTS' VENTURE.

The two small ships sent out to discover the northern parts of Virginia by the merchants of Bristol have now come home. They report that they have found in the islands very excellent fishing for cods, better than Newfoundland. Upon the mainland they saw many sorts of trees, oaks, beeches, fir-trees, hazels, and maples, and of beasts as deer, bear, wolves, foxes, lucerns (or lynx) and dogs with sharp noses. They had much intercourse with the savages, whom they used kindly. There was a youth in their company that could play upon the gittern, in whose homely music they took great delight, and gave him many things, such as tobacco and tobacco pipes, snake skins which they use for girdles, fawn skins and the like. They would dance round him twenty in a ring, using savage gestures and singing

'Jo, ja, jo, ja, ja, jo.'

They took with them also from Bristol two excellent mastiffs, whose names were Fool and Gallant, of which the Indians were more afraid than of twenty men; in such manner that one of the company, being parted from his fellows, and accompanied only by one of these dogs passed safely through six miles of their country. And when they would be rid of the savages they let the mastiffs loose, and with outcries they would flee away.

Their boats, whereof one is brought back to Bristol, are in proportion like a Thames wherry, 17 feet long and 4 foot broad, made of the bark of a birch tree, sewed together with strong osiers or twigs, the seams covered over with rosin or turpentine. This boat is open and sharp at both ends, save that the beak is a little bending roundly upwards. Nine men can stand upright, and it weighs not at most above 60 pounds. The oars are flat at the end like an oven-peel, made of ash or maple, very light and strong, about 2 yards long.

While they were there, they digged up the earth with shovels, and sowed wheat, barley, oats, peas, and sundry sorts of garden seeds, which in about seven weeks came up very well, giving certain testimonial of the goodness of the climate and the soil. The country also yields sassafras, a plant of sovereign virtue for the French pox and other diseases, of which they laded the small bark and sent her home. In the meanwhile the large ship was also laded with sassafras, and set sail about a fortnight after the other. While the men were busy in cutting down the sassafras they were in great danger from savages; for being asleep in the woods in the heat of the day about four score savages armed with bows and arrows came down and surrounded their barricade, wherein were but four men alone with their muskets; at the same time the master was in the ship with two others. When he saw the danger he shot off two pieces of great ordnance to warn those who were asleep. Those in the woods aroused themselves, and taking their weapons came down to the ship with the two mastiffs, whom, when the Indians saw afar off, in dissembling manner they turned all things into a jest and sport, and departed. They left their haven on the 8th or 9th of August, and came into the soundings of England within five weeks, but were long delayed by easterly winds. At length they reached King Road where they are anchored.

3rd October. A COMPLAINT OF THE COUNT AREMBERG.

The Count Aremberg, the Archduke's Ambassador, hath made great complaint to the King because of late a shallop and two prisoners of his master's were taken by a man-of-war of the States upon the main of England near Sandwich. To which Monsieur Caron, the Agent of the States, alleged that the shallop of the Archduke's did first set upon the States' ship within the river of Faversham, thinking her to be a merchant, but perceiving she was a man-of-war, the shallop ran herself aground and the men fled into the land to save themselves, where they were pursued and two taken, and carried away with the shallop into Holland there to be ransomed for some other prisoners with the

Archduke. Further, the Dutch Captain alleged that the men were delivered unto him by English men of the country because of some injuries they had committed. Hereupon the King demanded that the men with the shallop shall be sent back into England that thereby he may take occasion to see restitution made at the same time of some injuries likewise committed by the Archduke's subjects.

5th October. THE SPANISH AMBASSADOR.

The Spanish Ambassador hath now received two several audiences; the first in public consisting only of compliments and congratulations, as is usual among Princes at their first visitations. In the second, which was private before the King and some of the Council, many speeches passed by way of discourse to intimate the King of Spain's sincerity in embracing our King's friendship, wherein the Ambassador seemed so confident as he stuck not in his master's behalf to have our King's assistance to reduce his master's rebels in the Low Countries. Likewise he insisted very much to divert his Majesty from suffering the levy in Scotland to go forward. But the King in answer alleged many reasons very considerable between him and the Low Countries, such as their strict league with this Realm of England, the interest of debts and other weighty respects. He said that he would endeavour, upon assurance of reasonable conditions, to persuade them to acknowledge their obedience to the Archduke; but if they refused then he would leave them to their own ways. Besides, for the friendship of one, he would not enter into war with another but was resolved always to carry an even hand betwixt them both.

8th October. MONEY FOR GENEVA.

Of late agents from Geneva have petitioned his Majesty for succour by reason of the attacks made upon them by the Duke of Savoy, who would establish the Catholic religion among them by force. The King now commandeth that in parish churches collections shall be made, and the people exhorted to be liberal and forward in succouring a city deserving so well of the common cause of religion. Such moneys as shall be contributed shall be received by the churchwarden and sideman, with the privity of the incumbent, and at every month's end delivered to the Archdeacon, and by him to the Bishop who shall send them to the Archbishop. This collection is to be made monthly for the space of one year.

THE GARTER FOR THE DUKE OF WIRTENBERG.

The Lord Spencer, accompanied by Sir William Dethick, principal Garter King-at-Arms, has set out for Stuttgart, there to invest Frederick, Duke of Wirtenberg with the Most Noble Order of the Garter, to which he was elected six years ago.

9th October. COURT NEWS.

The Court, which is now at Winchester, is busied with the giving of audiences to the ambassadors that are come to perform the ceremony of congratulation. The King gave audience to the Spanish Ambassador immediately upon his coming; and within two days afterwards he desired to speak privately with the King; and since certain of the Lords have been appointed to confer with him upon three propositions; which are: first, the desire of his master to contract the strictest amity with his Majesty; the second an expostulation that the Lord of Buccleugh is licensed to transport troops out of Scotland for the service of the States; and the third a request for the future abandoning of the States. It was answered that the troops were passed with his Majesty's licence, and that howsoever he hath knowledge of them, yet he could not deny them also the benefit of that favour (living as he doth in neutrality with all States) and that the Archduke himself should also be permitted to make the like levies for his service; and that the King remaineth as yet engaged by so important interests with the States as doth behove him not to deal unkindly with them.

The great Scotch Lords that returned lately from England are discontented that there was no better respect shown unto them here, and specially for that they were not admitted, as well as others, to be of the Council; no good liking is conceived of their miscontent.

THE SERMON IN PAUL'S.

In his sermon in Paul's Church Master Christopher Hooke, preaching of the visitation of the plague and God's wrathful indignation, declared that God complaineth with grievous accusations both against Court and Country, against Church and Commonwealth, for the sins of blasphemy, of drunkenness, of pride and covetousness, of horrible witchcraft and sorcery, of immeasurable bribery; of buying and selling offices in the Commonwealth and dignities in the Church, of insatiable avarice, and ambition in both, and in neither a care or conscience to perform their duty to the common good but to their own gain and commodities. He spoke also of the great misery of the poor of the City, who with the winter so hard approaching want work and therefore food for themselves and their families, and exhorted the hearers to liberality. 'Rather than the poor should want,' quoth he, 'make a bank for the poor; it would be the most honourable bank that ever was made, and most profitable to the adventurers.'

13th October. THE PLAGUE DEATHS.
These two weeks past there died of the plague 1,641 and 1,146.

A TREATISE OF THE PLAGUE.
Master James Bamford, parson of Saint Olave's in Southwark, hath written a little book called *A short dialogue concerning the plague's infection* especially against that bloody error that denieth the plague to be contagious. Yet he would not have the people overfearful of the infection, since few ancient people die in comparison of the younger sort, and few are infected that keep a good diet, have clean and sweet keeping, lie in a good air, use reasonable and seasonable preservatives and be not pestered many in one house. Noteth, in answer to them who slandered the pesthouse, that when there were buried in and about London 3,385 in one week, yet of all pestered in that house there were buried but six.

15th October. THE MARQUIS SPINOLA.
The Marquis Spinola is now made Chief Commander of Flanders for the Archduke. He means to use his frigates at Ostend to hinder the coming in of ships and to be doing with the sloops. He has discharged the Dutchmen and means to use his own men.

17th October. COURT NEWS.

Yesterday the Council resolved upon the arrival of the Lord Chancellor that the term shall now be kept in Winchester, because it appears that Reading is much infected with the sickness. It is due to begin on the 12th of next month, and then to last but fourteen days. The Lord Admiral has made very good use of his marriage. Having bemoaned himself that he is much prejudiced by the ceasing of his accustomed profits of the Admiralty that he hath not the means to defray the ordinary charges of his diet, it is thought fit to bestow a pension of £600 a year on him for his diet, and £200 in land for his further maintenance.

21st October. THE NEW MONEYS PROCLAIMED IN IRELAND.

The proclamation for the new moneys in Ireland was signed in Dublin on the 11th of this month and publicly made on the day following.

27th October. THE PLAGUE GREATLY DIMINISHED.

The plague is now much fallen off, for in these two last weeks there are dead 642 and 500.

29th October. A STRANGE MIRACLE IN POICTIERS.

There is a book printing from the French called *A true and admirable history of a maiden of Consolens in the Province of Poictiers,* who for the space of three years and more hath lived (and yet doth) without receiving either meat or drink. This maiden (of the age of about 14 years) hath been seen by the French King himself, and by his command his best and chiefest physicians have tried all means to find whether this fast be by deceit or no. It is said that she was seized by a continued and severe fever on the 16 day of February 1600, since which time the *œsophagus* (or little belly) hath lost the force attractive, and no one can persuade her to eat, nor even to suck or lick meats delicate, fruits and sweet things agreeable to such young years. Her belly, intestines and bowels are all withdrawn or annihilated by want of food, yet in the other parts of her body there is no corresponding diminution. There comes no excrement or urine from her body, which moreover yields no sweat; yet doth she travail about the house, go to the market, spin at the wheel and gives herself to all serviceable offices in a family.

72

1st November. RECUSANCY IN THE NORTH.

Of late there has been great increase of recusancy in the north, since the penalty of the law has not been inflicted so absolutely as before, and many graces and favours have been shown to recusants. They begin to grow very insolent, and to show themselves more openly. Some go up and down to get out a petition for toleration of religion. The Papists take it very kindly that the King has restored the Lords Arundel, Westmorland and Paget, all known favourers if not practisers of the Romish religion. Moreover, he has knighted sundry famous recusants, and others whose wives are recusant have been put into the Commission for the Peace. Mr. Patrick Galloway, one of the King's Chaplains, for his forwardness in matters of religion has not only lost the King's favour, but by his direction is committed prisoner to the Tower. They make no question to obtain a toleration if not an alteration of religion.

10th November. 'HAMLET' PRINTED.

The tragical history of Hamlet, Prince of Denmark, which has been divers times acted by his Highness's men in London, and the two Universities, and elsewhere, is now printed, but from some mangled and imperfect copy.

12th November. THE PRISONERS AT WINCHESTER.

All the prisoners have now reached Winchester and are lodged there in the Castle. The two Lords Cobham and Grey were conveyed from the Tower in coaches at the beginning of the week. The others followed some days later, guarded in the journey by the warders of the Tower and fifty light horse of the county. They stayed the first night at Bagshot, and thence went to Winchester, 30 miles, in one day.

15th November. THE ARRAIGNMENT OF THE CONSPIRATORS.

This day at Winchester were seven of the conspirators arraigned before the Commissioners, namely, Mr. George Brooke, Sir Griffin Markham, Mr. Bartholomew Brooksby, Mr. Anthony Copley, Watson and Clarke the two priests, and Sir Edward Parham. The effect of the indictment was that they had consulted with the Lord Grey and others to surprise the King and the young Prince at Greenwich, to carry them to the

Tower, and after the slaughter of many of the guards to put on their coats. Further that they would have removed and cut off the Lord Chancellor, the Lord Treasurer and the Lord Chief Justice. They intended also to demand of the King and Prince a general pardon, a toleration of religion with equality of all Councillors and other officers as well Papist as Protestant; and that he would cut off the aforementioned officers. Mr. Brooke attempted some quibbling argument to the effect that the Commissioners had no power to try him, but this was soon answered; and then Mr. Attorney somewhat enlarged upon the treasons of Lord Cobham and Sir Walter Ralegh.

Mr. Brooke spoke little further, save to qualify or excuse his own confession, only he said that he had received a letter of the King wherein he had authority to deal in the sounding out of these practices; but neither before, or at the arraignment, could he produce it. Moreover, his Majesty being questioned upon this point by some of the Lords Commissioners demanded that the letter should be produced and denieth that he wrote any such letter.

Sir Griffin Markham answered exceeding well and truly to all things, denying nothing for his fault of treason, but that he deserved death upon the persuasions of Watson, by whom he was misled and assured that the King before his coronation was not an actual but a political King. He desired that his life might be exposed to any hazard or sacrifice, however desperate; but if the King would not grant this, then that he might die under the axe and not by the halter.

Of the priests, Watson spoke very absurdly and deceivingly, without grace or utterance or good deliverance, which (added to his other villainies) made him more odious and contemptible to the hearers; but Clarke, an excellent nimble-tongued fellow of good speech, more honest in his carriage of the business, boldly uttered his mind, being not unwilling to die but desired to avoid the imputation of a traitor.

Copley showed himself a man of whining speech but of shrewd invention and resolution. Brooksby and Sir Edward Parham also spoke in their own defence.

Sir Francis Darcy, being foreman of the jury and excellently commended for this day's carriage and behaviour made some doubts of Sir Edward Parham's guilt, receiving resolution from the Bench in some points, but the rest left to his conscience. The jury found all guilty save Parham, who is discharged; but upon the rest sentence of death is pronounced by the Lord Chief Justice.

My Lord Cecil showed himself very honourable in making way to the acquittal of Sir Edward Parham, who for anything that appeared knew not of any treason intended for the surprise of the King, but was abused by Watson, and made to believe that my Lord Grey had a plot against the Papists. This honourable dealing of my Lord Cecil did cause great and extraordinary applause in divers of the hearers by clapping of hands. Sir Edward Parham hath had better hap than any man these forty-five years to be acquitted upon an arraignment of high treason, but next to God he must thank Sir Francis Darcy, the foreman of the jury who first made the motion for him, otherwise it had passed *sub silentio*, and next he must thank my Lord Cecil.

17th November. THE TRIAL OF SIR WALTER RALEGH.

This day was Sir Walter Ralegh indicted at Winchester before the Commissioners, being Thomas Howard, Earl of Suffolk, Lord Chamberlain; Charles Blount, Earl of Devon; Lord Henry Howard; Lord Robert Cecil; Edward Lord Wotton of Morley; Sir John Stanhope, Vice-Chamberlain; Sir John Popham, Lord Chief Justice of England; Sir John Anderson, Lord Chief Justice of the Common Pleas; Mr. Justice Gawdy; Mr. Justice Warburton; and Sir William Waad. He was indicted on many counts, principally that he did conspire to deprive the King of his government; to raise up sedition within the Realm; to alter religion; to bring in the Roman superstition and to procure foreign enemies to invade the Kingdom.

The case for the King was opened by Sergeant Hele, who spoke briefly of the particulars of the indictment, which were that Ralegh had conference with Cobham on the 9th June last of an insurrection to be made to depose the King and to kill his children; and that the money for this was to be procured by the Count Aremberg (the Archduke's Ambassador) from the King of Spain, five or six hundred thousand crowns, and of this Ralegh should have 8,000. Furthermore that Ralegh would have Cobham go to persuade both the Archduke and the King of Spain to assist the pretended title of the Lady Arabella; 'and as for the Lady Arabella,' quoth Sergeant Hele, 'she, upon my conscience hath no more title to the Crown than I have, which before God I utterly renounce.' And after a few more words he gave way to Master Attorney-General.

The Attorney began a long speech to the jury, in which first he sought to include Sir Walter in the Bye plot, being the treason of the priest Watson, and then to speak of Cobham's treasons.

To which Sir Walter, after he had been speaking for some time, answered, 'Here is no treason of mine done. If my Lord Cobham be a traitor, what is that to me?'

To which Mr. Attorney replied,

'All that he did was by thy instigation, thou viper; for I "thou" thee, thou traitor.'

The examination of the Lord Cobham was then read, wherein he declared that he had never entered into these courses but by Ralegh's instigation, and that he would never leave him alone.

To these accusations of Cobham, Sir Walter answered in his own defence, saying that it would be a strange thing for him to make himself a Robin Hood, or a Kett or a Cade, for he knew England to be in a better state to defend itself than ever it was, Scotland united, Ireland quietened and Denmark assured. Moreover, he knew the Spaniard was discouraged and dishonoured. 'I knew,' quoth he, 'the King of Spain to be the proudest Prince in Christendom, but now he cometh creeping to the King, my master, for peace. I knew, whereas before he had in his port, six or seven score sail of ships, he hath now but six or seven. I knew of 25,000,000 he had from his Indies, he hath scarce one left. I knew him to be so poor that the Jesuits in Spain who were wont to have so large an allowance were fain to beg at the church door. Was it ever read or heard that any Prince should disburse so much money without a sufficient pawn?'

Then was Lord Cobham's second examination read, in which he said that his purpose was to go into Flanders and into Spain for the obtaining of the money; and that Ralegh had appointed to meet him in Jersey as he returned home to be advised of him about the distribution of the money.

76

Hereupon arose much argument between Sir Walter and the judges and Mr. Attorney; after which Copley's confession was read, together with Watson's and Grey's, a further confession of Cobham, and others, and lastly Sir Walter's own examination, in which he said that Cobham had offered him 8,000 crowns, which was for the furtherance of the peace between England and Spain, and that he should have it within three days. To which he gave answer that when he saw the money, he would tell more; for he accounted it but one of Cobham's ordinary idle conceits.

Then passed further passages between Sir Walter and his judges in the which he prayed that his accuser should be brought face to face and be deposed, but the Lord Chief Justice answered, 'You have no law for it; God forbid any man should accuse himself upon his oath.' And Mr. Attorney said, 'The law presumes a man will not accuse himself to accuse another.'

This matter of Lord Cobham's accusation was long disputed between Sir Walter and his judges, until at length he declared that they had not proved any one thing by direct proofs, but all by circumstances. Hereupon Mr. Attorney answered, 'Have you done? The King must have the last.'

To which Sir Walter replied, 'Nay, Mr. Attorney, he which speaketh for his life must speak last. False repetitions and mistakings must not mar my cause. You should speak *secundum allegata at probata*. I appeal to God and the King in this point whether Cobham's accusation be sufficient to condemn me.'

'The King's safety and your clearing cannot agree,' cried Mr. Attorney; 'I protest before God I never knew a clearer treason.'

To this Sir Walter replied that he never had intelligence with Cobham since he came to the Tower; but Mr. Attorney interrupted him, saying, 'Go to, I will lay thee upon thy back for the confidentest traitor that ever came at a bar. Why should you take 8,000 crowns for a peace?'

Hereupon the Lord Cecil spoke to Mr. Attorney willing him not to be so impatient, to which he answered in a chafe, 'If I may not be patiently heard, you will encourage traitors and discourage us. I am the King's sworn servant and must speak; if he be guilty, he is a traitor; if not, deliver him.'

Then he sat down and would speak no more until the Commissioners urged and entreated him. So after much ado he went on, and made a long repetition of all the evidence for the direction of the jury; and at the repeating of some things, Sir Walter interrupted him and said he did him wrong.

To which Mr. Attorney made reply, 'Thou art the most vile and execrable traitor that ever lived.'

'You speak indiscreetly, barbarously and uncivilly,' answered Sir Walter.

'I want words sufficient to express thy viperous treasons,' said Mr. Attorney.

And Sir Walter answered, 'I think you want words indeed, for you have spoken one thing half a dozen times.'

Then Mr. Attorney drew a letter out of his pocket written by Lord Cobham, upon which, before he read it, he made sundry speeches, declaring that Ralegh had taken an apple and pinned a letter to it and thrown it into Lord Cobham's window, the contents whereof were this: 'It is doubtful whether we shall be proceeded with or no, perhaps you shall not be tried'; and again, 'Do not as my Lord of Essex did: take heed of a preacher, for by his persuasion he confessed and made himself guilty.'

So Mr. Attorney read the letter of Lord Cobham, with sundry words of his own interspersed, which was to the effect that at Aremberg's coming, Ralegh was to have a pension of £1,500 a year for which he promised that no action should be taken against Spain, the Low Countries and the Indies, but he would give knowledge beforehand; that Ralegh had been the original cause of his ruin, and that he would have had no dealing with Aremberg but by his instigation.

To this Sir Walter replied that they had heard a strange tale of a strange man. And when the Lord Chief Justice asked him what he had to say of the letter and the pension of £1,500, he replied that Cobham was a base, dishonourable, poor soul. The Lord Chief Justice said, 'I perceive you are not so clear a man as you have protested all this while; for you should have discovered these matters to the King.'

And now Sir Walter pulled a letter out of his pocket which the Lord Cobham had written him and desired the Lord Cecil to read it because he only knew his hand, which was to this effect:

'Seeing myself so near to my end, for the discharge of my own conscience and freeing myself from your blood, which else will cry vengeance against me, I protest upon my salvation I never practised with Spain upon your procurement. God so comfort me in this my affliction, as you are a true subject for anything that I know I will say with Daniel, *Purus sum a sanguine huius.* So God have mercy upon my soul as I know no treason by you.'

Then said Sir Walter Ralegh, 'Now I wonder how many souls this man hath! He damns one in this letter and another in that.'

Here arose much ado, Mr. Attorney alleging that this last letter was politically and cunningly urged from Lord Cobham, and that the first was simply the truth; and lest it should seem doubtful, the Earl of Devonshire delivered that the first letter was voluntary and not extracted from the Lord Cobham upon any hopes of pardon.

This was the last evidence. So a marshal was sworn to keep the jury private. The jury departed and stayed not a quarter of an hour, but returned and gave their verdict of guilty. So Sergeant Hele demanded judgment against the prisoner, and Sir Walter being asked whether he had aught to say, desired that the King should know of the wrongs done him by Mr. Attorney. Further he desired them to remember three things to the King. 'First,' quoth he, 'I was accused to be a practiser with Spain: I never knew that my Lord Cobham meant to go thither. I will ask no mercy at the King's hands if he will affirm it. Secondly, I never knew of the practice with Arabella. Thirdly, I never knew of my Lord Cobham's practice with Aremberg, nor of his surprising treason.'

So the Lord Chief Justice made a speech to the prisoner, saying that he had two vices chiefly lodged in him, an eager ambition and a corrupt covetousness. Then he spoke somewhat of the heathen and blasphemous opinions with which the world taxes him, praying him not to go out of the world with these imputations upon him, for saith he, 'let not any devil persuade you to think there is no eternity in Heaven; for if you think thus, you shall find eternity in hell fire.' The Lord Chief Justice said further, 'You have showed a fearful sign of denying God in advising a man not to confess the truth. It now comes in my mind, why you may not have your accuser come face to face;

for such an one is easily brought to retract when he seeth there is no hope of his own life. It is dangerous that any traitors should have access to or conference with one another; when they see themselves must die, they will think it best to have their fellow live, that he may commit the like treason again, and so in some sort seek revenge.'

So judgment was passed upon him that he should be hanged and quartered.

It is much noted that Ralegh answered with that temper, wit, learning, courage, and judgment that, save that it went with the hazard of his life it was the happiest day that ever he spent. And so well he stifled all advantages that were taken against him that were not *fama malum gravius quam res* and an ill name half hanged, in the opinion of all men he had been acquitted. A Scotsman that brought the news to the King said that whereas when he saw him first he was so led with the common hatred that he would have gone a hundred miles to see him hanged, he would ere he parted have gone a thousand to have saved his life. Never was a man so hated, and so popular in so short a time.

18*th November*. THE LORD COBHAM CONDEMNED.

This day the Lord Cobham was tried at Winchester, found guilty and condemned before the Commission, which was the Lord Chancellor, and Lord Steward for both days, eleven Earls and nineteen Barons. The Duke of Lennox, the Earl of Mar, and many Scottish lords stood as spectators; and of the noble ladies the greatest part, as the Countess of Nottingham, the Lady Suffolk and the Lady Arabella who heard herself much spoken of these days (though chiefly at the arraignment of Sir Walter Ralegh who said that she was a woman with whom he had no acquaintance, and one whom of all that he ever saw he never liked).

The Lord Cobham, as is greatly noted, made such a fasting day's piece of work of it that he discredited the place to which he was called. He heard his indictment with much fear and trembling, and would some time interrupt it by forswearing what he thought to be wrongly inserted. He pleaded not guilty but admitted that he had hammered in his brain some such imaginations but never had purpose to bring them to effect.

Upon Ralegh he exclaimed as one who had stirred him up to discontent and thereby overthrown his fortunes, alleging against him that he had once propounded a means for the Spaniard to invade England by way of Milford Haven; further that Ralegh said that he had made himself a prisoner to Spain for 1,500 crowns to give intelligence; and for an earnest of his diligence had already related to the Count Aremberg the particularities of what passed in the States' audiences at Greenwich.

His brother's confession was then read against him wherein he accused him of a contract made with Aremberg for 500,000 to bestow amongst discontents, whereof Ralegh was to have 10,000, Grey as much, and Brooke 1,000. He excepted against his brother that he was an incompetent witness, and a viper. Hereupon a letter was produced which he wrote to Aremberg for so much money, and Aremberg's answer consenting to furnish that sum. He then declared that in this likewise he had no ill meaning. When particulars were urged of his intended travel he confessed imaginations but no purposes, and laid the fault upon his own weaknesses in that he suffered himself to be misled by Ralegh.

Being asked of his two letters to different purposes, the one excusing, the other condemning Ralegh, he said that the last was true, but the other was drawn from him by a device in the Tower by young Harvey, the Lieutenant's son, whom Ralegh had corrupted, and carried intelligence between them.

Having thus accused all his friends and so little excused himself, the Peers were not long in deliberation what to judge. After sentence of condemnation had been given, he begged a great while for life and favour, alleging his confessions as a meritorious act.

19th November. THE LORD GREY'S TRIAL.

The Lord Grey also is now condemned for his part in the conspiracy. He was tried by himself and spoke with great assurance, alacrity and eloquence so that he held his judges from 8 in the morning till 8 at night in subtle traverses and scapes. But the evidence was too perspicuous both by Brooke's and Markham's confessions that he was acquainted with the intended surprise of the Court. But the Lords were long ere they could all agree and loath to come out with so hard a censure against him, and most of them would fain have dispensed with their conscience to have showed him favour. At the pronouncement of the opinion of the Lords and the demand whether he had anything to say why sentence of death should not be given against him, he said, 'I have nothing to say'—and there paused long—'and yet a word of Tacitus comes into my mind, *non eadem omnibus decora*; the House of Wilton hath spent many lives in their Princes' service and Grey cannot beg his. God send the King a long and prosperous reign, and to your Lordships all honour.'

After sentence given he only desired to have one Travers, a divine, sent for to come to him if he might live two days. If he were to die before that, that he might have one Field, whom he thought to be near.

There is great compassion had of this gallant young Lord, for so clear and fiery a spirit hath not been shown by any at the like trials. Yet the Lord Steward condemned his manner much, terming it Lucifer's pride, and preached much humiliation; and the judges liked him as little because he disputed with them against their laws. No one yet knows what will become of him or the rest.

23rd November. A SAYING ABOUT RALEGH'S TRIAL.

That day Sir Walter Ralegh was tried the King demanded of someone that came from thence what news; and he answered that there was but one arraigned and two condemned, the one for a traitor, the other for a fool, meaning Sergeant Hele.

24th November. THE PLAGUE DEATHS.

The plague is now much abated in London, for during this month past the weekly deaths are reported to have been 594, 442, 251, and this week 105.

27th November. COURT NEWS.

Out of Ireland are come many captains and cashiered officers with their pockets full of brass; and sue to have it made good silver; but the Lord Treasurer's skill is not that of alchemy. The coffers are so empty that household officers are unpaid, and the pensioners and guards ready to mutiny.

29th November. WATSON AND CLARKE EXECUTED.

This day the priests Watson and Clarke were excuted at Winchester for their treasons. Watson acknowledged his offence and asked mercy of the King and State, desiring God to prosper them. He forgave and desired to be forgiven of all, namely that the Jesuits would forgive him if he had written over-eagerly against them, saying also it was occasioned by them, whom he forgave if they had cunningly and covertly drawn him into the action for which he suffered. He desired all to witness that he died a true Catholic. Clarke differed little from Watson, only he seemed not engaged in the action so much. He said he had written a dialogue between a gentleman and a scholar concerning the obedience and loyalty of subjects towards them, to the end that if it be hereafter printed it may be known for his. They both acknowledged that they died not for their religion or function of priesthood but for their treason, though Clarke said that he thought his priesthood at least by accident had hastened his execution.

They were very bloodily handled by the executioner, for after they had been turned off they were both cut down alive; and Clarke, to whom more favour was intended, had the worse luck, for he both strove to help himself and spoke after he was cut down. Their quarters are set on Winchester Gates, and their heads on the first tower of the Castle.

3rd December. THE IRISH MONEYS.

It is now proclaimed that the new money of Ireland shall be current in all the King's realms at their value in fine silver.

5th December. BROOKE EXECUTED.

Master George Brooke was this day beheaded at Winchester, in the Castle Yard, before no greater assembly than is usual at ordinary executions. The Bishop of Chichester who was sent from the Court two days before to prepare him for his end could not get loose from him, but by Brooke's earnest entreaty was fain to accompany him to the scaffold and serve for his ghostly father. After many exhortations and prayers used to him, Brooke uttered some few speeches with a very low voice and cheerful countenance; nor in the whole time of his being on the scaffold was he ever seen to make any show of grief until he came to talk of his wife and children, at which time the water stood in his eyes. He would not by any means seem to acknowledge himself guilty.

He was apparelled in a black damask gown, and a suit of black satin with a wrought nightcap. His gown being taken off, it was delivered to the Sheriff's man, which the headsman demanded; and when it was denied him, he answered that unless he had it, the Sheriff should execute the office himself.

When Brooke came to prepare himself to lay his head on the block, he told them they must give him instructions what to do, for he was never beheaded before. So he laid down his head; but his band not being fit, he rose again. The headsman pressed to help him, but he put him aside and called his own man to do this last service for him. He laid down his head again, and it was struck off at one blow, but when the executioner held up the head and cried 'God save the King,' no one save the Sheriff seconded him.

A BOOK FORBIDDEN.

Of late Valentine Sims printed a little book called *A Welch Bait to spare provender*, which is artificially written dialogue-wise and toucheth upon the state of the Realm at the Queen's death, concluding with the aptness of the English and the Scot to incorporate and become one monarchy, with the means of preserving their union everlastingly. But because Sims forbore to obtain licence for the printing of this book, and a ballad of the traitors lately arraigned at Winchester, he is fined 13s. 4d. and forbidden to meddle with printing or selling either hereafter.

'THE WONDERFUL YEAR.'

Dekker hath written a book of this year called *The Wonderful Year*, which was printed not long since without authority, but because the printers neglected to enter the same they are each fined 10s., and forbidden to print or sell the book, and are commanded to surrender all copies that remain on their hands. In this book is shown the great sorrow and apprehension at the death of Queen Elizabeth and the unspeakable joy at the entrance of King James, together with a lively description of the plague and sundry pathetical instances and merry jests of the same; as of two lovers that were wed, and at the instant when priest came to the words 'in sickness and in health' the bride was suddenly seized with the plague and so married by death; which fate was to be preferred to that of a cobbler's wife. This woman, being sick of the plague, and the worm of sin tickling her conscience, confessed to her sorrowful husband that she had often done him wrong with sundry of their neighbours, whom she named. But it fell out otherwise than she had foreseen; for the plague left her, and then see how the wives of those husbands with whom she had played at fast and loose came at her with nails sharpened and would have worried her to death with scratching and scolding; but that the matter was taken up in a tavern and all anger there reconciled.

A DESCRIPTION OF THE PLAGUE FROM THE SAME

What an unmatchable torment were it for a man to be barred up every night in a vast silent charnel house, hung (to make it more hideous) with lamps dimly and slowly burning, in hollow and glimmering corners; where all the pavement should instead of green rushes, be strewed with blasted rosemary, withered hyacinths, fatal cypress and yew, thickly mingled with heaps of dead men's bones; the bare ribs of a father that begat him lying there: here the chapless hollow skull of a mother that bore him; round about him a thousand corses, some standing bolt upright in their knotted winding sheets; others half mouldered in rotten coffins that should suddenly yawn wide open, filling their nostrils with noisome stench, and his eyes with the sight of nothing but crawling worms. And to keep such a wretch waking, he should hear no noise but of toads croaking, screech owls howling, mandrakes shrieking: were not this an infernal prison? Would not the strongest-hearted man, beset with such a ghastly horror, look wild? and run mad? and die? And even such a formidable shape did the diseased City appear in; for he that durst, in the dead hour of gloomy midnight, have been so valiant as to have walked through the still and melancholy streets, what think you should have been his music? Surely the loud groans of raving sick men; the struggling pangs of souls departing; in every house grief striking up an alarum; servants crying out for masters; wives for husbands, parents for children, children for their mothers. Here he should have met some franticly running to knock up sextons; there others fearfully sweating with coffins to steal forth dead bodies, lest the fatal handwriting of death should seal up their doors. And to make this dismal consort more full, round about him bells heavily tolling in one place, and ringing out in another. The dreadfulness of such an hour is unutterable.

6th December. LORD COBHAM AND RALEGH.

After the execution of Brooke yesterday, the Bishop of Chichester went to the Lord Cobham, and at the same time the Bishop of Winchester was with Ralegh, both being sent by express order from the King, as well to prepare them for their ends as likewise to bring them to liberal confessions, and by that means to reconcile the contradictions of the one's open accusation and the other's peremptory denial. The Bishop of Chichester had soon done what he came for, finding in Cobham a willingness to die; and readiness to die well, with purpose at his death to affirm as much as he had said against Ralegh. But the other Bishop had more ado with his charge, for though for his conscience he found him well settled, and resolved to die a Christian and a good Protestant, for the point of confession he found him so straitlaced that he would yield to no part of Cobham's accusation; only the pension, he said, was once mentioned but never proceeded in.

THE KING'S PLAYERS SENT FOR.

The Court is now at Wilton near Salisbury whence the King's players were summoned from Mortlake to play before his Majesty on the 2nd, and for their pains and expenses they are allowed £30.

8th December. COURT NEWS.

The ladies about the Queen spend their time these days in children's games such as 'I pray, my lord, give me a course in your park' or 'Rise, pig, and go'; or 'One penny, follow me' or the like. This exercise is sometimes used from 10 of the clock at night till 2 or 3 in the morning.

9th December. THE KING'S GREAT CLEMENCY.

About 10 of the clock Sir Griffin Markham, Lord Grey and Lord Cobham were bidden forth to execution in the Castle

Yard at Winchester. A fouler day could hardly have been picked out, or fitter for such a tragedy. Markham came first to the scaffold, and was at first much dismayed, and complained of his hard hap, to be deluded with hopes and brought to that place unprepared; but he seemed not to want resolution, for a napkin to cover his face being offered by a friend that stood by he threw it away, saying that he could look upon death without blushing. He took leave of some friends that stood near and betook himself to his devotions after his manner, and those ended, prepared himself to the block. But in the meantime the Sheriff was secretly withdrawn by one John Gibb, a Scotch groom of the bedchamber, who handed him a letter which he read. Hereupon the execution was stayed, and Markham left upon the scaffold. The Sheriff at his return told him that since he was so ill prepared he should have yet two hours' respite; and so led him from the scaffold without giving him any more comfort, and locked him into the Great Hall, to walk with Prince Arthur.

The Lord Grey, whose turn was next, was led to the scaffold with a troop of young courtiers, and was supported by two of his best friends; and coming in this equipage he had such gaity and cheer in his countenance that he seemed a dapper young bridegroom. At his first coming to the scaffold he fell on his knees, and his preacher made a long prayer, which he seconded himself with one of his own making, which for the phrase was somewhat affected and suited to his other speeches, but for the fashion expressed the fervency and zeal of a religious spirit. Then he entered into a long prayer for the King which held the standers-by a good half-hour in the rain. But being come to the full point, the Sheriff stayed him, saying that he had received orders from the King to change the order of the execution. Whereupon he likewise was led to Prince Arthur's Hall. Nor as yet could any man dive into the mystery of this strange proceeding.

The Lord Cobham was now to play his part and having by his former actions promised nothing but matter for laughter, did much cozen the world; for he came to the scaffold with good assurance and contempt of death. He said some short prayers after his minister, and did so outpray the company that helped to pray with him that a stander-by said, he had a good mouth in a cry but was nothing single. Some few words he used to express his sorrow for his offence and craved pardon; as for Sir Walter Ralegh, he took it upon the hope of his soul's resurrection that what he had said of him was true; and with those few words would have taken a short farewell of the world.

He likewise was stayed by the Sheriff and told that there rested yet somewhat else to be done, for he was to be confronted with some other of the prisoners, but he named none. So Grey and Markham were brought back to the scaffold, nothing acquainted with what had passed, looking strangely upon one another, as men beheaded and met again in the other world. And now, all the actors being together on the stage (as the use is at the end of a play), the Sheriff made a short speech by way of the interrogating, of the heinousness of their offences, the justness of their trials, their lawful condemnation, and due execution there to be performed. To all which they consented.

Then saith the Sheriff, 'See the mercy of your Prince, who of himself hath sent hither to countermand, and given you your lives!'

There was no need to beg a *plaudite* of the audience, for it was given with such hues and cries that it went from the Castle into the town and there began afresh, every man crying out 'God save the King.'

10th December. THE KING'S CLEMENCY.

Yesterday's resolution to save the prisoners was taken by the King without any man's help, for the Lords knew no other but that the executions were to go forward till the very hour of their performance, when the King called them before him, and told them how much he had been troubled to resolve in this business. To execute Grey, who was a noble, young, spirited fellow, and save Cobham who was as base and unworthy, were a manner of injustice. To save Grey, who was of a proud, insolent nature, and execute Cobham, who had showed great tokens of humility and repentance, were as great a solecism; and so went on with Plutarch's comparisons in the rest, till travailing in contrarieties but holding the conclusion in so indifferent balance that the

Lords knew not what to look for till the end came out, at last he added, 'and therefore I have saved them all.' Whereat there was a great applause as at Winchester, which began about the King, went thence into the Presence, and so round about the Court.

The manner of the action was that the King, having first called before him in his privy chamber at Wilton the Lords of the Council who had been Commissioners for the trial, commanded them to give a true narration of the nature and degree of their offences. Hereupon the King secretly determined that the executions should be stayed even at the instant. He therefore privately framed a letter to the Sheriff, written with his own hand, countermanding all the former directions, which he resolved to send by a man of no extraordinary rank that the standers-by might perceive no alteration, nor the delinquents themselves have any apprehension of what was to follow.

Accordingly he made choice of Master John Gibb, a Scottish man, who was but lately come to Wilton. Mr. Gibb therefore went to Winchester on the morning of the execution, and put himself in the throng of the people who were gathering on the Castle Green, and there waited till the Sheriff brought up Sir Griffin Markham. Two things had like to have marred the play: the letter was closed and delivered to Gibb unsigned, but the King remembered himself, and called for him back again: and the other was that Gibb had much ado, for the press of the people, to get near to the scaffold.

THE KING'S LETTER TO THE SHERIFF OF HAMPSHIRE WRITTEN WITH HIS OWN HAND.

Althouch it be true, that all vell gouernid and floorishing Kingdomes and common vealthis, aire establishid by justice, and that these tuo Noblemen by birth, that aire nou vpon the point of Execution, aire for thair treasonable practises condemnid by the Lawe, and adiudgit voorthy of Execution thairof, to the exemple and terror of otheris: The one of thaim having filthily practised the ouerthrow of the quhole Kingdome, and the other for the surprise of our owin Person: Yet in regaird that this is the first yeere of our Raigne, in this Kingdome, and that neuer King was so farre obleished to his people, as ve have bene to this, by our entry here vith so hairtie and generall an applause of all sorts; Among quhom all the kinne friendis, and allies of the saidis condemned personis, vaireas fordurat, and duetiful as any other our good Subiectis, as also that at the very time of thair Arrainment none did more freely and readily give thair assent to thair conuiction, and to deliuer thaim into the handis of Iustice, then so many of thair neerest kinsmen and allies (as being Peeris) vaire vpon thair Iurie; as likewise in regaird that Iustice hath in some sort gottin course already by the execution of the two Priests, and *George Brooke*, that vaire the principall plotteris and intisaris of all the rest, to the embracing of the saidis treasonabill Machinations, Ve thair fore (bing resoluid to mixe Clemency with Iustice) aire contented, and by these presentis command you, our present Sheriffe of Hampshire, to superseide the execution of the saidis two Noblemen, and take thaim backe to thair prison againe quwhile our further pleasure bee knowin. And since ve vill not haue our Lawis to haue respect to personis, in sparing the great, and strikking the meaner sort, It is our pleasure, that the like course be also taken with *Markeham*, being sory from our hairt, that such is not onely the heynous nature of the saidis condemnid personnis crime, but euen the corruption is so great of thair naturall disposition, as the care vee haue for the safety and quiet of our State, and good Subjectis, vill not permit vs to vse that clemency tovardis thaim, quhich in our owin naturall inclination, ve might vary easily bee perswadit unto.

15th December. THE PLOTTERS.

Sir Griffin Markham, Bartholomew Brooksby, and Anthony Copley, with the Lords Cobham and Grey, and Sir Walter Ralegh are all returned to the Tower of London, till his Majesty's further pleasure be made known.

18th December. PREPARATION AT COURT.

The Ambassador from Polonia who arrived in London some days since would fain be gone again because of the freezing of their seas; he is to be given audience on Thursday. This Christmas the Queen intendeth to make a mask, to which end my Lady of Suffolk and my Lady Walsingham have warrants to take of the late Queen's best apparel out of the Tower at their discretion. Certain young noblemen intend another; likewise certain gentlemen of good sort. A special choice is made of Mr. Sandford to direct the order and course of the ladies. It is said that there shall be thirty plays.

22nd December. THE PLAGUE.

This last month the weekly deaths from the plague were 102, 55, 96 and 74; so the sickness is much diminished. In this year past there have been buried in all 38,244, of which 30,578 died of the plague. And during the same time there were christened 4,789.

23rd December. COURT NEWS.

The King, Queen, and Prince are now arrived in Hampton Court, where they remain. There is a letter printed which sets down much of the circumstances of the proceedings after the arraignments. Some say it is the work of the Bishop of Durham's son, Master Toby Matthew, others think it the Prebend of Winchester. It is intended that the Parliament shall begin in March, if the sickness stays.

The Spanish Ambassador has the ill-hap to square in all places with his hosts for matters of reckoning, and unhappily there fell out a great quarrel on his removal from Salisbury. It drew a great number of rude townsmen upon him and his company, whereby one of his men was slain there. The King is very careful to see justice done, and a gentleman will be sent down to see to it.

24th December. 'NEWS FROM GRAVES-END.'

There is a new book called *News from Graves-end* dedicated to 'Him that (in the despite and never-dying-dishonour of all empty-fisted Mecæn-Asses) is the gracious, munificent and golden Rewarder of Rhymes; singular paymaster of Songs and Sonnets; unsquint-eyed Surveyor of Heroical Poems; Chief Rent-gatherer of Poets and Musicians; and the most valiant Confounder of their desperate debts; and (to be comfort of all honest Christians) the now only-only-supper-maker to ingles and players' boys, Sir Nicholas Nemo, *alias* Nobody'; with sundry verses at the end of *News from Graves-end, The Cause of the Plague, The Horror of the Plague, The Cure of the*

Plague (which is repentance) and *The necessity of a Plague*, concluding

> Of evils 'tis the lighter brood
> A dearth of people than of food!
> And who knows not, our land ran o'er
> With people and was only poor
> In having too too many living,
> And wanting living! rather giving
> Themselves to waste, deface and spoil,
> Than to increase, by virtuous toil,
> The bankrupt bosom of our Realm
> Which naked births did overwhelm.
> This begets famine, and bleak dearth.
> When fruits of wombs pass fruits of earth,
> Then famine's only physic; and
> The medicine for a riotous land
> Is such a plague.

26th December. THE PRINCE'S PLAYERS.

The Prince hath lately taken into his service the players of the Lord Admiral.

A Book for Gardeners.

A little book entitled *Profitable Instructions for the manuring, sowing and planting of Kitchen gardens*, gathered by Richard Gardiner of Shrewsbury showing the manner of growing carrots, cabbages, parsnips, turnips, beans (that is, the great white bean), lettuces, onions, pumpkins, cucumbers, radishes, artichokes, porrets and leeks.

'The Bachelors' Banquet.'

A book called *The Bachelors' Banquet*: wherein is prepared sundry dainties, dishes to furnish their table, curiously dressed, and seriously served in, pleasantly discoursing the variable humours of women, their quickness of wits and unsearchable deceits. Herein is shown the manners of many kinds of wives and how women of all degree combine to get the better of their husbands.

'Microcosmos.'

A long poem by Master John Davies of Hereford, entitled *Microcosmos; the discovery of the little world with the government thereof*, dedicated to the King, and adorned with many sonnets to the chief of the nobility.

Microcosmos

God is a sp'rit, the World a Body is,
Both which in Man are plain epitomiz'd,
Of God he's abstract in that soul of his;
And in his corpse the World is close compriz'd:
As if the divine Wisdom had devis'd
To bring into a centre's centre all
His greatness, that cannot be circuliz'd
And the large magnitude of the Earth's ball;
For Microcosmos men Man fitly call.

Montaigne's Essays.

The *Essays of the Count Michel de Montaigne* which Signor John Florio has been translating these many years.

The Epistle from the Same.

Reader, lo, here a well meaning book. It doth at the first entrance forwarn thee that in contriving the same I have proposed unto myself no other than a familiar and private end: I have no respect or consideration at all, either to thy service, or to my glory: my forces are not capable of any such design. I have vowed the same to the particular commodity of my kinsfolk and friends: to the end, that losing me (which they are likely to do ere long), they may therein find some lineaments of my conditions and humours, and by that means reserve more whole, and more lively foster the knowledge and acquaintance they have had of me. Had my intention been to forestall and purchase the world's opinion and favour, I would surely have adorned myself more quaintly, or kept a more grave and solemn march. I desire herein to be delineated in mine own genuine, simple and ordinary fashion, without contention, art or study; for it is myself I portray. My imperfections shall therein be read to the life, and my natural form discerned, so far forth as public reverence hath permitted me. For if my fortune had been to have lived among those nations which yet are said to live under the sweet liberty of Nature's first and uncorrupted laws, I assure thee, I would most willingly have portrayed myself fully and naked. Thus, gentle reader, myself am the groundwork of my book: it is then no reason thou shouldest employ thy time about so frivolous and vain a subject.

4th January. THE CONFERENCE AT HAMPTON COURT.

This day the King sent for the Archbishop of Canterbury and the Bishops of London, Durham, Winchester, Worcester, St. David's, Chichester, Carlisle and Peterborough to speak with them concerning the Conference to be held concerning the reformation of some things complained of in ecclesiastical matters, willing them to repair again to him on Saturday next.

5th January. THE KING AND SIR JOHN HARINGTON.

Of late the King received Sir John Harington in audience, enquiring much of his learning and showing forth his own in such sort as put the knight in remembrance of his examiner at Cambridge, for his Majesty sought much to know his advances in philosophy, uttering profound sentences of Aristotle and such like writers. Then he pressed Sir John to read to him part of a canto in Ariosto, praising his utterance and saying that he had been informed of many as to his learning in the time of the Queen. Moreover he asked many questions, as what Sir John thought pure wit was made of; and whom it did best become? Whether a king should not be the best clerk in his own country, and if this land did not entertain good opinion of his learning and good wisdom? He asked much concerning his opinion of the new weed tobacco, saying that it would by its use infuse ill qualities on the brain, and that no learned man ought to taste it, and wished it forbidden. He pressed Sir John much for his opinion touching the power of Satan in witchcraft, and asked with much gravity if he did truly understand why the devil did work more with ancient women than with others; to which Sir John replied with a scurvy jest that we were taught hereof in Scripture where it is told that the devil walketh in dry places. More serious discourse did then ensue, concerning the Queen, his Majesty's mother, and Secretary Davison. The King said that her death was visible in Scotland before it really happened, being spoken of in secret by those whose power of sight presented to them a bloody head dancing in the air. At length he dismissed the knight saying, 'Now, sir, you have seen my wisdom in some sort, and I have pried into yours. I pray you do me justice in your report; and in good season I will not fail to add to your understanding in such points as I may find you lack amendment.' Whereat Sir John made his courtesy and withdrew.

11th January. A PROCLAMATION CONCERNING THE PARLIAMENT.

A proclamation is come forth concerning the right choice of persons to serve in the Parliament (which hath not heretofore been summoned by reason of the infection), declaring, that since knights and burgesses are eligible by multitude, there are often many unfit persons appointed for that service. It is therefore straitly charged that the knights for the country shall be selected out of the principal knights or gentlemen of sufficient ability; and for the burgesses, that choice be made of men of sufficiency and discretion without any partial respects or factious combination. Also, that those chosen be of years and experience, without desire in any particular men to please parents or friends who often speak for their children and kin so that they be very young and little able to discern what laws are fit to bind a commonwealth. Above all, that choice be avoided of persons noted for their superstitious blindness one way, or their turbulent humours other ways. Further, that bankrupts and outlaws be not chosen; but men of good behaviour and such as are not only taxed to the payment of subsidies and the charges but have paid and satisfied them, nothing being more absurd in a commonwealth than to permit those to have free voices in lawmaking by whose own acts they are exempted from the law's protection.

14th January. THE CONFERENCE AT HAMPTON COURT.

At 11 of the clock this morning the conference concerning ecclesiastical differences was begun in a withdrawing-room within the Privy Chamber, the Bishops and the Council only being present. Dr. Reynolds (or Rainolds), and Dr. Sparks,

Master Knewstubs, and Master Chaderton were summoned to speak for those who are against conformity in the Church of England, but remained in a room without and were not called in.

The King first began with an oration of an hour's space wherein he declared that he had not called this assembly for any innovation, for he acknowledged the government ecclesiastical as it now is to have been approved by manifold blessings from God Himself; but because he had received many complaints since his first entrance into the Kingdom of many disorders, and much disobedience to the laws, with a great falling away to popery, his purpose was, like a good physician, to examine and try the complaints, and fully to remove the occasions thereof, if scandalous; to cure them, if dangerous; and take knowledge of them, if but frivolous, thereby to cast a sop into the mouth of Cerberus, that he bark no more.

Then he said that there were some special points wherein he desired to be satisfied, which might be reduced to three heads: 1st, Concerning the Book of Common Prayer: 2nd, Excommunication in Ecclesiastical Courts; 3rd, The providing of fit and able ministers for Ireland. In the Book of Common Prayer the King was concerned with three particulars, viz., confirmation, absolution, and private baptism.

On the first of these points, the Archbishop said that confirmation had been used ever since the Apostles, and that it was a very untrue suggestion that the Church of England holds baptism imperfect without it; and it was concluded to consider whether it might not be entitled an 'Examination with a Confirmation.'

In the point of absolution, the King read the confession and absolution of the Communion Book, and liked and approved them; as likewise the more particular and personal absolution in the visitation of the Sick; and it was concluded that the Bishops should consult whether to the rubric of the General Absolution the words 'remission of sins' might not be added.

To the point of private baptism the Archbishop said that the administration thereof by women and lay persons (for too commonly our midwives and other such persons practise it) is not allowed but censured by the Bishops in their visitations.

To which his Majesty replied that the words of the Book cannot but intend a permission of women and private persons to baptize. Upon which the Bishop of London spoke much and learnedly; and the King acknowledged himself to believe baptism to be necessary; but, quoth he, 'It may seem strange to you, my Lords, but I think you in England give too much to baptism, seeing fourteen months ago in Scotland, I argued with my divines there for attributing too little unto it: insomuch that a pert minister asked me, if I thought baptism so necessary that, if omitted, the child should be damned? I answered, 'No; but if you, called to baptize a child though privately, refuse to come, I think you shall be damned.'' The King would have baptism ministered by lawful ministers only, but he utterly misliked all re-baptization on those whom women or laics have baptized.

So it was resolved to consult whether in the Rubric of Private Baptism, which leaves it indifferently to all, these words 'curate or lawful minister' be not inserted.

For the point of excommunication, his Majesty propounded, whether in causes of lesser moment the name might not be altered but the censure retained; and secondly, whether in place thereof another coercion, equivalent thereunto, might not be invented? Which all sides yielded unto as long and often desired.

And so, after four hours spent in this conference, the further deliberation is deferred to Monday.

'THE DOWNFALL OF POPERY.'

Mr. Thomas Bell hath written a book entitled *The Downfall of Popery*, which he dedicateth to his Majesty, wherein he noteth the many barbarous and brutish dealings of the Jesuits in late years plainly set forth in the books of the secular priests, and challengeth a reply in seven articles of those things chiefly maintained by Papists, viz.: the supposed sovereignty of the Pope; the doctrine of the Mass; popish dispensations; original concupiscence in the regenerate; of the condign merit of works; the distinction of mortal and venial sins; the popish unwritten traditions; concluding with the impossibility of keeping God's commandments in popish sense.

15th January. A LEWD RHYME ON LORD CECIL.

One in sympathy with the conspirators of late made this rhyme upon the Lord Cecil:

> Backed like a lute-case
> Bellied like a drum,
> Like Jackanapes on horseback,
> Sits little Robin Thumb.

16th January. THE SECOND DAY'S CONFERENCE ABOUT RELIGIOUS MATTERS.

The conference about religious matters was resumed to-day in the same place, and the four speakers against the Conformity summoned to attend. Prince Henry also was present, sitting on a stool by his father. The King made a pithy speech to the same purpose as on Saturday, differing only in the conclusion which he addressed to the opposers of Conformity, whom (said he) he understood to be the most grave, learned, and modest of the aggrieved sort, and professing himself ready to hear at large what they would object, and so willed them to begin.

Dr. Reynolds therefore began to speak, saying that all things disliked or questioned might be reduced to four heads, viz.: 1st, That the doctrine of the Church might be preserved in purity according to God's word. 2nd, That good pastors might be planted in all churches to preach the same. 3rd, That the church government might be sincerely ministered according to God's word. 4th, That the Book of Common Prayer might be fitted to more increase of piety. He went on to speak of certain obscurities in the Book of Articles, but before he had gone far, Dr. Bancroft, the Bishop of London, interrupted him, alleging the ancient Canon *Schismatici contra episcopos non sunt audiendi*, and then, turning to Dr. Reynolds he said: 'And as for you, Dr. Reynolds, and your sociates, how much are you bound to his Majesty's clemency, permitting you, contrary to the statute, *primo Elizabethæ*, so freely to speak against the Liturgy and discipline established. Fain would I know the end you aim at, and whether you be not of Master Cartwright's mind, who affirmed that we ought in ceremonies rather to conform to the Turk than to the Papists. I doubt you approve his position, because here appearing before his

Majesty in Turkey gowns, not in your scholastic habits, according to your universities.'

But the King rebuked the Bishop, for though somewhat excusing his passion, yet quoth he, 'There is no order nor can be any effectual issue of disputation, if such party be not suffered, without chopping, to speak at large. Wherefore, either let the Doctor proceed, or frame your answer to his motions already made, although some of them are very needless.'

So the Bishop proceeded to speak of predestination (which was one of the points touched on by Dr. Reynolds); but the King wished that this doctrine might be handled tenderly.

Then they passed to the point of confirmation; upon which Dr. Reynolds said that seeing in some dioceses the Bishop hath 600 parishes, it is very inconvenient to permit confirmation to the Bishop alone, for it was impossible that he could take due examination of them that come to be confirmed.

To this the Bishop of London replied that the Bishops appoint their chaplains to examine them which are to be confirmed, and lightly confirm none but by the testimony of the parsons and curates where the children are bred and brought up. Further, said he, that none of the Fathers ever admitted any to confirm but the Bishops alone; even St. Jerome himself (otherwise no friend to bishops) confessed the same. Upon which the King said that he dissented from the judgment of St. Jerome in his assertion that Bishops are not of divine ordination, adding these words, 'I approve the calling and use of Bishops in the church, and it is my aphorism, NO BISHOP, NO KING; nor intend I to take confirmation from the Bishops, which they have so long enjoyed.'

Thence, after some further disputations of the nine Orthodoxical Assertions of Lambeth, Dr. Reynolds objected to the Catechism in the Book of Common Prayer that it is too brief, and that by Master Nowell (late Dean of Paul's) too long for novices to learn by heart, wishing that one uniform Catechism may be made and generally received. Which request the King thought very reasonable, yet so that the Catechism may be made in the fewest and plainest affirmative terms, with two rules observed; the first, that curious and deep questions be avoided in the fundamental instruction of a people; secondly, that there should not be so general a departure from the Papists that everything should be accounted an error wherein we agree with them.

Then Dr. Reynolds spake of the great profanation of the Sabbath Day, which found an unanimous consent. Then he said, 'May your Majesty be pleased that the Bible be new translated,' alleging certain instances of error in the present translation.

To this the Bishop of London replied that if every man's humour might be followed, there would be no end of translating. But the King said, 'I profess I could never yet see a Bible well translated in English; but I think that of all that of Geneva is worst. I wish some special pains were taken for an uniform translation, which should be done by the best learned in both Universities, then reviewed by the Bishops, presented to the Privy Council, lastly ratified by Royal Authority, to be read in the whole Church, and no other.'

To which the Bishop of London objected that no marginal notes should be added thereto, which caveat his Majesty well approved, for in the Geneva translation some notes are partial, untrue, seditious, and savouring of traitorous conceits.

Then Dr. Reynolds asked that unlawful and seditious books should be suppressed, which was taken as glancing at the Bishop of London, upon which the King said, 'Dr. Reynolds, you are a better college-man than a states-man, if meaning to tax the Bishop of London for suffering those books between the secular priests and Jesuits to be published, which he did by warrants from the Council to tolerate a schism betwixt them.' Which the Lord Cecil and the Lord Treasurer likewise affirmed, the one declaring that by them the title of Spain was confuted, and the other that by the testimony of the priests themselves it was shown that no Papists are put to death for conscience only, but for treason.

Dr. Reynolds then desired that learned ministers might be planted in every parish. But the King said it could not straightway be performed, the Universities not affording them. And the Bishop of Winchester added that lay patrons were a great cause of the insufficiency of the clergy, presenting mean clerks to their cures.

Next Dr. Reynolds spoke of subscription as a great impeachment to a learned ministry, for though many good men are willing to subscribe to the statutes of the Realm, Articles of Religion, and the King's Supremacy, they cannot subscribe to the Book of Common Prayer because it enjoineth the Apocryphal books to be read in the Church, although containing some errors repugnant to Scripture. On which point it is commanded that he do make a note of those offensive chapters against Wednesday next.

Then Mr. Knewstubs took exceptions at the cross in baptism, which bred some dispute of significant ceremonies, wherein he asked how far the ordinance of the Church bindeth, without impeaching Christian liberty; which moved the King to declare, that as for the opinion that every man for ceremonies is to be left to his own liberty, 'I will have none of that. I will have one doctrine, one discipline, one religion, in substance and in ceremony. Never speak more to that point, how far you are bound to obey.'

Mr. Knewstubs also took exception at the wearing of the surplice, alleging it to be a kind of garment used by priests of Isis; but the King said that he did not think till of late that it was borrowed from the heathen because commonly called a 'rag of popery'; yet he saw no reason but it may for comeliness' sake be continued.

Then Dr. Reynolds took exception to the words in the Marriage, 'with my body I thee worship.' To which the King answered, 'I was made to believe the phrase imported no less than divine adoration, but find it an usual English term, as when we say, "a gentleman of worship"; and it agreeth at the Scriptures, "giving honour to the wife." As for you, Dr. Reynolds, many men speak of Robin Hood who never shot in his bow. If you had a good wife yourself, you would think all worship and honour you could do her were well bestowed on her.'

Lastly, Dr. Reynolds desired that according to certain Provincial Constitutions, the clergy may have meetings every three weeks; first, in rural deaneries, therein to have prophesying, as Archbishop Grindal and other Bishops desired of her late Majesty; secondly, that such things as could be resolved on there, might be referred to the Archdeacon's visitations; thirdly, and so to the Episcopal Synod, to determine such points before not decided.

To these requests the King made answer, 'If you aim at a Scotch Presbytery, it agreeth as well with Monarchy as God and the Devil. Then Jack and Tom and Will and Dick shall meet and censure me and my Council.' And with that he went on to speak of his supremacy and of the dealings of Mr. Knox in Scotland, and of how they used his mother and himself in his minority, concluding, 'My Lords the Bishops, I may thank you that these men speak thus for my Supremacy. They think they cannot make their party good against you but by appealing unto it; but if once you were out and they in, I know what would become of my Supremacy, for NO BISHOP, NO KING. I have learned of what cut they have been who preaching before me since my coming into England passed over with silence my being Supreme Governor in Causes Ecclesiastical. Well, Doctor, have you anything else to say?'

To which Dr. Reynolds answered, 'No more, if it please your Majesty.'

Then the King said, 'If this be all your party hath to say, I will make them conform themselves, or else I will harry them out of the land, or else do worse.'

And so the second day's conference ended.

18th *January*. THE CONFERENCE CONCLUDED.

The third day's conference was held to-day and because the High Commission was the principal matter in dispute many knights, civilians, and doctors of the Law were admitted. There passed much discourse between the King, the Bishops and the Lords about the quality of the persons and the causes in the High Commission, rectifying excommunications in matters of less moment, punishing recusants, providing divines for Ireland, Wales and the Northern Borders. Afterwards the four preachers were called in, and such alterations in the Liturgy which the Bishops, by the King's advice, had made, made known; to which by their silence they seemed to consent. Dr. Reynolds promised to perform all duties to Bishops, as Reverend Fathers, and to join with them against the common adversary.

Then Mr. Chaderton, going down on his knees, begged that the wearing of the surplice and the cross in baptism might not be forced on certain godly preachers in Lancashire lest many won by their preachings of the Gospel shall revolt to Popery. To which the King replied that it was not his purpose out of hand to enforce these things without fatherly admonitions, conferences and persuasions; and further he commanded it to be examined whether such Lancashire ministers by their pains and preaching had converted any from popery, and were men of honest life and quiet conversation; and if so, then letters shall be sent by the Archbishop to the Bishop of Chester that favour be shown them. To this the Bishop of London objected that if it were granted all non-conformists will make the request, and so no fruit follow of this conference.

Then Mr. Knewstubs also went down on his knees to ask the like favour for some honest ministers of Suffolk; for which the King rebuked him as showing himself an uncharitable man, saying, 'We have here taken pains, and in the end have concluded on Unity and uniformity, and you, forsooth, must prefer the credits of a few private men before the peace of the Church. This is just the Scottish argument, when anything was concluded, which disliked some humours. Let them conform themselves shortly, or they shall hear of it.'

After a few more words had been spoken the King rose up to depart to an inner chamber. And so the Conference is ended.

20th January. THE CENSURE OF THE CONFERENCE.

It is generally said that in the late Conference the King went above himself, Dr. Bancroft (the Bishop of London) appeared even with himself, and Dr. Reynolds fell much beneath himself. But the non-conformists complain that the King sent for their divines not to have their scruples satisfied but his pleasure propounded; not that he might know what they could say, but they what he would do in the matter.

25th January. PURITAN REPORTS OF THE LATE CONFERENCE.

The Puritans give out sundry speeches alleged to have been uttered by Dr. Reynolds when he returned to Oxford after the late Conference at Hampton Court, as that the King gratified him in everything he proposed; that these things now obtained by the reformers are but the beginning of the reformation, the greater things are yet to come; that the King used the Bishops with very hard words but embraced Master Doctor Reynolds; that my Lord of Canterbury or my Lord of London falling on his knees besought his Majesty to take their course into his own hands, and to make some good end of it, such as might stand with their credit.

30th January.   A Mother's Books.

Mistress Elizabeth Grymeston, a lady of Norfolk, late deceased, left behind her sundry writings both prose and verse which are now printing, entitled *Miscellanea: Meditations: Memoratives;* with an Epistle to her son Mr. Berny Grymeston of advice in the sundry trials of this life.

31st January.   Things to be Reformed in the Church.

Following upon the Conference at Hampton Court, divers things are to be reformed in the Church of England. The Absolution shall be called 'The Absolution or General Remission of Sins.' The Confirmation shall be called 'The Confirmation or further Examination of Children's Faith.' The private baptism, now by laymen or women, shall be called 'The private baptism by the ministers' only, and all those questions in that baptism that insinuate it to be done by women taken away. The Apocrypha that hath some repugnancy to the Canonical Scripture shall not be read, and other places chosen which either are explanations of Scripture or suit best for good life and manners. The jurisdiction of the Bishops shall be somewhat limited. The excommunication, as it is now used, to be taken away both in name and nature. The Kingdom of Ireland, the Borders of Scotland, and all Wales to be planted with schools and preachers as soon as may be. As many learned ministers and maintenance for them to be provided in such places of England where there is want as may be. As few double beneficed men and pluralities as may be, and those that have double benefices to maintain preachers and to have their livings as near as may be to the other. One uniform translation of the Bible to be made and only to be used in all the Churches of England. One Catechism to be made and used in all places. The Articles of Religion to be made and used in all places, and no man to teach or read against any of them. A care had to observe who do not receive the communion once in a year; the ministers to certify the Bishops, who shall certify the Archbishops; and the Archbishops the King. An inhibition for popish books to be brought over, and if any come to be delivered into their hands only that are fit to have them. The High Commission to be reformed and reduced to higher causes and fewer persons, and those of more honour and better qualities.

1st February. 'THE MEETING OF GALLANTS AT AN ORDINARY.'

There is a little book of merry tales of the plague called *The Meeting of Gallants at an Ordinary*, noting how that since the term is once more held in London more coffins are made by cooks than carpenters, and the tailors again set at work by the return of gallants to the City. Telleth that in a county town a certain gallant, being overcome by drink, fell from his horse and lay as if dead. Whereupon the people of the town durst not touch him, no, not even with hooks and ropes. But at last one advised that they should heap straw about him and so burn out the infection; whereupon the drunkard upstarted supposing that the top of Paul's was on fire again. Noteth also the inhumanity shown to many that died of the plague in their journeyings, how they were buried near the highways in their clothes as they were, or rolled into ditches, pits and hedges.

2nd February   COURT NEWS.

The King has resolved that Parliament shall begin on the 19th March, and that he will shortly remove to Whitehall, but in the meantime he is going to Royston to hunt. He is to go to the Tower on the 12th March, and on the 15th to make his progress through London to Whitehall. In Court it is resolved that everyone shall then wear what apparel he listeth. The Lords determine to ride upon footcloths, some of one colour, some of another, but most choose purple velvet embroidered as fair as their purses will allow. The great ladies are appointed to ride in chariots, the baronesses on horseback, and they that have no saddles from the King must provide their own. The Queen's

Masque, presented on Twelfth Night, has lately been printed, as well as a ballad telling of it; but they are called in because of certain offence taken. The French Queen has sent to our Queen a very fine present, but not yet delivered. One part is a cabinet very cunningly wrought and inlaid all over with musk and ambergris, which giveth a sweet savour, and in every box a present of flowers for head-tiring, and jewels. She hath also sent divers presents to Councillors and ladies of the Court, but for what reason it is not yet known. There is much plotting and malice among the ladies of the Court striving for the offices of honour about the Queen.

4th February. THE CHILDREN OF THE CHAPEL.

The Children of the Chapel that play in Blackfriars are now become The Children of the Queen's Revels, to which effect a patent is directed to Edward Kirkham, Alexander Hawkins and others, and Mr. Samuel Daniel is appointed to have oversight of the plays which they shall act both before the Queen, and publicly.

8th February. THE KING'S PLAYERS.

Because they are forbidden to present any of their plays publicly in London by reason of the plague the King of his free gift hath given £30 to his players for their relief and maintenance.

12th February. TWO TREATISES ON TRADE.

Mr. Thomas Milles, customer of Kent, hath written two treatises of trade, the one called *The Customer's Apology*, being an abridgement of the larger work deposited in Sir Thomas Bodley's Library in Oxford; the other *The Customer's Reply, or second Apology*, in answer to a treatise in favour of the Merchant Adventurers printed some three years ago, maintaining that the abuse of subtle merchandising in exchanges in the Staple or mart towns abroad is so great that the English Merchants Staplers and Adventurers have come to fix the value of our coin so that in effect they govern the commonwealth; and through their vile and untrue valuation the Merchants keep the English pound so far under the price it ought to have that the excessive price of all commodities is enhanced and maintained.

15th February. THE TRANSLATION OF THE BIBLE.

It is said that both the Archbishop of Canterbury and the Bishop of London show some backwardness in this new translation of the Bible, lest the former translation done under Archbishop Parker be brought into disrepute, and hereby occasion given to the Papists of discrediting our common English Bible and the doctrines founded upon it, especially if the persons employed in the work of translating anew should affect many alterations and different readings from the former, more than be necessary.

22nd February. A PROCLAMATION AGAINST PAPIST PRIESTS.

Since the King's coming the Jesuits and seminary priests are greatly increased and use their professions with greater liberty than before they have durst, being assured of some innovation in matters of religion and of a general pardon. Wherefore his Majesty's pleasure is proclaimed that all priests, be they regular or without rule, having ordination from any authority by the laws of the land prohibited, shall depart out of the Realm before the 19th March and not return. Which severe course is justified by the late conspiracy, and out of necessary providence to prevent perils otherwise inevitable, considering that their absolute submission to foreign jurisdiction at their first taking of orders doth leave so conditional an authority to Kings over their subjects as the same power by which they were made may dispense at pleasure with the straightest band of loyalty and love between a King and his people. Nevertheless the good offices of the Bishop of Rome (in state and condition of a secular Prince) towards his Majesty are herein acknowledged, with the wish that a General Council may be freely called to the end that such a settled amity might by a union in Religion be established among Christian princes as may enable us to resist the common enemy.

26th February. THE ARCHBISHOP TAKEN SICK.

To-day, being Sunday, the Archbishop of Canterbury came to Whitehall, where he held long consultation with the King and the Bishop of London about the affairs of the Church; and going thence to the Council chamber to dinner, after long fasting, he was taken with a fit which ended in a dead palsy on the right side, and his speech taken away. He was carried to the Lord Treasurer's chamber where he lay for a while until he was conveyed home to Lambeth.

28*th February*. THE KING VISITS THE ARCHBISHOP.

The King came to visit the Archbishop, and declared that he would pray God for his life; and that if he could obtain it, he would think it one of the greatest temporal blessings that could be given him in this Kingdom. The Archbishop would have said something to his Majesty, but his speech failed him so that he uttered only imperfect words, but he was heard to repeat earnestly with his eyes and hands lifted up, '*Pro Ecclesia Dei, pro Ecclesia Dei*.' Being thus unable to speak his mind to the King he tried twice or thrice to write, but the pen fell from his hand.

29*th February*. THE DEATH OF THE ARCHBISHOP.

This day the most Reverend Father in God, John Whitgift, Archbishop of Canterbury, departed quietly in the Lord. He was bred up in the University of Cambridge, where, after some preferments taken in the Schools, as Master of Arts and Bachelor of Divinity, he became Master of Peterborough House, Master of Pembroke Hall, Master of Trinity College, and Doctor of Divinity and twice Vice-Chancellor. He became Chaplain to Queen Elizabeth, and after Dean of Lincoln in the year 1573. In the year 1577 he was installed Bishop of Worcester, and upon the death of Dr. Grindal he was made Archbishop of Canterbury in 1583. In the year 1585 he was sworn of her Majesty's Privy Council, wherein he continued during his life.

10*th March*. AN EXCESS OF LAW STUDENTS.

There is great complaint among those scholars of the University of Cambridge who have dedicated themselves to the study of the civil Law that when they leave the University there is no room for them in the State to exercise their profession, insomuch that the Vice-Chancellor and Senate petition the Lord Cecil, their Chancellor, to take up their cause.

12*th March*. THE COURT AT THE TOWER.

The King, the Queen and the Prince to-day removed to the

Tower, and were there welcomed by the chaplain with an oration congratulatory, wherein both the description of the Tower of London and the Union of the Kingdom were compendiously touched.

13th March. A LION BAITED.

The King, being told of the lions in the Tower, asked how they came thither, for in England there are bred no such fierce beasts. To which answer was given that the mastiff dog is of as great courage as the lion. Hereupon the King caused Mr. Edward Alleyn, Master of the Bear Garden, to fetch secretly three of the fellest dogs in the Garden. Which being done, the King, the Queen and the Prince went secretly to the Lion's Tower, and caused the fellest lion to be separated from his mate, and one dog alone put in the lion's den, who straightway flew to the face of the lion. But the lion shook him off, and grasped him fast by the neck, drawing the dog upstairs and downstairs. So another dog was put into the den, who likewise took the lion by the face, and he began to deal with him as with the former; but whilst he held them both under his paws they bit him by the belly, whereat the lion roared so extremely that the earth shook withal; and the next lion ramped and roared as if he would have made rescue. The third dog was them put in and likewise took the lion by the hip. The two first dogs are dead but the third is like to recover, concerning which the Prince hath commanded that he shall be sent to St. James' and there kept and made much of, saying that he that hath fought with the King of Beasts shall never after fight with any inferior creature.

15th March. THE TRIUMPHAL PROGRESS THROUGH LONDON.

Between ten and eleven o'clock in the morning the King, the Queen and the young Prince made their triumphal passage from the Tower of London through the Royal City of London towards Westminster, accompanied by all the Court in procession. First came the Messengers of the Chamber and the Gentlemen Harbingers, the Sergeant Porters; the gentlemen and esquires, who were the servants of the Prince, the Queen and the King; the Clerks of the Signet and Privy Seal, the Privy Council, the Parliament and the Council; the Chaplains;

the Aldermen of London; the Prince's Council at Law; the Queen's Council at Law; the King's Advocate and Remembrancer, the Attorney and Solicitor; Sir Francis Bacon, the King's Counsel at Law; the Sergeants at Law; the Masters of the Chancellery, the Secretaries of the Latin and French tongues, the Sewers, Carvers, Cup-Bearers; the Masters of the Tents, Revels, Armoury, Ordnance; the Barons of the Exchequer; the Judges of the Law; the Lord Chief Baron; the Lord Chief Justice of the Common Pleas; the Lord Chief Justice of England; the Knights and Gentlemen of the King's Privy Chamber and Bed-Chamber; the Knights of the Bath; Knights that have been Ambassadors, Presidents and Deputies; the Dean of the Chapel; the sons of Barons, Viscounts and Earls; the Knights of the Privy Council; the Knights of the Garter; the Barons of the Parliament; the Principal Secretary; the sons of Marquises and Dukes; the Lord Admiral and the Lord Chamberlain; the Heralds; the Lord Treasurer and the Lord Chancellor; the Lord Mayor of London; the Garter Chief-at-Arms; the PRINCE; the Sword borne by the Earl Marshal, with the Lord Great Constable on his right hand and the Lord Great Chamberlain on his left; HIS MAJESTY THE KING, richly mounted on a white jennet, under a rich canopy held up by eight Gentlemen of the Privy Chamber, as deputies for the Barons of the Cinque Ports; the Master of the Horse leading a spare horse; HER MAJESTY THE QUEEN, escorted by Gentlemen Pensioners, and Ushers; and following her the great ladies, all according to their degrees, Duchesses, Marchionesses, Countesses, Viscountesses, Baronesses, Knights' Wives and Maids of Honour, among them the Lady Arabella, the Countess of Oxford, the Countess of Northumberland, the Countess of Shrewsbury, the Lady Rich by special commandment, the Countess of Pembroke, the Countess of Essex, the Countess of Nottingham; and last of all the Captain of the Guard, the Guard following.

The Companies of the City, marshalled according to their degree, were placed ready first beginning at the upper end of Mark Lane, and the rest reaching to the conduit in Fleet Street. Their seats were double-railed; from the upper part whereof they leaned on a rail, with the ensigns and banners distinguishing each Company spread before them; in front, right through the City as far as Temple Bar, a single rail was erected to keep off the multitude.

The first object that the King's eye encountered was part of the children of Christ's Hospital, to the number of 300, who were placed on a scaffold erected for that purpose in Barking Churchyard by the Tower.

Along the way, which was gravelled, seven great gates had been erected. The first, at the east end of Fenchurch, on which was represented the true likeness of the houses, towers and steeples within the City of London. The second, of very sumptuous workmanship, was raised in Gracechurch Street by the Italians. The third was in Cornhill, by the Exchange, representing the seventeen provinces of the Dutch nation, and was their work. Close to St. Mildred's Church in the Poultry a scaffold was erected at the City's cost, to delight the Queen with her own country's music; here nine trumpets and a kettle-drum very actively sounded the Danish March. The fourth gate was raised at the charges of the citizens in East Cheap. Before the east front of the great Cross in Cheap was erected a square low gallery, about four feet from the ground, all set about with pilasters, where stood the Aldermen, the Chamberlain, the Town Clerk and the Recorder of the City, Sir Henry Montague, who made a short gratulatory oration, saying:

'High Imperial Majesty, it is not yet a year in days since with acclamations of the people, citizens and nobles, auspiciously here at this Cross was proclaimed your true succession to the Crown. If it was joyous then with hats, hands and hearts lift to heaven, to cry King James, what is it now to see King James? Come therefore, O worthiest of Kings, as a glorious bridegroom through your royal chamber; but to come nearer, *Adest quem quærimus.* Twenty and more are the Sovereigns we have served since our Conquest, but conquerors of hearts, it is you, and your posterity, that we have vowed to love, and wish to serve, whilst London is a City. In pledge whereof, My Lord Mayor, the Aldermen and commons of this City, wishing a golden reign unto you, present your Greatness with a little cup of gold.'

The oration being ended, three cups of gold were given in

the name of the Lord Mayor and the whole of the City to the King, the Queen, and the young Prince.

Thence they passed through the little conduit at Paul's gate. Here was placed the fifth gate, arbour like, and so called the Arbour of Music. From thence the King passed through St. Paul's churchyard, and upon the low battlements of the church an anthem was sung by the choristers of the church to the music of loud instruments. This finished, a Latin oration was delivered by one of Master Mulcaster's scholars in the door of the Free School.

The sixth gate was erected above the conduit in Fleet Street which, as also the conduits of Cornhill and Cheap, ran all day with claret wine very plenteously. This gate was very elaborate, being a tower 90 feet in height and 50 in breadth, with the globe of the world moving mechanical, and about it persons representing Justice, Virtue, Fortune and the like, in habiliments fitting to their nature. Likewise the four elements, in their proper shapes, which on the approach of his Majesty went round in a circle; and grouped about were all the estates of the land from the nobleman to the ploughman, on whose behalf a poetical oration was delivered by one Master Bourne, in the person of Zeal, written by Thomas Middleton. The seventh gate was in Temple Bar, where the forefront was proportioned in every respect like a temple dedicated to Janus, and there the King gave a gracious farewell to the Lord Mayor and the City. The City of Westminster and the Duchy of Lancaster had caused to be erected in the Strand an invention of a rainbow, with the sun, moon, and seven stars, advanced between two pyramids. It was nearly 5 of the clock before the King passed out of the City.

19th March. THE ASSEMBLING OF PARLIAMENT.

About 11 of the clock the King, apparelled in his Parliament robes, accompanied with Prince Henry and attended by the nobility, officers and servants in robes of scarlet passed in a chariot of estate from the Palace at Whitehall to the Abbey of Westminster where, according to former custom, he heard a sermon prepared for the time and occasion by the Bishop of Durham.

In the meantime the Earl of Nottingham, Lord High Admiral

of England, being appointed Lord Steward of the King's Household for the time of Parliament, withdrew himself into the great room, called the Court of Requests, where, being attended by the Clerk of the Crown and the Clerk of the Commons with the rolls of such names of the Commons as were returned, he commanded a crier to call them. Thereupon they came near in a great multitude (more than was ever seen on the first day of a Parliament) and answered their names. This done his Lordship gave the Oath of Supremacy to sundry of this assembly whom he appointed his deputies to minister the like oaths to the rest of the Commons; the form of which oath is as followeth:

'I, *A. B.*, do utterly testify and declare in my conscience that the King's Highness is the only Supreme Governor of this Realm, and of all other his Highness's dominions and countries, as well in all spiritual or ecclesiastical things or causes as temporal; and that no foreign Prince, person, prelate, State, or potentate, hath, or ought to have any jurisdiction, power, superiority, pre-eminence or authority, ecclesiastical or spiritual, within this Realm: And therefore I do utterly renounce and forsake all foreign jurisdictions, powers, superiorities, and authorities; and promise that from henceforth I shall bear faith and true allegiance to the King's Highness, his heirs and successors; and to my power shall assist and defend all jurisdictions, privileges, pre-eminences, and authorities granted or belonging to the King's Highness, his heirs and successors, or united and annexed to the Imperial Crown of this Realm. So help me God, and by the contents of this Book.'

This oath having been taken by at least 300 of the knights and burgesses, they took their place in the Commons House and there expected some message of the King's pleasure for their attendance in the Upper House.

In the meanwhile the King, being placed in his seat of estate and the Lords in their places, began this Parliament by his own speech.

His Majesty began by thanking the people of this Kingdom for their joyful receiving of him, and declared that in his own person he brought us two blessings; of which the first was outward peace abroad with all foreign neighbours, whereby the towns flourish, the merchants become rich, the trade doth increase, and the people of all sorts enjoy free liberty to exercise themselves in their several vocations without peril or disturbance. Moreover, in his person not only is the union of the princely houses of Lancaster and York reunited and confirmed, but the union of these houses is nothing comparable to the Union of two ancient and famous Kingdoms, which is the other inward peace annexed to his person. He spoke much of the advantages of this Union which shall ensue.

Then he went on to speak of religion, saying that at his coming in he found one religion by the law maintained, but another religion, besides a private sect, lurking within the bowels of this nation, namely, the religion falsely called 'Catholics' but truly 'Papists'; the third, a sect rather than a religion, the Puritans and novelists, who differ not so much in points of religion as in their confused form of policy and parity, being ever discontented with the present form of government. For himself, he would wish to be one of the members of such a general Christian union in religion, as laying wilfulness aside on both hands, we might meet in the midst, which is the centre and perfection of all things; and he would meet the Catholics in the midway, so that all novelties might be renounced on either side; but he warned them not to presume upon his lenity (because he would be loath to be thought a persecutor) as thereupon to think it lawful for them daily to increase their number and strength in the Kingdom.

Next he spoke of the relation of the King to his subjects, declaring that the King is as the head to the body, a righteous King ordained for his people, and not his people for him. Then he made a little apology for himself in that he could not satisfy the particular humours of every person that looked for some advancement, preferment or reward; and yet he was not so sparing but that without vaunting he might affirm that he has enlarged his favour in all three degrees, towards as many and more than ever King of England did in so short a space. Yet he confessed that two causes moved him to be so open-handed; the first was that being so far beholding to the body of the whole state he could not refuse to let run some small brooks out of the fountain of his thankfulness to the whole for the refreshing of particular members; the other was the multitude and importunity of suitors; but that he doubted not that experience would teach the subjects of the Kingdom not to be so importune and indiscreet in craving, and himself not so easily moved in granting that which may be harmful to his estate, and consequently to the whole Kingdom. And so, with brief apology that they might not have found such eloquence in his speech as they might have looked for, for it becometh a King to use plainness and sincerity that his speeches should be void of all ambiguity, the King ended his speech.

At the time of the beginning of the King's speech, it had been supposed that the Commons were present, for their place was filled by sundry gentlemen, who were indeed the King's servants and no members of Parliament; so that it was not until the King had been speaking for some good while that warning was given to the Commons for their attending; who, coming up to the Higher House of Parliament at the close of the speech, at the end made their wonted suit for leave to assemble themselves in their usual place of meeting, and to make choice of their Speaker. Which being granted and Thursday next appointed for their presentation to his Majesty, they returned back to the Lower House.

Hereupon Mr. Secretary Herbert, having attended all that occurred in the Upper House, made a brief report of the King's speech and in conclusion made known to the House that his Majesty was graciously pleased that they should with all liberty and freedom dispose themselves to the choice of a Speaker, wherein he thought no man more fit for that place and service than Sir Edward Philips, his Majesty's Sergeant-at-Law. There followed some silence, and then the names of others were mentioned, as Sir Francis Hastings, Sir Harry Neville, Sir Francis Bacon, Sir Edward Hoby, Sir Henry Montague, the Recorder of London, and others. But the more general voice ran upon Sir Edward Philips who therefore stood up and used some speech to disable himself. But the House, notwithstanding his excuse, was willing to proceed to the question and directed the Clerk to make the question: 'All that will have Sir Edward Philips Speaker, say Yea.' Which done, he was by general acclamation chosen for Speaker, and by two of the more eminent members of the House, Sir John Herbert and Sir Edward Stafford, placed in the Chair. Being set after some silence and pause, he stood up and uttered a speech of thanks.

Amongst his first acts, Master Speaker this day directed two warrants, the first to the Surveyor of his Majesty's Works to erect more seats in the Commons House so that the whole House may sit and attend the service with more ease and conveniency; the second to the Clerk of the Crown for a new writ for the return of a burgess for St. Alban's, because Sir Francis Bacon hath been chosen burgess both for St. Alban's and Ipswich and hath made choice to appear for the town of Ipswich.

An Insolent Yeoman.

Sir Herbert Croft complained that one of the Yeomen of the Guard keeping one of the doors of the Upper House, when Sir Herbert and some others of the Commons offered to come in, repulsed them, and shut the door upon them, saying 'Goodman burgess, you come not here.' Whereupon it was questioned whether the House should proceed to punish the contempt of itself, or address itself to the Lord Chamberlain or the Captain of the Guard: but it was left for the day.

21st March.   A Voyage for the Plantation of Guiana.

To-day Captain Charles Leigh in the *Olive Plant*, a proper bark of some 50 tons accompanied with forty-six men and boys, departed from Woolwich with intentions to discover and inhabit some part of the country of Guiana.

22nd March.   The Prince's Ship.

In order that the Prince might be instructed in the art of shipping and sailing, the Lord Admiral some weeks since commanded Mr. Phineas Pett, one of the King's shipwrights, to prepare a vessel of length 28 feet and breadth 12 feet, adorned with painting and carving within and without. This afternoon the Prince came on board, accompanied by the Lord Admiral and divers noblemen. They immediately weighed and fell down as far as Paul's Wharf under both topsails and foresail, and there coming to anchor, his Highness, in the usual form, baptized the ship with a great bowl of wine, giving her the name of *Disdain*. Then the Lord Admiral presented Mr. Pett to the Prince who hath received him into his service.

The King's Speech Repeated.

About 2 of the clock in the afternoon the King, having ascended his royal throne in the Upper House sent for the Commons; and when Mr. Speaker and the rest of the Commons were come into his presence he took occasion because of Monday's mistake to repeat the effect of his former speech delivered the first day.   After which the petitions made by the Speaker having been granted of course he, with the Commons, departed to their usual place.

CASES OF PRIVILEGE.

The first motion was made by Sir William Fleetwood on behalf of Sir Francis Goodwin, who upon the first writ of summons directed to the Sheriff of Buckinghamshire was elected the first knight for that shire, but the return of his election being made, it was refused by the Clerk as being one outlawed; whereupon, upon a second writ Sir John Fortescue was elected in that place.   Sir William moved that this return might be examined and Sir Francis Goodwin received as a member of the House. The House moved that (for a more deliberate and judicial proceeding in a case of privilege so important to the House) the Sergeant should give warning to the Clerk of the Crown to appear at the Bar to-morrow morning, and to bring with him all the writs of summons for the County of Buckinghamshire; and to give warning also to Sir Francis Goodwin to attend in person whom their pleasure is to hear *ore tenus*.

A second motion of privilege was made touching the arrest, on the 15th of the month, the day of the King's solemn entry through London, of Sir Thomas Shirley, elected one of the burgesses for the borough of Steyning in the County of Sussex. A warrant, according to ancient form under the hand of Mr. Speaker, was therefore ordered to be directed to the Clerk of the Crown for a writ of *habeas corpus* to bring the body of Sir Thomas Shirley into the House upon Tuesday next at 8 o'clock in the morning.

Another like matter having been concluded, a committee to consider all cases of returns and privileges was appointed. At the conclusion of this day's business some question was made whether the Commons House alone might of itself and by itself be adjourned, and thereupon a precedent in Queen Mary's time was cited by Sir Edward Hoby; and it was resolved by general opinion that it might.

A Book Against Enclosures.

Mr. Francis Twigge hath written a little book against the iniquity and inconveniences of enclosure which he entitleth *The humble petition of two sisters, the Church and the Commonwealth for the restoring of their ancient commons and liberties, which late enclosure with depopulation uncharitably hath taken away.* Herein he condemneth not the enclosure of woodlands but our covetous new devised enclosures which convert champaign and fruitful soils to pasture, whence cometh depopulation of towns and the ruin of houses.

23rd March.   The Parliament.

This day being the first day of business in the House of Commons, a beginning was made with prayers to God for good success, the prayers placed in front of the Book of Common Prayer were read by the Clerk of the House, together with a special prayer, fitly conceived for the time and purpose which was read by Mr. Speaker.

The House being now settled in expectation of what should be propounded for the weal of the common subject, Sir Robert Wroth moved that matters of most importance might first be handled, which were: the confirmation of the Book of Common Prayer; the wardship of men's children; the general abuse of purveyors and cart takers; particular and private patents commonly called monopolies; dispensations in penal statutes; transportation of ordnance; the writ of *Quo titulo ingressi.* The motion for some time passed with silence; and then Sir Edward Montague (one of the knights for Northamptonshire) proceeded in another, expressing three main grievances of his county, viz.: the burden and charge of commissaries' courts; the suspension of some learned ministers for matters of ceremony; depopulations by enclosures. These matters having been debated for some time, it was resolved that select committees should be named for their consideration.

Sir George Coppin, Clerk of the Crown in the Chancery, now appeared at the bar, being attended by the Sergeant of the House with his mace, and produced all the writs made of knights for Buckinghamshire, which were severally read by the Clerk of the House; and then the Clerk of the Crown was required to retire to the door. And after Sir Francis Goodwin himself, whom it specially concerned, was called and heard at large, and commanded again to retire until the House had determined what to do.

In this meantime the whole case was opened at large, and after much dispute it was resolved that Sir Francis Goodwin was lawfully elected and returned one of the knights for Buckinghamshire and ought to be received. It was further resolved that Sir Francis should forthwith take the Oath of Supremacy and his place in the House; which he did.

Hereupon that Yeoman of the Guard, by name Brian, of whom complaint was made on the first day was brought in by the Sergeant; and, upon his submission and confession of his fault, Mr. Speaker pronounced his pardon and dismission on paying the ordinary fees to the Clerk and the Sergeant, and in the name of the House, gave him advice and warning for his better care and carriage hereafter upon any the like occasion.

24th March. TILTING AT WHITEHALL.

To-day being *initium regium*, the anniversary of his Majesty's accession, solemn tilting was held before Whitehall, where the Earls of Cumberland and Southampton ran with greatest commendation, old Sir Henry Lee being constituted one of the judges. The Ambassadors of France, Spain and Venice were all present at the tiltyard, all placed at the farther end thereof opposite to the King in three several chambers. The French had the right hand who thought himself much honoured, the Venetian in the midst, and the Spaniard next the coming in, on the left hand nearest the tilt, where he did not only see best but was saluted by all the Lords as they passed in and out, which he held for a great grace. And so these two Ambassadors, emulous of each other as in other places, were here both pleased by supposing each was more highly placed and better seated than the other, and with like humour they apprehended the King's, Queen's and Prince's salutations to be done more affectionately to each of them.

DISORDERLY PAGES.

Certain pages upon the Parliament stairs of late took a cloak from one Richard Brock, a young youth and servant to a member of the House, and carried it to the Sign of the Sun, a tavern in Westminster. And the owner following and demanding his cloak, they offered it to the vintner's servant for such wines as they called for. When the reckoning was brought in, they left the cloak in lieu of payment and the vintner's man by force kept it from the rightful owner. When this abuse was reported in the House of Commons, the vintner and his man were sent for by the Sergeant, and order made that the cloak shall be restored to the owner, and the vintner and his man meantime to remain in custody until the particulars of the abuse be further considered by the Committee for Privileges.

26th March. THE PARLIAMENT.

In the House of Commons Mr. Hext moved against hissing to the interruption and hindrance of the speech of any man in the House, a thing (said he) derogating from the dignity, not beseeming the gravity, as much crossing and abasing the honour and privilege of the House as any abuse whatsoever. The motion was well approved.

Sir Oliver St. John then moved touching the wants and miseries of those who served in the rebellion in Ireland, and took occasion thereby to relate some particulars of it, remembering also the last exploit of invasion by the army of the Spaniards. In these wars the service of many captains was known to be used; some spent their fortunes, their best means and time to do her Majesty service there; some received wounds and disablement there. Their recompense was prevented by the Queen's death. In this alteration of state they were least thought on; most of them were like to perish for want, and all of them humble suitors, and he for them to this Assembly. It was appointed to take understanding of the particulars of their want and to consider the fittest course for their relief.

It is also agreed that a joint committee of both Houses shall consider the matter of Wardship, and the abuse of purveyors.

27th March. THE FUNERALS OF DR. WHITGIFT.

The corpse of the late Archbishop of Canterbury was honourably interred in the parish church at Croydon, the Earl of Worcester and my Lord Zouch, that formerly were his pupils, carrying his banners, and the sermon preached by Dr.

Gervase Babington, Bishop of Worcester, that was his pupil at Trinity College, upon II Chronicles xxiv, verses 15 and 16.

For his funerals one J. R. hath written an epitaph made to run upon the letters of his name. But certain Puritans show less charity, for there was found pinned upon his hearse a libel in defamation of the dead, containing a Commination wherein the colliers of Croydon were conjured to sing a *Dirige* in the company of Masked Impiety, Prelates' Pope, Old Virgin's Spectacle, Jesuits' Hope, Atheists' Cloaker, Devil's Proctor, True Pastors' Punisher, and such-like.

THE PARLIAMENT.

There was much disputing in Parliament concerning the case of Sir Thomas Shirley, who was arrested for debt. The sergeant being examined declared that he knew nothing of Sir Thomas's election to the Parliament, but understanding by the proclamation that no person outlawed for treason, felony, debt or any other trespass ought to be admitted a member of the Parliament, he was induced to think that Sir Thomas should not be elected a burgess. To this Sir Thomas answered that at the time of his arrest he informed the sergeant of his election as burgess for Steyning in Sussex, but notwithstanding he persisted in the arrest and carried his body to the Counter. The parties being withdrawn sundry members delivered their opinion, and it was concluded that a special commission should be named.

After this Sir Francis Bacon made report of the conference held yesterday with the Lords concerning the grievance of Wardship. Further, he showed in the conference one of the Lords touched on the case of Sir Francis Goodwin and desired to know further of it; but answer was made by the Committee of the House of Commons that they had no warrant from the House to speak of it.

A little later Sir Edward Coke, the Attorney-General, and Dr. Hone brought a message from the Lords, expressing their great acceptation of yesterday's motion touching wardship, and adding that their Lordships were desirous to couple in the same petition the matter of grievance of respite of homage. And as they conceived it likely that the conference between the two Houses might continue, they asked that (for the removal of all stumbling blocks) the Committee of the House of Commons might have authority to treat of the case of Sir Francis Goodwin.

Hereupon after some members had spoken it was resolved not to confer with the Lords touching Sir Francis Goodwin, and further that answer should be returned to their Lordships that it did not stand with the honour and order of the House to give account of any of their proceedings and doings.

Upon this last message to the Lords, their Lordships returned answer through the Attorney-General and others that their Lordships taking notice in particular of the return of the Sheriff of Buckinghamshire and acquainting his Majesty with it, the King conceived himself engaged and touched in honour and signified his pleasure that there might be some conference between the two Houses.

Upon this message so extraordinary and unexpected, the House entered into some consideration what were fit to be done and resolved that his Majesty might be moved for access the next day. The King signified that they should attend at 8 of the clock the next day. So, because the time was now somewhat spent, they ordered that the House with Master Speaker shall meet at 6 to-morrow morning: and in the meantime a committee to confer to set down the effect of what Mr. Speaker shall deliver.

A VIEW OF FRANCE.

A book called *A view of France*, written six years since by Sir Robert Dallington, is being printed wherein he describeth many things of that country and people, the King, the Court, the honourable Orders, the finances of the State and the manner of raising money. Of the city of Paris, noteth that the buildings are very fair, high and uniform, but that it is not yet one hundred years since this kind of building came first in request and that architecture was re-established in France. The streets both in the City, University and suburbs are very fair, straight and long; the shops thick but nothing so full of wares, nor so rich as they of London, in comparison whereof these seem rather pedlars. The faulxbourgs round about the City are ruined and desolate, except those of St. Germains. Of the King of France it is said that his stature is small, his hair almost white or rather grisled, his colour fresh and youthful, his nature stirring and full of life; and he hath this commendation which is very laudable in a Prince, he can endure that any man should tell him the truth, though of himself. He is naturally very affable and familiar, and more than befits the Majesty of a great King of France, insomuch that on a time when the Italian comedians were to play before him, he himself came whiffling with a small wand to make a place for the rascal players.

Of exercises noteth that the Frenchman is very immoderate, especially in those that are somewhat violent, particularly at tennis play, for there is not a little town in France that hath not one or two tennis courts. They be so apt to play well that you would think they were born with rackets in their hands, even the children manage so well, and some of their women also. As for their dancing, all sorts use it, save those of the Reformed religion.

28th March. THE PARLIAMENT.

Mr. Speaker with a great number of the House assembled at 6 of the clock this morning to resolve what should be delivered to his Majesty, but because the House was not thought full enough for a matter of that consequence, they proceeded to the reading of Bills. And at 8 of the clock in the morning Mr. Speaker, accompanied with a large committee of the House, went to attend his Majesty.

29th March. THE PARLIAMENT.

The Speaker offered the House to be read a petition given unto him in Westminster Hall by a poor minister whose name was subscribed as Brian Bridger. The petition being read contained words to the effect that the Bishops that enforce men to subscribe to the ceremonies of the Church of England are therein antichrists; that those Bishops that rule as Lords and Justices are imitators of antichrist; that the whole land is defiled by means of the Bishops, and therefore is subject to the judgment and wrath of Almighty God, of which we had a woeful taste last year, and may justly yet be more thoroughly plagued unless redress be had; wherefore the sound judgment of the Parliament with the especial approbation of the King is to be had.

The minister was then brought to the Bar by the Sergeant and twice urged to make known who were privy to that petition. He answered that he feared, if he should betray any, he might give occasion for murder to be committed. Being further wished to expound himself and to set down in writing what he meant by the petition he retired to the door and wrote to the effect that he had presented two supplications to his Majesty, and had been four times before the High Commissioners and Judges of Assize in Southwark and could have no judgment of his cause, but was retained still a prisoner.

It was therefore made known to the House that he had been sundry times examined by some of the Commissioners for Causes Ecclesiastical and committed to the prison of the White Lion in Southwark. Hereupon some spoke in his behalf affirming that they knew him to be a lunatic, which he denied; and Dr. Paddy, a physician and knight, being present as a burgess, gave some reasons that it was not likely. Whereat the major part of the house, which is generally thought to be Puritan, cried, 'Away with him to the Tower'; so he was committed to the Sergeant-at-Arms, and some appointed to know his complaint, which he will not confess. As yet he is a prisoner in the Gatehouse. By this accident the Puritans in the House were much confounded and have since been less malapert, all disclaiming that name, and many (before famous) are now most unwilling to be thought such, wishing his Majesty would make an inquisition and cashier all such. It was thought fit to appoint a committee to take his examination as one that had offered a petition of scandal and offence to the State, and in the meantime to commit him to the Tower.

Then Mr. Speaker related the effect of what had passed before his Majesty yesterday, in the matter of Sir Francis Goodwin. Divers precedents had been shown in general, and of Sir Francis in particular, for he served after his outlawry in the Parliaments of 1597 and 1601; and moreover that a sheriff is no judge of the outlawry and could not properly take notice it was the same man.

The King answered that he was loath he should now be forced to alter his tune, and that he should now change it into a matter of grief by way of contestation. He did not attribute his grief to any purpose in the House to offend him but only to a mistaking of the law. For his part, he was indifferent which of them was chosen, Sir John or Sir Francis; and they could not suspect in him any special affection in Sir John who was a Councillor not brought in by himself. He had no purpose to impeach their privilege, but since they derived all matters of privilege from him, and by his grant, he expected they should not be turned against him. There was no precedent did suit this case fully. Precedents in times of minors, of tyrants, of women, of simple kings, were not to be credited because of some private ends. By the Law the House of Commons ought not to meddle with returns, being all made with the Chancery, and are to be corrected or reformed by that Court only with which they are returned. By 35th Henry VIth it was the resolution of all the Judges that matter of outlawry was a sufficient cause of the dismission of any member of the House. The Judges have now resolved that Sir Francis Goodwin standeth outlawed, according to the Laws of this Land. The King's conclusion was that the House should truly report the course already taken; should debate the matter and resolve amongst themselves; should admit of conference with the judges, and make report of all proceedings to the Council.

This relation being made, the House did not enter into any consideration of it but defer it till next Monday.

30th March. THE CASE OF SIR FRANCIS GOODWIN.

There was much debate in the House of Commons concerning the case of Sir Francis Goodwin and the difference between the House and the King, wherein one said that the King hath been much misinformed, and hath too many misinformers, and that the case of Sir John Fortescue and Sir Francis Goodwin is become the case of the whole Kingdom. After many divers opinions had been uttered, it was resolved that the reasons of the House should be set down in writing by a committee chosen for that end, and that the committee should have warrant to send for any officers or to view any record which might help their knowledge in this service.

31st March. RECUSANCY IN THE NORTH.

There are so many recusants in the northern parts that at the last assizes 900 of them were indicted at York, and there be many more, for the Archbishop's courses are so slack (he being now more fit to sleep than to govern a province) that but little is done by his authority. Two priests were condemned at these assizes for seducing the King's subjects from their allegiance, but their execution is forborne until the King's pleasure be known. These two when asked whether, if the Pope should invade any of his Majesty's Kingdoms, they would fight against him, refused to answer. Another notable recusant in these parts was condemned for beating a minister in church and uttering very seditious speeches against the King. He was made to stand in the pillory and lose his ears, which sentence was carried out which will no doubt give great stay to the irregular courses which many in the northern parts do run.

1st April. THE FRENCH AMBASSADOR AND THE CATHOLICS.

The French Ambassador is an earnest suitor to the King in behalf of the Catholics, and seemeth to retain the patronage of the secular priests whose books, petitions, and memorials he exhibits to his Majesty; but, as appeareth from the King's late speech, neither they nor any other priests are likely to find much favour. The time limited in the late proclamation is now expired, but little is yet done against priests or Papists; few or none have departed, nor is any certainty yet known when the priests in prison shall be sent into exile. The French Ambassador also presented to the King a copy of that book called *A Supplication to the King's Most Excellent Majesty*, written by Colleton. When the King began to read it he fell into great passion and with many oaths trod it under his feet, and yet after took it up and perused it.

2nd April. THE CASE OF SIR FRANCIS GOODWIN.

The Sheriff of Buckinghamshire, being examined before the Committee, delivered the manner of the first election of Sir Francis. He said that he was present at the first election and had sent word to Sir Francis before the election that he should not bring any freeholders, for he thought the election would be without scruple for both Sir John Fortescue and Sir Francis Goodwin. About 8 of the clock he came to Brickhill (where the County was by reason of the plague), and being informed that the first voice would be given to Sir Francis, he answered that he hoped it would not be so, and desired every gentleman to deal with his freeholders. Then he went to the election, a great number being children, never at the County. After the writ had been read, he first intimated the points of the proclamation, then jointly propounded Sir John Fortescue and Sir Francis Goodwin. The freeholders cried first, 'A Goodwin! A Goodwin!', but the justices of the peace all said, 'A Fortescue! A Fortescue!' Sir Francis himself also endeavoured to persuade the freeholders, saying that Sir John was his good friend and he would not do him that injury. Notwithstanding the freeholders would not desist, crying, 'A Goodwin! A Goodwin!'; some to the number of sixty crying, 'A Fortescue,' but those for Sir Francis being about two or three hundred. Being in London on the 2nd of March, Mr. Attorney-General delivered him two writs of outlawry against Sir Francis Goodwin; and before he made his return he further advised with Mr. Attorney who penned it.

A Notable Contempt.

Yesterday the King was minded to have gone from Royston to Huntingdon, but on hearing from the Lord Cecil of the troubles in Parliament he stayed till the coming of the Earl of Northampton. Such is the disorder at Royston that there was no man about the King of authority to command horses to be ready or to give warrant for them so that the King was fain to sign warrants with his own hand. These warrants were delivered to the post who brought them back again saying that no man would obey them. This strange contempt was concealed from the King lest he should learn that his own warrants had been disobeyed in so vulgar a manner.

Four Paradoxes of War.

Mr. Dudley Digges hath completed certain *Paradoxes* concerning military discipline written long since by his father Thomas Digges, Esquire; wherein the first maintaineth that no Prince or State doth gain or save by giving too small entertainment unto soldiers, officers, or commanders martial; but do thereby extremely lose and unprofitably waste their treasure, besides the dishonour and foils that necessarily thereof ensue. The second paradox is that the antique Roman and Greek discipline martial doth far exceed in excellency our modern, notwithstanding all alterations by reason of that late invention of artillery, or fire shot: and that (unless we reform such corruptions as are grown into our modern militia, utterly repugnant to the ancient) we shall in time lose utterly the renown and honour of our nation, as all other also that have or shall commit or tolerate like errors. To these are added that the sometimes neglected soldier's profession deserves much commendation, and best becomes a gentleman that desires to live virtuously or die honourably; and that wars are sometimes less hurtful and more to be wished in a well-governed state than peace.

3rd April. THE PARLIAMENT.

A Bill for the better exercise of sundry statutes touching purveyors and cart-takers being read for the second time, one Griffin Payne, one of the burgesses for Wallingford in the County of Berkshire, entered into a bitter invective against the proceeding of the House, taxing it in unseemly terms as that they sought to dishonour the King, disgrace the Council, discredit the opinion of the Judges and did now, by this Bill, go about to hang some of his servants. Nevertheless, though troubled with this sudden speech, the House proceeded to the committing of the Bill to the former committee; but then it was moved that Mr. Payne might be called to the Bar as for a great indignity and contempt.

He therefore came to the Bar, and kneeling, he denied that he had said the words 'dishonouring the King.' But by the next he said that he meant the disgrace of Sir John Fortescue. The other, he said, concerned himself, being a purveyor. Upon further examination it appeared that he is Mayor of Wallingford, and therefore drawn into question that being a Mayor of the town, and an offender in the point of grievance complained of, whether he ought to serve in the House. After some debate, it was upon question ordered that he should be suspended until the point was cleared.

THE COMMONS' ANSWER TO THE KING

The answer drawn up by the committee was brought in and read by the Clerk, being in the form of a petition, wherein the objections to their proceedings in the case of Sir Francis Goodwin are reduced to four heads or objections, viz. :

1st. That they assumed to themselves power of examining of the elections and returns of knights and burgesses, which belonged to his Majesty's Chancery and not to themselves. To which, after sundry precedents alleged, they declare that the use, reason and precepts do occur to prove the Chancery to be a place appointed to receive the returns and to keep them for the Parliament, but not to judge of them. And the inconvenience might be great if the Chancery might upon suggestions or Sheriffs' returns send for new elections, and those not subject to examination in the Parliament: for so, when fit men were chosen by the counties and boroughs, the Lord Chancellor or the Sheriffs might displace them, and send out new writs until some were chosen to their liking, a thing dangerous in precedents to times to come, howsoever they rest securely from it by the now Lord Chancellor's integrity.

2nd. That they dealt with the cause with too much precipitation and without respect to the King. They answer that they in no way knew that the King had taken an especial notice of that cause. And concerning their refusing conference with the Lords, there was none desired until after their sentence passed. And further for any matter of privileges of the House, they are and ever have been a court of themselves to discern and determine.

3rd. That by their sentence of receiving Goodwin admitted that outlaws may be the makers of laws, which is contrary to all laws. To this they show reasons why Goodwin was never properly outlawed.

4th. That they proceeded to examine the truth of the fact of outlawry and gave sentence upon it, whereas they ought to have been bound by the Sheriff's return of the outlawry from further examining, whether the party were outlawed or not. To which the answer is that the precedents cited do prove the use of the Commons House to examine *veritatem facti* in elections and returns.

These reasons being set down and published to the House, Mr. Secretary Herbert was sent with message to the Lords that the House had resolved of their answer and had set it down in writing and that it should be sent to their Lordships.

5th April. A Second Voyage to the East Indies.

The second voyage set forth by the company for trading in the East Indies has now sailed, which consisteth of four ships, with Sir Henry Middleton, General, in the *Red Dragon*, which is the Admiral, the *Hector*, Vice-Admiral, the *Ascension* and the *Susan*. They passed the Lizard on the 2nd of this month and are now put to sea.

The King's Answer to the Commons.

At 8 o'clock this morning Mr. Speaker by private commandment attended the King and stayed till 10. When he came into the House, he brought a message from the King to this effect, that he had as great desire to maintain their privileges as ever any Prince had or they themselves. He had seen and considered of the manner and the matter; he had heard his judges and Council; and he was now distracted in judgment. Therefore for his further satisfaction, he desired and commanded, as an absolute King, that there might be a conference between the House and the judges; and that for this purpose there might be a select committee of grave and learned persons out of the House; and that his Council might be present, not as umpires to determine but to report indifferently on both sides.

Upon this unexpected message there grew some amazement and silence. At last one stood up and said, 'The Prince's command is like a thunderbolt; his command upon our allegiance like the roaring of a lion. To his command there is no contradiction; but how, or in what manner, we should now proceed to perform obedience, that will be the question.' And in the end it was resolved to confer with the Judges in the presence of the King and Council.

6th April. Court News.

Ostend is greatly distressed, thirty or forty slain in the town every day. They have had three Governors slain within this month; and yet there is news newly come that they have slain 1,200 of the enemy, and whensoever the enemy shall enter the town, they doubt not but to make good shift with them, for it is thought that the town is well manned.

A Scotchman coming from Greenwich to London killed

the waterman that brought him, very beastly running his rapier through him.

Mr. Churchyard, the poet, is lately dead; and not past a fortnight before his death being in a pair of loose gascoines, being hard by the Maids of Honour, he shot off his piece and all the powder ran down upon his stockings, which drove away the Maids and all the company.

THE SERMON AT COURT.

To-day, being Good Friday, Dr. Lancelot Andrewes, Dean of Westminster, preached before his Majesty upon the Lamentation of Jeremy, Cap. I, v. 12, concluding that 'it is kindly to consider *opus diei in die suo*, the work of the Day in the day it was wrought; and this day it was wrought. This Day therefore, whatsoever our business be, to lay them aside a little; and whatsoever our haste, yet to stay a little, and to spend a few thoughts in calling to mind and taking to regard what this day the Son of God did and suffered for us; and all for this end, that what He was then, we might not be; and what He is now, we might be for ever.'

11th April. THE CASE OF SIR F. GOODWIN.

In the House of Commons to-day Sir Francis Bacon reported what had taken place at the conference between the Judges and the Lords of the Council in the presence of the King, and that after the King's speech he moved that neither Sir John Fortescue nor Sir Francis Goodwin should have place. Hereat there was some question of the action of the committee, that they had no authority to consent; but it was resolved that both should be excluded and a warrant for a new writ be drawn. It was resolved also that thanks should be presented by the Speaker to his Majesty for his presence and direction in the matter.

13th April. THE KING AND THE SPEAKER.

Upon Mr. Speaker's declaring the message of thanks from the House of Commons the King said that the question had been unhappily cast upon him for he carried as great a respect of their privileges as ever any Prince did; and he thought that the ground of their proceeding was their not understanding that he had intermeddled before they decided. In the second part of his speech, directed to those of both Houses, he said that they should treat first of such matters as most concerned the commonwealth, the three main businesses in their hands being the Union; sundry public and commonwealth bills; and matters of religion and reformation of ecclesiastical discipline; and lastly, that his occasions were infinite and much beyond those of his predecessors, and therefore that in the first Parliament we would not take from him that which we had yielded to others.

18th April. THE UNION OF THE TWO KINGDOMS.

In the House of Commons Mr. Speaker to-day desired that they would fall into resolution for conference concerning the Union of the two Kingdoms whereupon some spoke by reason and persuasion of the thing itself, and others of the course in proceeding; but it was resolved to debate the matter further to-morrow.

19th April. THE UNION DEBATED.

The matter of the Union was further debated in the House of Commons to-day, but again deferred until to-morrow.

20th April. THE UNION.

The Union was again debated to-day in the House of Commons, especially the matter of the name, whether the name of the Kingdom should become 'Britain'; and at the conclusion Mr. Speaker put several questions, which were: Whether there should be a conference? Which is resolved. Next whether the Union in Name should be treated and resolved before the Union in Government, which was resolved in the negative. Then a Committee for the Union to confer was set up which was appointed to attend the King at Whitehall at 2 of the clock this afternoon, to hear him explain his own meaning in the matter of the Union.

21st April. THE UNION.

In the House of Commons Sir Francis Bacon made report at large of what had passed from the King to the Committee for the Union. The King, said he, had delivered him a frame or model of the Union now in question, and moreover, at Sir

Francis's request, was pleased to dictate his words concerning it; not, said his Majesty, to prejudge the liberty of their Conference but to serve Sir Francis as a piece of crystal to deliver him from mistaking. Herein the King declared that the substance of the thing which he now craved to be done consisted only in two points; the first that by a Bill or Act there should be recognition that his just possession of the Crowns of both the famous, ancient and honourable nations of England and Scotland whereby they are united under one allegiance should be rightly understood of all men. The second was that commissioners might be appointed to confer with Scottish commissioners for the making of a resolution to be propounded to the next two Parliaments of England and Scotland.

25th April. An Answer to the Puritans.

Dr. William Covell hath answered that book entitled *The plea of the innocent*, put forth by the Puritans two years since, in a work entitled *A modest and reasonable examination, etc.*, dedicated to the Bishop of London, and treating of such matters as the authority of Princes in Church matters; of ceremonies; of archbishops, bishops and ministers; of toleration; and ending with a humble conclusion to his Majesty.

26th April. The Union.

The matter of the Union is still discussed in the House of Commons and to-day many reasons are alleged for and against the use of the name of Britain for the two United Kingdoms. In the end it is concluded that when the Lords do sit the House of Commons shall give them notice of their desire for a conference; and in the meantime the Committee to set down reasons and objections; the lawyers for matters of law; the inconvenience in state by such as are fit for it; and the inconvenience in reason by others.

27th April. The Union.

Sir Francis Bacon reported in the House of Commons the objections of the Committee made against the change of the name or style of England and Scotland into Great Britanny. It was argued that the maintenance of the several objections to be urged at the conference with the Lords shall be distributed amongst those best able to sustain them.

A Petition Against Purveyors.

A petition was presented to the King by a Committee of the House concerning purveyors, setting out at length the grievances that arise by the action of cart-takers who take up carts and carriages, many more than be needed that they may discharge the rest for money. Horses also are taken, sometimes out of carts or ploughs or upon the highway. As for purveyors of victual, wood, coal and the like, they commit many wrongs and abuses, as that at divers times they take great quantities of timber, squared in the wood, and charge the country to carry it by carts to the waterside, and often sell all that timber for money.

The petition was delivered to the King by Sir Francis Bacon who made a speech of introduction and explanation. The King answered that he would ease the burden and desired that there should be some conference with the Privy Council. Certain of the great officers of the Household in some measure tried to disprove the petition saying that when complaint was made they did justice, and that these things were done according to ancient usage. To which answer was made that usage contrary to a positive statute was void and that it was a great marvel that the King could not be served if his laws were observed.

30th April. Master William Alexander's Works.

There are to be printed in England certain pieces of Master William Alexander of Menstry, being the monarchic tragedies of *Crœsus* and *Darius*, *A parænesis to the Prince*, and *Aurora*, containing the first fancies of the Author's youth.

1st May. An Apology of the Roman Church.

The Catholics have of late caused to be printed abroad a book called the *Apology of the Roman Church*, which is divided into three several tracts, the first concerning the antiquity and continuance of the Catholic Roman religion ever since the Apostles' time; the second that the Protestants' religion was not so much as in being at or before Luther's coming; and the last that the

Catholics are no less dutiful and loyal to their Sovereign than
Protestants; all of which is undertaken and proved by testi-
monies of learned Protestant writers themselves. This book is
dedicated to the Parliament and to his Majesty.

THE KING'S LETTER ON THE UNION.

In the House of Commons a letter from the King to the
House in the matter of the Union was delivered by Sir Roger
Ashton to the Speaker, and read publicly at the board by Sir
Thomas Lake, as one best acquainted with the King's hand and
phrase; which was to the effect that the Union is not so willingly
embraced by the House as the worthiness of the matter doth
well preserve, and that nothing stays them from harkening unto
it but jealousy and distrust either of himself, the propounder, or
of the matter.   And, saith he, 'it is in you now to make the
choice, either by yielding to the Providence of God, and embracing that which He hath cast in your mouths to procure the
prosperity and increase of greatness to me and mine, you and
yours; and by the away-taking of that partition wall, which
already by God's Providence in my blood is rent asunder, to
establish my throne and your body politic in a perpetual and
flourishing peace; or else, contemning God's benefits so freely
offered unto us, to spit and blaspheme in His face by preferring
war to peace, trouble to quietness, hatred to love, weakness to
greatness, and division to union; to sow the seeds of discord to all
our posterities; to dishonour your King; to make both me and
you a proverb of reproach in the mouths of all strangers, and all
enemies of this nation, and enviers of my greatness; and our
next labour to be to take up new garrisons for the Borders, and
to make new fortifications there.' But, concluded the King, he
hoped for better things.

A MASQUE AT HIGHGATE.

The King and Queen visited Sir William Cornwallis at his
house at Highgate, where they were entertained by a masque
written by Ben Jonson.   As they entered in at the gate, the
Penates received them, attired after the antique manner with
javelins in their hands, and so led them through the house into
the garden where Mercury received them, and sundry others in
the guise of Aurora, Zephyrus, and Flora, singing songs of wel-

come. After dinner, the King and the Queen came again into the garden, where Mercury and Pan accosted them, offering wine from a fountain in the garden to the King and Queen and certain of the courtiers.

2nd May. THE HOUSE OF COMMONS.

The matter of the King's letter was this day discussed, and it was urged that every man that hath access to the King should purge himself of tales, and that detractions should be sifted out. In conclusion it was moved that Mr. Speaker shall pray access to the King and on behalf of the House give him some satisfaction, and in the meantime some committees to be named to consider of the matter.

4th May. THE CASE OF SIR THOMAS SHIRLEY.

This day in the House of Commons a petition was presented to the effect that his Majesty would signify his assent to the Bill passed for the release of Sir Thomas Shirley from the Fleet, and indemnifying the plaintiff and his keepers. Upon which it was resolved that Sir Thomas should be delivered forthwith, and to this end a writ of *Habeas Corpus* was ordered for the bringing of his body into the House to-morrow morning.

7th May. THE CASE OF SIR THOMAS SHIRLEY.

There is much ado about the case of Sir Thomas Shirley, for when the writ for his release was presented to the Warden of the Fleet he denied to execute it till the King's Royal Assent be procured for the safety of Simpson (the goldsmith at whose suit Sir Thomas Shirley was first arrested) and himself. He was therefore brought to the Bar and there questioned, but still denied that he would surrender the body of his prisoner, even upon a new writ. He is left in the custody of the Sergeant, and threatened that if he do not submit to-morrow he shall be sent to the Tower.

9th May. SIR THOMAS SHIRLEY.

Sir Thomas Shirley is still a prisoner, and the Warden of the Fleet hath been sent to the Tower, for he refused to deliver Sir Thomas save upon conditions. To-day the Sergeant with the Mace went to the Fleet and demanded the body of Sir Thomas, but Mistress Trench, the Warden's wife, had taken all the keys and discharged their attendance upon the prisoners; and she cried out to him that if they would call her husband he would satisfy the House. The Sergeant being loath to use violence (and indeed having no commission thereto) came away empty-handed. There was a motion in the House to send six gentlemen to fetch Sir Thomas away by force, whereupon Mr. Speaker put the House in mind that all that did enter the prison in that manner were in law subject to an action, and so thought meet to stay the proceedings.

10*th May*. THE CONSTABLE OF CASTILE AND THE JEWELLERS OF ANTWERP.

From Antwerp it is reported that the Constable of Castile, who is expected for the making of the treaty with Spain, there bespoke many and sundry jewels of great price, which when they were brought unto him, he refused unless the jewellers would be content to receive them again at the same price, if at his return out of England, whither he did intend to carry them, he should bring them back. The jewellers found strange this demand, but he more strange that he was refused.

11*th May*. THE WARDEN OF THE FLEET.

The Warden of the Fleet was again brought to the Bar of the House, and asked if he would yield, which he still obstinately refuses and so is sent back to the Tower to be committed to the prison called Little Ease.

12*th May*. THE REPORT OF THE CONFERENCE AT HAMPTON COURT.

The publishing of a true copy of what passed at the Conference at Hampton Court hath been long desired and expected, and the charge thereof was laid upon Dr. Barlow, who hath completed the work which is now ready for the press. The King is pleased with it.

14*th May*. THE WARDEN OF THE FLEET.

To-day, according to the order of the House, six gentlemen went to the Tower to see that the orders about John Trench, the Warden of the Fleet, are being duly performed. They bring back word that the place called Little Ease (or 'Skevington's Daughters,' so named from Mr. Skevington that was sometime

Lieutenant) is a very loathsome place, unclean and not used for a long time either for prison or other cleanly purpose. Hereupon the Lieutenant is much taxed for not making ready the place, and the House waxing indignant many harsh measures were propounded as that the Lieutenant should pay a fine of £1,000, that the Warden should be fined £100 a day till Sir Thomas be released, and the like.

15th May. SIR THOMAS SHIRLEY RELEASED.

The Warden of the Fleet hath now yielded his prisoner and Sir Thomas Shirley took his seat in the House.   And afterwards a letter was read from the Warden complaining that he remaineth in Little Ease, and that his prisoners do mutiny because of his absence.

16th May. THE PRISONERS IN THE TOWER.

The Lieutenant in the House to-day put the House in mind of the prisoners in the Tower, viz., Bridger, the poor minister, and John Trench, the Warden of the Fleet.   It was resolved to release Bridger, being a poor simple man, if indeed not mad; and that the Warden be released from Little Ease but remain a prisoner still until he do petition the House, acknowledging his fault, for his release.

18th May. SIR FRANCIS BACON'S APOLOGY.

Being sensible of the common speech that he was false and unthankful to the unfortunate Earl of Essex, Sir Francis Bacon hath written a defence or *Apology* of all his actions and dealings with the Earl, which is written in form of a letter to my Lord of Devonshire and now to be printed. He denieth that in any way he did thrust himself officiously into the business of the Earl's arraignment, but declareth that it was laid upon him; and as for what he performed at the bar in his public service, it was his duty to do it honestly and without prevarication.

19th May. THE WARDEN OF THE FLEET RELEASED.

The Warden of the Fleet was to-day called to the Bar of the House, and on his knees confessed his error and presumption, professing that he was unfeignedly sorry that he had so offended the House. Hereupon, by direction of the House, Mr. Speaker pronounced his pardon and discharge, on paying ordinary fees to the Clerk and Sergeant.

21st *May*. THE BILLS FOR FREE TRADE.

Two Bills for Free Trade, the first for all merchants to have free liberty of trade into all countries as is used in other nations, the second for the enlargement of trade for his Majesty's subjects with foreign countries, were reported to the House from the Committees. The Committees from the whole of Commons have sat for five whole afternoons on these bills, being attended by a great concourse of clothiers and merchants of all parts of the Realm and especially of London, who were so divided as that all the clothiers, and in effect all the merchants of England, complained grievously of the engrossing and restraint of trade by the rich merchants of London; and of the London merchants, three parts joined in the same complaint against the fourth; and of this fourth part some stand stiffly for their own Company and yet repine at other Companies.

Sir Edwin Sandys made a large report of the travail and proceeding of the Committee, showing what reasons had been urged for and against the Bills. For the Bills, it is shown that merchandize being the chief and richest of trades and of greater importance than all the rest, it is against the natural right of the subjects of England to restrain it in the hands of some few as now it is, for the Governors of the Merchant Companies so handle it that the mass of the whole trade of the Realm is in the hands of some 200 persons at the most. The increase of wealth generally will follow by the ready vent to the merchants at a higher rate, for where there are more buyers, ware grows dearer. There will also be a more equal distribution of the wealth of the land, which is a great stability to the Realm, and the contrary inconvenient to all estates, oftentimes breaking out into mischief when too much fullness doth puff up some by presumption, and too much emptiness leaves the rest in perpetual discontent, the mother of desire of innovation and troubles. Moreover, free traffic is the breeder and maintainer of ships and mariners. Under the King, we are like to be in amity with all nations and so have greater opportunity abroad, as there will be greater necessity at home, for what else shall become of gentlemen's younger sons, who cannot live by arms when there is no wars, and learning preferments are common to all, and mean, so that nothing remains for them save only merchandize, unless they turn serving men, which is a poor inheritance.

For the continuing of the restraint of trade it was urged that the Companies are not monopolies, and these Companies keep up the price of our commodities abroad by avoiding an overglut of commodities, so that of late years our cloth is much dearer, whereas when trade is free many sellers make cheap ware. The Companies that now are do vent all the commodities of the land, and yet are they hardly able to live one by another. These and many other reasons are alleged against the Bill, and answered by those who support it.

A DIALOGUE ON WAR.

Master Barnaby Rich hath written a dialogue entitled *The fruits of long experience*, discoursed between Captain Pill in his humorous fit and Captain Skill in his temperate judgment, wherein they fall to talk of many things appertaining to the soldier's profession; as of the difficulty of the Art Military and the need for great experience, and especially in these days when there be so many tuft-taffeta captains that will impose upon noblemen by their boasting talk. Toucheth also on the foolishness of those constables that will abuse the Prince's service by impresting rogues, vagabonds and other excrements of the commonwealth whereby the manners and disciplines of the ancient militia are corrupted, and the name and estimation of the noble soldier utterly despised.

26th *May*. A COMPLAINT AGAINST THE BISHOP OF BRISTOL.

Mr. Tey informed the House of Commons of a book published by a Bishop during the present sitting of Parliament tending to the derogation and scandal of the proceedings of the House in the matter of the Union, answering the objections made against the Union in name, and taking knowledge of many other passages of the House touching the matter, unmeet to be questioned by any, much less by any member of the Higher House. Whereupon there was much indignation in the House, and several motions propounded, and at length a committee named to consider the heads of a message to be sent to the Lords.

1st June. THE SIEGE OF OSTEND.

The town is now in very desperate terms. The Spaniards have blown up a ravelin of ours called the Porcespy, opposite to Helmont, and thirty of the guard of eighty were slain, the captain, a Dutchman, either slain or taken. At the same day they made an alarm at Sandy Hill and the West Bulwark and assaulted the Poulder Bulwark with 400 men that were at push of pike for half an hour before our men beat them back. Of our men twenty-five were slain, of whom five were serjeants.

4th June. THE TREATY OF PEACE.

The treaty of peace with Spain is now being debated between the commissioners of both sides. When the commissions of both sides had been examined, their commissioners asked first what manner of treaty was best liked, either defensive and offensive, or defensive *sine offensione*, or of friendship and amity only with mutual trade to each other's dominions; which last was accepted. Thence they fell into debate of many particulars, as of our trade with the United Provinces which they would gladly have interrupted; but on this point the King was resolved not to permit anything to prejudice the same. Since then, they have pressed the redelivery into their hands of the Cautionary Towns; which being denied them, our commissioners propounded unto them that we might have free trade and commerce with the East and West Indies wherein they are as stiff not to yield to ours. As yet no point is concluded but debate only to sound each other's dispositions.

5th June. THE KING SENDS A MESSAGE TO THE HOUSE.

In the House of Commons Mr. Speaker delivered a message from the King to the effect that when he looked into the gravity and judgment of the House and of the long continuance of the Parliament, so few matters of weight passed, and that matter of privilege had taken much time (which notwithstanding he was as careful to preserve as they), he was moved with jealousy that there was not such proceeding as in love he expected. This was the cause of unkindness. This declaration is not in any way condemnation of ingratitude or forgetfulness of himself, but by way of commemoration or admonition as a father to his children; neither doth he tax the House, but only put them in remembrance of expedition, omitted and desired.

6th June. THE BILLS FOR FREE TRADE PASSED.

The Bills for Free Trade having been debated for three several days were this day passed at the third reading with great consent and applause of the House of Commons, as being for the exceeding benefit of all the land, scarce forty voting against them.

8th June. DR. DEE'S COMPLAINTS.

Three days since Dr. John Dee exhibited a petition to his Majesty that he might be tried and cleared of that horrible and damnable slander which for many years last past is made current against him *videlicet*, that he is a conjuror or invocator of spirits. To the members of the House of Commons he hath also addressed a petition in rhymed verses to the like effect.

9th June. A MURDER IN LINCOLNSHIRE.

There is news of a very foul murder committed at Bourne in Lincolnshire, by one John Dilworth upon his wife. This man, by trade a wheelwright, is a great company keeper and drunkard which caused his wife to reprehend him in a more sharp manner than he could or would brook. On a time, he coming home half drunk, his wife began to tell him sharply of his gross faults and spoke for a long while very bitterly to him. Whereupon once or twice he roughly willed her to hold her tongue, but she continuing her sharp reprehension, he suddenly heaved up his fist and gave her such a box under the ear that she fell flat to the ground and before she could rise again, he took up the spoke of a cart wheel and gave her two deadly blows upon her head, saying, 'Now I trow thou art past rising or scolding again in haste.' Then he made a very great fire of wood and turfs, and laid the dead carcase thereon, clothes and all, not forgetting to hang up blankets before the windows to hide the great light this fire cast. But when it drew to day the carcase was but half consumed. As soon therefore as the heat would suffer him, he dragged out the remainder of the burned body and hid it under a great heap of thatch.

By this time his three children (the eldest whereof was seven), missing their mother, began to cry out for her; so at last he took them up, and as best he could made them ready. When night was come he made great haste to give them their supper and get them to bed; which being done and they fast asleep, he made another fire greater than the first and having fetched the half-burned body he threw it again on the fire, forgetting (as Almighty God would have it) to hang up the blankets.

The watch of the town being now set and sitting not far off from the house, they began to espy a great light and to feel an evil smell, which made them search from whence it should come; and being come to the door they knocked hastily thereat, but he would neither answer nor open the door. So they brake it open and came in upon him; where seeing this pitiful spectacle and assuring themselves that it was a piece of some Christian creature, some went to seek for his wife and children. Having found the children but not the mother, they came again and asked for her.

'Why,' quoth he, pointing to the fire, 'there is all is left of her.'

So they laid hands on him and bound him, and in the morning had him before Mr. John Tailor, the coroner, to whom he did not only confess the fact and the manner of it, but in a graceless and godless sort justified it, saying he had done God and the world good service in sending so unquiet a creature out of it.

10th June. SIR THOMAS SMITH GIVEN AUDIENCE.

This day Sir Thomas Smith, who is chosen Ambassador for Russia, came with sundry gentlemen to the Court at Greenwich where they were brought into the King's presence by the Lord Cecil. Whereupon the King demanded of Sir Thomas the length of his voyage, the time of his return, the nature of the climate and other questions touching the country; unto all which Sir Thomas answered, declaring that the voyage will be full fifteen months by reason of the winter's cruelty whose frosts are so extreme that the seas are not at those times navigable. Whereupon the King pleasantly said, 'It seems then that Sir Thomas goes from the sun'; to which the Earl of Northampton, standing, he replied, 'He must needs go from the sun departing from his resplendent Majesty.' At which the King smiled, giving his hand to Sir Thomas to kiss, and bestowing the like grace upon all the gentlemen that are for the voyage.

The Passionate Shepherd.

Master Breton hath written a book of verses entitled *The Passionate Shepherd*, of many excellent conceited poems and pleasant sonnets fit for young heads to pass away idle hours, being five pastorals and eleven sonnets and passionate poems.

12th June. Sir Thomas Smith Sets Forth for Russia.

Sir Thomas Smith, formerly Alderman of London, who is sent as Ambassador from the King to the Emperor of all Russia, this day began his journey.

15th June. A Poem about the Earl of Essex.

A poem by Robert Pricket entitled *Honour's Fame in Triumph Riding*, or *The Life and Death of the late honourable Earl of Essex*, wherein he runneth over his life and death, praising his nobility and generosity.

> He was no churl, nor wretch-like covetous,
> 　　His noble breast, as dross, base gold esteem'd,
> Valiant, liberal, wise and virtuous,
> 　　His honour more than all world's wealth he deem'd.
> Some could in print his honoured bounty scorn,
> That largely have from him great sheaves of corn.
> 　　　　Such tricks as these time-servers use.
> 　　　　What virtue will they not abuse?

Noteth also that Queen Elizabeth was deceived, else would she have pardoned him:

> Her royal breast was falsely oft accus'd,
> 　　Of cruel deeds but she was Mercy's child;
> For honour's death she may well be excus'd,
> 　　By private tales rough work was smoothly fil'd.
> Could he but once her glory's sight have gain'd,
> And unto her, his wrongs and woes complain'd:
> 　　　　Then had he liv'd, and that they knew,
> 　　　　Whose hate her heart from him withdrew.

But could her eyes these weeping lines peruse,
   Her princely tears would show her sorrow's grief;
Herself would say, they did her grace abuse,
   That in that action were the actors chief.
And truth to say, I think her Majesty,
Was chiefest mourner in that tragedy,
    Though now a fluent nimble wit,
    Can boldly play the politic.

20th June. THE HARD CASE OF MR. RICHARD HAWKINS.

To the many misfortunes of Master Richard Hawkins at the hands of the Spaniards is added yet another: for since the coming of the Spanish Ambassador into England, he was partner with Sir Thomas Middleton and others in a voyage unto the West Indies in a ship and a pinnace which went for trade. Being allowed to trade by the Lieutenant-General of the Island of Santo Domingo, the pinnace was sent into the port with £1,500 worth of goods, where his people, being busy in their trade, were suddenly murdered by those who come to buy and sell with them, and the pinnace and goods surprised, so that the voyage is clean overthrown with a loss of £3,000.

22nd June. THE CASE OF SIR ROBERT DUDLEY.

The hearing is begun in the Star Chamber of Sir Robert Dudley's case. Sir Robert is son to the late Earl of Leicester by the Lady Sheffield; and notwithstanding that the Earl in his will seventeen times named him bastard, yet he hath endeavoured to prove himself legitimate, and the Lady Sheffield truly married to the Earl of Leicester, to the great dishonour of the Countess of Leicester. He was also charged by Mr. Attorney that he had given his men the badge of the Ragged Staff, and calleth himself Earl of Warwick and Leicester. But this Sir Robert denied, declaring that Mr. Attorney did cast forth many scandalous aspersions and rumours to prejudge his cause, and therefore desired that bill and answer might be heard in open court, which is so ordered.

This is generally observed to be a very great cause, and many honourable personages are interested in it either in blood or right. To this end there came with Sir Robert and stood by him within the Court the Lord Dudley, the Lord Sheffield, and the Lord of Effingham; whereupon the Attorney said that it was strange precedent that so great and honourable personages should come in Court to countenance and embrace any cause contrary to the law. Hereat the Lord Sheffield seemed to be very much offended and took it ill that Mr. Attorney should so indiscreetly tax them who came but to hear and see how the world went.

25th June. AN ALARM AT COURT.

Last night, being Sunday, by order of the King and Council, the Earl of Southampton, Lord Danvers and others were arrested and each confined apart. To-day, upon examination, all are released. My Lord had been slanderously charged by some enemy unknown that he was plotting to slay certain Scots about the King. He declared that if he knew the slanderer he would challenge him to the field, but as he did not he could only appeal to the King who gave him fair answer but no more.

26th June. THE DEATH OF THE EARL OF OXFORD.

Edward de Vere, Earl of Oxford, is dead. In former times this noble Lord was among the first at Queen Elizabeth's Court, but in his later days, having spent up all his wealth, he became a poor almsman of the Queen, who allowed him a pension of £1,000 per annum for his life. In the year 1575 he went travelling into Italy and brought back many new fashions as gloves, sweet bags, perfumed jerkins and other pleasant things. The Queen took such pleasure in these gloves that she was pictured with them upon her hands and the perfume was for many years called the 'Earl of Oxford's perfume.' Many scandalous reports are made of him as that in his travels he lived at Florence in more grandeur than the Duke of Tuscany. The occasion of his travelling is said to have been a mischance in the Presence, for, making his congée to Queen Elizabeth, he had the ill fortune to break wind. He did not return to Court for seven years space when the Queen welcomed him back, saying, 'My Lord, I had forgot the fart.'

27th June. 'A LOYAL SUBJECT'S LOOKING GLASS.'

One William Willymat hath written a book called *A loyal subject's looking glass*, wherein a man may examine himself that he may the better frame the whole course of his life according to the true grounds of the duties of an honest and obedient subject to his King, and arm himself against all future syren songs of unnatural conspiration and rebels. Noteth especially six causes of the undutifulness of subjects, viz.: pride; ambition; envy; lack of wisdom and knowledge in the subject; discontent of mind, especially in the proud and ambitious sort of great men, and in those that have prodigally consumed their patrimony and who want but a leader whom they may follow and they would redress commonwealth matters and divide every man his share, share and share alike; and lastly the misliking of due and deserved punishment of malefactors.

29th June. THE KING HURT BY A HORSE.

The King hath been hurt in the instep of his foot by a stroke of the Queen's horse whilst hunting and is confined to his bed. Whereupon the House of Commons sending certain members to visit him, the King sent answer saying that he would ever be as careful of any sore or grievance that should come to the House as they were of his hurt.

COMMISSIONERS FROM THE HANSE TOWNS.

Commissioners from the Hanse towns are on their way hitherwards to solicit a return of those privileges allowed them in this Realm until six years ago, when they were deprived of them. In ancient times the Society of the Hanse consisted of many rich cities, who by their conjunction were of great power, which gave occasion to Princes to embrace their friendship. But in times more recent most of those cities found by dear experience that their being of the Society served only to increase the greatness of Lubec, Hamburg and Danzig, and refused either to appear or to contribute. At the assembly of the Hanse at Lubec in March last past, but two towns appeared though more were summoned, which were Lubec, Cologne, Bremen, Hamburg, Rostock, Stralsund, Wissmar, Dantzig, Lunneburg, Magdeburg, Hildesheim and Brunswick. It was then concluded that six of these towns should each send two principal persons to the King.

30th June. THE LORD COBHAM.

The Lord Cobham spends his time in the Tower translating

the first of Seneca *De Clementia* out of the Latin with the help of the French translation, and would dedicate it to the King, presenting it by the hands of the Lord Cecil.

5th July. MARSTON'S MALCONTENT.

John Marston's play of *The Malcontent*, which was lately played both by the Children at Blackfriars and also by the King's Men, is now printing, with the Induction written by Webster for the King's Men, wherein Burbage, Sly, Condell, Sinklo, and Lowin speak in their own persons. In this play Altofronto, formerly Duke of Genoa, but driven from his kingdom by Pietro, returned disguised as a malcontent about Court, known only to Celso, and being unsuspected he can speak as he listed to all. The Duke Pietro, being of a phlegmatic humour, disappointeth his Duchess so that she taketh for her lover Mendoza, who would persuade the Malcontent to poison the Duke; and upon the false report of whose death Mendoza proclaimeth himself and would force into marriage Maria, Altofronto's constant wife; but at the last the Malcontent is revealed the rightful Duke and the usurper cast out.

6th July. COPLEY SENT INTO EXILE.

Anthony Copley, that was first to be arrested for the plots last year, is now to be released from prison, but must go overseas as an exile.

7th July. PARLIAMENT PROROGUED.

The Parliament was this day prorogued until the 7th of February of next year.

A NOTE OF THE CHIEF STATUTES ENACTED IN THE PRESENT PARLIAMENT.

A most joyful and just recognition of the immediate, lawful and undoubted succession, descent, and right of the Crown, whereby it is recognized that immediately upon the decease of the late Queen, the Imperial Crown of the Realm of England did descend upon his present Majesty as being lineally, justly and lawfully next and sole heir of the Blood Royal.

An Act authorizing certain commissioners of the Realm of England to treat with commissioners of Scotland for the weal of both Kingdoms, whose proceedings shall be subscribed and sealed in tripartite, to be presented to the King, and the Parliaments of England and Scotland for their considerations of their next Sessions.

An Act for the continuance and explanation of the Statute made in the Parliament of 1597 for the banishment of rogues, vagabonds and beggars, and ordaining that any rogue that shall be judged incorrigible or dangerous shall be branded on the shoulder with a great roman R of the breadth of a shilling.

An Act to take away benefit of clergy for manslaughter when the party slain shall not first have his weapon drawn or have first stricken his slayer, provided that the fact be not committed *se defendendo*, or by misfortune, or by chance in preserving the peace.

An Act to restrain the inordinate haunting and tippling in inns, ale-houses, and other victualling houses whereby an inn-keeper that doth permit any person to continue tippling unless he be invited by a traveller, or be a labouring or handicraftsman of a city or town taking his diet upon working days for one hour at dinnertime, shall be fined 10s.

An Act for the better execution of justice to prevent the taking of inordinate fees for certificates by clerks of the Courts, who are empowered to take for their pains for the writing of certificates 12d. for every first side, and 2d. for every side after, and no more.

An Act to restrain all persons from marriage until their former husbands (or wives) be dead; which is enacted because divers evil-disposed persons being married run out of one county into another or into places where they are not known and then become married again. Those that offend in this manner hereafter shall be regarded as felons and suffer death accordingly. To this there are added certain exceptions, *videlicet*: any person whose husband or wife shall continually remain beyond the seas for seven years together, or shall absent himself (or herself) for seven years together, the one not knowing the other to be living; also any person divorced by a sentence of an Ecclesiastical Court, or whose former marriage has been declared void.

An Act against conjuration, witchcraft and dealing with evil spirits, repealing the Act made in 5th Elizabeth, and making more severe the punishment. Hereby it is enacted that any person, that shall use any invocation or conjuration of any wicked spirit for any purpose, or shall take up any dead body or part thereof to be used for sorcery or enchantment, or shall practise witchcraft whereby any person shall be killed, wasted or lamed, shall suffer death as a felon. And further, to the end that all practice of witchcraft shall be abolished, any person that shall take upon him any witchcraft, charm or sorcery to declare where any treasure may be found, or goods lost or stolen, or shall provoke any person to unlawful love, or cause goods or cattle to be destroyed or impaired, shall suffer imprisonment for one whole year, and once in every quarter stand for six hours in the pillory upon market day or at a fair and confess the error; and if they offend again, then to suffer death.

An Act for the better relief of creditors against such as shall become bankrupts, to prevent fraudulent actions by bankrupts, and to declare the description of a bankrupt more fully.

An Act concerning wherrymen and watermen, by reason of the great hazard and loss of lives and goods through the unskilfulness and lack of experience of divers watermen.

An Act against brokers to prevent the fraudulent practices of counterfeit brokers and pawntakers upon money, who imbolden lewd persons to rob and steal.

An Act to encourage the seamen of England to take fish, whereby they may increase to furnish the Navy of England, re-enacting that old Statute that no flesh be killed in Lent.

An Act for the charitable relief and ordering of persons infected with the plague.

An Act of subsidy of tonnage and poundage, similar to like Acts passed in former times whereby for the defence of the Realm and the keeping of the seas safe for merchandise certain sums are levied upon all manner of goods coming in and going forth of the Realm.

8th July. THE DUKE CHARLES.

The little Duke Charles is reported to be much improved in health in Scotland, his strength and the amendment of his going improving daily, so that he is now able to walk alone without the aid of a staff for five and six times the length of the great chamber at Dunfermline. He is said to be a very lively image of his most royal father.

10th *July*. THE EARL OF LINCOLN'S HIGHHANDED ACTION.

The Earl of Lincoln of late conceiving some dislike for Mr. Lodovick Bryskett, that is his neighbour in his house at Chelsea, caused the pale to be taken down which protected Mr. Bryskett's garden and sent his workmen to carry away Mr. Bryskett's cabbage plants and caused cattle to be driven in which utterly spoiled his barley then beginning to shoot ear.

16th *July*. THE FRENCH KING'S MIRACULOUS ESCAPE.

From Paris there is a strange tale that the French King hath been miraculously delivered. His Majesty was about to partake of the communion upon the day of Corpus Christi, and had opened his mouth to receive the Host when suddenly there appeared a dog which pulled him backwards. A second time the King essayed to receive the Host and again the dog prevented him. Hereupon he commanded the priest to partake of the Host himself, which at first he would have refused, had not the King importuned him. When the priest had taken it, he swelled up and his body was burst in twain. Thus was the plot discovered and some of the noblemen who were privy to it are now in the Bastille.

22nd *July*. THE TRANSLATION OF THE BIBLE.

The King hath concluded that fifty-four learned men shall undertake the translation of the Bible, and since divers of them have either no ecclesiastical preferment at all or else so very small as the same is unmeet for men of their desert, it is required none shall be admitted to any prebend or parsonage rated at £20 and upwards until his Majesty's pleasure be known. Moreover, the Bishops shall inform themselves of all learned men in their dioceses who, having special skill in the Hebrew and Greek tongues, have taken pains in their private studies of the Scriptures for clearing of obscurities in the Hebrew or Greek, or touching any difficulties or mistakings in the former English translation. These men shall be written unto and earnestly charged to send their observations either to M. Lively, the Hebrew Reader in Cambridge, or Dr. Harding, the Hebrew

Reader in Oxford, or to Dr. Andrewes, Dean of Westminster, to be imparted to the rest of their companions.

Of late Mr. Hugh Broughton took upon himself to propound to his Majesty directions and rules how to proceed in this work. He would have many to translate a part, and when they have brought a good English style and true sense, others should make an uniformity that divers words might not be used where the original word was the same. He would have seventy-two persons set to translate in memory of the ancient seventy-two Greek translators, and that artificers should be brought in to help for terms, as embroiderers for Aaron's ephod, geometricians, carpenters, masons about the Temple of Solomon and Ezekiel; and gardeners for all the boughs and branches of Ezekiel's tree.

23rd July. THE SIEGE OF OSTEND.

The enemy gain much upon the town. They have blown up a mine between the Poulder Bulwark and West Port. A sloop laden with 2,000 weight of powder, being foul upon the entrance of the haven, was struck with a shot and the powder all blown up in the air and fourteen men lost in it.

25th July. DUTCH CRUELTY.

Some days since the Dutch captured at sea a small ship from Sandwich with goods belonging to certain English. They wrapped the mariners in the sails and drowned them that the deed might not be known; but the owners learnt of it and so roused the people of Sandwich against some Flemings, subjects of the Hollanders, who live in their town, that they killed three of them and threaten death to the rest.

30th July. THE PRISONERS IN THE TOWER.

There is some complaining by the principal prisoners in the Tower of the restraints which have been newly laid upon them by the Lieutenant. Upon their return from Winchester, the Council ordered that Lord Cobham, Lord Grey, and Sir Walter Ralegh should each have two servants, one to attend, the other to go about their business. Since then this order has been somewhat relaxed, and many come to them, their ladies and some courtiers. Once or twice, the gates of the gardens where they are allowed to walk being open, Lord Grey and Sir

Walter have walked and talked together; but now the Lieutenant has caused locks to be put on their gates, and more straitly prevents too much access, which moves them to complain. Lord Cobham declares that he is translating Dion out of the Spanish, and asks for aid.

1st August. THE SPANISH COMMISSIONERS.

The Commissioners to ratify the treaty of peace sent by the Spanish King are on their way hither. They are Don John de Velasco, Constable of Castile, Pedraca de la Sierra, Great Chamberlain accompanied with Marquises, Earls, Barons and Knights to the number of 100 persons.

3rd August. GREAT RAIN.

To-day about 10 of the clock in the forenoon great claps of thunder were heard in London, and great rain and hail followed, such as hath not been seen in the memory of man, for one hour's space; and the channels and water-courses rose so high that many cellars were overflowed or filled, and the goods in them drowned.

5th August. A LIONESS WHELPS.

To-day the lioness in the Tower, named Elizabeth, brought forth a lion's whelp, the rarest thing which in this country has happened in any age.

7th August. THE LIONESS'S WHELP.

The matter of the lioness and her whelp so greatly entertained the King's mind that he gave order to the Lieutenant of the Tower to have special care for the feeding and warm keeping of it, and that much resort, as to a strange thing, and the often opening of the place do not annoy it. Nevertheless the whelp died yesterday. So soon as it was delivered from the dam she carried it in her mouth from place to place so that the keeper, to save it, hazarded to take it from her and used the best means to preserve it, but whether by the dam's bruising of it, or by some other accident it is dead. It is now bowelled and embalmed to be presented to the King.

8th August. THE CONSTABLE AT DOVER.

The Constable of Castile with his train is at Dover, having

landed on the 5th, being forced by contrariety of winds to land at the Downs, whither Sir Lewis Lewkenor and the Spanish Ambassador repaired to him with as many coaches, horses and waggons as could be procured, and brought to him to Dover, where he is delayed because some of his gentlemen are not yet recovered of their sea-sickness. He is determined to go through the City in full bravery by daylight. He has brought great store of provisions and amongst the rest two loads of ice to put in his wine. He is all in his Spanish *grandeza*, permitting no one of his train to stand covered before him, or to sit covered at his table. He has in his train 234 persons, and is said to be a very grave gentleman, courteous enough, his behaviour void of vanity and no tedious complimenter.

10*th August*. THE COMMISSIONERS FOR THE PEACE.

The Commissioners for the Spanish King and the Archduke have now reached London. They were brought up from Gravesend to Somerset House, where the Spanish Commission keeps residence. The Archduke's Commission remains at Durham House. In both houses they are dieted at the King's cost and attended by the Gentlemen Ushers, sewers, cooks, Yeomen of the Guard, and Grooms of the Chamber. The King's Players, being Grooms of the Chamber Extraordinary, are summoned for the purpose.

12*th August*. THE COMMISSIONERS FOR THE HANSE TOWNS.

The Commissioners for the Hanse towns, who arrived some weeks ago, have submitted their articles, but complain that they receive no answer. They claim ancient privileges in England granted by Edward the Second, and afterwards confirmed by patent and parliament of Edward the Fourth. Their chief claim is to be free of all customs as English born for all transactions and importations, and to be free of all trades and towns in England. This continued till Edward the Sixth made an order by his Council proving those liberties forfeit; first, because they were no corporation capable thereof; but chiefly by abusing the liberties in colouring foreigners' goods, denying us like mutual commerce with them, enlarging their Hanses and their trade to the ruin of the English. Queen Mary, at the instance of King Philip, condescended to some liberties, but they never accepted thereof;

and when some moderations of those liberties were offered them by Queen Elizabeth, they refused, and caused the Emperor by strict mandate to inhibit us the Empire.

13th August. THE ARCHBISHOP OF YORK'S LETTER TO LORD CECIL.

The Archbishop of York, upon receiving a letter from the Council concerning a loan of money to be raised from the clergy of his Province for his Majesty, hath written to the Lord Cecil complaining that the King's subjects hear and fear that his excellent and heroical nature is too much inclined to giving, which in short time will exhaust the treasure of this Kingdom and bring many inconveniences. His Majesty in Scotland lived like a worthy and noble King of small revenues in comparison, because he wisely foresaw that *expensa* should not exceed *recepta*, which he doth not in England, but not minding his yearly *recepta* and *recipienda* (though great yet not infinite), yields almost to every man's petition. If this should continue, this Kingdom will not serve but that his Majesty, contrary to his princely nature, must be compelled to be burdensome and grievous to his subjects.

14th August. SUNDRY ACCIDENTS.

The sickness which is at Oxford increases, and has taken away Master John Eveleigh, Principal of Hart Hall, which gave them such an alarm that the Colleges were ready to rise and make away.

The Lord Sanquahar, being at Rycote, there fell to practise or play with Turner the fencer, who by mischance ran him in the eye so that he is in great danger to lose it, and the pain and anguish have put him into an ague.

19th August. THE PEACE SWORN.

The peace with Spain was sworn to-day, the Earl of Devonshire accompanying the Spanish Ambassador to the Court where the King, in the presence of all the Commissioners, English and others, took his corporal oath upon the Holy Bible religiously to upkeep the Articles of Peace lately agreed upon, the Ambassador holding the King's hands between his hands. The solemn oath having been performed, the King feasted them at the Banqueting house, and after dinner at the outer gate they saw bull-baiting and bear-baiting, and in the preaching place running and dancing upon ropes, with other feats of activity. This afternoon the peace was proclaimed at the Cross in Cheapside by William Segar, Garter King-at-Arms, assisted by Master William Romney, Sheriff of London, in his scarlet robes, eight heralds and sergeant-trumpeters, and seven others all on horseback.

The Articles of Peace.

Among the Articles of this Peace it is to be noted that neither side shall give assistance to the prejudice of the other, nor shall they supply soldiers or provisions or victuals, money, or instruments of war. All letters of reprisal and licence to take prizes shall be withdrawn. The towns of Flushing, Brille, and Ramekins and other places which the States pledged to Queen Elizabeth shall remain in the King's hands. The King will not allow his garrison soldiers to succour the Hollanders, or other enemies of the King of Spain and the Archduke. Ships of either party may have access to the ports of the other. The King's ships shall not carry merchandises out of Holland and Zealand into the kingdoms of the Spanish King and the Archduke. The King's ships may trade in the Spanish ports, paying only the usual customs and tolls. Prisoners serving in the galleys shall be released and dismissed. Further, the King's subjects shall not be molested by the Inquisition for anything they may have committed out of Spain, nor shall they be compelled to enter the Spanish churches, but if they do then they shall perform their duty and reverence towards the Holy Sacrament of the altar; and if they shall see the Holy Sacrament coming towards them in any street they shall do reverence by bowing their knees, or else pass aside into some other street, or turn into some house. Further, if any ship's master or officer offend, then the Inquisition shall proceed against them by sequestering only their own goods, and leave free the ship and other goods not belonging to the offenders.

The Peace is more joyfully accepted than the people make show of, for the multitude of pretended gallants, bankrupts and unruly youths that are settled in piracy are disdainful, only because they see an end to their livelihood. But honest citizens are exceeding glad, hoping henceforth to have free trade with all nations, and to see an end to the continual pressing of their sons and servants for foreign service.

20th August. LORD CECIL PROMOTED.

This day the Lord Cecil was created Viscount Cranborne.

24th August. JESUITS TO BE BANISHED FROM MUNSTER.

Of late the Lord President and Council of Munster made proclamation that all Jesuits, seminaries and massing priests shall depart from that province by the last day of September, and so to continue for the space of seven years: and any that shall relieve or receive one of them shall be fined £40, one-half to be given to the informer and the other half to the King's use.

26th August. THE SPANISH AMBASSADOR DEPARTS.

The Constable of Castile and his train departed from London towards Dover.

29th August. THE ILL-FEELING OF THE STATES.

The very name of our peace with their enemies is so unpleasing to those of the States that in a short time all pleasures past will be forgotten, though our men of war would rather that we had kept the pathway of the old Queen; for then our old enemy, and now reconciled friend, had been at Death's door, and Christendom no more had feared his usurping ambitions. Already this peace breeds some grudgings. Already some English ships trading to the Archduke's havens in Flanders have been taken and one burned, with some English drowned, which our men will not much digest; and the matter is come to bloodshed in revenge, a skipper of Flushing being killed at Sandwich, and two Hollanders said to be slain at Dover.

4th September. THE TREATY AND THE STATES.

Although by the strict letter of the Treaty it seemed that no small disadvantage is threatened to the States, yet upon more curious examination it appeareth that they will not be deprived of English succours, because there is no article to revoke those companies that are there already; and for the passage of voluntaries the King promiseth neither to punish nor to stay, but only not to consent to them, and to treat both sides alike. The Archduke now beginneth to form some companies of English.

7th September. OSTEND.

The enemy now hasten themselves very diligently at Ostend and are already come to the middle point in the first of the new works that were set up behind the old. In a ravelin before this new Helmont they blew up a mine, and covered some sixty of the enemy.

12th September. THE PLANTATION OF GUIANA.

News is come of the voyage of the *Olive Plant* and of the plantation of Guiana. After leaving the Downs on the 28th of March last Captain Charles Leigh reached the mouth of the River of Amazons upon the 10th of May. Thence they sailed to the River of Wiapogo in the latitude of 3 degrees and a half to the north of the Line, where they found the people ready to give them the best entertainment they could, bringing forth honey, pines, plantains, potatoes, cassavo (of which they make their bread and wine), hams, coneys, hogs and the like. Then, after divers conferences with the chief Indians, and especially two that have been before in England and could speak some English, Captain Leigh found them very willing to have him and his people abide in their country. Further, when he would have sought some other place, they offered him their own dwelling-houses and gardens already planted, which he accepted. So they held a great feast together, and it was concluded that Captain Leigh with thirty-five Englishmen should remain, and the rest returning home with letters to Sir Olive Leigh, his brother, have now reached England with four principal Indians as pledges.

As yet they have found no gold, but the country will yield through industry sugar canes, cotton and fine flax. Captain Leigh asks that 100 men at least may be sent out, all labouring men and gardeners, with a few carpenters.

17th September. OSTEND TAKEN.

The memorable siege of Ostend which hath ministered so large a subject of discourse to the world, and for so long, is now at an end, rendered upon terms as honourable as the law of arms could permit or the extremity of the town demand. It was long before the Governors would resolve to hearken to a parley, but seeing the succours so solemnly assured from day to day to be deferred, and the enemy within one day's working likely to be masters of the Greule, on the 10th entered into treaty, and the 11th rendered up the town. The conditions were that the garrison should march forth with their arms and goods, their colours flying, with sound of drums, bullets in their mouths, and match burning; the ships in the haven, which were to the number of 50 vessels, should depart at the first wind, with such munitions and artillery as then were embarked, with other great pieces then within the town; that waggons and chariots be furnished for their transport to the Count Maurice's army, and they in safety thither convoyed. At the capitulation there were in the town 1,600 men and 400 women besides children. The honour for this accord the Marquis Spinola shall receive to the reproach of the Spaniard, who has been accustomed to serve himself at all advantages without mercy, and sometimes to fail of treaties, the memory whereof is engraved on the hearts of that people to all posterity.

The summer's service is now at an end, for the season is far spent, as the Archduke is reinforced by French supplies out of Italy as well as by those men employed before Ostend; and besides the States must attend the conservation of this summer's conquest, which doth require many fortifications.

21st September. THE KING VISITS ETON.
The Court is now at Windsor, whence the King was taken to see Eton College, and after a banquet there knighted Master Henry Savile, the Provost.

23rd September. THE COMMISSIONERS FOR THE HANSE TOWNS.
After much conference between the Commissioners for the Hanse towns and the Council these past weeks, an answer was given to-day, which was delivered by word of mouth in Latin by Sir Christopher Perkins at Hampton Court. The King and Council find their liberties void, and denied to them these sixty years. Touching their desire to have some new treaty for more moderate liberties, the answer is that the State of England may not endure them to be as free as the English, especially in customs, for so the trade of our merchants would be overthrown and our navy decay. To allow them equal freedom in custom with the English (for all strangers pay double custom) is that the Hanses carrying in bottoms far cheaper and having more alliance

and freedom in passing the Sound, they may sell better cheap, and ingross our cloths, and stop and open our vent at their will. But they are offered as great liberties as any foreign nation in amity with the King; and to grant them more would draw on the King the daily importunity and mislike of other Princes.

The Commissioners did not expect so final an answer, but hoped at least to have a return of their Stillyard. This Stillyard (or Steelyard) was first granted as *Guilda Aula Teutonicorum* for the merchants of Almain that used to bring hither as well wheat, rye, hemp, linen cloth, wainscots, wax, steel, and other merchandises in the year 1259 by Henry the Third; and they held it till they were dispossessed by order of Queen Elizabeth in January, 1598.

25th September. A COLOUR NAMED AFTER THE ARCHDUCHESS ISABELLA.

It is said that at the beginning of the Siege of Ostend the Archduchess made a vow that till Ostend was taken, she would not change her linen, which being now (after three years) of a yellow-dingy hue they call this colour *l'Isabeau* or the 'Isabella.,

30th September. COURT NEWS.

The Court return in a few days to London for pursuing the commission of the Union, the meeting of the commissioners being appointed for the 27th of next month. The most of the Scottish commissioners are already arrived, and they begin to consult how to reconcile our money with theirs, wherein there will shortly be order taken. Most men are of opinion that there will be so great difficulty to change the state of the present constitutions that little can be done to satisfy what is proposed. No one is yet chosen to take the oath of the King of Spain and the Archduke. Much dislike is caused that the States' ships do take our men that carry corn into Spain, which we may not suffer; neither that they buy up our ships to serve upon the coast of Spain as they go about; so that if we do not come to an agreement for the ordering of things between them and us, we shall quickly fall into discontent against each other.

The King hath now declared his resolution for the making of the Bishop of London to be Archbishop of Canterbury, and Dr. Vaughan, the Bishop of Chester, to be Bishop of London.

2nd October. A BOOK OF PASCALE TRANSLATED.

A book called *False complaints*, or the censure of an unthankful mind, the labour of Carolus Pascalius, is now translated into English, a work very learned and fit for all estates in this age of unnecessary discontentments, showing how all complain, but all without cause.

3rd October. COURT NEWS.

Dr. Richard Bancroft, Bishop of London, is to be our new Archbishop of Canterbury. The Lady Arabella spends her time in lectures and riding, hearing of services and preachings, and visiting the princesses. She will not hear of marriage. Indirectly there was speech used in recommendation of Count Maurice.

8th October. THE DUKE CHARLES.

The little Duke Charles, who has remained in Scotland since the King's coming because of his weakness, has now reached Windsor. Before his coming, many great ladies were suitors to be his guardian, but when they saw how weak a child he is and hardly likely to live, none is any longer desirous for that office. The Queen has now chosen the lady of Sir Robert Carey. The Duke is still unable to walk or to stand alone, he is so weak in his joints; and he is so slow in beginning to speak that the King was desirous that the string of his tongue should be cut, and that he should have the child put in iron boots to strengthen his sinews and joints, but the Lady Carey will not allow it.

10th October. A COUNTERBLAST TO TOBACCO.

There is come forth a little book called *A Counterblast to Tobacco*, with no author's name to it (but credibly said to be written by his Majesty's own hand), very invectively condemning the taking of this herb. Herein the author noteth that tobacco is used by the barbarous Indians as an antidote to the pox (which disease was likewise brought thence), denieth it to be a sovereign remedy for diseases, and declareth the taking of it to be a custom loathsome to the eye, hateful to the nose, harmful to the brain, dangerous to the lungs, and in the black stinking fume thereof nearest resembling the horrible Stygian smoke of the pit that is bottomless.

15th October. A NEW LORD DEPUTY FOR IRELAND.

The King is now pleased to license Sir George Carew, that

hath been Lord Deputy in Ireland since the coming over of the
Earl of Devonshire, to return to England, and to deliver over the
Sword to Sir Arthur Chichester to be Lord Deputy in his place.
Further there shall be a Parliament of the three Estates of the
Realm to consult and resolve of all things that shall be good for
the Realm.

ENGLISH SHIPS NOT TO BE SOLD.

There is a proclamation expressly commanding all merchants,
owners of ships, mariners and all others that from henceforth
they forbear to sell, truck, exchange or alienate any English ship
without special licence first obtained under the Great Seal.
Further, that if it shall appear that any of his Majesty's officers
have used negligence or connivance therein, his Majesty will
extend the pain of his displeasure unto them, and cause them to
feel the smart thereof.

16th October. A BETROTHAL AT COURT.

After long love and many changes of affection Sir Philip
Herbert, the younger brother of my Lord of Pembroke, on
Friday last was betrothed to the Lady Susan Vere, daughter of
the Earl of Oxford, without the knowledge of his or her friends.
The next day she acquainted her uncle, my Lord Cranborne,
who seemed much troubled; but the King took it upon himself
and has since made peace on all sides.

17th October. A TAX ON TOBACCO.

To restrain the immoderate taking of tobacco a tax of 6s. 8d.
is to be levied upon every pound of it brought into the Realm, for
nowadays this herb (which was formerly used only by the better
sort as physic to preserve health) is through evil custom and the
toleration thereof so excessively taken by disordered persons of
base condition that they consume their wages, impair their
health, and weaken their bodies, and are driven thereby to
unthrifty shifts to maintain their gluttonous exercise.

23rd October. COMPLAINTS AGAINST THE STATES.

Of late the States have not only sent new order to their men-
of-war on the coasts of Flanders to impeach our trade with the
Archduke's ports by all means possible, but also to burn all ships
of foreign Princes as they shall take. Certain merchants of

London, a few days since, despatched some vessels with currants, cloth, lead, salt and other merchandises to Dunkirk, which were taken by the men-of-war of the States and sent to Rotterdam, and there confiscated without yielding the owners any restitution. These courses are very strange and contrary to expectation. Moreover many of their own people, under cover of private licences, carry all manner of victuals to the Archduke's ports and daily resort thither underhand.

24*th October*. THE KING'S NEW STYLE.

At the great Cross in Westminster the King was in most solemn manner proclaimed King of Great Britain, France and Ireland, Defender of the Faith, &c., in the presence of Sir Thomas Bennet, the Lord Mayor of London, the aldermen in scarlet, with the heralds and trumpeters, all mounted.

28*th October*. THE SERMON AT COURT.

To-day Dr. John Gordoun, Dean of Sarum, preached before his Majesty and the Court upon the union of Great Britain in antiquity of language, name, religion, and Kingdom, declaring the restitution of the ancient name of Britain by his Majesty to have come by the very motion and instigation of God's Holy Spirit that it may be a perpetual memorial that God hath restored His true covenant of eternal life, which He hath promised to all those that do worship Him faithfully and truly; and moreover that it is great honour to be called Britans, that is to say 'the people of God's covenant,' which after the name of Christian is the most glorious and honourable name that any man in the world may enjoy.

30*th October*. A TAX ON PLAYS PROPOSED.

The Lord Say and Sele, being very desirous at this time to benefit both the King and himself in his necessities, hath proposed to the Viscount Cranborne certain devices for raising of money; as, that since interludes and common playhouses are unnecessary and yield no penny to the King, although for every comer in 3d., 6d. or 9d. is taken before they come to the best places, the King should have 1d. for from every comer in. And if it may be granted to my Lord for four years to collect a penny a poll of all that come into playhouses throughout England, he will give 1,000 marks to him whom Viscount Cranborne shall name, and £40 rent to the King.

1st November. 'THE MOOR OF VENICE.'

This night the King's players played in the Banqueting House at Whitehall before his Majesty a play called *The Moor of Venice*, by Shakespeare, whereof the plot is that Othello, a Moorish captain serving the Venetians, is privily married to the daughter of a noble senator. He chooseth as his lieutenant Cassio, and for his ancient Iago, an old and well-experienced soldier. This Iago is so eaten up with jealousy that Cassio should be preferred before him that in revenge thereof he worketh upon Othello to believe that he is made cuckold by Cassio; by which means Othello, being a man very passionate and without any experience of women, is so greatly moved that he strangleth his wife, but when the truth is known stabbeth himself in remorse.

7th November. THE KING'S HOUND.

The King came to Whitehall to-day from Royston but returns thither in two days. At Royston one of the King's special hounds called Jowler was missing one day. The King was much displeased, but notwithstanding went hunting. The next day, when they were on the field, Jowler came in amongst the rest of the hounds. The King was told of him and was very glad, and looking upon him spied a paper about his neck in which was written, 'Good Mr. Jowler, we pray you speak to the King (for he hears you every day so doth he not us) that it will please his Majesty to go back to London, for else the country will be undone; all our provision is spent already, and we are not able to entertain him any longer.'

10th November. THE ORDER FOR THE NEW TRANSLATION OF THE BIBLE.

For the new translation of the Bible the King hath set down that the work shall be divided among three bodies of translators, the one at London, the other two at Cambridge and Oxford, and the books are divided as followeth. At Westminster, the *Pentateuchon* and the story from *Joshua* to the first Book of *Chronicles*; and the translators are Dr. Lancelot Andrewes, Dean of Westminster, Dr. John Overall, Dean of Paul's, Mr. Dr. Saravia,

Mr. Dr. Richard Clark, Mr. Dr. John Leifield, Mr. Dr. Robert Tighe, Mr. Burleigh, Mr. Geoffrey King, Mr. Richard Tomson and Mr. William Bedwell.

At Cambridge, from the First of *Chronicles* with the rest of the Story and the *Hagiographi*, viz., *Job, Psalms, Proverbs, Canticles, Ecclesiastes*; and the translators Mr. Edward Lively, the Regius Professor of Hebrew, Mr. John Richardson, Mr. Lawrence Chaderton, Master of Emmanuel College (that was present at the Conference), Mr. Francis Dillingham, Mr. Thomas Harrison, Mr. Roger Andrewes, Mr. Robert Spalding and Mr. Andrew Byng. Also at Cambridge, the *Prayer of Manasses* and the rest of the Apocrypha, to be undertaken by Dr. Duport, Master of Jean's College, Dr. William Branthwart, Dr. Jeremiah Radcliffe, Mr. Ward of Emmanuel; Mr. Andrew Downs, the Regius Professor of Greek, Mr. John Boyes, Mr. Ward of King's College.

At Oxford, the four Greater Prophets, with the *Lamentations*, and the twelve lesser Prophets, which are assigned to Dr. John Harding, Regius Professor of Hebrew, Dr. John Reynolds (who was also at the Conference), President of Corpus Christi College, Dr. Thomas Holland, Regius Professor of Divinity, Dr. Richard Kilby, Rector of Lincoln College, Mr. Miles Smith, Mr. Richard Brett, and Master Richard Fairclough.

The places and persons agreed upon for the Greek are, at Oxford, Dr. Thomas Ravis, Dean of Christchurch, Dr. George Abbot, Dean of Winchester, Dr. Edward Edes, Dean of Worcester, Dr. Giles Tomson, Dean of Windsor, Sir Henry Savile, Provost of Eton, Dr. John Perne, Regius Professor of Greek, and Mr. John Harmer. These undertake the four Gospels, the *Acts of the Apostles*, and *Apocalypse*.

At Westminster, Dr. William Barlow, Dean of Chester, Dr. Ralph Hutchinson, President of St. John's College in Oxford, Dr. John Spenser, Mr. Roger Fenton, Mr. Michael Rabbett, Mr. Thomas Sanderson, and Mr. William Dakins, Professor of Divinity in Gresham College.

THE RULES TO BE OBSERVED IN THE TRANSLATION.

It is laid down that the ordinary Bible read in the Church (commonly called the Bishop's Bible) shall be followed and as little altered as the truth of the original will permit; and old ecclesiastical words shall be kept, viz., 'church' not to be translated 'congregation.' No marginal notes at all to be affixed, save for explanation of the Hebrew or Greek words which cannot without some circumlocution be briefly expressed in the text. Quotations of places as shall serve for the fit reference of one scripture to another to be set down in the margin.

As for the manner of work, every particular man of each company to take the same chapters, and, having translated or amended them severally by himself where he thinketh good, then all to meet together to confer and agree; and as soon as one company shall have despatched any one book in this manner they shall send it to the rest to be considered of; and of this point his Majesty is very careful. If any company, upon review, should doubt or differ upon any place then to send word, and if the translators agree not, the difference to be compounded at the general meeting at the end of the work. When any place of special obscurity is doubted of, letters are to be directed by Authority to any learned man in the land for his judgment; and the Bishops are to send letters to all learned men amongst their clergy, admonishing them of this translation in hand, and to move as many as be skilful in the tongues to send his particular observations to the company, either at Westminster, Cambridge or Oxford. The directors in each company are the Deans of Westminster and Chester for Westminster, and the King's Professors in either the Hebrew or Greek in the Universities.

MASTER CAMDEN'S 'REMAINS.'

Master Camden hath sent to the press anonymously a book entitled *Remains of a greater work*, concerning Britain, the inhabitants thereof, their language, names,. surnames, wise speeches and the like.

14*th November*. THE DUKE OF HOLST IN LONDON.

The Queen's brother Ulric, Duke of Holst, has come to court, but with no great following. He lodges in the Court in the Lord Treasurer's lodging, and his company in my Lord of Derby's house in Cannon Row. He has twenty dishes of meat allowed at every meal, and certain of the knights are appointed to attend him. To-morrow the King goes towards Royston and the Duke with him.

26th November. COURT NEWS.

It is said that the King likes exceedingly well all things that have been done about the Union. Moreover, he would not have the Archbishop of Canterbury to deal too hastily with the ministers that do not conform themselves precisely by the day, so that where any shall be found that give disposition of conformity, though not in the present, all proceeding may be forborne for a month or two, and that if this disposition of theirs be but counterfeit and to win him they be the more soundly dealt with afterwards.

30th November. THE TRUE COPY OF 'HAMLET' PRINTED.

There is a new copy of *The tragical History of Hamlet, Prince of Denmark* imprinted, and enlarged to almost as much again as it was in the former, according to the true and perfect copy.

5th December. COURT NEWS.

The matter of the Union hath entertained the Lords of the Council in so continual employment that little other business is despatched. The matter is now concluded and would have been interchangeably signed but the King misliked the form of the preamble which hath brought him back to Whitehall from Royston to resolve thereof with the Council. My Lord of Worcester who is with the King at Royston greatly complaineth that since his departure from London he hath no rest but upon Sundays, for in the morning they are upon horseback by 8 of the clock, and so continue in full career from the death of one hare to another until 4 at night, by which time, for the most part, they are four miles from home. The ladies in the Court prepare to solemnize the Christmas with a gallant Masque which doth cost the Exchequer £3,000.

8th December. AGREEMENT CONCERNING THE UNION.

The Conference about the Union of the Kingdoms is at length concluded to the King's very good satisfaction, as he witnessed by his speech when the Commissioners presented the instrument under their seals. The substance of the agreement is that all hostile laws made between either Kingdom shall be

168

abolished; that Border laws and customs likewise abolished, and justice ministered hereafter according to the ordinary laws of both Kingdoms; that there be free intercourse of trade between the Kingdoms without paying any customs for all commodities (except sheep, wool, wool-fells, cattle, hides and leather, which are wholly prohibited), so as a caution be given not to transport any of the said commodities into any foreign ports; that either nation shall be enabled to be free of any company or corporation of the other; that it shall be declared by Parliament that the law already is, (for so the judges have declared it) that the subjects of either Kingdom born since Queen Elizabeth's death are naturalized in the other to all intents and purposes. These be but the heads of the agreement for all copies are utterly prohibited till the Parliament.

DISAPPOINTMENTS OF THE PEACE.

It is commonly reported that our merchants are ill used in Spain by the Inquisition, and besides that the trade proves nothing as beneficial as was expected; partly by reason that the merchants there are become poor by these wars and not able to buy but upon days; and many of those that have been trusted have proved bankrupt, insomuch as some of ours have brought back their commodities rather than sell upon credit; partly also, by reason that in this long restraint of trade, they have been forced to betake themselves to making of cloth there, and do make it now in that quantity as they care not much for ours which was wont to be our chiefest trade thither. As for corn, the French both by reason of their nearness and better abundance will ever furnish better cheap. So there appears little hope of any fruit of our peace in that regard; which begins to cool that ardent affection which carried us to the Treaty, and begets some discourses that this will be but a short peace.

10th December. BORDER FEUDS.

The North Borders are reported to be much infested with stealing, and now and then disordered persons of the Scottish side stir up the ancient and barbarous custom of deadly feuds. Of late some unruly persons, lying in wait upon the night, have outrageously wounded divers Englishmen upon a former feud, eighteen years old.

11th December. A QUARREL AT COURT.

The Duke of Holst, going up to the Queen attended by Sir Thomas Somerset and the Master of Orkney, as they entered in at the Privy Chamber, being thrust one upon another by the press, conceived each of them that the other had thrust and strived to go in before. Whereupon one looking big upon the other, after they were in the Privy Chamber, they fell to multiplying of words so far that the lie passed from Sir Thomas to the Master of Orkney. So they were sent for by certain of the Council; but Sir Thomas having in the meanwhile passed into the Balloon Court to play, the Master of Orkney came to Sir Thomas and gave him a blow with his fist which was returned. Hereupon each drew his sword but the gentlemen parted them. By this time the Yeomen of the Guard who had been sent had found them and brought them before Viscount Cranborne, the Lord Chamberlain, the Earl of Devonshire, Lord Knollys, Lord Wotton, who examined the cause of the quarrel and admonished them of their great peril in quarrelling in the Court. So Sir Thomas is sent to the Fleet, and the Master of Orkney commanded to tarry in his house till the King's pleasure be known.

12th December. COURT NEWS.

The assembly for the Union is now broken up, only three copies of their resolutions being made and those, closely sealed, remain the one in the King's hands, the other with the commissioners for England, and the third with those from Scotland, and so to remain until the assembly in Parliament in February next. The Puritans about Royston, to the number of seven or eight and twenty, presented to the King, as he was hunting there, a petition in favour of their ministers. The King took in ill part this disorderly proceeding, commanding them to depart forthwith, and to depute ten of the wisest among them to declare their grievances. These ten were sent before the Council and are bound over to answer before the Lords when they shall be summoned.

13th December. COURT NEWS.

The Lords of the Council have set down an order that because one day in the week is too little for dispatch of suitors, they will assign every Wednesday afternoon to assemble themselves for all business that shall occur. The Duke of Holst is still here trying to procure a levy of men to carry into Hungary, but few are like to adventure so far with a man that can do them so little good. My Lord Admiral prepareth against March to go to Spain very magnificently; all his gentlemen shall have black velvet cloaks. He carries with him the title of Excellency, and hath £15,000 allowed for his expense, besides two of the King's best ships to transport him. The King sends a present of certain horses and hunting geldings with two rich saddles, and eight or ten horsecloths of several coloured velvets with rich embroidery whereby they are hot and heavy, and so very improper for the climate. There is great preparation for the Queen's Masque, wherein besides her Majesty will be eleven ladies, my Ladies of Bedford and Suffolk, Susan Kerr, Lady Dorothy Rich, Lady Walsingham and others. The Lady of Northumberland is excused by sickness, and Lady Hertford by measles. My Lady of Nottingham hath the polypus in her nostril, which some fear must be cut off. The Lady Hatton would fain have had a part, but some unknown reason they left her out; whereupon she is gone to her house and will not let her Master Attorney be with her or within her chamber till he has performed all convenants made to her at her marriage.

17th December. THE COUNCIL'S PROTEST TO THE KING.

The Council are much perturbed at the masque proposed for Christmas which the King would have performed, lest by its lack there should be come conceit of ominous presage. They have therefore represented to the King that in time past many Christmases have passed without such mark of note, dancing, comedies and plays being thought sufficient marks of mirth except some great strange Prince or extraordinary marriages fell at that time. As for the Queen's intention to take a part in a masque wherein there shall be fine ballets and dancing, they are bold to say it were a ready way to change the mirth of Christmas to offer any conditions where her Majesty's person is an actor. Moreover, it will be very disadvantageous that the expense should be laid on noblemen and gentlemen, for few are able to undergo such charges. Nevertheless the Council would not now have the masque abandoned, for though a saving of £4,000 would follow, yet the change would be more pernicious than the expense of ten times that value; for the ambassadors of foreign Princes will believe that the masque has been forborne because the King or the Queen lack £4,000.

18th December. A Play of the Gowry Conspiracy.

The tragedy of Gowry with all the action and actors hath been twice represented by the King's Players with exceeding concourse of all sorts of people; but whether the matter or the manner be not well handled, or that it be thought unfit Princes should be played on the stage in their lifetime, some great Councillors are much displeased with it, and so 'tis thought it shall be forbidden.

20th December. 'Westward Ho.'

The Children of Paul's have a new play called *Westward Ho* written by Dekker and Webster, showing how divers citizens' wives cozened those who would have cuckolded their husbands.

21st December. The French King's Mistress.

From Paris the news is that Madame D'Entragues, the King's mistress, and her father are committed to prison for some treasonable matter. The father protesteth that last summer he delivered up the contract made with the King, who then promised a full abolition of all faults. The lady herself, desperate in her misery, and with more audacity avoucheth a fact, saying that what she did was to assure the future of her son, lawful heir to her husband the King. There is much perplexity in this matter, for although the contract was delivered up, yet they doubt not that before the delivery copies were taken by a notary, which are as authentical as the original. These matters come to light through a confession of the Count D'Auvergne, and it is thought that he and Monsieur d'Entragues shall be put to death, and the lady confined in a nunnery.

23rd December. Papists in the North.

The Archbishop of York, on receipt of the Council's letters that he should proceed according to law against those Puritans that will not conform themselves, hath written to my Lord Cranborne that he would have the like order taken with the

Papists; for the Puritans, though they differ in ceremonies and accidents, yet they agree with us in substance of religion; and all or most of them love his Majesty and the present State. But the Papists are opposite and contrary in very many substantial points of religion and cannot but wish the Pope's authority and the popish religion established. Many are gone from all places to London and some are come down into the north in great jollity, almost triumphantly.

The Archbishop also complaineth, as one that loveth and honoureth his Majesty, that he would wish less wasting of the treasure of the Realm and more moderation in the lawful exercise of hunting that poor men's corn be less spoiled and his Majesty's subjects more spared. This letter by the indiscretion of his Grace's clerks is become generally talked of.

24th December. PARLIAMENT AGAIN PROROGUED.

The Parliament that was to have met again on 7th February next is now prorogued by proclamation until the 3rd of October next year, and in the meantime all who have repaired to London about the Commission concerning the Union or in expectation of the Parliament may return to their own homes. Upon which some say that this proroguing is because of the bringing in of the privy seals which are yet most behind, the avoiding of the clamour of Puritan ministers, and giving time to our Union-makers to play upon the bit.

THE BISHOP OF LONDON INSTALLED.

This afternoon Dr. Richard Vaughan, formerly Bishop of Chester, was installed Bishop of London in Paul's Church.

28th December. A MARRIAGE AT COURT.

Yesterday, being St. John's Day, the marriage of Sir Philip Herbert and the Lady Susan Vere was performed at Whitehall, with all the honour could be done a great favourite. The King gave the bride; and she in her tresses and trinkets bridled it so handsomely that the King said if he were not married he would not give her but keep her himself. The marriage dinner was kept in the great chamber, and at night there was a masque in the hall. The presents of plate and other things given by the noblemen are valued at £2,500; but that which made it a good marriage was a gift of the King's of £500 land for the bride's jointure. No ceremony was omitted of bride cakes, points, garters and gloves; and at night there was sewing into the sheet, casting off the bride's left hose, with many other pretty sorceries. They were lodged in the Council chamber, where in the morning the King in his shirt and nightgown gave them a *reveille matin* before they were up, and spent a good time in or upon the bed.

30th December. A DISORDER IN DUBLIN.

Of late one Shelton being chosen mayor of Dublin ought by ancient custom to have taken the oath both of supremacy and of his office, but the Barons of the Exchequer, being absent because of the contagion, he took only the oath of his office. Hereupon the priests gave out that the mayor was the only champion of the Catholic religion. The Lord Deputy, being advertised of this matter, awarded a commission to the Lord Chancellor and Chief Baron to call the mayor before him and offer him the oath of supremacy, but when he came before them he made great scruple. First he made a doubt whether he was required to take his oath because the words of the oath expressed in the statute 2nd Elizabeth are that the Queen's Majesty is the only supreme governor, etc., and so the force of the law ceased upon her decease. To which answer was made that by the word 'Queen,' the politic royal body was intended, which never dieth. Then he offered a new form of oath of his own. The Chief Baron, being not a little displeased at the mayor's fond and inconstant carriage in this business, peremptorily offered him the usual oath, which he refused. Whereupon the Chief Baron instantly abolished the commission, and advertised the Lord Deputy, by whose command the aldermen elect a new mayor.

31st December. THE YEAR'S MORTALITY IN LONDON.

It is much noted that in this year past, though other cities, and most villages and towns corporate, of the Realm were visited with the pestilence, yet it pleased Almighty God to spare the city of London; for notwithstanding the great multitudes of people from all places that came together to behold the King ride in triumph through London, there died in all in the City and liberties but 4,353 persons.

A DISCOURSE OF CLIMACTERICAL YEARS.

Master Thomas Wright hath written *A succinct philosophical declaration of the nature of climacterical years*, occasioned by the death of Queen Elizabeth to be added to his treatise *Of Passions of the mind* formerly printed. Noteth the different opinions of physicians, that in some men of solid and virile constitution the ninth are the climacterical years, but in others the seventh; and that the most dangerous years of all are the 49th (compounded upon seven times seven), and next to these the 70th (which containeth ten times seven). The cause of the notable alterations and dangers of death are by some physicians assigned to the influence of the heavens, to wit, that so many courses of the sun, moon, and planets from a man's nativity work such effects, so that some men, live they never so orderly, after so many circular motions of the sun and moon have warbled over their heads, upon necessity they must fall into one sickness or another and so die.

THE UNMASKING OF A FEMININE MACHIAVEL.

A poem by Mr. Thomas Andrewe, gentleman, called *The Unmasking of a feminine Machiavel*, of the misfortunes of one Andrea that went to the Flanders wars and being preserved at the late bloody battle of Newport was afterwards betrayed by a faithless mistress; which poem, saith the author, is set forth neither for profit nor for malice. But Mr. Samuel Rowlands in a poem dedicatory declareth this woman to be no fiction but a damn'd monster of deformed evil.

GRIMELLO'S FORTUNES.

Grimello's Fortunes in form of a dialogue between two travellers, Grimello and Ganuzido, wherein they discourse of sundry matters with sundry merry tales by the way, as of a certain page that with his fellows played a trick upon a gallant in the Court. This lob-lolly would for ever be making love to ladies, to the no small gain of the pages, who would feign to bring him commendations and tokens from the ladies in return for angels. At last one of them, dressing himself in the apparel of a gentlewoman, so fooled him that he went away into the country and was seen no more in Court.

A Book of Jests.

A book of more than sixty merry tales entitled *Pasquil's Jests*, mixed with Mother Bunch's Merriments, whereunto is added a dozen of gulls.

An Apology of the Brownists.

Certain of our English Brownists living in exile at Amsterdam have a book which they entitle *An Apology or defence of such true Christians as are commonly (but unjustly) called Brownists*, against the imputations laid upon them by the Heads and Doctors of the University of Oxford in their answer to the former petition. Herein they maintain sundry positions, alleging that the hierarchy and ministry of Popes, Archbishops, Lordships, Archdeacons, Priests, etc., are antichristian, and that ministers may not bear civil offices, and that marriage and burial of the dead are not ecclesiastical actions but civil. They would do away with degrees in Theology, and enforcement to single life in Colleges; nor would they tolerate the works of profane heathen writers in schools, alleging this, 'because the Scriptures are fully sufficient for all instruction and conviction, both for faith and conversation, and therefore all other studies, learning, and courses had in Schools and Universities to be no further nor otherwise used or allowed than may be warranted by the word of God, and be serviceable thereunto.' This *Apology* is dedicated to his Majesty, trusting that it may find favour in his eyes, lest otherwise He by whom Kings reign see it and it displease Him if His will be not obeyed; 'for,' quoth they, 'He can as easily loose the collar of Kings and put down the mighty from their seats; in His hand is your breath and all your ways, and, behold, He cometh shortly, and His reward with Him, to give every man according as his work shall be.'

Two Treatises by William Bradshaw the Puritan.

The first, *A Treatise of Divine Worship*, without author's or printer's name, wherein he goeth about to prove that the ceremonies imposed upon ministers are in their use unlawful. Declareth that though ceremonies are in themselves comely and decent, yet all ceremonies of religion must be commanded by God Himself else they are a mock. Noteth 'All civil furtherances and necessary circumstances of God's solemn worship, though they be not essential parts of the same, nor by special nomination commanded, yet are they to be esteemed ordinances of God, and not human inventions. As God having ordained that His saints, dwelling together both men, women and children of all sorts and degrees, should ordinarily at appointed times meet together, it must needs be presupposed to be His ordinance that they meet together in some such ordinary places as are fittest for to receive most commodiously such assemblies; for God having ordained that his ministers should preach or proclaim salvation to a multitude gathered together, and that they should sit at his feet, hath also ordained that the minister's seat should be higher than the rest of the people's: and the like may be said of all other such circumstances of divine worship, which are matters of so base and low consideration, and so subject to common sense, that it neither beseemeth the majesty of the Word of God in special, or human authority derived from God, to make any laws in particular about them; no more than to make laws that one should not sit in the congregation upon another's lap, or one spit upon another's clothes or face, or that men should not make antic faces in the church.'

The second little book, printed at Amsterdam, and called *A short treatise of the cross in baptism*, contracted into this syllogism: No human ordinance becoming an idol may lawfully be used in the service of God: But the sign of the cross being a human ordinance is become an idol: Ergo, the sign of the cross may not lawfully be used in the service of God.

The Siege of Ostend.

A true history of the memorable siege of Ostend, setting out in the form of a Journal all that passed from first to last in that famous action, with a cut of the defence works, and the engine called Pompey's bridge that was designed to give an assault upon the Half Moon. This work is translated from the French by Master Edward Grimestone.

2nd January. HOLIDAYS AT COURT.

New Year's Day passed without any solemnity and the exorbitant gifts that were wont to be used at this time are so far laid by. The present of the purse and gold was hard to be had without the asking. To-day the King played in the presence of the bridegroom, and threw for him, and had the great fortune to win £1,000, which he had for his pains. The great part was lost by my Lord of Cranborne.

4th January. NEW KNIGHTS OF THE BATH.

This afternoon Charles, Duke of Albany, the Lord Willoughby, the Lord Chandos, the Lord Compton, the Lord Norris, William Cecil, son of Lord Cranborne, Allan Percy, brother of the Earl of Northumberland, Thomas Somerset, second son to the Earl of Worcester, Francis Manners, brother to the Earl of Rutland, Francis Clifford, brother to the Earl of Cumberland, Thomas Howard, second son of the Earl of Suffolk, and John Harington, son of Lord Harington, were appointed to be made Knights of the Bath. The Earls of Oxford and Essex, being esquires to the Duke of Albany, took up their lodging at Whitehall in the first gate-house. Here, after supper, they all sat together in a row on one side, with the arms of each over the seat where he was placed. Their baths were provided for them in the chamber underneath.

MASTER SAMUEL DANIEL IN TROUBLE.

Master Daniel, unhappily for himself, has turned play-maker for the stage with a tragedy in the ancient manner called *Philotas,* which because it treats of a favourite come to destruction was by some taken to glance at our late troubles. Being therefore called before Lords of the Council, he declared that he had written three acts of the play before my Lord of Essex's troubles, purposing to have had it presented in Bath by certain gentle-men's sons as a private recreation for Christmas; but being called upon by his printer for a new impression of his works he laid aside until, driven by necessity to make use of his pen and the stage to be the mouth of his lines, he allowed it to be per-formed, never supposing that it could be so misapplied. Further, he told the Lords that it had been perused by the Master of Revels and that he had read some part of it to the Earl of Devonshire, which my Lord takes somewhat offensively. He has now written to Lord Cranborne protesting that the affairs of men in all ages bear the same resemblances; no time but brought forth the like concurrences, the like interstriving for place and dignity, the like supplantations, risings and overthrows. He petitions further that he may withdraw the book, pretend-ing some other occasion, that the suppressing it by authority may not make the world to imagine other matters in it than there is.

5th January. THE KNIGHTS OF THE BATH.

This morning the Knights of the Bath went through the gallery down into the Park, in their hermits' weeds, the musicians playing and the heralds going before them into the Court and so into the Chapel; where, having made solemn courtesies first to the altar and then to the Cloth of State, everyone took his place in the stalls of the choir, and heard solemn service. This done, each with his esquires went and offered, the Dean of the Chapel in a rich cope holding the basin. After they went into their lodgings, and newly attired them-selves in robes of crimson taffeta, with hats and white feathers. Then they went back to the Great Chamber where the King sat under the Cloth of Estate, and by him were they girded with the sword, and had the gilt spurs put upon them. This done, they were solemnly led to dinner, and after dinner went again to the Chapel where they offered their swords.

6th January. SOLEMNITIES AT COURT.

The Knights of the Bath, in robes of purple satin and doctors' hoods on their shoulders, and hats with white feathers, proceeded out of the revestry with the Duke of Albany into the Hall, where the King sat very royally under the Cloth of Estate, the heralds going before, the Knights of the Bath following; the Lord Chamberlain, the Earl of Suffolk, in his robes of estate going alone, Henry Howard, Earl of Northampton, and Charles Blount, Earl of Devonshire, carrying the robes of estate for the Duke; after came Henry Wriothesley, Earl of Southampton, carrying the coronet, the Earl of Cumberland carrying the gold rod, the Earl of Worcester the cap of estate, the Earl of Nottingham bearing the little Duke of Albany himself in his arms, supported by the Earl of Dorset, the Lord Treasurer, and the Earl of Northumberland. They all came in that order before the King. Then the Duke of Albany, after the patent had been read by my Lord Cranborne, was there created Duke of York, the robes and coronet being put on him, and the golden rod delivered into his hand. When this had been performed, they went to dinner, the Duke and the Earls sitting at one end of the upper end of the Great Chamber, in their robes of estate, and the Knights of the Bath being together at another table on the side of the Chamber.

At night was enacted the Queen's Masque in the Banqueting House. There was a great engine at the lower end of the room, which had motion, and it were images of sea-horses and other strange fish, which were ridden by Moors. At the other end was a great shell in the form of a scallop, wherein were four seats; on the lowest sat the Queen with my Lady Bedford; on the rest were placed the Ladies Suffolk, Derby, Rich, Effingham, Anne Herbert, Susan Herbert, Elizabeth Howard, Walsingham and Beville. Their apparel was rich but, some said, too light and courtesan-like for such great ones. Instead of vizards their faces and arms up the elbow were painted black, which was disguise sufficient and they were hard to be known, but it became them nothing so well as their own red and white.

This *Masque of Blackness* was made by Ben Jonson, the bodily parts and devices designed and carried out by Master Inigo Jones. For the scene was drawn a landscape consisting of woods and hills, and here and there a void place filled with huntings; which folding, an artificial sea was seen to shoot forth as if it would flow to the land, lashed with waves that seemed to move. In front of this sea were placed six Tritons; from their backs were borne out certain light pieces of taffeta, as if carried by the wind, and their music was made with wreathed shells. Behind these a pair of sea-maids were singing, and two great sea-horses conspicuously set, as big as the life, upon whose backs sat Oceanus and Niger, these two introducing the masquers, which were twelve nymph negroes, supposedly the daughters of Niger, attended by so many Oceaniæ, which were their torch-bearers. The attire of the masquers was all alike, the colours azure and silver, but returned on the top with a scroll in antique dressing of feathers and jewels, interlaced with ropes of pearls; and for the front, ear, neck and wrists the ornament was the most choice Orient pearl. For the torch bearers, seagreen, waved about the skirts with gold and silver; their hair was loose and flowing, garlanded with sea-grass and branches of coral.

The Spanish and Venetian Ambassadors were both present at the masque, and sat by the King in state, at which Monsieur Beaumont quarrels so extremely that he says the whole Court is Spanish. But in this he should fall out with none but himself, for all were invited to come as private men to a private sport; which he refused, but the Spanish Ambassador accepted at once, and then saw no cause but that he should cast off the private man and become the Ambassador. In the first masque he sat amongst his men disguised, but afterwards he took out the Queen and did not forget to kiss her hand, though there was danger that it would leave a mark on his lips. The night's work was concluded with a banquet in the Great Chamber, which was so furiously assaulted that down went tables and tresses before one bite was touched.

9th January. THE PLAYERS AT COURT.

At Court these Christmas holidays the King's players played *Measure for Measure, The Comedy of Errors, Love's Labour's Lost, Henry the Fifth* and *Every Man out of his Humour*; the Queen's players played *How to learn of a woman to woo* (by Heywood); and the Boys of the Chapel played *All Fools* by Chapman.

RELUCTANCY AT CAMBRIDGE.

There is small eagerness in the University of Cambridge amongst the fellows to conform in matters of ceremony with

the King's orders or to subscribe to the three articles lately set
out by Convocation. When the Vice-Chancellor proposed a
grace to that effect, it was stayed. Yet it is thought that in time
all will conform in the performance of divine service, except
some few in Emmanuel College.

10*th January.* COURT NEWS.

The King is gone to Royston two days ago where he con-
tinueth, and finds such felicity in that hunting life that he hath
written to the Council that it is the only means to maintain his
health, which being the health and welfare of us all, he desires
them to take the charge and burden of affairs, and foresee that
he be not interrupted or troubled with too much business. He
continues still his wonted bounty, and hath lately given the
Duke of Holst £4,000, besides £100 a week he is allowed for
his expense. The Parliament is put off till October, for what
reason is unknown, unless it be that they would have the matters
of the Church thoroughly settled; wherein it is hard to say what
cause were best to take, for more show themselves openly
opposite than was suspected, and the Bishops themselves are
loath to proceed too vigorously in casting out and depriving so
many well reputed for life and learning, only the King is
constant to have all come to conformity. Though he seek to be
very private and retired where he is, yet he is much importuned
with petitions on their behalf, and with foolish prophecies of
danger to ensue; and there is great speech of a strange apparition
lately seen at Berwick of two armies that fought a long time
with horse, foot and ordnance. These last days there was above
£200 worth of popish books taken about Southampton and
burned in Paul's churchyard.

11*th January.* A TREATISE OF SPECTRES.

A translation has been made into English of that book of
Peter de Loyer called *A treatise of spectres or strange sights,
visions and apparitions appearing visibly to men,* written in twelve
chapters, treating of such matters as the definition of a spectre
or apparition, and of the imagination; of things natural mistaken
by the sight or hearing as things prodigious; of things natural or
artificial which may deceive the sight and hearing and drive men
into a passion of terror; what persons are most commonly subject

to receive false imaginations and phantoms; and how the devil doth sometimes convey himself in the corrupted senses and the like.

14*th January*. 'THE POOR MAN'S PASSIONS.'

One Arthur Warren hath written two poems, called *The poor man's passions*, the other *Poverty's patience*, lamenting the hard lot of the poor in these hard-hearted times:

> What is't to beg, but to be counted base?
> What is't to borrow, but to be denied?
> When Poor are trespassed, they learn Ployden's cave,
> And must for recompense content abide:
> > Yet give the Rich but an uncourteous look,
> > It proves a forfeit by their statute book!

> It's wrong to them, if any pleasant live:
> It's pain to them, if any sit in ease:
> It's grief to them, if any one do thrive:
> It's death to them, if any them displease:
> > They do prohibit that a horse should bear
> > But golden him that silver spurs doth wear.

> Degrading us with contumelious spells,
> They touch, attack, and summon us with shames,
> To our discredit ring reproachful bells,
> And catalogue us with inhuman names,
> > Vagabonds, varlets, villains, vassals, slaves,
> > Rogues, caterpillars, runagates and knaves.

16*th January*. THE KING AND THE BISHOP OF PETER-BOROUGH.

The King, who is now at Hinchinbrooke, has had long conference with the Bishop of Peterborough, concerning disobedient ministers, to his small satisfaction; for he finds the Bishop aged and fearful, and unwilling to act, pretending sometimes that he has received no express directions from any public authority, sometimes that he has no example of any other's proceedings, and especially of my Lord Archbishop of Canterbury, of whom, he says, that it were fit that he should

show the way to the rest because his place is most eminent,
and with more access to the King and his Council. This weakness of the Bishop is much misliked of the King.

THE LEVANT MERCHANTS AND THE KING.

The Levant merchants, being much distressed by the impost
laid upon currants, sent four or five of their company to present
a petition to the King himself at Huntingdon. They arrived
in the afternoon, finding his Majesty at cards. Hereupon Sir
Thomas Lake came out to them and rebuked them for their
indiscretion, and especially as the matter had long been debated
in the Council, and their arguments against it heard. The
merchants made many protestations that they could not pay
the imposition. Nevertheless they waited, and watching their
time delivered a petition to the King as he came to supper.
Sir Thomas again rebuked them for their persistence, showing
them how impertinent it was that they should trouble the King
at his sports. They replied that they had been advised by my
Lord Cranborne, and that since their ship had come in the
matter was urgent. They determine, moreover, to send the
ship away unladen, whereby the imposition will be lost by him
who has farmed it from the King.

20th January. THE KING AND A PROPHET.

The King in his stay at Hinchinbrooke has been greatly
troubled by sundry impostors who would put about strange
prophecies, of whom some are taken, but the principal is yet at
large. One William Morton in examination is charged with
prophesying that there will be fire and sword throughout all
this land (one place only excepted) for religion. Another named
Butler is much reported in those parts as a witch and for
supposed miraculous cures.

26th January. THE PROPHECIES IN HUNTINGDON.

The man Butler, whose prophecies have caused some stir
in Huntingdon, was lately brought before the King who closely
examined him for his meddling in witchcraft. The King has
now sent him to be examined by the Lord Chief Justice. He is
a poor creature who was whipped in the Queen's time for like
matters of prophecies.

28th January. MR. EGERTON, THE PREACHER.

The Archbishop of Canterbury, when conventing the ministers of London before him before he departed, passed over Mr. Egerton of the Blackfriars, saying that he was not to proceed against lecturers; but my Lord of London hath now suspended him from his preaching to the great discontent of his hearers, who be many in the City. He preaches in a little chapel upstairs, and commonly to a great congregation, specially of women of the more fashionable sort.

10th February. THE KING AND THE PAPISTS.

To-day being Sunday, the King made a long and vehement apology for himself in the Council Chamber against the Papists who flatter themselves with a vain hope of toleration, declaring that he never had any such intention, that if he thought his sons would condescend to any such course he would wish the kingdom translated to his daughter, that the mitigation of their payments was in consideration that none of them had lifted up his hand against his coming in, and so he gave them a year of probation to conform themselves, which seeing it had wrought none effect he had fortified all the laws that were against them and made them stronger (saving for blood from which he had a natural aversion), and commanded that they should be put in execution to the uttermost.

12th February. 'THE MERCHANT OF VENICE.'

On Sunday the King's players played *The Merchant of Venice* at Court, which was so pleasing to his Majesty that he commanded them to play it again to-night. Yesterday they played *The tragedy of the Spanish Maze.*

13th February. THE LORD CHANCELLOR'S CHARGE.

At the beginning of the term the Lord Chancellor delivered his customary charge in the Star Chamber to all judges and justices of peace. He began with the justices of peace, who, said he, generally throughout the Kingdom forget their oath to God, their duty to their King and Country. Their multitude daily increaseth, and they should be men of best desert who study to execute justice and to maintain peace, but they rather make war; and there are too many that do no good, and too few

186

that execute the duty of their place, but live in London the most part of the year, and only in the summer go down for pleasure. He charged them also that the law for the eating of fish, and fasting be specially looked to, for at this season the increase and breeding of young things of all kinds being preserved and spared, the plenty thereof is more abundant all the year afterward. The multitude of all houses also should be looked to, and the general want of mending the highways.

Then he went on to speak of maintainers and movers of sedition, which be of two sorts; the one speaking or writing libels about the King, State and Government; the other are those petitioners that either come in multitudes, or presume of multitudes of subscription of hands as Papists, or sectaries, or Puritans; *hoc est mouere seditionem regni*, which is treason. He touched especially those that tax the King and Council with a disposition for toleration of religion, declaring that such a report deserved great punishment.

And to the like effect spoke the other Lords of the Council, giving instances of the King's great hatred for popery, though for the Puritans he accounted of them in another rank and would go half way to meet them.

16th February. PURITANS SUPPRESSED.

Our Puritans now go down on all sides and though the new Bishop of London proceed but slowly, yet at last he hath deprived, silenced or suspended all that continue disobedient, in which course he hath won himself great commendation of gravity, wisdom, learning, mildness and temperance, even amongst that faction, and indeed is held every way the most sufficient man of that coat. Yet those that are deprived wrangle, and will not be put down, but appeal to the Parliament, and seek prohibitions by law; but the judges have all given their opinions that the proceedings against them are lawful and so they cannot be relieved that way.

Then they take another course to ply the King with petitions, the ringleaders whereof were Sir Richard and Sir Valentine Knightly, Sir Edward Montague with some three or four score gentlemen more that joined in a petition for the ministers of Northamptonshire a week ago, which was so ill taken that divers of them were convented before the Council and told what danger they had put themselves in by these associations little less than treason, and Sir Francis Hastings for drawing the petition and standing to it when he had done, is put from his lieutenancy and justiceship of peace in his shire; and others receive like treatment.

The sword now begins to cut on the other edge also, and to fall heavily on the Papists' side, whereof there were twenty-eight indicted at the last sessions in Newgate. If this strict course be held on both sides, either party will have less reason to complain.

23rd February. A SAUCY MINISTER.

The King has returned to Royston. He had no sooner arrived but he was waited on by some of the Puritans. One of them, by name Thomas Bywater, presented a book, most saucy and dangerous, in which he spares neither King, Councillor nor Court. He has been arrested by the command of the Dean of the Chapel.

25th February. THE KING AND THE ARCHBISHOP OF YORK.

That letter which the Archbishop of York wrote to Lord Cecil (of which copies have been spread abroad) was lately shown to the King, together with the answer. The King was merry at first till he came to the wasting of the treasure and the immoderate exercise of hunting. He began then to alter countenance, and in the end said it was the foolishest letter that he ever read, and the Lord Cecil's an excellent answer, paying him soundly but in good and fair terms.

1st March. A PROCLAMATION TO RECALL MARINERS FROM FOREIGN SERVICES.

All mariners and seamen of the realm that have betaken themselves to the services of other Princes to continue their ungodly course of living by spoil, using the service of those Princes but for colour and pretext but in effect making themselves commonly no better than pirates, are now commanded to return forthwith and to betake themselves to their vocation in the orderly course of merchandise; and none shall employ themselves in any warlike courses of any foreign state upon the sea without special licence.

Moreover, seeing that chances may happen, as in the past, of difficult interpretation concerning the subjects of the King of Spain, the Archduke, and of the United States, it is declared that no force or violence shall be done within the King's ports. Men-of-war of the one part shall not be allowed to hover about the skirts of the ports to seize upon ships of the other at their going out.

Further, if a man-of-war of one side shall come into a port where there shall be a merchant of the other side, then the merchant, if they shall require it, shall be suffered to depart two or three tides before the other. Likewise a ship of war shall be allowed to depart a tide or two before the other.

Officers and inhabitants in the ports, many of whom do receive goods brought in from the sea by such as are indeed pirates, are warned of the severe laws in that case established.

A PROCLAMATION FOR BUILDINGS IN AND ABOUT LONDON.

There hath been such consumption of timber in the Realm that in the very City of London they are now daily driven to build with beech and other timber of small continuance which in time will be the notorious peril and decay of the city. It is now commanded that no part of a tree that may serve for any use of timber shall be converted to coal or firewood; and, for the better preservation of timber, from the Feast of St. Michael no one shall erect any new house, or the forepart of any house within the City and suburbs except all the utter walls and windows be made wholly of brick, or of brick and stone. Moreover, the forefront thereof shall be made of that uniform order and form as shall be prescribed for that street where the building shall be by the chief magistrates of the City.

3rd March. THE KING'S HEALTH.

The King hath for long suffered from a cold but it is now almost gone, though he was for a time very ill and heavy with it. The reason that it hath so long continued hath been the sharpness of the air and wind, for every day he hunteth he taketh a new cold; for being hot with riding a long chase, he sitteth in the open air and drinketh, which cannot but continue if not increase a new cold. He is now at Thetford and liketh exceeding well of the country; but hath been but once abroad hunting since his coming thither; and on that day he was driven out of the field with press of company that come to see him; wherein he took no delight but so went home and played at cards. Sir William Woodhouse, that is the sole director of these parts, hath devised a proclamation that none shall presume to come to him on hunting days; but those that come to see him or prefer petitions shall do it going forth or coming home.

6th March. THE PURITAN BYWATER.

The Puritan Bywater, being released from the arrest of the Dean of the Chapter that he may present himself for examination before Lord Cranborne, was very saucy at his departure, and high words passed between them, the Dean declaring that in all his life he never saw so much poison spit out by atheist, Papist or Puritan against the sweetest Prince that ever the sun of the Gospel did shine upon.

This Bywater is a Cambridge man that about twenty years since was preferred to be schoolmaster to my Lord Sheffield's children, being then a young Master of Arts. He continued in that place for about five years, in which time he so well applied his own study by neglecting his charges that they proved ill scholars. Nevertheless Lord Sheffield, seeing him so religiously bent, was willing to further him until his zeal became so hot that he wrote a book of my Lord's faults and presented it to him, which were for the most part hunting and hawking too much. Thereafter he grew more precise every day, maintaining to his Lordship's face that hounds and hawks were not ordained by God for man's recreation, but for adorning the earth and the heavens. Thereafter Lord Sheffield dismissed him from his service.

10th March. COURT NEWS: MANY ROBBERIES.

Pilling and polling is nowadays grown out of request and plain pilfering comes into fashion. Sir John Davies hath been robbed by his man of £30 in gold, and gold buttons which he sold for as much more. The thief is fled over into the Low Countries. Sir Henry Goodyere had his chamber broken up at Court and £120 stolen. Sir Adolphus Carew was robbed at the last remove from Whitehall of £50 and three suits of apparel which were provided for the Spanish journey; and at the same time my Lady Dorothy Hastings (who lay in the chamber above him) was spoiled of all that God ever sent her, save that she had on her back and her belly. Moreover, Sir Robert Hampson, an alderman of London, is cheated of merchandise to the value of £8,000 which he put into the hands of his factor who is now lurking in Holland.

The Tilting this year is to be at Greenwich, where there is much practising, and the Duke of Holst is a learner among the rest, whose horse took it so unkindly to be spur-galled on the shoulder that he laid his little burden on God's fair earth.

The Lord Admiral takes with him 500 to Spain. There was great execution done lately upon Stone, the fool, who was well whipped in Bridewell for a blasphemous speech that there went sixty fools into Spain besides my Lord Admiral and his two sons; but he is now at liberty again, and for that unexpected release gives his Lordship the praise of a very pitiful Lord.

12th March. ANOTHER LION'S WHELP.

On the 26th February the lioness Elizabeth again whelped in the Tower. The whelp was taken from the dam to be brought up by hand by his Majesty's commandment, but it likewise hath died.

21st March. THE DEPARTURE OF THE LORD HIGH ADMIRAL
    FOR SPAIN.

To-day the Lord High Admiral assembled his company, that go with him into Spain to receive the King's oath at Nottingham House, and proceeded in many barges and boats to the Court at Windsor. For his company he hath ordained six trumpeters clad in orange-coloured damask, with cloaks of cloth of the same colour, and banners of damask with his honour's arms thereupon; six footmen in orange tawny velvet alike suited; six pages clad likewise in velvet of the same colour, with their cloaks suitable; thirty gentlemen with cloaks of black velvet; four-score yeomen well apparelled with livery cloaks of orange tawny cloth, garded with silver and blue lace. With this company, the Earl went from Nottingham House about noon, and so shooting the Bridge, arrived at Greenwich immediately after dinner, and there presenting himself and his company unto his Majesty was most graciously entertained. After some time spent in receiving the King's commandment as well concerning himself as also touching the conducting and presenting of Sir Charles Cornwallis, who is appointed his Majesty's lieger ambassador with the King of Spain. The Ambassador and their company having humbly taken their leaves are for this night dismissed everyone to his lodging.

There accompany my Lord on this embassy the Earl of Perth, the Lord Howard of Effingham (my Lord's son and heir), the Lord Willoughby, the Lord Norris, Sir Richard Leveson, Vice-Admiral of England, Sir Robert Drury, Sir Robert Mansell, Sir George Buc, and many other nobles and gentlemen. The ships appointed to attend his Lordship are the *Bear*, the *Due Repulse*, the *Wastspite*, being ships royal, together with the *Mary Anne*, the *Amity*, the *Resistance* and the great hoy called the *George*.

A BOOK ABOUT THE ENGLISH NATION.

One Master Richard Verstegan, an Englishman born though descended of a stranger born in the Duchy of Geldres, hath written a book called *A restitution of decayed intelligence in antiquities*, wherein he makes distinction between Englishmen and Britons, showing how that the true ancient Britons be now the Welsh, and Englishmen descended of the Saxons, that were originally a people of Germany. He speaketh much of the ancient English tongue, declaring it to be much discredited by the daily borrowing of words from other tongues, and hardly to be understood of many Englishmen, as of him that told how 'as he itinerated he obviated a rural person, and interrogating him concerning the transitation of the time, and the demonstration of the passage, found him a mere simptician,' whereas if in his true speech he had asked him what was the clock and which had been his way, his ignorance might have been informed of both.

23rd March. A LIBEL AGAINST THE LATE ARCHBISHOP.

The study of the Puritan Bywater that some days since delivered a book to his Majesty has been searched, and therein is found a libel of the late Archbishop Whitgift and my Lord

Bishop of London, entitled 'The lamentation of Dickie for the death of his brother Jockey,' of which the burden is—

> Jockey is dead and gone
> And dumb Dickey is left to moan.

Being examined concerning it, he now declares that he had it from Mr. Lewis Pickering, who did dictate it to him.

25th March. A CHARITABLE ACT.

Such is the desperate estate of many of the condemned prisoners in Newgate that after judgment of death and even at their very execution they remain careless of their souls' health, deriding their imminent danger and dying reprobate. In consideration whereof, Master Robert Dow of London, merchant-taylor, hath given competent maintenance unto St. Sepulchre's parish for the tolling of the great bell and for some especial man to be appointed the midnight before execution to ring a handbell and then to pronounce a godly exhortation beginning thus: 'O ye prisoners, within condemned this day to die, remember your sins; call to God for grace whilst yet you have time.' And in the morning when they are in the cart he shall again put them in mind of their former lives and present death, saying, 'The great bell of this church, which I told you last night should toll for you from six of the clock until ten, now tolleth to the end to move good people to pray to God for you whilst yourselves with them may pray for remission of your sins.'

26th March. THE EMBASSY FOR SPAIN.

The Earl of Nottingham and his company departed early this morning with the tide from Nottingham House and the fleet is now come to Chatham.

28th March. COURT NEWS.

The King, Queen and all are now at Court, and there purpose to remain some time. The Queen expects delivery within a month; and there is great preparation of nurses, midwives, rockers and other like officers to the number of forty or more. Yesterday a son of the Earl of Southampton was christened at Court, the King and my Lord Cranborne, with the Countess of Suffolk, being gossips. The oldest officers at Court complain that they are in a measure rather neglected than countenanced, and so retire themselves, and those more young with their money are suffered to purchase preferment. The King is now purposed to take all woods into his hands within the compass of three miles from the water's side and near unto his Houses, and will allow to such as out of time have enjoyed them as their own recompense according to discretion, which course will breed in many much discontent.

The Impudency of the Players.

It is much observed that the players do not forbear to present upon their stage the whole course of this present time, not sparing either King, State or religion, in so great absurdity and with such liberty as any would be afraid to hear them.

31st March. The Pope Dead.

From Rome the news is that Pope Clement the Eighth died on the 6th of this month, who for his virtue, temperate life and discreet government was held in great estimation amongst all Christian Princes. He reigned full thirteen years and died of the gout.

4th April. The Hollanders' Discontent.

From the Hague it is reported that there is great discontent in the minds of the Hollanders by reason of the late proclamation recalling our seamen from the service of foreign states, for they fear that this revocation of those that serve by sea will be followed by a recall of those who are at their service by land, wherein the force of their state and the support of their war doth chiefly consist. These diffidences are multiplied by a report that the King will shortly discontinue his favours towards them.

6th April. Court News.

The time of the Queen's delivery is now at hand and prayers are said everywhere for her safety. Three midwives are attending, but she will not speak with any of them till she hath need of their help, neither will she yet signify which of them she will employ until the easiness or hardness of her travail doth urge her to it. There is great preparation for the christening chamber and costly furniture provided for performance of other ceremonies. In the meanwhile the time of the year forbids the King his common exercise, and somewhat the ordinary complaints of poor country farmers to endure continual wrong by the hunting spoils and misgovernment of the unruly train. On Easter Tuesday Master William Herrick, a goldsmith in Cheapside, was knighted for making a hole in the great diamond the King doth wear; he little expecting such an honour, but did the work so well as won the King to an extraordinary liking of it.

THE EMBASSY FOR SPAIN.

The Earl of Nottingham with his fleet sailed from Dover yesterday, having been delayed by contrary winds, and also because the hoy called the *George* was disabled by spending of her mast so that it was necessary to unload the provisions out of her and to disperse the baggage amongst the other ships.

8th April. THE DEATH OF JOHN STOW.

This day is buried in St. Andrew Undershaft the body of Master John Stow, of London, merchant-taylor, a painful writer of the English Chronicle for the space of forty-seven years. He was tall of stature, lean of body and face, his eyes small and crystalline, of a pleasant and cheerful countenance, his sight and memory very good, very sober, mild, and courteous to all that required his instructions. He retained the true use of all his senses unto the day of his death, being of an excellent memory. He protested never to have written anything either for malice, fear or favour, nor to seek his own particular gain, or vain glory; and that his only pains and care was to write truth. He could never ride but travelled on foot unto divers cathedral churches, and other chief places of the land to search records. He was very careless of scoffers, backbiters and detractors. He died of the stone colic on the 5th of this month being fourscore years of age.

9th April. THE QUEEN'S DELIVERY.

Last night between 11 and 12 of the clock the Queen was delivered of a daughter, for joy whereof the citizens make bonfires throughout London, and the bells continued ringing all day.

13th April. A STRANGE CASE OF A SLEEPING PREACHER.

From Salisbury comes a strange story of one Mr. Richard

Haydock (or Haddock), a physician newly arrived in that city from Oxford. Divers persons declare that in the night time, when he is asleep, he preaches excellent sermons, to the great astonishment of all who hear him. Some days since the Dean of Salisbury and Mr. Hyde of that city sat up to listen to him. About 3 of the clock in the morning he began to preach and continued for an hour and a half. His method was very formal, full of learned discourse, and his metaphors and sentences of the poets and the Fathers all very apt. The Dean set the candle to his face, but his eyes did not move at all. His hands and his arms remained closed within the sheets without any moving; his lips and tongue only moved. At the end of his prayer he said 'Amen' as in a sleeping man's speech, and then he groaned as a man wearied with sickness. He has now been summoned to London that the King himself may witness this strange marvel.

13th April. TROUBLE AT CAMBRIDGE.

There are great complaints from Cambridge of the behaviour of some of our new-made knights who usurp the place of ancient doctors very ill-manneredly. It is the custom at sermons and other scholastical acts that next after the Vice-Chancellor sit the doctors according to their order, and after them the young sons of noblemen. But for this year past some of these knights take upon themselves to usurp the chief places, not only in the Church of St. Mary, but even in the common schools, which is much resented in the University, for the young knights are of no noble birth.

14th April. A SUPPLY SHIP FOR GUIANA.

Sir Olive Leigh has now sent out a supply ship to his brother Captain Charles Leigh for his plantation in Guiana. She is called the *Olive Blossom* and departed from Woolwich with a good supply of men under the conduct of Captain Catlin and Captain Nicholas St. John.

15th April. THE SPANISH AMBASSADOR INSULTED.

This night the Spanish Ambassador would have made shows upon the news of the birth of the young Spanish Prince which were prevented by the disorder of the apprentices and other lewd persons. He had prepared to burn certain lights in a frame of iron

196

set upon the gate house of Somerset House, but they were spoiled and torn down with violent and indecent words. He had also good store of money in readiness to throw down into the street, but at the casting down of some of it, the people, instead of thanks, began to hurl stones at those which were above so that by the rebounding of these stones some of the people that stood thick in the press received some hurt. Moreover, certain counters were spread in the street (through malice as is said) to give occasion of the false liberality of the Spaniard. Howbeit these same disorders saved the Ambassador a good deal of gold and silver which he then stayed but would otherwise have bestowed among them.

19th April. THE EMBASSAGE TO THE ARCHDUKE.

The Earl of Hertford, who goes as Lord Ambassador to the Archduke Albertus and the Archduchess Isabella to receive their oaths for the confirmation of the Articles of Peace ratified last August, took shipping at Dover in the *Vauntguard*. He is accompanied with two barons, sixteen knights and many gentlemen of quality, two chaplains and others to the number of 300, most being his own servants in rich liveries. Sir Thomas Edmondes goes with him as Ambassador lieger.

A DEPUTY PURVEYOR'S MISCONDUCT.

To-day in the Star Chamber one Stokes, a poor carpenter, servant to Sir Henry Seckford, Master of the Tents, was in question, because acting, contrary to law, as deputy purveyor to his master he took divers timber trees of oak and elm growing near men's dwelling-houses at Fulham under colour of his master's right of purveyance. Hereby wrong and oppression is offered to the subject and the King's prerogative abused. The matter was referred to all the judges for their opinion whether his prerogative did warrant the taking of trees, for the ancient and Great Charter of England saith '*Nec nos, nec ballini nostri, nec alii, capiemus boscum alienum ad castra vel ad alia agenda nostra, nisi per voluntatem illius cuius boscus ille fuerit.*' And all the judges upon deliberate advice have resolved that none of the King's officers can take any trees growing, for they are a parcel of a men's inheritance and thereunto fixed, nor take anything but such as the owner hath a purpose to sell for gain.

So the whole Court much condemned this usage and sentenced him to be fined, set upon the pillory, and whipped; and to have three years' imprisonment.

MEASURES AGAINST RECUSANTS IN THE NORTH.

There has been much zeal shown against Catholic recusants in the northern counties. In the late assizes about 1,000 were indicted at York, and 600 at Lancaster, and few of the better sort omitted.

20th April. THE DEATH OF THE POPE.

It is reported from Rome that the Cardinals have chosen a Pope with the title of Leo the Eleventh; but he reigned less than a month after his election and then died on the 26th of last month.

23rd April. THE GARTER FEAST.

The King kept the Feast of St. George at Greenwich, where the old custom that gentlemen attend their lords in chains of gold and liveries is wholly omitted. The King made two new Knights of the Garter, the Duke Ulric, heir of Norway and brother to our Queen, and the Lord Henry Howard, Earl of Northampton and Lord Warden of the Cinque Ports.

27th April. THE SLEEPING PREACHER.

At Court there is much talk of Dr. Richard Haydock, a doctor of physic, who uses oftentimes to make long sermons in his sleep. The King hath heard him one night; the next time the Dean of Windsor and Sir Thomas Chaloner; and the third time my Lord of Cranborne caused a bed to be put up in his drawing chamber at Court, and heard him preach, and sent for my Lord Pembroke, Lord Chandos, Lord Danvers, Lord Mar and others. He doth very orderly begin with his prayer; then to his text, and divides it; and when he hath well and learnedly touched every part, he concludes it, and with groaning and stretching awakes and remembers nothing he said. The man seems to be very honest, of a good complexion, of civil conversation and discreet. He hath no books or place to study; and twice or thrice a week he usually preaches. Yet the King will not say what he thinks of it; he will hear him and sift him ere he depart from Court.

28th April. A Cuckoo in Paul's.

Dr. John Milward, preaching at Paul's, in the midst of the sermon a cuckoo came flying over the pulpit (a thing never heard of before), and very lewdly cried out at him with open mouth.

29th April. The Sleeping Preacher's Confessions.

Yesterday Dr. Haydock, the sleeping preacher, sent to the King that if it would please his Majesty to pardon his offence and deliver him from punishment, he could confess the whole trick of this deceit. And so told how at his first coming to Oxford he had a great desire to become a preacher, but being disabled by reason of a stutter he betook himself to physic. Then it came to his remembrance that his school-fellows at Winchester had told him many times how he used to speak in his sleep, and make verse and speak Latin with much more quickness of invention and readier utterance than at any time else. Upon this he took a conceit that he would try to come to that ability of utterance by speaking about that same time of night. So he determined as soon as he was out of his first sleep to speak some discourse concerning physic; which he did, and found in himself such a ripeness of invention and so perfect and ready utterance as he wondered at himself. He resolved therefore to try if the same conceit would hold in divinity. So he took a text and prepared himself to preach of it three or four days before he put it in practice; and that night, as soon as he waked of his first sleep, he sat up in his bed and in his own conceit made an excellent good sermon. This he used twice or thrice, not intending that any should hear him; but the next time he preached, by chance some that lay in the next chamber were awake and heard all that he said, who reported next morning that Mr. Haydock had made an excellent sermon in his sleep. This coming to his ears, he took a pride in it, and practised it every other night, and so continued for this year and a half, preaching in Latin at Oxford, and in English in the country; and, as he confessed when he came to the King, he thought to have confessed the truth at once; but then thinking that he had gotten such a reputation of his honesty amongst learned and judicial men that heard him preach, he continued his former course, and preached four sermons at the Court, one of which the King heard. The King hath forgiven him graciously, upon promise he shall never practise the like again, and sent him back to Oxford.

1st May. SIR ROBERT DUDLEY'S CASE.

This day was the beginning of Sir Robert Dudley's case heard in the Star Chamber. For his part Sir Robert declareth that the Earl of Leicester did indeed marry the Lady Sheffield, but in secret, for the Earl would not have the Queen hear of it; and after understanding that she was with child (who was Sir Robert), he rejoiced greatly at it, writing her many letters by the name of wife. But afterwards growing in some mislike with her, he got these letters away and would have poisoned her, and soon after married with the Lady Lettice (at that time widow of the Earl of Essex), the now Countess of Leicester, so that the Lady Sheffield was forced to marry Sir Edward Stafford, a man very adverse to the Earl of Leicester.

The case for the King was opened by Mr. Solicitor Doddridge and Sir Edward Philips the King's Sergeant, which was in four parts, viz.; First, the magnitude of the case; secondly, that the five witnesses for the first marriage were not worth a frieze jerkin, and the minister could not be known, whereas at the second marriage were present the Earls of Warwick and Pembroke, the Lord North and Sir Francis Knollys, and, moreover, Leicester himself did solemnly protest before Almighty God that he was free, and later did on oath deny the second marriage; thirdly, as to the accusation itself, one Thomas Drury, a knight of the post, insinuated with Sir Robert Dudley that if he might be well rewarded he would prove a marriage; fourthly, the subornation of these practices.

So they began to read their witnesses, offering some examined in the Ecclesiastical Court and others taken before the Attorney General. But the Lord Chancellor disallowed both, whereat Mr. Attorney was very much moved, and after some dispute, would not speak again this day. So the Court sat silent a pretty space, and at last the King's Sergeant read many witnesses to the third and fourth heads.

4th May. NEW PEERS CREATED.

To-day in the Hall at Greenwich which was richly hanged

with arras, and under a cloth of estate, the King, accompanied with the Princes, his sons, the Duke of Holstein, the Duke of Lennox, and most of the nobility of England and Scotland, created three Earls, one Viscount, and four Barons, viz., Robert Cecil, Viscount Cranborne, is created Earl of Salisbury; Thomas Cecil, Lord Burghley, his elder brother, is created Earl of Exeter; Sir Philip Herbert, younger brother to the Earl of Pembroke, is created Earl of Montgomery; Sir Robert Sidney, Baron of Penshurst, is created Viscount Lisle; Sir John Stanhope is created Lord Stanhope of Harington; Sir George Carew is created Lord Carew of Clopton; Master Thomas Arundel is created Lord Arundel of Wardour; and Master William Cavendish is created Lord Cavendish of Hardwick.

There is now general expectation that my Lord of Salisbury will shortly resign his office of Secretary and assume some greater office of State, and many surmises who will succeed him, some favouring Sir Thomas Lake, and others my Lord Carew.

5th May. THE LADY MARY CHRISTENED.

Between 4 and 5 of the clock in the afternoon, the Lady Mary was christened in the Chapel at Greenwich. The child was brought from the Queen's lodgings through both the great chambers, and through the presence, and down the winding stairs into the Conduit Court, at the foot whereof attended a canopy borne by eight Barons, before which went the officers of arms, and divers Bishops and noblemen. The Earl of Northumberland bore a covered gilt basin, after followed the Countess of Worcester bearing a cushion covered with lawn and thereon many jewels of inestimable price. Under the canopy went the Countess of Derby bearing the child, who was supported by the Dukes of Holstein and Lennox. Then followed the godmothers, the Lady Arabella and the Countess of Northumberland, after whom came many Countesses and great ladies.

At the entrance of the Chapel, the Archbishop of Canterbury, assisted by the Deans of Canterbury and of the Chapel Royal in rich capes, received the child, and passed into the traverse, the choir singing anthems whilst the Lords took one side of the stalls and the Ladies the other. In the midst of the choir was erected a most stately canopy of Cloth of Gold, and within it stood a very rich and stately font of silver and gilt, curiously wrought with figures of beasts, serpents and other antique works. After a while the gentlemen ushers opened the barriers of the canopy, and the Archbishop with the Deans entered; and then followed the Countess of Derby with the child, the Duke of Holstein, the godfather and the two godmothers. Then the solemnity of baptism was fully read and performed according to the Church of England, the child being named Mary; after which the godfather and godmothers ascended to the altar and there made offerings.

Then the Earl Marshal and the Lord Chamberlain placing Sir William Segar, Garter Principal Knight at Arms, between them, Master Garter making low reverence to the King, who stood in the closet window, proclaimed the child's name and descent. Which being ended, the gentlemen ushers and servers brought in a voidy of wine and confectures. The trumpets sounded, and the whole train returned as they had come.

6th May. RECUSANTS IN THE NORTH.

There is great complaint of recusants in the north, particularly in Hexham and Bywell where one Roger Woodrington, a gentleman of great weight in those parts, is able to raise two or three thousand of a sudden upon any occasion. He gives harbour and resting place to Jesuits and seminary priests, and no sheriff dare go against him.

8th May. SIR ROBERT DUDLEY'S CASE.

The defendant's cause in Sir Robert Dudley's case was partly heard to-day, and it was shown that his witnesses were persons of good credit; but the matter is not yet determined. At the rising of the Court, my Lord of Cumberland desired to be heard, being much stirred that Mrs. Chancellor, one of the witnesses in the case, had affirmed that the Earl of Leicester begot a bastard of the late Countess of Derby, his sister; and he desired the Lords to have consideration of it that so great a scandal might be punished. To the like effect spoke the Earl of Salisbury, whose niece is married to that lady's son, the present Earl of Derby, and my Lord of Northampton. Whereupon it is ordered by the Lord Chancellor that messengers be sent for the witnesses to be dealt with by the King's Counsel or the Privy Council, and to receive punishment.

A Play of King Leir.

That play of King Leir and his three daughters which hath lately been acted is to be printed. This Leir, being king of Britain in the ancient times, when he grew old determined to divide his kingdom amongst his daughters, but first for a trial demanded that they should express their love for him; which the two eldest did in many flattering terms, but the youngest (by name Cordella) could not frame her speech to flatter him. Hereupon King Leir in great wrath cast her forth, and divided the kingdom amongst the elder two, who turned on their father and forced him to flee, accompanied only with a faithful servant called Perillus. At length, after many dangers, the King is saved by Cordella, now married to the king of Gallia, and restored to his kingdom.

10th May. Sir Robert Dudley's Case Concluded.

This day was the case of Sir Robert Dudley concluded in the Star Chamber, and the Lords gave their opinions, which differed very much, some were for fining Sir Robert for his misdemeanour, but others would have acquit him. My Lord of Salisbury said that it was natural for Sir Robert to revive his legitimacy, but all men must take notice of the law, and he was somewhat indiscreet in his proceedings, so that he was for fining him £100. And in conclusion the Lord Chancellor said that Sir Robert's chief fault was want of discretion, ignorance and ill advice, and his sentence was to fine him £100. Of the others in this case, one is fined £100, and others £30 and £20 and the rest acquitted. So this great cause was at 6 of the clock at night sentenced, but not like yet to be ended.

14th May. The Archbishop's Libeller Punished.

This day Lewis Pickering, a gentleman of Northamptonshire, a scholar religiously disposed, was charged before the Star Chamber with uttering that libel against the late Archbishop of Canterbury. Pickering denied it not, but said that since it concerned a dead man he took it to be no offence. The Attorney-General spoke vehemently against him and his opinions, declaring that *nefas super mortuos gloriari*, it is a poison, and so went about to prove Pickering guilty of treason against God. Although, saith he, a libel be true and the person infamous yet it is a great offence; for the state and government is delivered to the magistrate, and therefore any private delivery or writing of a libel is a great offence; yea, to see it, hear or report it. The Lords of the Council spoke variously in condemnation of the offence and praise of the departed, especially my Lord of Salisbury. Pickering is condemned to imprisonment for a year and then during the King's pleasure; to stand in the pillory in London, Northampton and Croydon; and to wear a sack if it might stand with the sentence of the Court; and to pay a fine of £1,000.

15th May. A PROJECT FOR VIRGINIA.

Captain Bartholomew Gosnold, that made a voyage to Virginia three years ago and came back with very good accounts of the place, hath ever since most vehemently urged that another plantation should be made there.

For a long while he was unable to persuade anyone to renew the attempts, but at length several gentlemen and others now declare themselves willing, such as Captain John Smith, Master Edward-Maria Wingfield, Master Robert Hunt and others.

Note that another attempt was made to found a plantation in Virginia some twenty years ago, when Sir Walter Ralegh sent Sir Richard Grenville with a fleet of seven sail, in the year 1585, who then left behind about 100 persons. These quarrelled with the savages, and were taken off by Sir Francis Drake in June, 1586. But in the meanwhile Sir Walter Ralegh had sent a ship of 100 tons laden with provisions which arrived after the departure of Sir Francis. From this ship fifteen men were left behind to hold possession of the country, with provision for two years. In the year following, 1587, Sir Walter continuing his purpose of plantation sent another colony of 150 persons under the government of Master John White, to whom he gave a Charter. When they went on shore they learnt that the savages had secretly assaulted the fifteen English, slaying some and forcing the rest to flee, it was not known whither. This project likewise failed, for after a few weeks the company persuaded their Governor to return to England to supply their wants.

19th *May* (*Whit-Sunday*). THE QUEEN CHURCHED.

The Queen was solemnly churched to-day. First the King, accompanied by most of the peers, went into the Closet and there heard a sermon preached by Dr. Watson, Bishop of Chichester; whence he went down into the Chapel and offered. Then he withdrew into the traverse on the right side of the altar. Then came the Queen from her lodging, and having stayed awhile in her Closet was brought thence with a great train of ladies into the Chapel by the great Lords, supported by the Duke of Holst and the Duke of Lennox. When she came before the altar she made a low reverence, and offered her besant, and then went into the traverse on the left side of the altar. After the usual prayers, according to the Book of Common Prayer, sundry anthems were sung to the organ, cornet and sackbut, and other instruments of music. Then the King and the Queen both advanced from their traverses, and came before the altar, and embraced each other with great kindness; and so went hand in hand together to the King's Presence Chamber door, where they parted, doing great reverence each to the other.

The King dined openly in the Presence Chamber, accompanied with the Archduke's Ambassador, Prince Henry, and the Duke of Holst.

20th *May*. THE EARL OF HERTFORD RETURNS.

My Lord of Hertford has returned from his embassage to the Archduke. He landed at Dunkirk on the 20th of April, and was received in great state by the Governor, staying there two days. From thence he passed to Nieuport, Bruges, Ghent, Alst, and so to Brussels, which he reached on the 27th. At all these places he bountifully feasted the chief Commanders and head burghers at his own cost. He remained at Brussels for twelve days, being entertained with all state and honour, with shows and pastimes, and great triumphs in the market place, and revels at night. On the 1st of May the Archduke and Archduchess took their oaths. First the Ambassador's commission was read out, then the oath; and during the reading the Archduke and Archduchess held hand in hand as at a marriage, the Ambassador holding both their hands within his hands. The oath being ended, they laid their hands upon the Gospel which was held by the Archbishop of

Malines, and the Ambassador signified to the Archduke that the King's new style of 'King of Great Britain' neither was nor should be an impeach of the performance of the articles of peace formally sworn. At his departure, my Lord, in honour of the King, gave to the Duke's servants and others who had attended him the sum of £3,000. The Archduke presented him with jewels worth £900 and a suit of arras worth £300. All the time he stayed in Brussels the Archduke defrayed his costs.

23rd May. A COMMOTION OF THE PAPISTS IN HEREFORDSHIRE.

Of late a certain Papist named Alice Wellington of Allen's Moor near the city of Hereford died, whose body the vicar of the parish refused to bury because she was excommunicate. Hereupon many Papists in those parts determined among themselves, come what come would, the burial should be performed after their manner; and about 6 of the clock in the morning they brought the corpse to the churchyard with ringing of a bell, tapers burning and the like, many of them bearing weapons. When they had all departed the vicar certified the Bishop of Hereford of these proceedings, together with the names of some persons whom he had seen in that action. So the Bishop directed a warrant to the high constable of the hundred for their apprehension, by virtue of which the high constable with sundry petty constables apprehended two, being weavers, but they resisted the arrest and escaped; but while they were thus contending another of the men named in the warrant came in, and him they seized. At length the high constable, summoning to his aid divers such as he met with in the King's name, with some fifteen men began to escort the prisoner towards Hereford city; but when they came within a quarter of a mile of the city, suddenly they espied themselves beset with men, forty or fifty, weaponed with bows and arrows, bills, swords and other weapons. These men asked the high constable whither he conveyed the prisoner, and for what purpose; to which he answered that when he came there, they should know. At which words one of them set a javelin to his breast and charged him, unless he meant to see his own guts, to let go the prisoner. And so the high constable, his company being too weak to make resistance, was forced to let go the prisoner.

After this the high constable gave present notice to the Bishop of Hereford, whereupon the Council are advertised, and some such as are known to have been chief actors herein are sent for to London.

1st June. THE DUKE ULRIC DEPARTS.

The Duke Ulric has departed homewards, he having taken ship for Denmark from Rochester whither the King, the Prince and divers lords, knights and gentlemen accompanied him.

3rd June. THE KING AND THE LIONS.

This last spring the King hath caused a walk and breeding place for the lions to be made in the moat of the Tower. This afternoon his Majesty, being accompanied with divers noblemen and many knights and gentlemen, came to the Lions' Tower. Then Mr. Ralph Gill, keeper of the lions, was commanded that his servants should put forth into the walk the male and female breeder, but the lions would not go out until they were forced out with burning links, when they stood looking about in amazement. Then were two racks of mutton thrown down to them, which they straightway ate. Then a lusty live cock was cast down, which they killed and sucked his blood; and then another live cock which they likewise killed but sucked not. After that the King caused a live lamb to be easily let down by a rope, but the lions stood in their place and only beheld the lamb. But the lamb rose up and went towards the lions, who very gently looked upon him and smelled on him without sign of any further hurt. Then the lamb was softly drawn up again in as good plight as he was set down. Then they caused these lions to be put into their den, and another lion to be put forth and two lusty mastiffs at a by-door to be let unto him. These flew fiercely upon him, and perceiving the lion's neck to be defended with hair they sought only to bite him by the face. Then was a third dog let in, as fierce as either let in, a brended dog, that took the lion by the face and turned him upon his back; but the lion spoiled them all.

5th June. A NEW POPE CHOSEN.

On the 16th of May a new Pope of Rome was elected, with the title of Paul the Fifth. He is 58 years of age and was born in Sienna.

7th June. SIR ROBERT DUDLEY'S CASE.

In the Star Chamber the Lords were lately moved to alter the order made against Sir Robert Dudley, especially in two points, namely; the one, that where his witnesses were censured as suspected, now they should be set down only as subject to suspicion; the other where the Earl of Leicester's lands were said to be reverted to the Crown, it should be only supposed to be reverted. These things because they seemed much to prejudice the legitimation were far pressed; but the order was entered as it was first set down upon the speeches, especially of the Earl of Salisbury, the Lord Treasurer and Chief Justice, the Earl of Northumberland holding hardly for the contrary.

ENGLISH PIRATES.

In spite of the recent proclamation for recalling mariners from foreign services and for repressing of all piracies there come many complaints, especially from the Ambassador of the King of Spain, that our mariners still rob the subjects of that King and other Princes with whom we are at amity. Others go to sea as merchants but become men of war and turn pirates. These enormities are in part imputed to the great negligence of the officers at the ports, whereby ships are not properly searched, and the pirates allowed to buy and sell. A warning has now been sent to all officers at ports that if this negligence continues the burden of satisfying the losses done by pirates shall be laid on them.

8th June. 'THE SOUL'S IMMORTAL CROWN.'

There is a book of poems by Mr. Nicholas Breton called *The Soul's Immortal Crown* consisting of seven glorious graces, viz., virtue, wisdom, love, constancy, patience, humility, infiniteness, divided in seven days' works, and dedicated to his Majesty.

9th June. THE KING AND THE LATE RIOTS.

Matters are like to proceed in hard terms with our English Catholics. To-day all the judges in their robes appeared before the King who made a speech to them of three hours long and gave them a most straight charge to enquire of all recusants in their circuits. And as for the rebellious behaviour used in Herefordshire, he thinks it needless any longer to spare their blood who contemning his clemency have broken forth into so manifest a demonstration of their disloyalties towards his laws and his officers. Sir Charles Morgan, a Justice of the Peace of that county, leaving but the shire the next day after this matter and coming to London is committed to the Fleet for neglecting his place in a time of such disorder.

THE FRENCH KING'S ESCAPE.

News is come from Paris that the French King and the Queen were very near drowning. They had been at St. Germains to see the Dauphin and the rest of their children and in the evening took their coach with six horses to return to Paris again. At one of the ferries the hindmost horses in the descent of the bank, being wet and slippery, fell into the water and drew the coach into the water after them, but the coach falling upon a little flat-bottomed boat was thereby supported. The King was much wet but soon recovered, and had out by gentlemen that put themselves into the water to help; but the Queen was in the lower side of the coach a great while under water. The King caught at her gown at first and held it but it rent off. Then he returned into the water himself and lamented much, thinking she must have perished. But at length the Queen and the Princess of Conti, who was with her in the coach, were both gotten out, the Queen's gown and hair and all that came next to hand being laid hold on, so that she lost all her head tire, and some of her hair and jewels of value, and came to Paris in a man's hat. The Princess got in a manner as much hair as the Queen lost, for the first thing she laid hold on was his beard that came to help her, and that she held so fast as hath made the places of his face, where it grew, bare. The next day the *Te Deum* was sung in many places of Paris for this deliverance.

15th June. THE CASE OF THOMAS DOUGLAS.

Thomas Douglas, that is accused of forging the King's seal, was this day committed to the Tower, having been sent over in irons by the County Palatine of the Rhine.

20th June. THE LORD CHANCELLOR'S CHARGE IN THE STAR CHAMBER.

To-day being the last Star Chamber day the Lord Chancellor delivered his customary charge wherein he took occasion to speak of the late commotions in Herefordshire declaring that the number of Papists in England is mightily increased since his Majesty's coming into England, and that Papist priests and Jesuits (factors for the Pope) lie lurking in many corners of this land to seduce his Majesty's subjects from their due and lawful allegiance unto their rightful Prince to the acknowledgement of a foreign power and authority, namely, the Pope of Rome.

Then also that his Majesty marvelled how it happened that Papists could so increase daily, or priests or Jesuits be entertained within his kingdoms, considering that his laws are in force against them. And thereupon entering into a consideration where the fault lay, the Lord Chancellor alleged that justices are too slack and negligent in their places, it being impossible that priests and Jesuits should swarm so thick unless justices are careless of their place and office. Moreover, he said that many justices are either so affected themselves or leastwise for special respects favour them that are.

Likewise in his charge to the judges, he bade them in their circuits to have an especial care to make diligent inquiry for such as be Papists, and especially Justices of Peace, that they may be removed out of the commission likewise for obstinate Papists, and especially such as have become Papists since his Majesty's coming.

Moreover also he showed that Papists in divers parts do brag that they are in good hope of a toleration, to which he added a speech of his Majesty concerning the folly of Papists how they are so besotted, yea and more than bewitched, to suppose any such matter.

26th June. 'THE DUTCH COURTESAN.'

The Dutch Courtesan, a play written by Mr. Marston and lately played at the Blackfriars by the Children of the Queen's Revels, is to be printed, whereof the argument is the difference betwixt the love of a courtesan and a wife, intermixed with the deceits of a witty city jester.

27th June. THOMAS DOUGLAS QUARTERED.

Yesterday Thomas Douglas was brought from the Tower to the Sessions House without Newgate and there arraigned and condemned of high treason. This Douglas was counsellor and coadjutor with that James Steward who was executed last

year for counterfeiting the King's hand to procure the Great
Seal of England, for forged letters patents for passing a hundred
marks a year of Crownland unto himself. Douglas, when he
saw Steward apprehended, prepared to gain wealth or preferment by foreign employment. He caused the King's Privy
Signet to be counterfeited, and therewith sealed six letters unto
six Princes of Germany, counterfeiting the King's hand, and
in divers of them changing his own name.

To-day he was drawn on a hurdle into Smithfield and there
hanged and quartered, at his death acknowledging all to be
true, and protesting before God that there was not any one
person so much as accessory in any one point of his treasons.

28th June. A FIERCE AFFRAY AT DOVER.

Some time since ten ships laden with Spanish soldiers, being
in all twelve companies, put forth from Lisbon with a purpose
to go for Flanders for the Archduke's service, and were met
in the Narrow Seas with the Fleet of the States that had lain
in waiting for them for six weeks and more. The Spaniards
were assaulted on the high seas, and pursued very furiously even
to the limits of the harbour of Dover. Nor did the States' ships
cease to pursue them with acts of hostility. Five of the ships,
with loss of 400 men, were taken or sunk by the Hollanders,
who would have destroyed all the rest had not the cannon of
the fort at Dover forced them to retire from further violence
within his Majesty's limits, killing some 100 of them, for they
would have assaulted the Spaniards even upon our shore. The
next day the Hollanders presumptuously came and burnt a
Scottish ship within the harbour.

1st July. AN AMBASSADOR FROM THE EMPEROR.

The Prince George Lodovic who is Lord Chamberlain to
the Emperor has come to London as Ambassador Extraordinary
from the Emperor Rudolph the Second, and is lodged in Lom-
bard Street. He is attended with three Earls, one Baron,
twenty-four gentlemen, twelve musketeers, and others to the
number of 100 persons.

SIR ROBERT DUDLEY.

Sir Robert Dudley is moved to such indignation by the
late censure of the Court of Star Chamber that he has sought

leave to travel for three years. He has moreover turned Catholic, and thereby pretends to find some scruple with his marriage to his present wife, in that he took her when his former wife was still alive. Last night he ran away from the Court taking with him Mistress Elizabeth Southwell, one of the Maids of Honour to Queen Elizabeth, who the better to escape discovery dressed herself as a boy and pretended to be his page. She is but nineteen, Sir Robert thirty-two. Sir William Monson is now commanded to use the King's ships to stop them in their flight.

4th July. A Proclamation Against Toleration in Ireland.

There is a proclamation made for Ireland denying the King's intention, which is very generally spread abroad there, to give liberty of conscience or toleration of religion to his subjects in that Kingdom. The people are hereby commanded to resort to their parish churches to hear divine service every Sunday and holy day; and further all Jesuits and priests ordained by any authority derived from the See of Rome shall depart from that Kingdom before the 10th of December, unless he shall conform and repair the Church according to the Statute.

6th July. A Brawl at Flushing.

There has been a fierce brawl in the garrison at Flushing. It happened in the place called Venus Street, which is the standing for victuallers and lewd houses, a Dutch Guard had been set to prevent disorders. In this street an Englishman took up a handful of cherries without weighing but said he would pay for them. Whilst this was debating a Dutchman of the guard gave him a box on the ear. Scots and Englishmen standing by drew to revenge the blow, thereupon the guard put themselves in array and discharged their muskets. A sergeant of my Lord of Buccleugh's regiment drew the Scots together and charged upon the guard, and the fight could hardly be stopped till the Count Maurice himself appeared with a troop of horse.

7th July. A Great Contempt of Scottish Ministers.

On the 2nd of this month certain Scottish ministers, to the number of seventeen, contrary to the King's express command, held a solemn assembly at Aberdeen. Being convented before the Council of Scotland they utterly denied not only their Lordships' authority in the matter, but the King's also, declaring that in matters ecclesiastical they neither own nor ought to acknowledge themselves in any subjection either to the King or to any temporal Council, and that all spiritual differences should be tried and determined by the Church.

8th July. THE LORD ADMIRAL'S RETURN.

Two days since the Lord Admiral and his company, having set out from the Groin on 20th June, landed at Portsmouth, being received with many shot of great ordnance from the castles, forts and walls of the town. On the shore stood Sir Lewis Lucas accompanied with the Mayor and officers of the town, being appointed by the King and Lords of the Council to receive his Lordship.

MISTRESS SOUTHWELL.

Mistress Southwell who ran away with Sir Robert Dudley last week was stayed at Calais by the Governor there. But when she declared that she had not left England for love but in order that she might enter a nunnery and serve God in the Catholic Faith, he let her go.

11th July. THE EARL OF NOTTINGHAM'S RETURN.

The Earl of Nottingham to-day rode to Windsor Castle, where the King lieth for the hunting, and is very graciously entertained and welcomed by his Majesty, who will give audience to the Spanish Ambassador on the 14th at Whitehall.

AN ACCOUNT OF THE EMBASSY TO SPAIN.

The Lord Admiral and his fleet reached the Groin on 16th April where the Governor prepared for his landing a bridge of timber above 40 yards long painted yellow, red and blue, and garnished with silk of like colours very formally, and planted the way into the town with bows of bays and orange trees, and strewed the same with rushes and flowers. So the Lord Admiral entered the town in great state and was lodged at the Condé's house. Whilst they remained at the Groin one of the mariners, becoming tippled amongst lewd company, violently struck one of the churchmen of the town. When the

Lord Admiral heard of it, he caused diligent enquiry to be made, and at last finding the offender he committed him to the bilbows; and the next day he was brought before Sir Richard Leveson and the other Admirals and Captains of the fleet who adjudged him straightway to be hanged; but the Condé and the Condess very vehemently pleaded for him, so with a halter round his neck he was delivered to the Condé, who sent him to wait in the buttery and took pity on him.

On the 24th of April his Lordship solemnized the Feast of St. George, being served in the English manner by his own servants, very magnificently, but the Condé would not dine with him, fearing to do anything that might impeach the honour of his master or be present to hear anything pronounced which might offend him. At the coming of the second course, according to our English fashion, the King's style was proclaimed in three several languages by Somerset Herald, crying 'largess,' who had a liberal reward for his pains.

His Lordship and his company reached Madrid on 16th May from Simancas, where they were met by divers noblemen, the chief whereof was the Duke of Fryas, Constable of Castile, the King's late Ambassador in England, together with Lords, Knights and Ladies in great number. The weather all this time was extraordinary hot, but suddenly to the great disordering of the company there fell a great shower of rain, which continued till they could get to the town, so that they were all throughly wet before they reached their lodging. That night came divers noblemen, as also the Major Domo to the Queen to visit his Lordship, which was much wondered at by the Spaniards themselves who said that they never knew the like favour done to any Ambassador whatsoever. Upon the 18th May the King appointed the first audience, and the Lord Admiral and his company came to the Court in twenty coaches, very honourably accompanied, and waited upon by the King's guard of 300, all newly suited in coloured velvet, yellow and red; and such was the courtesy of the Spaniards that they spared not to put out of the audience chamber all manner of people of what condition soever to give place even to the meanest of the English. His Lordship having delivered his mind in oration by the mouth of Mr. Giles Porter, his interpreter, and also our King's letters into His Highness's own hands, the King descended from his chair and gave most kind and affable behaviour to his Lordship, appointing him to sit by him very near. Some short time being spent in conference, the King was pleased to take notice of the nobles and gentlemen who had accompanied his Lordship in this long and painful journey. So they drew near to do their reverence after their customary manner which is only in bowing low to the ground, without touching either hand or foot or other part of his garments. His Lordship and his company were likewise conducted to the presence of the Queen. At length his Lordship taking leave of her Majesty, for it began to be late, all his lords, knights and gentlemen, were called up to the Queen, and all after bowing themselves in obeisance and kissing the skirt of her kirtle were conducted back again to their lodging.

On Sunday the 19th May his Lordship was present at the christening of the infant prince Philip, and upon the Tuesday following at the churching of the Queen. On 30th May, being Corpus Christi Day, after the customary festivities, the King sent word that he would take the oath, formerly agreed upon, on that day. When the Lord Admiral arrived at the Court gate, his own gentlemen were waiting for him, and divers noblemen of Spain, amongst them the Duke of Lerma, and some other grandees. By them his Lordship was conveyed up a long gallery into a Presence, and so to another room, the gentlemen, knights and lords ever going before him in very good order. In this room the King received him with affable and kind congratulation, and took him along with him by his side, the sergeants at mace going first, after following all the grandees and lords of Spain one among other; then the four Kings of Arms; then the Duke of Lerma bearing the Sword naked, but on his right shoulder, and not upright as is the custom of England. So the King and his Lords went together into a very fair banqueting house, the Ambassador Lieger and the Lords and others following.

The King sitting in his Estate, his Lordship and the Ambassador Lieger were placed upon his left hand, the grandees, and other of the noblemen of Spain being seated on the other two degrees lower. Before the King was brought a little table,

whereon lay the Bible and a crucifix upon it. The Archbishop
of Toledo read the oath with a reasonable loud voice; and at
one part of the oath his Lordship held the King's hand between
his, to which the King swore kneeling and laying his hand
upon the book; and afterwards subscribed to the articles and
agreements drawn and concluded by both Kings.

Upon the day following there was a great bullfight at which
fourteen bulls were slain, and afterwards the sports of *Inego de
Canas* wherein the King and his noblemen to the number of
four-score took part. Other sports and devices were shown
during his Lordship's stay, as a muster of armed men, and a
great masque and dancing. His Lordship took his leave on
8th June and on the 15th came to S. Andreas, whither he had
summoned his ships; and here he embarked on the 19th of
the month.

13th July. THE EMPEROR'S AMBASSADOR GIVEN AUDIENCE.

The King came yesterday from Windsor to Whitehall, and
to-day gave audience to the Prince Lodovic, who was accompanied to the Court by the Duke of Lennox. The Prince
made an oration in high Dutch and then presented his letters to
the King. He comes principally for three causes; firstly to
deliver a gratulation from the Emperor to the King for the
peaceful obtaining and enjoying of his kingdom, and for the
preservation of the amity that was between the Emperor and
Queen Elizabeth; secondly for continuation of the treaty which
was begun a little before the Queen died, concerning the Hanse
towns and their privileges, and thirdly for aid and assistance
against the Turk.

16th July. THE PRINCE LODOVIC.

The King has begun his progress to Oxford. Yesterday in
all state he feasted the Prince Lodovic at his own table, the
Queen and the Prince being present, and drank and pledged
a health to the Imperial dignity of the Emperor. After dinner
they saw bear-baiting and bull-baiting. The Ambassador makes
his departure on the 22nd of the month.

THE COMMOTION AT HEREFORD.

After the late broils at Hereford the Earl of Worcester came
down to those parts to his place of Raglan in Monmouthshire,

when most of the principal offenders came in and yielded themselves to his Lordship; of whom some were straightway committed to prison till his Majesty's further pleasure be known; but with others who were carried away by popish factors his Lordship took a milder course, seeking to win them to the truth, and hath so effectively dealt in the case that from stiff recusants many are converted. The county is now quieted.

20th July. AN EXPLORATION OF VIRGINIA.

Two days ago Captain George Waymouth and his company in the *Archangel* came to anchor in Dartmouth. This ship was set out at the charges of the Earl of Southampton and Lord Thomas Arundel to examine and explore the country of Virginia. They bring back very favourable report of the richness of that land and the pleasing temperance of the climate.

They left England upon Easter Sunday (3rd March), being very well victualled and munitioned, and the whole company but twenty-nine persons, but all seamen.

After some dangers by reason of the falseness of the sea-charts they came to a very fair harbour in an island off the main of Virginia, where there is abundance of trees of all kinds, with fresh water, and many fish to be caught. They reached a safe anchorage amidst the islands of the mainland and there anchored upon Whit Sunday, and the next day the pinnace was fitted together and launched, and on the 22nd May they went ashore, and there felled trees and cut wood for the ship's use, and scoured their wells. Likewise they digged wherein to sow some garden seeds, pease and barley, of which such as the birds spared grew eight inches in sixteen days, and so continued every day more than half an inch. They had much to do with the savages who came to them in their canoes, and were wondrous friendly, trading with them for trifles worth four shillings or five shillings forty good skins of beaver, otter and other beasts. Moreover they came aboard ship and were very many. Captain Waymouth showed them a strange thing, at which they wondered, his sword having been touched with a loadstone took up a knife, and made it turn when laid on a block, and by giving their knife a touch with the sword made it take up a needle. Thus for several days our men went on shore, one or two of them even sleeping with the savages, whilst some of them slept on the ship; and besides they brought tobacco of very excellent quality.

On 11th June, after Captain Waymouth had coasted about the islands to take soundings, they weighed anchor and passed up to survey a great river, forty miles wide at the mouth and narrowing to half a mile at the narrowest. On either side they noted excellent places where there are natural docks to grave and careen ships of all burdens, secured from all winds. The river yields many salmons, and is well wooded. Some among the company who had been in these parts before declare that it is to be preferred to the Orinoque which Sir Walter Ralegh discovered. The ground is very pleasant and fertile, and fit for pasture. The farther they went up, the more pleasing was the prospect.

They set sail for England upon Sunday the 16th June.

25th July. THE ARCHPRIEST'S COMMAND TO CATHOLICS.

The Archpriest Blackwell, having received a mandate from the Pope, now writes to his Catholic brethren that they endeavour to suppress all suspected attempts and proceedings for liberty because they will bring many grievous inconveniences upon Catholics.

28th July. PARLIAMENT AGAIN PROROGUED.

The Parliament is again prorogued until Tuesday, the 5th of November.

5th August. THE PAUL'S CROSS SERMON.

This day the thanksgiving sermon at Paul's Cross was preached by the Lord Bishop of London who spake of his Majesty's care for religion, declaring that he had made a protestation before God and His angels that he was so constant for the maintenance of the religion publicly in England professed as that he would spend his own dearest blood in the defence thereof rather than that the truth should be overthrown; and that if he had ten times as many more kingdoms as he hath, he would dispend them all for the safety and protection thereof; and likewise, that if he had any children that should overlive him, if they should maintain or uphold any other religion, he desired of God that he might see them brought to their graves before him, that their shame might be buried in his lifetime, never to be spoken of in future ages.

JONSON'S 'SEJANUS' PRINTED.

That play of *Sejanus* which was played some two years since at the Globe is now at length printing with sundry commendatory verses by Jonson's friends, as Chapman, Marston and others, praising the play and condemning the people for their ill receiving of it. Blount is the printer, having taken it over from Thorp, who entered it in November last but forbore to print. Certain speeches written by another and spoken from the stage have now been taken out, so all that remains is pure Ben.

6th August. A SCHOOLMASTER STABBED.

The Court is now at Sir Anthony Mildmay's at Apthorp, with a great train; but there is neither public nor private business stirring, but all very quiet and excellent hunting. Here came news from Norwich that young Mr. Sidney, my Lord of Lisle's son, that was with the Prince, hath stabbed his schoolmaster with a knife for offering to whip him so dangerously that it is thought he cannot live. The King when he was told of it was very much displeased, and gave instant commandment that he should be discharged from attending the Prince any longer, and so he is sent away to his father. My Lord had gone over to Flushing before this mischance happened.

9th August. STRANGE CRUELTY.

On the 5th of the month Walter Calverley, of Calverley in York, esquire, was executed at the Castle of York. He murdered two of his young children, stabbed his wife into the body with full purpose to have murdered her, and instantly went from his house to have slain his youngest child at nurse but was prevented. At his trial, he stood mute and was condemned to be pressed to death.

10th August. THE DESPERATE ACTIONS OF SIR JOHN FITZ.

This day was buried at Twickenham Sir John Fitz of Fitzford in the County of Devon. This gentleman formerly took to wife the daughter of Sir William Courtney of those

parts. Some years ago he quarrelled with his particular friend
Mr. Slanning, whom with the aid of certain of his servants he
waylaid and slew, and himself got safe away to France until
he had procured a reprival of the offence upon his good behaviour. But upon his return he began little by little to follow
the humours of depraved company. At the time of his Majesty's
coronation it pleased the King to bestow upon him the honour
of knighthood, whereupon this Sir John now became bolder
in his riots, and entertaining to his company one commonly
named Lusty Jack caused much disorder and riot in the town
of Tavistock. So wholly was he addicted to all vicious defama-
tions that it even shamed him not to bring his queans with him
to the great distress of his wife, who at length returned to her
father.

It fortuned that not long since Sir John fell out with an
officer of the town whom he assaulted and wounded very
grievously, thereby bringing himself into great peril. Hereupon
Master Slanning's son, knowing that Sir John's pardon was
but conditioned upon his good behaviour, used means for his
attachment. Sir John, therefore, being in some fear of his life,
and suspecting also that Sir William Courtney, his father-in-
law, would take some action against him, hastened towards
London, and alighted at an inn in Kingston upon Thames;
but being afflicted by fearful visions he would not stay there,
and calling for his gelding he rode away in the dead time of
night, crying that Sir William Courtney was at hand to apprehend him. Whilst he was so doing he met the watch in the
streets; at the sight of whom he cried aloud that they were
come, they were come; but the watch, being more certainly
informed by his man of this sudden malady, assured him that
they were not Sir William but the neighbours of the town.

So he went on to the village of Twickenham where at
length about 2 in the morning he came upon a little victualling
house kept by one Daniel Alley, of whom he demanded lodging.
This poor man having no guest chamber caused his wife to lay
clean sheets upon their own bed which they gave up to Sir John.
Sir John bade the goodman stay with him, which he did till
about 4 and 5 of the clock; at which time, seeing Sir John
between sleeping and waking, he went out about his own

labour with his man. But as they were filling a bottle of drink to take to the field, they heard something give a jump, and forth comes Sir John in his shirt, with his naked rapier in his hand, his countenance terrible and ghastly. Whereupon the men gave way before him, Sir John following. Then perceiving the goodman about to shut the gate upon him he cried out, 'Ah villain! art thou one that should apprehend me? I will surely kill thee,' and therewith ran at him with his rapier; but as the goodman was shutting the gate, Sir John's rapier passed through a little hole of the gate and thrust him quite through the body so that he fell down straightway and died, only with a hideous shriek crying out, 'I am killed.' Hereat the goodwife leaps out of bed in her smock, and running out of doors meets Sir John, all on gore with the blood of her husband, who, though she knelt for mercy, thrust twice at her body, and twice missed, but at the third thrust wounded her grievously in the arm.

Now Sir John, not yet satisfied with blood but he must needs shed his own, espying a mud wall close by, takes his rapier and laying the hilts thereto, and the point thereof unto his own breast, ran forcibly thereon, and pulled it forth, and again ran on it, and a second time pulling it forth, runs into the house after the woman; but his strength failing, down he falls on the floor of the house, where he was anon found wallowing in his own blood.

Surgeons were sent for, who tented his wounds, but he always pulled them out again saying that he would die and not live. Nevertheless he lived some forty-eight hours after his hurts before he died. On Thursday (7th) the Coroner sat upon the man of the house and by verdict there given Sir John Fitz was found guilty both of the man's death and his own also, if he should die thereon. Nevertheless because he was a gentleman born and of good kindred, he is buried in the chancel at Twickenham.

Before he died the Earl of Northumberland sent a gentleman to him of his old acquaintance to persuade him to repentance. He did at length say that he was sorry for the death of the poor man leaving three wretched children upon the mother's hands; and being asked whether he would willingly give anything unto the poor woman in recompense of the loss of her husband, he was contented to bestow upon her £100; but whether he had anything in his own power to give is not known.

12*th August.* Mistress Southwell.

There is a bruit that Mistress Southwell is now become a professed nun of the Order of St. Clara at Brussels, and there was received with all the solemnity that may be.

19*th August.* Sir William Waad made Lieutenant of the Tower.

Four days ago Sir William Waad was sworn Lieutenant of the Tower, his oath being taken by the Earl of Devonshire and the Lord Treasurer. Then he went to see the prisoners. Sir Walter Ralegh, after using some speech of dislike, acknowledges his error and seems satisfied. Lord Cobham used him very sullenly, and so far forgot himself that he spoke very loud and passionately. Mr. Lieutenant therefore had him shut up in his lodging, but the next morning he confessed his fault and entreated that it might be forgotten. The new Lieutenant is likely to be more severe with the prisoners who hitherto enjoy many liberties. Sir Walter Ralegh has access to the Lieutenant's garden, where he has converted a little hen-house to a still-house, and spends all his time in distillation.

24*th August.* The Tower Ditch.

There have long been disputes between the Lord Mayor and the Lieutenant of the Tower. Now the Lord Mayor and the Aldermen, not content with voiding the town ditch into the Tower ditch, have caused a sluice to be opened which will bring all the soil from the Minories into the town ditch and so into the Tower ditch, which stinks very vilely, and puts those in the Tower to great shifts for sweet water.

The King's Progress.

The King and Queen proceeded to Woodstock on the 21st and are now gone to Langley whence they will visit the University of Oxford, where great preparations are made for their receiving, and divers ordinances for the proper behaviour of the scholars, as that the scholars, bachelors and masters do diligently frequent the ordinary lectures during the King's abode; that the scholars which cannot be admitted to see the plays do not make any outcries or indecent noise about the hall, stairs, or within the quadrangle of Christchurch upon pain of present imprisonment and other punishment; further, that verses are to be provided to be set upon St. Mary's, which verses shall first be corrected by the Deans of colleges or some other appointed by the Head; and at every College a short oration shall be provided to entertain his Majesty if it be his pleasure to visit the same. Both in the Colleges and the streets the rails, posts and pumps have been freshly painted, and all coats-of-arms newly tricked out.

27th August. THE KING'S VISIT TO OXFORD.

Some days before the King's visit, the Earl of Suffolk, with the Earls of Worcester and Northampton, came to Oxford to see that all things were in readiness. They utterly misliked the stage at Christchurch and above all the place appointed for the chair of estate, because it was no higher and the King so placed that the auditory could see but his cheek only; which much troubled the Vice-Chancellor and all the workmen, yet they stood in defence of the thing done, maintaining that by the art perspective the King should behold all better than if he sat higher. The Chancellor when he came likewise took their part, but on the Sunday following it was debated in the Council Chamber; and in the end it was removed and set in the midst of the hall so far from the stage that there were many long speeches delivered which neither the King nor any near him could hear. My Lord of Dorset, Chancellor of the University, came very late the next night, and was entertained at Christchurch with an oration, which he heard very unwillingly because he had commanded the contrary.

On the 27th (being Tuesday) at one of the clock in the afternoon the Vice Chancellor and the doctors went to the Chancellor at New College, and from thence went out to meet the King. First rode three esquire bedells, in fair gowns, with gold chains and velvet caps, carrying their staves, and the Sergeant of the mace. Immediately after rode the Chancellor, talking with the Vice-Chancellor (who bore back about half the length of his horse). After them some six or eight doctors in scarlet; then the two proctors; and after them some ten or twelve in black gowns riding two and two. These were some of them Heads of Halls, and all wore square caps. They stayed first at a place called Aristotle's Well, about a mile from the city, but because it was narrow and much annoyed with dust, the Lord Chamberlain sent word for them to come a little forward into a fair meadow, where they alighted and stayed beside the highway. But the Mayor of the city, with twelve aldermen in scarlet, and some six-score commoners passed forward by them, to the great discontent of the Vice-Chancellor, so that the Chancellor sent the Sergeant-at-arms to tell the Mayor and his brethren that they had forgot themselves, and bidding them on their peril to come back behind him and not to dare to speak to the King until they had done.

Immediately after the King came riding on horseback, with the Queen on his left hand, and the Prince before them, the Duke of Lennox carrying the Sword. The nobility attending the King was very great and richly attired. So the Chancellor went towards the King and kneeled down, and the King gave him his hand and pulled him up. Then the King came nearer and the Vice-Chancellor began his speech which he delivered upon his knee with good grace and clear voice, wherein he commended the University above all others in the world *ratione cœli et soli, antiquitatis, pulchritudinis, ædificorum, multidinis collegiorum, studentium, et doctorum virorum.* After that they presented to the King a Greek Testament in folio, and two pair of Oxford gloves with a deep fringe of gold, and likewise to the Queen two pair, and a pair unto the Prince.

So they went forward and came to Mr. Mayor and his brethren. The Town Clerk made a long speech in English, extolling greatly the late Queen and her government, the great fear at her death, the exceeding joy and infallible hope that succeeded upon it. After this the Mayor surrendered his mace to the King who put it upon him again, and then the Mayor gave the King a fair standing cup, having £50 of gold in it, in all worth £100; also to the Queen they presented another worth £40, and to the Prince another worth £30.

So then they marched on slowly to the City until they came near unto St. John's College, where coming against the gate three young youths, in habit and attire like nymphs or sibyls, confronted the King, saluting him and putting him in mind of

that ancient prophecy made unto Banquo, his Majesty's
ancestor, that though the sceptre should not come to him yet it
yet should be for ever with his posterity. These things were
said first to the King in Latin, and then to the Queen and the
Prince in English, the conceit whereof the King did very much
applaud. Thence they passed to the Carfax, the scholars standing all on one side of the road, arranged according to their
degree, and the strangers of all sorts on the other. Here the
Greek Reader made an oration in Greek which the King heard
willingly, and the Queen much more because she said she had
never before heard Greek.

From thence they went on to Christchurch where at the
hall-stair's foot the University Orator made an oration. Then
the King went to the church to solemn prayers, a fair canopy
of crimson taffety being carried over the heads of their Majesties
by six canons of the church. The service was very solemn,
the choir full, with excellent voices mixed with instruments.
When prayers were done they all went to the King's lodging,
and a while after the Prince, accompanied with three coaches
full of noblemen, came to Magdalen College to his lodging
where he was entertained.

At night they had a comedy which began between nine and
ten and ended at one. It was a pastoral named *Alba*, and in
the acting thereof, they brought in five or six men almost
naked which were much misliked by the Queen and Ladies,
and also many rustical songs and dances, which were so tedious
that if the Chancellors of both Universities had not earnestly
entreated the King, he would have gone before half was ended.

28th August. THE KING AT OXFORD.

At 8 of the clock a sermon was appointed, but the King was
asleep and so word was brought that nothing should be done till
his coming. About 9 he came in great state to St. Mary's
Church, the Earl of Southampton being Sword-bearer for the
day. After the King was placed in his estate and the nobility
had taken their places, Dr. Holland, the Father in Divinity,
asked leave of the King that he might create his son, after the
manner of the University, whereunto the King gave his consent. So he spake first of his gown, the colour and dye thereof,

225

then he felt whether he was booted or not, and gave reason why he should be booted; then he gave him a Bible; and then a cap, ring and *osculum pacis*, and so the Act began. He could have been long but the proctors bade him conclude.

So they proceeded next to the Divinity Acts. The Vice-Chancellor read the questions, which were:

I. '*An sancti et angli cognoscunt cogitationes cordium?*' (Whether the saints and angels know the cogitations of men's hearts);

II. '*An peste grassante teneantur Ecclesiarum pastores ægros inuisere?*' (Whether at the onset of the pestilence pastors should visit the sick.)

The King was most attentive and would show when he liked the argument by word or other outward gesture. Both questions were concluded in the negative.

After dinner, about 2 of the clock, the King came again with the Queen and the Prince, and the Law Act began, wherein were disputed these questions:

I. '*An iudex in iudicando teneatur sequi legitimas probationes in iudicio deductas contra ueritatem sibi priuatim cognitam?*' (Whether a judge in giving judgment should follow the legal proofs produced in the court of justice contrary to the truth known privately to himself);

II. '*An iudicia uel fœdera sint bonæ fidei uel stricti iuris?*' (Whether judgments or convenants be of good faith or of strict law.)

All the disputants replied very well and the King observed them much, and talked to divers about him, but of a sudden three or four times he spake and interpreted the law. He determined the first question himself in these words: '*elaborandum inprimis iudici, ut Principi suo uel etiam Regi lucem ueritatis sibi priuatim cognitæ producat, atque ita auctoritatem huic ueritati conciliet; sin id maxime contendens parum effecerit, exeundam potius iudicis personam ut indicat priuati testis, et sic quouis modo integram seruet conscientiam in promouenda ueritate, quam ut iudicis personam ad extremum conscientiæ et ueritatis naufragium diutius sustineat.*'

In the second Act, after the King first spoke the scholars began a *plaudite*; at the second time the graver men cried '*uiuat Rex*'; but at the third time the Prince, nobility and all, applauded with great vehemency.

In the evening after supper, about 9 of the clock, they began to act a tragedy called *Ajax Flagellifer* wherein the stage was adorned with stately pillars, which turned about, so that with the aid of other painted cloths, the scene was varied three times. For the contriving of this and the seats and scaffolds, they entertained two of the King's Master Carpenters, and had the advice of the Controller of the works; they also hired Master Inigo Jones, who undertook to furnish them with rare devices for which he had for his pains, as was said, £50, but performed very little to what was expected. The King was very weary before he came thither, but much more wearied by the tragedy, and spake many words of dislike.

THE SPANISH AMBASSADOR'S PASSAGE.

Now that the Spanish Ambassador is about to depart, the King sent for Sir Noel Caron and told him that he expected the States not to molest the homeward journey of an ambassador. To this Sir Noel replied that he had received orders from his superiors to observe the King's command, but seeing that the Lord Arundel of Wardour is going out to fight for the Archduke, they presumed that he would not be countenanced or protected in or by the King's ships. To this the King agreed, and when he heard that the Lord Arundel was on his way to Dover he caused the Council to write to the Ambassador from Oxford that he should not carry him over. They wrote likewise to Sir Lewis Lewkenor in like manner. When these orders were imparted to Lord Arundel he was very passionate and perplexed.

29*th August*. THE KING AT OXFORD.

The King attended a Physic Act which began at 9 and lasted till noon, the Earl of Worcester being Sword-bearer. The questions were:

I. '*An mores nutricum a puerilis cum lacte imbibantur?*' (Whether the manners of nurses are sucked in by children with their milk);

II. '*An creber suffitus nicotianæ exoticæ sit sanis salutaris?*' (Whether the frequent fumigation of *nicotiana exotica* be wholesome for the health.)

Thence the King went to New College and dined with the Chancellor in great state. In the afternoon there were two Philosophy Acts very well performed, that of Natural Philosophy being first, after which the Queen and the Prince went away immediately. The second replier, one Mr. Simon Baskerville, disputed so well that when the proctor would have cut him off, the King bade him continue, and after said to the nobles about him, 'God keep this fellow in a right course, he would prove a dangerous heretic; he is the best disputer that ever I heard.' Of the next he said that he had never heard a worse who would have proved that tobacco must needs be good because Kings and persons of all degree (naming a number) loved it; for, said the King, there was one King which neither loved nor liked it; which moved great delight.

The King himself determined one of the questions in Natural Philosophy, which was '*An aurum artis opera possit confici?*' (whether gold can be made by the care of art), saying that if gold could have been made by human art, then Solomon would have known of it, which he did not, for he had to fetch gold from the Indies for his Temple. The King heard all to the last word and until it grew dark. Then he stood up, moved his hat off his head, and spake very graciously in Latin, approving all their exercises, and exhorting them to worship God, His word, and His pure doctrine, fleeing from Romish superstitions, schisms and novel opinions. So doing they would bring glory to God and joy to himself, and would fulfil the expectation he had of them.

At night, after supper, there was acted a comedy called *Vertumnus*, much better than the other. But the King was so over-wearied by the disputations at St. Mary's that after a while he distasted it, and fell asleep. When he awaked, he would have been gone, saying 'I marvel what they think me to be,' with other such-like speeches, yet he did tarry till they had ended it, which was after one of the clock.

30th August. THE KING'S VISIT TO OXFORD.

There was a play acted before the Queen and the Prince with all the ladies and gallants attending the Court, which was penned by Mr. Samuel Daniel, and entitled *Arcadia Reformed*. Before this play began, at about 6 in the morning a bedell went around calling all doctors and masters to convocation at 7 of the clock. At 8 divers of the nobility began to arrive, and graces were passed for the Earls of Northumberland, Oxford, Essex, and in general for all other noblemen, knights and officers of the royal household (which were men of account) to be admitted; which was performed in the accustomed manner so long as they came slowly, but afterwards they pressed so thick that the Register being there with pen and ink could not take their names, nor did he nor any other man ask who they were; so that provided they looked like gentlemen and had gotten a gown and hood they were admitted. There was great labour made that the Prince might be made Master of Arts but the King would not consent to it.

After 9 the King came to view the Library, upon whom attended a great part of the nobility. There he spent at least an hour taking into his hands several books which he perused and gave his learned censure of them.

Thence he returned by Brazennose College, where he heard an oration, and coming out of his coach walked about the square and viewed the college. From whence he went by All Souls' College where he heard an oration, and from thence to Magdalen College and there also heard an oration; and so back to Christchurch for dinner where in the time of dinner Dr. Lylly of Balliol College made a learned oration but too long.

After dinner the King entered the Court, and both he and the Queen giving their hands to be kissed of the Vice-Chancellor and the rest of the doctors, bade them farewell and trouble themselves no further, though they had horses and footcloths ready to carry them out of their liberty. Then the King, Queen and Prince went all in one coach and passed through the town by Magdalen College, not staying anywhere. The Mayor and the officers of the town rode before his Majesty to the farther end of the bridge and there stopped. There were verses set up on the walls of such Colleges as were in his way (*videlicet* All Souls', Corpus Christi and Magdalen) which the King regarded not, nor did any step out of the train to read them, so they were by the boys rudely pulled down.

There was likewise some incivility amongst the scholars, for the morning before the King came they sat at the sermon hard by the Vice-Chancellor with their hats on and afterwards 140 of them were sent to prison by command upon their oaths, and so went without any officer of their own accord. While the King spake in the exercises they applauded him by clapping their hands and humming, which though strange to him, yet when he understood upon enquiry what the noise meant, he was well contented.

From Oxford the Court is gone to Gray's.

31st August. AN AMBASSADOR FROM DENMARK.

The King of Denmark has now sent his principal secretary Henry Ramelius to be solemnly installed on his behalf in the Order of the Garter to which he was elected two years since. He is accompanied only with thirty gentlemen and twenty others. At the King's appointment he is lodged at Somerset House and served by the King's gentlemen ushers, servers, yeomen of the guard, and grooms of the chamber.

4th September. A PLAY CALLED 'EASTWARD HO.'

The Children of the Queen's Revels at Blackfriars of late had a new play called *Eastward Ho*, made by Chapman, Jonson and Marston which is now sent to the press, which in the prologue they dedicate to the City, showing how prodigals are brought to ruin and the industrious apprentice to prosperity. There is presented also one of these forty-pound Knights, by name Sir Petronel Flash, that married a young wench for her fortune and would then away to Virginia leaving her bare of all but the name of Lady. Of Virginia quoth one Seagull, a sea captain, it is as pleasant a country as ever the sun shined on, where a man may live freely without Sergeants or courtiers or lawyers or intelligencers, 'only a few industrious Scots perhaps, who indeed are dispersed over the face of the whole earth. But as for them, there are no greater friends to Englishmen and England (when they are out on't) in the whole world than they are. And for my part, I would a hundred thousand of 'em were there, for we are all one countrymen, ye know, and we should find ten times more comfort of them there than we do here.'

9th September. LORD ARUNDEL'S GREAT CONTEMPT.

When the Spanish Ambassador landed at Gravelines, he was met by the Lord Arundel, who declared that he had passed over by way of Calais but it is now known that he went over in the fleet on board the *Adventure*, the Vice-Admiral, having disguised himself with a false beard, and raggedly clothed, pretending to be a servant of the Lord Lisle's. He is now to be called home again, as soon as he shall have put in order the troops under his charge, and ended the summer service.

15th September. THE AUTHORS OF 'EASTWARD HO' IMPRISONED.

The King being informed by Sir James Murray of the taxing censure of the Scots in the play of *Eastward Ho* was so angry thereat that both Jonson and Chapman have been arrested and sent to prison, whence they petition his Majesty, my Lord of Salisbury, the Lord Chamberlain and other honourable persons for their favour and release. Jonson especially complaineth that he is committed unexamined and unheard, and that it hath ever been his destiny to be misreported and condemned on first tale, and moreover that since his first error he hath ever so attempered his style that he hath given no cause of grief to any good man, nor offence to a nation, a public order, or state, or any person of honour or authority. Moreover they declare that the offensive clauses are not of their own writing.

18th September. THE LORD LISLE'S MISUNDERSTANDING.

Some days ago the Lord Lisle, supposing that the Queen would not need his services on the progress, asked leave of absence to visit Flushing of which place he has long been Governor but has left in charge of his Deputy. On his way thither his ship was driven by storm into Gravelines, which is held by the Archduke. Hereupon his enemies declared that he had made that voyage to meet with some Spanish minister. This report by Sir Noel Caron, the Agent of the States, was carried to the King who was so angry that he caused the Council to command my Lord Lisle to return upon pain of death, loss of estates, and proclamation as a traitor. My Lord has now come back and easily cleared himself of those charges, proving that he was forced to enter Gravelines and that he saw no Spanish minister. So Sir Noel is now much blamed for an overfoolish credulity.

SIR THOMAS SMITH'S VOYAGE INTO RUSSIA.

Sir Thomas Smith, who set out as his Majesty's Ambassador to Russia in June of last year, is now returned. During the whole time of their stay in Russia he and his train were very kindly entreated by the Emperor, and twice received in audience. At the first audience, which was on 11th October of last year, when his Majesty's letters were presented, the Ambassador and Master John Merrick, the English agent in Moscow, were invited to dine with the Emperor Boris Theodorwich in great state, and honour. But the business of their ambassage was much interrupted because at this time then came news that the infant son of the late Emperor, named Demetre Evanowich Beola, who was (as was thought) murdered in his infancy, was alive and up in arms for his right and inheritance. By reason of these troubles the Ambassador did not receive his second audience until the 10th March of this year when letters for his Majesty were delivered, and the Emperor, by the mouth of his Chancellor, declared his great desire for the continuance of peace and amity with our King, and further granted a new privilege for the Company. Shortly afterwards the Ambassador began to take his journey towards Archangel, and on 29th March having reached a place called Vollagde they abode at the English house over Easter; and here came heavy news that the Emperor had died very suddenly, though whether it were by natural sickness, or grief at the ill success of the wars, or by poison, it was not certainly known.

Here they lodged until the 6th May, when the ambassador resolved to pass down the river to Colmigro, as well that he might the sooner have news from England as to be out of fear of any disaster, for many strange reports came from Moscow, where the people rose against the young Emperor and committed great riot in the city. Whereupon his mother, the Empress, persuaded him to drink poison, which she gave also to the Princess, and took herself rather than they should fall into the hands of the invader. So the Prince Demetrius Evanowich was chosen Emperor, who hath renewed the favour shown to our English merchantmen; and on 3rd August Sir Thomas Smith set sail from Archangel for England.

24th September. A SPANISH FOOL.

There came out of Spain with the Lord Admiral in the company of his Spanish Ambassador a Spanish jester in whom the

King and Queen of Spain take great delight, for he has a humour of ranging abroad, and on his return giving out the most foolish and extravagant discourses of his adventures, and yet he is one of the fearfullest creatures alive. Now this fool must needs go to see the Count Maurice, which causes my Lord of Salisbury, albeit very reluctantly, to condescend to write on his behalf that our people in the Low Countries may look to him well, for he is sickly.

27th September. Dogs for the King's Use.

The commissions granted to certain officers for the taking up of hounds, greyhounds, spaniels and dogs of other sorts accustomed for venery, falconry or other sports of Princes, are now discontinued since gentlemen and others who delight in the pastime of hunting and hawking have shown themselves ready to furnish his Majesty with dogs of all sorts.

'Wit's Pilgrimage.'

Master John Davies of Hereford hath compiled a book of divers poems called *Wit's Pilgrimage*, wherein are many amorous sonnets and soul passions, and divers poetical essays upon certain sentences and upon more serious and sacred subjects; which is dedicated to the Lord Philip Herbert, and Sir James Hayes.

THE BOOK TO HIS PATRON
If I thy blood do kindly warm or move,
Warm my sire's blood with comfort of his love.

28th September. The King of Denmark's Ambassador.

The King of Denmark's Ambassador was installed at Windsor on the 8th of this month, feasted at Hampton Court on the 15th, and to-day is embarked.

29th September. The Archbishop Made a Councillor.

To-day (being Sunday) Dr. Bancroft, Lord Archbishop of Canterbury, is sworn a Privy Councillor.

A Strange Present.

Captain Christopher Newport came to the Court bringing two young crocodiles and a wild boar from Hispaniola which he presented to his Majesty.

1st October. A Strange Miracle at Dort.

A strange miracle is reported from Dort of a young man that

was hanged five days, and yet, by God's special mercy, is preserved alive. This young man, by name John Johnson, being employed by his uncle, one John Peterson a merchant of Antwerp, was by him taken to Frankfort Fair, and thence being sent back towards Antwerp he lodged on the way at an inn in Bonn; but, as he slept, the host of the inn secretly laid in the young man's wallet certain money and other goods that he had stolen from a merchant that lay in the inn. Next morning the young man departed, and a while after the merchant, missing his money, he with the host pursued after Johnson who was taken and the goods discovered in his wallet. The young man was therefore brought to the place of trial and adjudged to be hanged, which sentence was carried out, though he protested his innocence very vehemently, praying God to show some miracle upon him. Five days afterwards his uncle coming to the same inn learnt that a young man had been hanged, and suspecting from the host's description that it was his nephew went with other merchants to see the corpse. So they came to the gallows and when he perceived that it was indeed his nephew he fell down in a swoon, but the young man there hanging spake to him, declaring that God had placed a stool under his feet, albeit unperceived by others, and that an angel had fed him these five days. So the merchant went straightway to the magistrates who forthwith caused the young man to be taken down, who was then in perfect health, although he had hanged five days. Hereupon he was brought into the town and thoroughly examined of the matter. So they sent for the host; but when he beheld the young man still to be alive he confessed the deed. So he was condemned to be burnt, which was accordingly performed. It was likewise ordered by those judges that the young man should possess to his own use the sum of 3,000 guilders of the host's money in recompense of the injury done to him.

These things the magistrates of Bonn caused to be printed to set forth the mighty power and glory of God. As for the young man, he yet remaineth at Antwerp with his uncle.

5th October. SIR ROBERT DUDLEY AND HIS MISTRESS.
Sir Robert Dudley and Mistress Southwell are now at Lyons, where they hope for a dispensation that they may be married.

234

They go about constantly in public lest it should be said that there is any guilty concealment between them.

10*th October*. THE KING AND AN IMPOSTOR.

Of late a woman named Ann Gunter was brought before the King, who was by many supposed to be bewitched, and at such times would cast pins out of her mouth and the like. In outward show she was a creature most weak and impotent; yet when she was brought before the King she began to dance with great strength and comeliness, and leapt with great agility. Hereupon his Majesty, marvelling to see such a change, examined her himself very closely, when she confessed that she had been cured of her former weakness by a potion given her by a physician and a tablet hanged about her neck; that she never was possessed with any devil, nor bewitched; and that this practice of pins grew at the first from a pin that she put in her mouth, affirmed by her father to be cast therein by the Devil; and after that with other pranks such as a swelling of her belly, which was caused by the disease called the 'mother,' she persuaded many that she was bewitched.

12*th October*. GENERAL NEWS.

The King went lately to Royston and is now at Huntingdon; the Queen lies at Hampton Court. The Council sit much at Whitehall about ordering the household and bringing it to the French fashion of board wages. The sickness rose suddenly to thirty in a week, and the infecting of nineteen parishes made it appear that the term or parliament or both might be put off, but the abating of a few this week make all hold on. The Bishop of Chichester (Dr. Anthony Watson) is dead, rich for so mean a living, and bestowed the greatest part of his wealth on his kindred and servants. Dr. Launcelot Andrewes is like to be Bishop and Almoner in his place.

THE STATE OF IRELAND.

Of late the Lord Deputy made a journey in Northern Ireland to compose certain differences and to view the state of the Kingdom, and is now returned to Dublin. Noted that among the impediments to that Kingdom's tranquillity are the corruption of under officers and the scarcity of good Justices of the Peace, which can only be remedied by planting of English and others well affected. In the matter of banishing the Jesuits and priests, few or none but English will help them, and the Government can do little. Nor do our Englishmen fulfil their duty, for many are content to receive the pay and suck the sweets of Ireland, but few love the service or the country, accounting it base and obscure in that it is not countenanced with greatness.

As for remedies, declareth the King would more conform and strengthen his state, and leave a more honourable memory behind him by reforming and civilizing Ireland than by conquering France. It is much wasted and unpeopled, and the replenishing of it with civil men would be a great strength in every way to his Majesty in all his wars and defences. It must needs be a folly that many should run to Virginia and Guiana and other remote and unknown countries, whilst this of our own is left waste and desolate.

16*th October*. A PURVEYOR SENTENCED.

In the Star Chamber a purveyor was censured for misdemeanour in his office to ride with his face to the horse's tail. Herein one of his judges dissented from the rest and would rather have it upon an ass, and this for two reasons; first, it would cause more wonderment and gather more boys about him, and secondly, the slow pace of the ass would prolong his punishment.

20*th October*. THE KING AND QUEEN ENTERTAINED BY SIR WILLIAM POPE.

The King and Queen were entertained at Hanwell by Sir Anthony Cope, and later in the day visited Sir William Pope at Wroxton, where they were entertained by hawking and bearbaiting. His lady having been lately delivered of a daughter, the child was presented to the King, holding a paper on which were written these verses:

> See this little Mistress here,
> Did never sit in Peter's chair,
> Or a triple crown did wear,
> And yet she is a Pope.

No benefice she ever sold,
Nor did dispense with sins for gold;
She hardly is a sevenight old,
    And yet she is a Pope.

No King her feet did ever kiss,
Or had from her worse look than this;
Nor did she ever hope,
To saint one with a rope,
And yet she is a Pope.

A female Pope, you'll say; a second Joan!
No, sure; she is Pope innocent, or None.

21st October. THE EARL OF CUMBERLAND DYING.

My Lord of Cumberland is very sick and in the opinion of
the physicians like to leave his life ere many hours. My Lord of
Salisbury was with him at five o'clock this morning, and he hath
made to Dr. Andrewes a religious and penitent confession of his
faith, clearly condemning all popish and corrupt opinions. He
hath received the Communion, forgiven all the world lovingly,
and discreetly reconciled all dryness between him and his lady.

22nd October. MEANS OF CURTAILING THE KING'S EXPENSES.

The Lords of the Privy Council have considered means of
cutting off the great expense for the King's household, and make
certain propositions for saving of charges in unnecessary diet,
and amongst others that the Prince's house should be dissolved
and he to remain in his Majesty's house which would save
£2,000 a year. In all they would save by diet alone £9,600; and
further by abating the officers of the household, chamber and
stable another £12,000 per annum.

23rd October. THE PRIVILEGES OF COUNTESSES.

One Milwarde, a goldsmith in Cheapside, was to-day in question in the Star Chamber, for he caused a sergeant to arrest the
Countess Dowager of Rutland for a debt of £90, which was done
very unreverently and irregularly whilst the lady was in her
coach. So it was argued at length what were the privileges of the
wives of noblemen, and concluded that they have the like

privileges as their husbands, unless they marry ignobly or live dishonourably. Because of certain irregularities in the proceedings, the goldsmith is fined £200 and imprisonment; the sergeant is fined the like amount, to stand upon the pillory with papers, and be disabled from ever holding that place. The Lord Chancellor delivered that Ladies should be tried by their peers, but that it was a good course that great Ladies and Countesses should pay their debts so they would have no use of this privilege.

24th October. GENERAL NEWS.

It is reported that the Spaniards have met Sir Edward Michelbourne at sea and massacred him and all his company. Likewise that they have converted or perverted Sir Charles Cornwallis's Chaplain, a fellow that preached at Paul's Cross this twelvemonth, and hath a benefice and a wife here in England. The young Earl of Essex and Lord Cranborne (my Lord of Salisbury's son) shall marry two of the daughters of the Lord Chamberlain at Court very shortly; the only stay is for the King's coming, who is looked for next week. He cannot well stay longer, for the Parliament is to begin on the 5th of November. He finds such variety of sports that he cannot easily leave Royston; he is now fallen into a great humour of catching larks and takes as much delight in it or more than in hunting. The sickness keeps still much at a stay; there died this week one hundred and twenty in all, whereof twenty-two of the plague.

29th October. INDIGNATION AT PURVEYORS.

There is much secret murmuring at the King's great expenses and his desire for a subsidy from the Parliament. It is noted that there is now no war with Spain, nor in Holland, nor on the Borders, and the King has his revenues of Scotland. The people are more heavily burdened now than in Queen Elizabeth's time, for the King stays continuously in the country, and the country people are forced to furnish beasts and carts to carry the Court from place to place. The Court is larger than in former times, and the people are forced by the purveyors to supply goods at a low price. The old Queen demanded only what was necessary; the officers nowadays exact twice as much as is needed at their own value and sell the remainder at a high price.

1st November. DANGEROUS RUMOURS.

Now that the assembling of the Parliament draws near there are many rumours and daily throwing of scandalous libels in the Court and City. Some say that there is a practice of discontented Catholics at home and abroad by way of combination amongst themselves against this Parliament, for enabling them to deliver some petition to his Majesty for toleration of religion, which shall be so cunningly delivered and so strongly backed as the King shall be loath to deny their requests. Others speak of the discovery of some terrible treason, especially by a letter which the Earl of Salisbury showed the King; and to the like effect daily increasing. Others say that an obscure letter has been delivered to the Lord Mounteagle advising him not to appear at the Parliament House the first day, and that no sooner had he read it but instantly he carried it to the Earl of Salisbury.

THE FRENCH AMBASSADOR.

Monsieur Beaumont, the French Ambassador, has gone homeward and has blotted his former reputation with very mechanical tricks at parting; for having 2,000 ounces of plate given him he cavilled for 500 ounces more, as having seen a precedent of the list. This being granted, he begged two horses more by the name of the King, besides pictures great and small with jewels at his own appointment, and not a nobleman or other of his near acquaintance but he got horses, geldings or somewhat of him; and the import of sixty tun of wine of the Lord Treasurer which he sold to French merchants for £60, with divers other such petty larcenies as if he made no conscience to rob the Egyptians.

Certain books have lately been brought over from France and great search is made after them to call them in. It is said, moreover, that our Ambassador moved the French King for the suppressing the whole press and received but a slight answer. It containeth a history of some eight years since written by one Dampmartin. There is another book written in Spanish, much in disgrace of the Admiral, and the carriage of our countrymen there.

3rd November. THE ADVANCEMENT OF LEARNING.

Sir Francis Bacon's book, *Of the proficiency and advancement*

of Learning human and divine, is now come out, being dedicated
to the King. This work is in two parts, in the first of which he
defends learning against its detractors, and those who bring it into
disrepute, amongst whom are the learned men themselves. Noteth that the first distemper of learning is when men study words
and not matter. Justifieth it as of all pleasures that which lasteth
longest and breeds no satiety. In the second book considereth
and ordereth the branches of human learning, making as it were
a small globe of the intellectual world wherein is shown those
parts which are well studied and those which are neglected.
Urgeth that the Readers in the Universities shall be of the most
able and sufficient men which cannot be unless their endowment
be answerable.

5th November (Tuesday). A MOST HORRIBLE CONSPIRACY
    DISCOVERED.

Very early this morning a most horrible conspiracy of the
Papists against the King and the whole realm was discovered,
being no less than to destroy the Parliament House and all
therein by gunpowder this day.

About ten days since, the Lord Mounteagle (son and heir to
the Lord Morley), being in his lodging in the Strand ready to go
to supper about 7 of the clock, one of his footmen was met in the
street by an unknown man who delivered him a letter, charging
him to put it straightway into his lord's hands. The Lord
Mounteagle, perceiving it to be in an unknown and somewhat
unlegible hand, called one of his men to help him to read it, the
tenor whereof was that my Lord should devise some excuse to
shift off his attendance at this Parliament, 'for,' said this unknown writer, 'God and men have concurred to punish the
wickedness of this time; and think not slightly of this advertisement, but retire yourself into your country, where you may
expect the event in safety; for though there be no appearance of
any stir, yet I say, they shall receive a terrible blow this Parliament, and yet they shall not see who hurts them. This counsel
is not to be contemned, because it may do you good, and can
do you no harm; for the danger is past so soon as you have burnt
the letter.'

Hereupon my Lord was greatly perplexed what construction

to make thereof, whether it was a matter of great consequence, or some foolish pasquil (such as at this time abound), or some device of his enemies. Nevertheless, notwithstanding the darkness of the night, he went straightway to the Court at Whitehall and delivered the letter to the Earl of Salisbury, who gave him condign thanks and encouragement. So the Earl of Salisbury showed the letter to the Lord Chamberlain, and to the Lord Admiral, and the Earls of Worcester and Northampton, who all agreed to acquaint the King withal when he should return from Royston, which was on Friday last.

Therefore the Earl of Salisbury alone in the Privy Gallery acquainted the King with all their proceeding. The King having read the letter once, paused awhile and read it again, and said he thought it was not to be contemned, for the style seemed to be more quick and pithy than is usual in pasquils and libels or superfluities of idle brains. The Earl, perceiving the King to apprehend it deeplier than he had expected, replied that he thought by one sentence in it, it should be written by a fool or a madman, viz., 'for the danger is past so soon as the letter is burnt,' for then the warning was of small avail. But the King, considering the former sentence in the letter viz., 'they shall receive a terrible blow in this Parliament and yet shall not know who hurts them,' joining it to the other sentence, conjectured that the danger should be some sudden danger by blowing up with powder, for it was not possible for them to endanger the King and State either by insurrection, invasion, rebellion or any other of like nature that might be suddenly attempted in this time of Parliament. The King was not in any way amazed, but wished that a very secret and exact search should be made in the Parliament House and all rooms and lodgings adjoining.

So the Earl of Salisbury went back to the Lords and told them all that had passed between the King and himself. The next day (which was Saturday) the Earl renewed the matter with the King, the Lord Chamberlain being then present, and it was determined that the Lord Chamberlain (according to the virtue of his office) should view the Parliament House and all other places adjoining, and should do it with such coverture as would prevent idle rumours, or giving of any suspicion to the workers of this mischievous mystery.

Yesterday therefore in the afternoon the Lord Chamberlain, accompanied with the Lord Mounteagle, entering the cellar under the upper House, found great store of faggots, billets and coals, which he learnt were Master Thomas Percy's, who is kinsman to my Lord of Northumberland. As the Lord Chamberlain looked about him, with a seeming careless survey of things, he espied a fellow standing in a corner who said that he was Percy's man and keeper of the house for him. So the Lord Chamberlain went back to the King, whom he met in the Gallery accompanied with the Lord Treasurer, the Lord Admiral and the Earls of Worcester and Salisbury, to whom he made report, adding further that when the Lord Mounteagle heard the fellow (whose name is John Johnson) declare himself to be Mr. Thomas Percy's man, remembering Percy's backwardness in religion and his friendship to himself, he thought that he was a very desperate fellow and would have the chamber very narrowly searched.

The King instantly agreed to search thoroughly. But then arose a question among them upon what pretence they should make search, lest, finding nothing worthy their labours, a general scandal might grow upon King and State in being too credulous of the evaporation of idle brains, and also for laying an imputation upon the Earl of Northumberland, because this Percy is very inward with him, and by his means became the King's servant. Hereupon it is given out that special search was to be made for certain robes and other furniture stolen out of the Wardrobe, and Sir Thomas Knivett was selected for the business, accompanied with a small number specially fit for that employment.

At midnight therefore Sir Thomas went about the search, and coming before the entry to Percy's house, he perceived the pretended servant standing without the door, booted and spurred, whom he apprehended and was very desirous to search; but this Johnson, being wondrously unwilling to be searched, violently gripped one Mr. Doubleday by his fingers of the left hand, who would have drawn his dagger, but bethought himself and did not; and in the heat he struck up the fellow's heels, fell upon him and searched him, and in his pocket found his garters, wherewith they bound him, together with some touchwood, a tinder box and a match. Within the house, when they had removed some billets and coals, they found a small barrel of powder, and afterwards many others, great and small, to the number of thirty-six, with other instruments fit for the purpose.

When Johnson saw his treasons discovered, he instantly confessed his own guiltiness, saying that if he had been within the house when they first laid hands upon him, he would have blown up them, himself and all.

So Sir Thomas Knivett comes to the Lord Chamberlain and the Earl of Salisbury, who forthwith draw together all the rest of Council which lay within the Court, and this morning about 4 of the clock they come to the King's bedchamber, where the Lord Chamberlain, in a confused haste, tells the King that all is discovered, and the traitor taken. Immediately upon this all the Council that lay abroad were summoned to Court, where they sit in council and examine the fellow, who will acknowledge no other name but John Johnson, flatly denying to know any other complotters in this treason, justifying the deed, and denying the King to be his liege Lord or God's anointed. He is quick and careless in his answers unto all objections, fleering and scoffing all that mislike him, repenting only that the deed was not done.

Hereupon order is given to the Lord Mayor of London, and the City of Westminster to set a civil watch at the gates; and a proclamation is set forth for the apprehending of Thomas Percy.

It is not as yet known how far this treason may extend, though it is well perceived to be practised and commenced by some discontented papists; and everywhere there is a general jealousy. The common people mutter and imagine many things, and the nobles know not whom to clear or whom to suspect. The King hath deferred his coming to Parliament till Saturday next.

This night there were as many bonfires in and about London as the streets could permit, the people praising God for His mercy, and wishing that the day may for ever be held festival. The Spanish Ambassador made bonfires and threw money amongst the people; and the like gladness is shown by the Ambassador of the Archduke, and by those of the French and Dutch Churches.

6th November. THE POWDER PLOT.

This Thomas Percy hath been a servant of the Earl of Northumberland, and was put in great trust by him concerning his northern business, and is lately made by him a Pensioner. Early on the Monday morning the Earl of Worcester was sent to Essex House to signify the matter to the Earl of Northumberland, whom he found asleep in his bed, and who hath done since his best endeavour for his apprehension. This Percy, my Lord of Northumberland confesseth, had £4,000 of his in his hands.

When Johnson was brought to the King's presence, the King asked him how he could conspire so hideous a treason against his children and so many innocent souls which never offended him. He answered that it was true; but a dangerous disease required a desperate remedy. He told some of the Scots that his intent was to have blown them back to Scotland.

7th November. THE EARL OF NORTHUMBERLAND.

The Earl of Northumberland is committed to the charge of the Archbishop. There hath been some insurrection in Warwickshire, begun the very same day that the plot should have been executed. The chiefest names are such as were swaggerers in Essex's action, as Catesby, and some say Tresham, the two Wrights, and one of the Winters. If the practice had taken effect the King of Spain's Ambassador and the Archduke's had been blown up too. Some say that Northumberland received the like letter that Mounteagle did, but concealed it. Captain Whitlock is committed to the Tower. Sir Walter Ralegh is much suspected to be privy to this action, for Whitlock has had private conference lately with him. The prisoner's right name is now held not to be Johnson but Faux.

9th November. THE KING PROROGUES THE PARLIAMENT.

In the Lower House Sir Edward Hext moved that the Speaker should make manifest the thankfulness of the House to God for the King's safe deliverance, and that they would be ready, every one of them, with the uttermost drop of their blood.

Later the King himself came to the Parliament, and being sat in his seat of state, the Lord Chancellor began his speech with a brief rehearsal of that which passed between the Commissioners of England and Scotland, and thereupon presented the King and the House some of the tripartite writings, which was then delivered to the Clerk of the Parliament to be kept in his custody. This done, he went on to speak of the horrible treason.

Then the King himself began to speak, declaring that though it was not usual for any of his predecessors to repair to any Session of the House held by prorogation, yet he had resolved to come to the Parliament for the receiving of his writing.

After which, he spoke much of this late intended treason, saying, 'In this great and horrible attempt, whereof the like was never either heard or read I observe three wonderful, or rather miraculous events.

'First in the cruelty of the plot itself, wherein cannot be admired enough the horrible and fearful cruelty of their device, which was not only for the destruction of my Person, nor of my wife and posterity only, but of the whole body of the State in general; wherein should neither have been spared, or distinction made of young or old, of great nor small, of man nor of woman. The whole nobility, the whole reverend clergy, bishops and most part of my good preachers; and if any in this society were favourers of their profession, they should all have gone one way. The whole judges of the land, with the most of the lawyers and the whole clerks; and as the wretch himself that is in the Tower doth confess, it was purposely devised by them, and concluded to be done in this House; that where the cruel laws (as they say) were made against their religion, both place and persons should all be destroyed and blown up at once.'

Further, the King said that the discovery of this plot was not a little wonderful, for he was himself so little suspicious that he was wont to contemn all advertisements or apprehensions of practices; but yet at this time when the letter was shown him, wherein a general obscure advertisement was given of some dangerous blow at this time, he did upon the instant interpret some dark phrases to be meant by this horrible form of blowing up all by powder. Wherefore they had all cause to thank and magnify God for this his merciful delivery.

Then, when he had spoken somewhat of the Union, he proceeded to declare the nature of the High Court of Parliament, which is nothing else but the King's great Council, which the King doth assemble either upon occasion of interpreting, or abrogating old law, or making of new, according as ill manners shall deserve, or for the public punishment of notorious evil doers, or the praise and reward of the virtuous and well deservers.

'As for the thing itself,' saith the King, 'it is composed of a Head and a Body: the Head is the King, the Body are the members of the Parliament. This Body again is subdivided into two parts: the Upper and Lower House: the Upper compounded partly of Nobility, temporal men, who are heritable councillors to the High Court of Parliament by the honour of their creation and lands; and partly of Bishops, spiritual men, who are likewise by virtue of their place and dignity councillors, life renters, or *ad vitam* of this Court. The other House is composed of knights for the shire; and gentry, and burgesses for the towns. But because the number would be infinite for all the gentlemen and burgesses to be present at every Parliament, therefore a certain number is selected and chosen out of that great body, serving only for that Parliament, where their persons are the representation of that body.

'Now the matters whereof they are to treat ought therefore to be general, and rather of such matters as cannot well be performed without the assembling of that great Body, and no more of these generals neither than necessity shall require; for as *in corruptissima republica sunt plurimæ leges*, so doth the life and strength of the Law consist not in heaping up infinite and confused numbers of laws, but in the right interpretation and good execution of good and wholesome laws. If this be so, then neither is this a place on the one side for every rash and harebrain fellow to propone new laws of his own invention; nay, rather I could wish these busy heads to remember that law of the Lacedemonians, that whosoever came to propone a new law to the people, behoved publicly to present himself with a rope about his neck, that in case the law were not allowed, he should be hanged therewith. So wary should men be of proponing novelties, but most of all not to propone any bitter or seditious laws, which can produce nothing but grudges and discontents between the Prince and his people.'

Then he went on to say that men should not propone laws for their own private benefit, not make show of their eloquence with long-studied and eloquent orations but remember that they were present as sworn councillors to their King, to give their best advice for the furtherance of his service, and the flourishing weal of his estate. Moreover they should be ashamed to make show of the quickness of their wits here, either in taunting, scoffing or detracting the Prince or State in any point, or yet in breaking jests upon their fellows, for which the ordinaries and alehouses are fitter places than this honourable and High Court of Parliament.

And so, after the Lord Chancellor had spoken concerning the proroguing of the Parliament, the King declared that the next session shall meet upon the one-and-twentieth day of January next.

GUNPOWDER PLOT.

Curious folks observe that this deliverance happened to the King the 5th of November answerable to the 5th of August, both Tuesdays, and this plot to be executed by Johnson as that at Johnstown.

THE ARCHPRIEST'S LETTER TO CATHOLICS.

George Blackwell, the Archpriest, has sent out a letter to all Catholics protesting that this plot is against the prescript of a general Council and against the sentence of the best Catholic writers of this age; for their divines say that it is not lawful for private subjects by private authority to take arms against their lawful king, albeit he become a tyrant; and that without most grievous offence of God and holy Church, private violent attempts cannot be thought of, much less aided and maintained by Catholics. For his own part, if any notice had been given him, he would have been most forward by all possible means to have stayed and suppressed the attempt.

NEWS FROM IRELAND.

Sir Arthur Chichester, the Lord Deputy, complaineth that divers young gentlemen of the Pale and borders do now run to the wars, so that the King's subjects serve foreign States and Princes, one against another in bands and companies, a course which the Switzers have found base and dangerous. Most of them serve with the Archduke, and these will be, as much as in them lies, firebrands for a new rebellion in Ireland, to which they are much affected, though at present lacking the means.

FAWKES' SULLENNESS.

Fawkes (or Johnson) for three days hath remained in a most stubborn and perverse humour, being resolved to declare nothing which shall touch other than himself. But last night Sir William Waad persuaded him to set down a clear narration of his wicked plots from the first entering in, with the discourses and projects which were thought on amongst them; which he promised to do, and craved the night to bethink him the better. But this morning he had changed his mind and still continued obstinate; until the coming of the Lords Commissioners when he told all; but still conceals the names of all, save Percy; though he remains so far obdurate that he will not set his name to the examination.

10th November. THE SERMON AT PAUL'S CROSS.

This Sunday the sermon at Paul's Cross was preached by Dr. William Barlow, Lord Bishop of Rochester, upon Psalm xviii, ver. 51, 'Great deliverances giveth he unto his King and showeth mercy to his annointed David and to his seed for ever,' wherein he spake much of the plot, calling it a cruel execution, an inhuman cruelty, a brutish immanity, a devilish brutishness and an hyperbolical, yea, an hyperbolical devilishness. He read moreover the parties' confessions, concluding with hearty prayer to Almighty God for the continuance of our good King, our State and our Religion.

THE PLOTTERS TAKEN OR SLAIN.

News is come out of the country that most of the plotters are taken or slain. As soon as they learned from Fawkes of the search made by the Lord Chamberlain, two of them, by name Catesby and John Wright, fled, but Percy and Christopher Wright remained in London until they heard of the arrest of Fawkes. Two others, named Rookwood and Keyes, who were not known in London, stayed until the next morning; but perceiving everywhere the amazement and terror in the countenances of all whom they met, and the guards in the streets who allowed no one to pass, they also fled away. Now it had been agreed that they should all meet together again at a place of rendezvous, which was at Dunchurch where Sir Everard Digby had gathered together a company of Catholic gentlemen, who did not indeed know of the plot but only that some notable blow was to be struck in London for the Catholic religion. But when Catesby and the others who had come from London appeared, they perceived that the plot had miscarried and most of them departed home again, so that at last but few remained save those who were sworn complices and believed that by this time their names would be known to the Council through the discoveries of Fawkes.

So that night they departed from Dunchurch and on the next day (which was Thursday) they came to the Lord Windsor's house at Whewell, whence they took a large store of arms and armour, and the same night came to a house at Holbeach near Stourbridge. And here, being much wearied and knowing that Sir Richard Walsh, the Sheriff of Worcestershire, with a great company of gentlemen and their servants was coming, they resolved to make a stand, and so began to prepare the house for defence. It happened by reason of the rain that some of the powder which they had taken from the Lord Windsor's house was wetted. So Catesby and some of the others set about drying it upon a platter over a fire when a coal fell among it, and it exploded with such violence that some of the party were severely burned. This accident put them in amaze, for it seemed as a judgment from God who would destroy them by the same means with which they had sought to destroy others.

About noon yesterday Sir Richard Walsh and his company arrived at Holbeach, and having surrounded the house, he summoned them to surrender themselves; and when they refused he gave order that part of the house should be set on fire and the assault made on the gate of the courtyard. So the Sheriff's men began to discharge their pieces at the rebels, and soon Thomas Winter was struck in the arm with a shot from a cross-bow, and the two Wrights were both mortally wounded. Catesby and Percy resolved to die fighting and stood back to back waiting for their enemies, but they were both shot through the body by two bullets discharged from one musket. Catesby made his way into the house, and taking hold of an image of the Virgin there died. Percy was taken, but is since dead of his wound. The others are also taken, to the number of ten, and the rest of the rebellious assembly so dispersed that they are likely to be speedily apprehended.

11*th November*. THE EARL OF NORTHUMBERLAND.

The Earl of Northumberland, who is now under restraint at the house of the Archbishop in Croydon, being in question for some matter concerning Thomas Percy his Steward, protesteth that though Percy saw him at Sion House upon the Monday before the plot yet it was but by chance, and that Percy had cheated him of his Northern rents by some lying tale, five horse-loads of money, £3,000 and more.

12*th November*. MR. FRANCIS TRESHAM ARRESTED.

Mr. Francis Tresham, who is among those said to be privy to the plot, was this day arrested and taken before the Council to be examined. He confesseth that he had seen and conversed with Catesby and Wright a few days before the discovery of the plot, but will not answer more clearly.

13*th November*. A CASE OF ENCLOSURES.

In the Star Chamber five men and five women were fined for riot for diverting the ditch and paling of a common in the night. It was declared in defence that the women had acted without the privity of their husbands; and it was agreed by the Court that it is not good to make enclosures of commons, for this causes great offence, though it is warranted by law. Further it is ruled that if a woman offend in trespass, riot, or otherwise and an action is brought against her and her husband, the husband is answerable notwithstanding the action was without his privity.

16*th November*. THE PORTS REOPENED.

Now that the plot is thoroughly discovered, the ports and havens may now be opened, and carriers from the ambassadors and merchants, and any honest known merchant or his factor allowed to trade freely; but all others who repair to any port in the quality of a soldier or traveller shall be stopped unless they can show a passport from the Council.

20*th November*. A DISCOURSE OF BODIES NATURAL AND POLITIC.

One Mr. Edward Forset hath written *A comparative discourse of the bodies natural and politic*, wherein out of the principles of nature is set forth the true form of a Commonweal, with the duties of subjects, and the right of the sovereign: together with many good points of political learning. Noteth that the commonweal with all her parts, orders, qualities, and requisites whatsoever, is (for better apprehension) set forth by sundry fit resemblances, as by the architecture of an house, by the swarming and cohabiting of bees in an hive, by a ship floating on the sea, and such-like; but by none more properly than by the body of man, being the lesser world, even the diminutive and model of that wide extending universal.

21st November. THE LADY RICH DIVORCED.

My Lord Rich and his Lady (who have been separated these many years) were divorced before the High Commissioners, when my Lord of Canterbury chid Lord Rich very much, and gave my Lady great commendations, telling what an honourable house she was of, and how hardly my Lord hath used her, and in the end bade my Lord go amongst his Puritans.

22nd November. A SORCERER SENTENCED.

One Whitehead was to-day charged before the Star Chamber with forging letters of the Earl of Salisbury and Sir John Fortescue, commanding the justices of Essex to remove Sir Thomas Gardener from the bench, which was a thing no Councillor of State could do. Further, it was shown that he had travelled in Germany for learning of the magical art, and received lessons in conjuration that he should baptize a dog, and take the skin of a Christian body and make him a girdle, and with these he should command all spirits, and rolls, and books. Moreover in his examination he did confess that he could turn all the rushes in a room into spirits and serpents. For these offences the Court resolved that they would impose the greatest punishment they could, except death; so they sentenced him to stand in two several places upon the pillory and lose both his ears, and have perpetual imprisonment.

25th November. A RIOT IN SOUTHWARK.

This night there was a notable outrage in Southwark committed by certain insolent priests which put the whole town into an uproar. The constable took three of them who behaved very insolently. When they were searched for letters, one of them answered, 'If thou hadst searched me three weeks since, thou mightest have found a hundred about me.'

27th November. NOBLEMEN SENT TO THE TOWER.

My Lord of Northumberland is committed to the Tower, as
also are the Viscount Montagu, Lord Mordaunt and Lord
Stourton. These three last are suspected because they were
Catholics and were absent from the Parliament, and besides
known friends of the principal conspirators. As for my Lord
of Northumberland, though not intending to be absent, yet
there are certain matters presumed against him, for Percy was his
Steward and very inward with him, and came out of the north
three days before the time, and resorted to the Earl not twenty
hours before his villainy should have been acted; and moreover
the Earl had declared often to the King that the Catholics had
offered themselves to depend upon him in all their courses so
far as his Majesty's pleasure was concerned. The truth as yet is
not known but it is thought not improbably that Percy may
have given him some general warning. Yet he is unfortunate
in that Catesby and Percy being dead the proof of his innocency
or guiltiness must depend upon circumstances of other persons
and times.

28th November. THE ARCHPRIEST'S SECOND LETTER TO THE
    CATHOLICS.

The Archpriest Blackwell has written a second letter to all
priests and Catholics within the Realm declaring that no violent
attempt against the person of our Sovereign can be other than
a most grievous and heinous offence to God, scandalous to the
world, utterly unlawful of itself, and against God's express
commandments. Further he heartily entreats all Catholic persons living under obedience of his authority upon the utter pain
that can or may ensue thereby that none of them dare or do
presume to attempt any practice against the King, the Prince,
councillors or officers of State.

5th December. THE PILGRIMAGE OF MAN.

A little book called *The Pilgrimage of Man*, wandering in a
wilderness of woe, wherein are briefly set forth the miseries of
man in his birth, youth, age and death, and the many abuses of
this age. Denounceth the wickedness of many mothers here in
England that learn their daughters to dance, to use rhetoric
terms, to haunt companies, to scoff and flout, to paint and colour

their faces, to deck their fingers with rings, and their necks with jewels, as though they were jewel sellers pretending to keep a shop. Of marriage noteth that the Athenians ordained certain magistrates whom they called Reconcilers of Marriage, whose office was to set agreement between husband and wife.

The Romish Doctrine in the Case of Conspiracy and Rebellion.

There is printing a little book called *An exact discovery of Romish doctrine in the case of conspiracy and rebellion*, collected (not without direction) out of the express dogmatical principles of popish priests and doctors; wherein it appeareth that neighbours, if heretics, may lawfully be spoiled of their goods by force, though it be better to be taken from them by authority; that parishioners may lawfully defraud Protestant ministers of their tithes; that all keepers of forts are freed from their oaths of subjection; that wives are not bound to render due benevolence unto their husbands if heretics; that the commonwealth hath authority to choose a King and to limit him laws at pleasure; that the right of Kings Christian must depend rather upon their religion than upon order of succession; with many like pregnant observations, directly proving Romish schools to be seminaries of rebellions in all Protestants' government.

9th December. 'The Double PP.'

There is a book of riddling rhymes against the Papists called *The Double PP*: a Papist in arms, bearing ten several shields, encountered by the Protestant at ten several weapons; a Jesuit marching before them.

12th December. My Lord of Northumberland.

The Earl of Northumberland's business stands where it did, for he will answer no questions upon examination, demanding that if there be any charges against him a commission of his peers shall be appointed to try them. To this the Earl of Salisbury replied that he ought not to refuse that which others had done, naming my Lord of Essex who always answered what was asked of him. To which my Lord of Northumberland answered that Essex was a brave gentleman but in the latter part of his life not in his right mind, which brought him to his death. Last

Sunday the Countess went to the King with a petition praying not for grace but for justice; that her Lord might have speedy trial; and that the King would not allow the ill will of a certain great one to ruin the Earl in fame, fortune and life. The King treated her gently; but those in Court reminded themselves that never a nobleman of his greatness committed to the Tower on such a charge came out alive.

15th December. RELIGION IN IRELAND.

The Lord Deputy goes about to repress popery in Ireland, summoning those by whose example the rest of the people are most led to come to church upon pain of the King's displeasure and further penalties; by which course it is hoped either to bring them to what is desired or by law to have good grounds to lay sound fines upon them, which may be employed upon the ruined and decayed churches, bridges and such good works. But the chiefest cause that the people are misled by the doctrine of Rome and are now so hard to be reconciled is the sluggish and blockish security and ignorance of the unworthy Bishops.

In Ireland there are ten Archbishops and under them should be twenty Bishops at least. The dowry of the Church by the book of first-fruits is very great, but the churchmen for the most part are mere idols and ciphers, and such as cannot even read if they should stand in need of the benefit of their clergy; yet most of them, though many be but serving-men and some horseboys, have two or three benefices apiece, for the Court of Faculties doth dispense with all manner of non-residence and pluralities. And yet for all their pluralities they are most of them beggars, for the patron taketh the greater part of their living by plain contract before their institution; it is even said that the Agent of the Pope hath £40 or £50 a year of the profits of a parsonage within the Pale. For an example of pluralities the Archbishop of Cashell is worthy to be remembered, for he hath in his hands four bishoprics, and seventy-seven spiritual livings besides.

To make a beginning with those that will not obey the proclamation, of late the Lord Deputy caused some sixteen principal personages in the Pale, that had refused to obey, alleging that the proclamation was against their consciences, to be censured by the Irish Star Chamber and fined £100 or £50 apiece, and to be imprisoned and put from all offices until they shall conform themselves and take the Oath of Supremacy.

Nevertheless, certain noblemen and gentlemen within the Pale protest against the proclamation and propose a petition to the Privy Council; in anticipation whereof the Lord Deputy prays the Lords of the Council that neither the petition nor the agent shall receive any favour; for if the Lords of the Council would hold that course which was held in the Queen's time that no suitor from Ireland should be regarded, but rather be punished, if he come without a certificate or letters of recommendation, they will be less troubled with them.

18th December. BODIN'S COMMONWEALTH.

The six books of a Commonweal written by Jean Bodin, a famous lawyer and a man of great experience in matters of State, have now been done into English, out of the French and Latin copies, by Mr. Richard Knolles, wherein are considered all sorts of commonweals in general, their rising and declining and their several manners of government. This book when first published in France was seven times printed in three years' space.

19th December. A PETITION FROM THE RECUSANTS IN THE PALE.

The Viscount Gormanston and others within the Irish Pale have made a petition against the late proclamation that Jesuits should be banished from the Pale, protesting that they could never be alienated in their loyalty to his Majesty by the inducements of priests, but they find themselves not a little grieved both at the imputation and at the severity of the proclamation against themselves and the priests for mere matter of religion and conscience. This petition was signed by more than 220 of the principal persons of those parts. When it was presented to the Lord Deputy, he caused the Viscount Gormanston, Sir Patrick Barnewell, and one Flashbury, a lawyer, to be committed to the Constable of Dublin Castle. The petition has now been sent to the Privy Council, with the complaint of the Viscount Gormanston that very harsh measures are taken with the recusants beyond the law. Some in authority in Ireland are of opinion that though the entry be difficult, yet there will be good success in this work of reformation, if it be constantly pursued. If this one corporation of Dublin be reformed, the rest will follow; for the multitude is ever made conformable by edicts and proclamations. So it happened in King Edward the Sixth's days, when more than half the Kingdom of England were Papists; and again in the time of Queen Mary when more than half the Kingdom were Protestants; and again in Queen Elizabeth's time, when they were turned Papist again.

21st December. THE LORD MAYOR AND THE TOWER.

Notwithstanding a command given a fortnight ago not to renew any quarrels with the Lieutenant of the Tower, last night the Lord Mayor compassed the greater part of the Tower with the sword carried before him, accompanied with the sheriffs, and a rabble of sergeants, and took possession of the postern, and so came back again in great bravery, bidding the people bear witness of his triumph. At this the Lieutenant complains very bitterly to the Council that these are intolerable courses, and especially at this unseasonable time.

23rd December. A POWDER PLOTTER DEAD.

Francis Tresham who was sent to the Tower after his arrest died very early this morning, with very great pain, for though his spirits were much spent and his body dead, he lay about two hours in departing. Not long before his death he caused a paper to be written wherein he declared upon his salvation that his former confession that Garnet was privy to the sending of Thomas Winter was false, and further that he had not seen Garnet for sixteen years, nor never had letter nor message from him. His head has been cut off that it may be set upon London Bridge when the others are executed.

27th December. MY LORD OF DEVONSHIRE'S ILL-ADVISED
       MARRIAGE.

Yesterday was the Earl of Devonshire married to the Lady Penelope Rich by his chaplain, Master William Laud, which occasions great scandal whether it be a lawful marriage, by the laws ecclesiastical or civil, she being a divorced person and her husband yet living. The King is greatly offended.

This love is of long standing, for when my Lord was but a younger son with small hope of advancement they pledged each

other in private but without such witness as would make their
pledge of force by law. The lady was married against her will
to the Lord Rich, but not long afterwards they conversed first in
private, and then, after he had unexpectedly succeeded to the
title of his father on his brother's death, they came together more
openly. She bore her husband several children, and after she had
separated herself from him *a thoro et mensa* she bore five children
to my Lord of Devonshire. My Lord was in great perplexity
about his marriage, and consulted many. He wrote a tractate on
the matter which he showed to his chaplain, but his friends
persuaded him to it, principally that he might legitimate his
children.

OTHER BOOKS PRINTED IN THE YEAR 1605

SIR THOMAS BODLEY'S LIBRARY.

Dr. Thomas James hath completed and caused to be printed a catalogue of the books of the public library which Sir Thomas Bodley of late set up in the University of Oxford, wherein the books are disposed alphabetically according to the four faculties, to which is added an index of the authors.

THE HONOUR OF VALOUR.

A poem by Master Breton called *The Honour of Valour* dedicated to the Earl of Devonshire. Verses from the same:

> The chamber music that enchants the ear,
> Gives sudden silence to the trumpet's sound;
> And crying Cupid doth but willow wear,
> While worthy Mars is with the laurel crowned;
> The man of war the merchant runs aground,
>   And resolution cannot quench his fire,
>   Till he hath either death or his desire.
>
> Ease hath no part in passion's happiness,
> Nor safety lulls his watchful eye asleep,
> And working spirit loves no idleness,
> Which have the key of honour's care to keep;
> The noble mind can•never learn to creep;
>   No princely honour is the royal prize,
>   For which true valour either lives or dies.

THE LONDON PRODIGAL.

A play called *The London Prodigal*, showing how one young Mr. Flowerdale, believing his father to be dead becomes prodigal, squanders his inheritance and deserts his wife, but at the end is brought to repentance by her loyalty and the kindness of his father and his former friends. This play was played by the King's men and written by William Shakespeare.

NEWS FROM HELL.

A book by Dekker called *News from Hell*, brought from the Devil's carrier, in the form of a sequel to that book of *Piers Penniless, His Supplication to the Devil* which Nashe wrote in 1592, whom he praiseth as one 'into whose soul (if ever there were a Pythagorean Metempsychosis) the raptures of that fiery and inconfinable Italian spirit were bounteously and boundlessly infused, thou sometimes secretary to Piers Penniless, and Master of his Requests, ingenious, ingenuous, fluent, facetious T. Nashe, from whose abundant pen honey flowed to thy friends and mortal aconite to thy enemies.' Herein is told how the post fetched the Devil's answer to Piers' Supplication, and what and whom he saw in hell.

THE OPINIONS OF THE PURITANS.

A little book privily printed entitled *English Puritanism*, containing the main opinions of the rigidest sort of those that are called Puritans in England; set out in six chapters concerning the worship of God in general; the Church; the ministers of the Word; the elders; the censures of the Church; the civil magistrate. They hold *imprimis* that the Word of God contained in the writings of the Prophets and Apostles is of absolute perfection, given by Christ the Head of the Church to be unto the same the sole canon and rule of all masters of Religion and the worship and service of God whatsoever; that all ecclesiastical actions invented and devised by man are utterly to be excluded, and that to add mystical rites and ceremonies in the worship of God is a fearful sin. They would have no church or congregation subjected to any superior ecclesiastical jurisdiction, allowing every church to chose their own spiritual and ecclesiastical officers, for, say they, it is a greater wrong to have any such forced upon them against their wills than if they should force upon men wives, or upon women husbands. They hold that their churches are in no way repugnant to any civil state whatsoever, whether monarchical, aristocratical or democratical. As for ministers, the people of God should have reason rather to doubt of any office than of the peculiar office or jurisdiction of Primates metropolitan, Archbishops and prelates of the world. Concerning the elders, they would as soon allow tradesmen and artificers, that are able to maintain themselves, to be overseers of the Church as that persons ignorant of religion and all good letters should become pastors and teachers of a congregation. Further, they hold that the spiritual keys of the Church should not be used to lock up civil rights, or to open men's treasuries, or as keys of prisons; nor should the officers of the Church proceed unto the extremest censure against any man without the free consent of the whole congregation. Finally they hold that all archbishops, bishops, deans, officials, etc., have their offices only by will and pleasure of the King; and whosoever holdeth that the King may not without sin remove these offices out of the Church and dispose of their temporalities according to his own pleasure denieth a principal part of the King's Supremacy.

TWO BOOKS ABOUT RATSEY THE HIGHWAYMAN.

Two books about Gamaliel Ratsey the highwayman, that was hanged at Bedford on 26th March last, entitled *The Life and Death of Gamaliel Ratsey,* showing how he cozened many by divers merry devices; the other called *Ratsey's Ghost,* setting forth other of his mad pranks, to which is added his Repentance, in verse.

1606

3rd January. THE DEVIL OF THE VAULT.

One J. H. hath written a poem of the late plot entitled *The Devil of the Vault, or the unmasking of murder,* beginning:

> Come thou obdurate flinty heart,
>   With mourning melt in twain:
> To hear my weeping pen howl forth,
>   Melpomen's tragic strain:
>
> So dreadful, foul, chimera-like,
>   My subject must appear:
> That Heaven amaz'd, and hell disturb'd,
>   The earth shall quake with fear.
>
> If murders, furies, fates and death,
>   Be clad with bloody weed:
> Would all concur with Night's black hours,
>   To plot some dismal deed.
>
> Let them but congregate themselves,
>   And silent stand awhile:
> To draw death's sampler from the sense,
>   And sequel of my style.

4th January. A PRESENT FROM THE KING OF SPAIN.

To-day the Spanish Ambassador delivered to the King as presents from his master six jennets of Andalusia, with saddles very richly embroidered and saddle cloths of cloth of tissue, embroidered with the arms of Spain and all other furniture suitable. They were led blindfold through the streets by grooms of the stable, bare-headed and clad in crimson velvet trimmed with gold lace. One of these jennets is snow-white, and his mane reaches to the ground.

5th January. THE MARRIAGE OF THE EARL OF ESSEX AND
MISTRESS FRANCES HOWARD.

To-day the young Earl of Essex was married to Mistress
Frances Howard, daughter to the Earl of Suffolk. The bridegroom carried himself very gravely and gracefully. He had
greater gifts given him than my Lord of Montgomery, his plate
being valued at £3,000 and his jewels, money and other gifts
at £1,000 more.

The masque was held on Sunday wherein both Inigo Jones,
Ben Jonson, and the actors did their parts with great commendation. The conceit of the masque was Hymen bringing in a
bride, and Juno's priest a bridegroom, that these two should be
sacrificed to nuptial union; and here the poet made an apostrophe
upon the Union of the two Kingdoms. But before the sacrifice
could be performed, Ben Jonson turned the globe of the Earth
standing behind the altar, and within sat eight men maskers
representing the four Humours and the four Affections, who
leaped forth to disturb the union. But amidst their fury Reason,
that sat above all, crowned with burning tapers, came down and
silenced them. About the globe of the Earth hovered a middle
region of clouds, in the centre whereof stood a grand consort of
musicians, and upon the horns sat the ladies, four at either horn
who descended upon the stage not after the stale perpendicular
fashion (like a bucket in a well) but came gently sloping down.
These eight after the sacrifice was ended represented the eight
nuptial powers of Juno. The men were clad in crimson and the
women in white; they had everyone a white plume of the richest
heron's feathers, and were very rich and glorious in jewels upon
their heads, for it seems that they hired and borrowed all the
principal jewels and sets of pearl in Court and City. The Spanish
ambassador seemed but poor to the meanest of them. They
danced all variety of dances, both severally and promiscuously,
and then the women took on the men, namely the Prince (who
danced with great perfection and settled majesty), the ambassadors and others; and the men gleaned out the Queen, the bride
and the greatest of the ladies.

6th January. THE BARRIERS AT COURT.

To-night was held the solemnity of the Barriers. There

appeared in the lower end of the hall as it were a mist made of delicate perfumes, out of which, a battle being sounded under the stage, there seemed to break forth two ladies, the one representing Truth, the other Opinion, but both attired so alike that there could be no noting any distinction. The colour of their garments was blue, their socks white. They were crowned with wreaths of palm, and carried palm boughs. Then they began to examine each other with question and answer, which turned to a debate about marriage, Opinion urging virginity, and Truth wedlock. So they both came down from the hall, where at the lower end, a march being sounded with drums and fifes, the Earl of Nottingham, who was Lord High Constable for the night, and the Earl of Worcester, Earl Marshal, led in sixteen knights armed with pikes and swords, their plumes and colours carnation and white; they marched by, making an honour to the State as they passed, and were ranked on one side of the hall; and after these sixteen others, accoutred in like manner, only that their colours were watchet and white, passed up and were placed on the opposite side. Then the bar was set up, and the champions on both sides fought at the barriers, first single, after three to three. The barriers being ended, on a sudden a striking light seemed to fill the hall, and an Angel or Messenger of Glory appeared. The Duke of Lennox led those on the side of Truth, and the Earl of Sussex those of Opinion; Jonson devised the entertainment and wrote the words to it.

10th January. TWO PLOTTERS TAKEN.

Two more of the plotters in the Powder Treason have now been taken, who have remained lurking in the country since the discovery of the plot, which are Robert Winter and Stephen Littleton. These two escaped from Holbeach before the coming of the Sheriff and his men, and for two months' space went disguised from farm to farm, being informed by Master Humphrey Littleton of the searches made for them. They came at last, on New Year's Day, to the house of one Perkes in Hagley who brought them to a barley mow in his barn, where he sent them food and drink by his man and his maid. Now this Perkes had been warrener to Mrs. Littleton but dismissed from her service for some unbecoming usage; he was wont with a companion of his called Poynter, a lusty youth, to steal Mrs. Littleton's conies. These two went forth after their manner to steal conies upon the 3rd of this month and being both much tippled with drink and venturing home somewhat late, Poynter would have lodged in Perkes' house; but Perkes was unwilling, and Poynter, being thus left abroad in the open field and the weather wet and cold, bethought himself of Perkes' barn. In the dead time of the night therefore he entered the barn, and climbing up upon the mow fell down into the hole where Winter and Littleton lay hid, to the terror and amazement of all three of them.

Now it happened this Poynter had a wound in his leg which with their rough handling of him and his struggling to get away began to grieve him very sore; yet they felt it no policy to let him go lest he should tell tales abroad. So for four days Poynter remained in the barn. In the meantime he pretended great pain of his leg and besought the man and the maid who brought the victuals to get him a salve. They brought him salves, and he getting up upon the top of the mow began to dress his leg, creeping more and more towards the light, dissembling he could not see how to apply his salves to the sore. At last he slipped down quite off the mow and so got out of the barn before they could lay hold of him.

When Master Humphrey Littleton heard that Poynter had so escaped, doubtless with an intent to betray Winter and Littleton, about eleven of the clock at night he conveyed them into Hagley House, not making any of the servants of his counsel save one John Fynes of Fynwood, who was the cook. Master Littleton bade the cook prepare food for them, which he did very speedily, but they could not obtain any drink, for the butler was in bed and calling so late to him for the key might breed suspicion. Whereupon the cook said that his mother sold drink in the town and he would step forth thither and fetch some. As soon as he was come to his mother, this seeming honest cook told her in secrecy that Mr. Robert Winter and Mr. Stephen Littleton, the traitors that were sought for by the King's proclamation, were at that instant in Hagley House; and therefore he prayed his mother in the morning to raise the town to take them. Then the cook went back with the drink to Hagley House.

In the morning the cook told Master Hazlewood, the steward, of the traitors being in the house, and how his mother was to raise the town. In the meantime Poynter also had raised a great number to make search in the barn. Soon the officers of the town came to Hagley House, when they demanded of Master Humphrey Littleton for such men as he had then with him in the house. Master Littleton stoutly made denial of them and sought to outface them with his power and presence. But the butler betrayed him, and soon afterwards the two traitors were apprehended in the stable yard. They have now been sent up to London and are lodged in the Tower with their fellows.

18th January. THE ESCAPE OF GREENWAY.

Greenway the Jesuit was of late seen about London streets. He was standing in a crowd that were gathered reading the proclamation for his own arrest, which was set up at the corner of a street, when a certain man, noting that his person greatly resembled the description of him in the proclamation, took him by the arm purposing him to lead him before the Council. Greenway assured him that he was not the man and suffered himself to be led quietly away until they came to a remote and unfrequented street, where, being a powerful man, he suddenly seized upon his captor and struggling with him broke loose and is fled away.

21st January. THE PARLIAMENT CONTINUED.

The Parliament met again to-day after the proroguing. In the Commons House Sir George Moore made a motion out of a sense of the late conspiracy that the House should enter into consideration what course may be fittest to settle the safety of the King and prevent the danger of papistical practices. After much debate a committee was appointed to consider of timely and severe proceedings against Jesuits, seminaries and all other popish agents.

23rd January. A BILL FOR A THANKSGIVING.

A Bill was read and committed for a public Thanksgiving to Almighty God every year on the 5th day of November.

THE SEARCH FOR THE JESUITS.

Master Humphrey Littleton, that harboured the plotters Robert Winter and Stephen Littleton, being condemned to death at Worcester for that fact, and thinking to save his own life hath declared to the Sheriff that some of the Jesuits are harboured at Hendlip, the house of one Master Abington, who is married to a sister of the Lord Mounteagle. Wherefore Sir Henry Bromley who is a magistrate in those parts is sent by the Council to make a narrow search of the house by drawing down the wainscot, measuring of rooms, probing with gimlets and the like wherever there seem to be likely places of hovering.

24th January. EXTRAORDINARY PUNISHMENTS PROPOSED.

In the Lower House to-day divers members proposed that extraordinary measures should be taken with the conspirators. Sir Thomas Holcroft would have them tried in the House. Sir Robert Wingfield moved for some extraordinary punishment for the miners, but not to make a petition to the King for he is so compounded of mercy and piety that he will deny it.

THE COUNCIL'S ADVICE TO THE LORD DEPUTY.

The Council have written to Sir Arthur Chichester, the Lord Deputy of Ireland, advising a temperate course between two extremes, for (considering how recently the people have been reduced from an almost general revolt, how apt they may be to relapse, and how deeply this superstition is rooted, and how widely spread), a main alteration in religion is not to be suddenly obtained by forcing against the current, but by gaining little by little, as opportunity may be taken.

25th January. TWO JESUITS TAKEN AT HENDLIP.

Sir Henry Bromley now reporteth that two more of the Jesuits are taken at Hendlip. At his coming there he could never get from Mistress Abington (for Master Abington was not at home at the time), nor from any other in the house, the least glimmering of any these traitors. Nor could he by any means persuade the lady to depart the house unless he should have carried her, which he held uncivil, she being so nobly born. But having certain presumption to remain there, as finding beds warm and certain parcels of books and apparel, he continued the search, and on the morning of Thursday last (which was the 23rd) two men came forth from their hiding for hunger and cold, that give themselves other names but are believed to be Greenway and Hall.

A Book of Faults.

There is a new book by Mr. Barnaby Rich called *Faults, faults and nothing else but faults*, overrunning some of the many corruptions of these times. Herein the author declareth that he doth not altogether dislike of our satirists and critics that do chide at vice, but cannot allow them to aim at any one particularly. Speaketh much of true and false love and marriage. Of our clergy, noteth their disagreement about rites, about ceremonies, about worshipping, about apparel, about discipline, as if they thought by these contentious matters to ascend into heaven for the which in times past Lucifer was thrown down into hell. Of printers, complaineth that to make the book more readable they rather desire a glorious title than a good book, so that many times being deceived by a flourishing title posted on a post he hath bestowed his money upon so vain a book that it served but as warning against the foolish humour of him that writ it, good for nothing but to set the printers a work.

26th January. Great Fishes in the Thames.

It is reported that a very great whale came up the Thames to within eight miles of London, whose body was seen divers times above water, and judged to exceed the length of the longest ship in the river; but when she tasted the fresh water and scented the land she returned into the sea. A few days ago a great porpoise was taken alive at West Ham in a small creek.

27th January. The Powder Plotters Arraigned.

Early this morning the eight principal plotters, namely Sir Everard Digby, Robert Winter, Thomas Winter, Ambrose Rookwood, John Grant, Guido Fawkes, Robert Keyes, and Thomas Bates were taken in a boat from the Tower to Westminster Hall, where they waited together in the Court of Star Chamber until the Lords Commissioners had taken their seats. Then they were straightway brought in and set on a scaffold in front of the Court. The Queen and the Prince were in a secret place to hear, and some say the King also in another. The commissioners were the Earls of Nottingham, Suffolk, Worcester, Devonshire, Northampton and Salisbury, the Lord Chief Justice (Sir John Popham), Sir Thomas Fleming, Lord Chief Baron of the Exchequer, and Sir Thomas Walmis and

Sir Peter Warburton, Justices of the Common Pleas. In the indictment, which was long, the prisoners were principally charged that they, with Henry Garnet, Oswald Tesmond (*alias* Greenway) and John Gerrard, the three Jesuits, together with Catesby, Percy, the two Wrights, and Tresham (who are all dead) traitorously conspired to kill the King and the Queen and the Prince Henry; to raise sedition and to produce a miserable slaughter in the realm; to cause rebellion and to subvert and change the government and true worship of God established in the Realm; and also to invite foreigners to invade the Realm and make war against the King; all of which charges were set forth at large.

To this indictment all the prisoners pleaded not guilty, which caused some astonishment, for their previous confessions are notorious, insomuch that the Lord Chief Justice asked Fawkes how he could deny the indictment, having been taken in the cellar with the powder, and having never before denied the fact. To which he replied that he pleaded so in respect of certain conferences set forth in the indictment.

Then Sir Edward Philips, Sergeant-at-Law, opened the indictment, and afterwards Sir Edward Coke, the Attorney-General, spoke at great length. He began by answering those who had grieved that no speedier expedition has been used in these proceedings, considering the monstrousness and continual horror of so desperate a cause, saying that there had been already twenty-three several days spent in examinations, and that the King had appointed this trial in time of assembly of Parliament because it concerned those especially of Parliament. Thence he went on to speak of the crime, which is without name and without example; and of foreign Princes whom he went about to clear of all imputation, for the King of Spain's first listening to Winter, it was when the Spanish nation was at war with England.

The first beginning of this plot, he declared, was in December 1601 when Henry Garnet, Superior of the Jesuits in England, Oswald Tesmond (*alias* Greenway), a Jesuit, and Robert Catesby, together with Tresham and others, on behalf of the English Catholics employed Thomas Winter into Spain, that he should make proposition to the King of Spain on behalf of the English Catholics that the King should send an army hither into England, and that the forces of the Catholics in England should be prepared to join with him; and further that the King should bestow some pensions here in England upon sundry persons devoted to his service; and because in all attempts upon England the greatest difficulty was ever found to be in the transportation of horses, the Catholics in England would assure the King to have always in readiness 1,500 or 2,000 horses. These propositions the King willingly embraced, and promised to bestow 100,000 crowns, the half to be paid that year, and the rest the next spring when he hoped to set foot in England. Thomas Winter, laden with these hopes, returned into England about a month before Christmas (1602) and delivered answer of all that had passed to Garnet, Catesby and Tresham. But shortly after the Queen died.

Christopher Wright was therefore sent into Spain by Garnet, Catesby and Tresham as well to carry the news of her Majesty's death as to continue the negotiation begun by Thomas Wright; and in the Spanish Court Christopher Wright met with Guy Fawkes, who was employed out of Flanders by Sir William Stanley, Hugh Owen, and Baldwin, the legier Jesuit in Flanders, to give advertisement to the King of Spain how the King of England was like to proceed vigorously with the Catholics, and to entreat him that he would send an army to England to Milford Haven where the Romish Catholics would be ready to assist him. But the King answered that he would not further listen to any such motion as having before despatched an embassy into England to treat concerning peace. Therefore this course by foreign forces failing, they fall to the Powder Plot; Catesby and Tresham being in all the treasons of this time, in the treason of the Earl of Essex, in the treason of Watson and Clarke, and also in this of the Jesuits.

Then the Attorney went on to speak of sundry considerations, as of the persons who undertook it, who are all gentlemen of good houses, and of the pernicious courses of the Jesuits therein, concluding with a comparison of the Powder Plot and Ralegh's treason. 'I say not,' quoth he, 'that we have any proofs that these of the Powder Plot were acquainted with Ralegh or Ralegh with them; but, as before was spoken of the

Jesuits and the priests, they all were joined in the ends like Samson's foxes in the tails, howsoever severed in their heads.'

In conclusion the Attorney spoke of the admirable clemency of the King who, although these traitors have exceeded all others their predecessors in mischief, will not exceed the usual punishment of the law nor invent any new torture or torment for them. 'And,' saith he, 'surely worthy of observation is the punishment by law provided and appointed for high treason; for first, after a traitor hath had his just trial, and is convicted and attainted, he shall have his judgment, to be drawn to the place of execution from his prison, as being not worthy any more to tread upon the face of the earth whereof he was made: also for that he hath been retrograde to nature, therefore is he drawn backward at a horse-tail. And whereas God hath made the head of man the highest and most supreme part, as being his chief grace and ornament, he must be drawn with his head declining downward, and lying so near the ground as may be, being thought unfit to take benefit of the common air; for which cause also he shall be strangled, being hanged up by the neck between heaven and earth, as deemed unworthy of both or either; as likewise, that the eyes of men may behold, and their hearts contemn him. His bowels and inward parts taken out and burned, who inwardly had conceived and harboured in his heart such horrible treason. After, to have his head cut off, which had imagined the mischief. And lastly, his body to be quartered, and the quarters set up in some high and eminent place, to the view and detestation of men, and to become a prey for the fowls of the air. And this is a reward due to traitors, whose hearts be hardened; for that it is a physic of state and government, to let out corrupt blood from the heart.'

After this speech the Attorney-General desired that although that which had already been confessed at the bar might be sufficient for the declaration and justification of the course of justice, yet for further satisfaction to so great a presence and audience, he prayed that the proofs of the treasons and the voluntary and free confessions of the several traitors should be openly and freely read.

So the several confessions which have been made by the traitors were then read at length, declaring in all particulars the full course of this treason. And upon the end of the reading the Lord Chief Justice spake to the jury and directed them to consider of their verdict; upon which they retired into a separate place and returned with a verdict of guilty.

As soon as the trial of the conspirators was ended, Sir Everard Digby was arraigned upon a separate indictment. Having heard the indictment read he showed a disposition to confess the principal part of it and so began to enter into a discourse; but being advertised that he must first plead directly to the indictment guilty or not guilty, and that afterwards he should be licensed to speak his pleasure, he forthwith confessed the treason and so fell into a speech, whereof there were two parts, viz., motives and petitions.

The first motive, said he, which drew him into this action was not ambition or discontentment but the great love he bore to Catesby. The next was the cause of religion, for which alone he resolved to neglect his estate, his life, his home, his memory, his posterity and all worldly and earthly felicity whatsoever. His third motive was the promises broken with the Catholics. And lastly that they generally feared harder laws from this Parliament against recusants. His petitions were that his punishment might extend only to himself, and not be transferred to his wife, children or others. Then he prayed pardon of the King and the Lords for his guilt, and lastly he intreated that he might be beheaded, desiring all men to forgive him, and that his death might satisfy them for his trespass.

To this speech Sir Edward Coke, the Attorney-General, forthwith made answer, but in respect of the time, for it grew now dark, very briefly, point by point. As for his petitions for his wife and children, how, quoth he, 'doth he now put on the bowels of nature and compassion in the peril of his private and domestical estate! But before, when the public state of his country, when the King, the Queen, the tender Princes, the Nobles, the whole kingdom were designed to a perpetual destruction, where was then this piety, this religious affection, this care?' And as for his wife and children, whereas for the Catholic cause he was content to neglect the ruin of himself, his wife, his estate and all, he should have his desire as it is in the Psalm, 'Let his wife be a widow and his children vagabonds, let his posterity be destroyed, and in the next generation let his name be quite put out.'

After this speech of the Attorney-General, the Earl of Northampton made address to Sir Everard Digby, particularly upon the point of the King's supposed breaking of promise with the Catholics, wherein my Lord declared of his own knowledge that the King had given him many directions in the Queen's time to take heed that no further comfort might be given to Catholics than he did intend, which was to bind all subjects in one kingdom and to one law concerning the religion established, howsoever in civil matters he might extend his favour as he found just cause. It was Watson and Percy that were first devisers of the report that toleration should be showed to Catholics: which afterwards in prison Watson acknowledged to be false. As for Percy, after his first and second return from the King (in the late Queen's time) he brought the Catholics no spark of encouragement.

Then the Earl of Salisbury also spake, especially of this point of his Majesty's breaking of promise with recusants, and concluded by commending the Lord Mounteagle for his loyal and honourable care of his Prince and country in his speedy bringing forth of the letter sent unto him; wherein he had showed both his discretion and fidelity.

Which speech being ended, Sir Everard Digby acknowledged that he spake not of the breach of promise out of his own knowledge but from their relation whom he trusted; and namely from Sir Thomas Tresham.

Then Sergeant Philips prayed the judgment of the court upon the verdict of the jury against the seven first prisoners, and against Sir Everard Digby upon his own confession. And first the prisoners being severally asked what they could say, wherefore judgment of death should not be pronounced against them, there was none of them, excepting Digby and Rookwood, who would make any continued speech, either in defence or extenuation of the fact.

Then the Lord Chief Justice Popham, after a relation and defence of the laws made by Queen Elizabeth against recusants, priests and receivers of priests, pronounced judgment of high treason upon all the prisoners.

Upon the rising of the court, Sir Everard Digby, bowing himself towards the Lords, said, 'If I may but hear any of your Lordships say you forgive me, I shall go more cheerfully to the gallows.' Whereupon the Lords said, 'God forgive you, and we do.'

28th January. SLANDERS ON THE EARL OF SALISBURY.

Of late some Catholics unknown sent a letter to my Lord of Salisbury warning him that, since he was taking advantage of the late foul plot either by sudden banishment, massacre, imprisonment, or other means to root out all memory of the Catholic religion, there are five that have taken the sacrament to undertake his death. This letter is now printed, together with an answer thereto, written by my Lord himself.

29th January. THE ABUSE OF PURVEYORS.

A Bill for the better execution of sundry statutes against purveyors and cart-takers was read for the first time, which arises because of the great complaints made of many abuses. It is now proposed that no warrant shall be made out in the King's name unless it is warrantable by his statutes; that ready money shall be paid for carts and carriages; and that the appriser of things to be taken shall be sworn to deal indifferently between the King and the subjects.

30th January. THE ARCHDUKE'S UNFRIENDLY ACTION.

Amongst those greatly suspected as a partaker in the plot of the Gunpowder is one Owen, also Baldwin, a Jesuit, and Sir William Stanley, all of whom dwell in Brussels. The King therefore sent by his Ambassador to the Archduke asking that they might be sent over; but although he caused Owen to be arrested and his papers taken, yet by no means will he send these traitors over until the King of Spain's pleasure be known. . So the King debated the matter in the presence of the Ambassadors of the King of Spain and of the Archduke, showing that though there be no example for it, yet the plot itself having no example in former ages might afford a new precedent in the punishment of offenders. The next day this and other matters were debated between the Earl of Salisbury and the Spanish Ambassador, which bred some dryness between them, for the Ambassador for his part declared that our King likewise harbours rebels of his master, meaning some few merchants and tradesmen of the Low Countries. To which my Lord replied that in contending so much for the caitiff Owen, they did not advert to the suspicion to which they exposed themselves in the judgment of the world.

Four of the Plotters Executed.

This day four of the plotters, namely Sir Everard Digby, Robert Winter, John Grant and Thomas Bates, were drawn upon sledges and hurdles to St. Paul's churchyard to a scaffold made on purpose for their execution. And lest there should be any tumult, the aldermen of each ward of the city were required by the Lord Mayor to cause one able and sufficient person, with a halberd in his hand, to stand at the door of every dwelling-house in the open street in the way that the traitors were drawn towards the place of execution, and there to remain from seven in the morning until the return of the Sheriff.

When they came to the place of execution Sir Everard Digby was first despatched. He spake not long, protesting that from the bottom of his heart he asked forgiveness of God, the King, the Queen, the Prince and all the Parliament, and if that he had known it at first to have been so foul a treason, he would not have concealed it to have gained a world, requiring the people to witness he died penitent and sorrowful for this vile treason. He prayed kneeling about half a quarter of an hour, often bowing his head to the ground. After him went Winter up to the scaffold where he made few words and stayed not long for his execution. Then came Grant, who confessed his offence to be heinous, yet excused it by his conscience for religion. Last of them came Bates, who seemed sorry for his offence, and asked forgiveness of God and the King and of the whole kingdom. He prayed to God for the preservation of them all, and said that it was only his love to his master that drew him to forget his duty to God, his King and country.

Garnet the Jesuit and Oldcorne Apprehended.

The two men that were taken at Hendlip are now said to be the servants of the Jesuits, named Chambers and Owen. Sir Henry Bromley upon their capture renewing his searches, on the eighth day there was found the opening into a little chamber wherein were discovered the two Jesuits Garnet and Oldcorne (*alias* Hall). Marmalade and other sweetmeats were found lying by them, but their better maintenance was by a quill or reed, thrust through a little hole in a chimney, by which candle and books were conveyed to them. The place where they lay was so straightened that they could not even stretch themselves. When they came forth they appeared like two ghosts, and the fellow that found them ran away for fear, thinking they would have shot a pistol at him. Sir Henry Bromley knew Garnet straightway by the proclamation, nor indeed doth he deny it himself.

31*st January*. THE OTHER PLOTTERS EXECUTED AT WEST-
    MINSTER.

To-day, being Friday, were drawn from the Tower to the Old Palace at Westminster, Thomas Winter, Rookwood, Keyes and Guido Fawkes, whom they call 'the devil of the vault.' Winter was first brought to the scaffold where he made a little speech, in which he seemed sorry for his offence, protesting that he died a true Catholic. He went up the ladder with a very pale and dead colour and after a swing or two with the halter was drawn to the quartering block and there quickly despatched.

After him came Rookwood, who made a speech of some longer time, confessing his offence and asking mercy of God, whom he besought to bless the King, the Queen and all his royal progeny and that they might long live to reign in peace and happiness over this kingdom; but he prayed also that God would make the King a Catholic. And so beseeching the King to be good to his wife and children, and protesting that he died a Catholic, he went up the ladder. He was left hanging until he was almost dead.

After him came Keyes, who made small show of repentance, but went stoutly up the ladder, where staying not the hangman's turn, he turned himself off with such a leap that he brake the halter. Whereupon he was drawn to the block and quickly divided into four parts.

And last of all came Fawkes, *alias* Johnson, that should have put the fire to the powder, who at his death was more penitent than any of the rest, beseeching all Catholics never to attempt any such bloody act, being a course which God did never favour nor prosper. His body being weak with torture and sickness, he was scarce able to go up the ladder, but yet with much ado by the help of the hangman went high enough to break his neck with the fall.

The quarters of these traitors are placed over London Gates and their heads set upon the Bridge. The heads of Catesby and Percy that were killed in the fighting are set up on the top of the Parliament House, where it had also been intended to set Tresham's head; but the Judges will not agree, for they make this difference, that the two former were in open rebellion, but Tresham was not ever indicted.

2nd *February.* CERTAIN SURVIVORS FROM THE GUIANA VOYAGE RETURN.

Certain that survive from the company sent out by Sir Olive Leigh last year have now returned, bringing news of the massacre of the most part of their fellows. After they set out, by contrary winds, unknown currents of the sea and the unskilfulness of the master, they were put to leeward of their port, without any hope of recovering it in any due time. They were fain therefore to touch first at the Isle of Barbados and then at Santa Lucia in the West Indies; and here Captain St. John and the rest of the passengers that had purposed to stay with Captain Leigh in Guiana resolved to stay and take their fortune in this fruitful island. Thus sixty-seven of them were left on shore, with swords, muskets, and powder, one falcon, and one barrel of biscuit. The next day the ship departed with some discontentment because they seized the boat. For the space of five or six weeks they lived very peaceably, trading with the Indians for food, and killing wild fowl and tortoises.

It then happened that Captain Nicholas St. John, seeing certain square plates which the Indians wore on their arms, asked one Brown, a gold-finder, his opinion, who replied that three parts was gold. And when they asked the Indians where they got them they pointed to a high mountain on the northwest part of the island. This caused Captain St. John, and as many of the chief men as could go in the boat on a Monday to go thither, promising Master Alexander St. John and others whom he left to govern at home that he would return the next Saturday. In the meantime they were very merry with the Indians, and especially one called Augramert and his father. At length upon the Thursday Master St. John and others to the number of eighteen went with this Augramert as if to see his house where he promised that they should have hamaccos to lie on. So they went along the sands very careless, young Master St. John jesting with the Indian captain until they came within sight of their houses where they had placed an ambush of 300 Caribs; when suddenly Augramert took Master St. John's rapier and poniard, while the old man struck him to the ground with his sword. Then out of the woods the arrows came so thick about their ears that they had not time to put the matches in their cocks; and many had their matches still to light, insomuch they discharged not six pieces amongst them. Such was the slaughter that only one man, by name John Nicol, escaped back to the rest of his fellows. Thereafter for seven or eight days they fought against the Indians to the number of 1,300 or 1,400, having nothing but their chests to defend them against the arrows; and besides on the very first day the Indians shot five with their arrows and burnt their houses, but they kept them back with their falcon. By this time of nineteen men that now remained twelve were sore wounded with arrows. But the next day, quite contrary to their expectations, certain of the Indians offered to trade with them again, which was a miracle, for they had no food left, nor any means to get any. At length it was agreed that they should have a periagua (or country boat), which with all speed they made ready with a sail, for they heard that Augramert and his party were coming again with arrows.

So they put to sea, with but one barrico of fresh water and one small firkin of rice and very little other food, being nineteen persons and not one having skill in the mariner's art, and without card or compass. Nevertheless at last they reached an island in desperate case, where five more of them died; but now certain Spaniards succoured them, and treated them very kindly, and sent them to Carthagena, whence at length after many further chances John Nicol and two others are at length come home.

3rd February. 'FOUR BOOKS OF OFFICES.'

Mr. Barnabe Barnes hath written *Four books of offices*, divided according to the four virtues cardinal (which he dedicateth to his Majesty), to enable private persons for the special service of all good Princes and policies. The first book which treateth of the office of treasurers is included under Temperance. Prudence is the substance of the second book, deciphered in the secret councillor's office. The third treateth of Justice; and the forth of Fortitude, containing certain qualities of a true soldier.

5th February. 'THE ISLE OF GULLS.'

There is much speech of a comedy which the children play at the Blackfriars called *The Isle of Gulls* wherein from the highest to the lowest all men's parts are played of both nations. It is said that some have been committed to Bridewell because of it. This comedy is written by John Day, prefaced with an induction wherein one of the children, as Prologue, complaineth greatly of this nice and difficult age which is become so critical of plays that 'tis grown a custom if anyone rise (especially of the fashionable sort) about what serious business so ever, the rest thinking it to be in dislike of the play, cry 'Mew! by Jesus, vile!', and leave the poor heartless children to speak their epilogue to the empty scene. Spectators, saith he, be of three kinds; one will have railings and invectives or the author will never content him; another is all for bawdy and scurril jests; and the third for swelling comparisons and bombast epithets which the others cannot abide.

6th February. RECUSANTS' CHILDREN.

It was said in the Commons to-day upon a question of recusancy that 2,000 children under the age of sixteen are gone beyond the seas for their education within these two years.

9th February. SEDITIOUS BOOKS PRINTED ABROAD.

There are sundry factious and schismatical persons, who have planted themselves in the Low Countries where they have liberty without impeachment or contradiction to publish in

278

print many books and anabaptistical pamphlets slandering the ecclesiastical government in England. And to this end Sir Noel Caron hath written, at the King's request, that certain books now in hand to be printed at Amsterdam be stayed, and all others likewise suppressed and restrained.

10th February. A SUBSIDY PROPOSED.

To-day in the Commons the question of a subsidy was propounded and many members spoke on it, and the manner in which it should be given. Sir Edwin Sandys said that a subsidy in time of war was a necessity; but in peace 'twas a matter of love, virtue and thankfulness. It was resolved to appoint a committee to consider of it.

A STRANGE ACCIDENT.

The minds of men are much troubled with a strange accident lately fallen out, which yet by no means can be discovered, about the City of London and some of the shires adjoining. Whole slaughters of sheep have been made, in some places to the number of 100, in others less, where nothing is taken from the sheep but their tallow and some inward parts, the whole carcasses and fleeces remaining still behind. Of this are sundry conjectures, but most agree that it tendeth towards some fireworks.

FEARS OF THE TURKEY MERCHANTS.

This last summer one Cockaine sent out a ship called *The Merchant Royal* and got her to be entertained of the Duke of Florence to go against the Turks, in which service she took a great galleon of Constantinople of 1,200 tons called *The Sultan*, and belonging to their Queen Mother, richly laden at Alexandria with inestimable wealth; in which fight were slain 500 Turks, and 300 more brought to Leghorn, the best of the goods taken out, and the rest sunk with the galleon. For this piece of service our merchants stand in doubt to lose all their goods in Turkey, and to be debarred of their trade in those parts. Cockaine in the meantime lieth in the Fleet.

11th February. THE KING'S THANKS.

Master Speaker did not take his place in the Commons till past 9 of the clock, when he reported that he had been sent for to the King, who learning of the proceeding of the House touching the subsidy takes more joy in the manner that if the value of ten times as much had fallen unto him by any other accident.

STRANGE NEWS FROM CARLSTADT.

Very strange news is reported from Carlstadt in Croatia, which happened in June last, where the sun did shine like blood nine days together, and two armies were seen in the air, the one encountering the other. Moreover, in the same city a woman was delivered of three sons, of which the first had four heads that spake and uttered strange things; the second child was black like a Moor, and the third like unto Death. Such things together with the Earth's and Moon's late and horrible obscurations, the frequent eclipsations of the fixed bodies, within these four years more than ordinary, shall without doubt have effects no less admirable than the positives unusual, portending, as ancient authors affirm, new leagues, traitorous designments, catching at kingdoms, translation of empire, downfall of men in authority, emulation, ambition, innovations, factious sects, schisms and much disturbance.

12th February. A COMMITTEE OF BOTH HOUSES.

At a Committee this afternoon of both Houses of Parliament, Master John Hare, Clerk of the Court of Wards, spoke first at some length of the grievances caused by purveyors. This the Lords took unkindly, for the chief purpose of this Committee is to consider of the King's present state and necessities, and not of matters of grievance. Then the Lord Treasurer spoke of the King's state, that his ordinary receipts are not able to supply the ordinary expense, and of his great debts. Queen Elizabeth left the Crown in debt some £400,000, to which must be added the charge of the King's coming £10,000, the burial of the late Queen £20,000, the coronation £20,000; and the augmentation of the King's yearly charge which is *per annum* £55,000; so that the debt is now some £734,000.

THE JESUITS BROUGHT TO LONDON.

To-day the two Jesuits, Garnet and Oldcorne, were brought to London and are lodged at the Gatehouse. They have been very kindly used since their taking, Garnet being lodged in the

house of Sir Henry Bromley where he dined and supped every
day with Sir Henry and his family. On Candlemas Day there
was a great dinner made to end Christmas, and all drank the
health of the King bareheaded. There came in, accompanying
the wine, a white wax candle lighted, taken at Hendlip, with
'Jesus' on one side and 'Maria' on the other. So Garnet,
desiring to see the candle, took it in his hands and gave it to
Oldcorne, saying that he was glad yet that he had carried a
holy candle on Candlemas Day. At his parting from the gentle-
women of the house, such was the kindness used towards him
that Sir Henry was afraid they would be perverted. All the
way to London Garnet was exceeding well used at the King's
charges and by the express orders of my Lord of Salisbury.
There was some bickering with ministers by the way.

13th *February.* THE LORD CHANCELLOR'S CHARGE.

In the Star Chamber to-day complaint was made against the
excessive length of a bill containing 125 sheets of paper close
written, which Sir Francis Bacon would have excused, but the
Court did much condemn, fining the plaintiff at £40. The
ancient order of the Court is now confirmed that no bill shall
contain above 15 sheets of paper. The Lord Chancellor wished
that another precedent could have been put in execution, that
is, that the counsellor, being a man of infamy, should have had
the bill slit with a hole in the middle thereof, and worn it as a
herald's coat through all the Courts in Westminster.

Then the Lord Chancellor, according to usage, delivered
his charge to the Judges that they shall diligently observe all
such Justices of Peace as be careful and diligent, and such that
be troublesome and contentious, that they may be removed
with disgrace, for there are very many laws made and referred
to them, but few executed by them. He exhorted the justices
to be very careful in the execution of justice, and of the law
against wanderers, priests and Jesuits, and the multitude of
beggars. Also he spoke of the great fault in the making of
constables of the baser, poorer, and simpler sort of people.

14th *February.* GARNET SENT TO THE TOWER.

Yesterday Garnet was brought to the Council Chamber at
Whitehall and there examined before the Lords. Both at his

going and coming a great multitude surrounded him. He was examined for about three hours yet with all courtesy, principally upon the matter of equivocation, and of the supremacy of the Pope. To-day he is sent to the Tower where he is lodged in a fair chamber.

17th February. THE PARLIAMENT.

In the Commons there was proposed a Bill for the better observing of the Sabbath Day or Sunday, which was agreed but with some difficulty and dispute. A Bill to restrain many abuses of players was also read.

23rd February. THE IRISH RECUSANTS.

Some months since fines were imposed upon certain recusants at Dublin; and these fines being estreated into the Exchequer, the Sheriffs impanelled a jury to inquire of their lands and goods, and to value them that the fines might be raised. Whereupon there were offered to the jury certain deeds of gift, by which it appeared that they had given in general words all their goods and chattels, not reserving so much as their wearing apparel, to their children, prentices or friends. Moreover, the deeds were antedated six months at least, and the donors themselves continue in possession of their goods, so it is a manifest collusion and mockery. Notwithstanding this clear fraud, the jury found that there was nothing for the King.

26th February. THE PRECEDENCE OF OXFORD.

A Bill concerning Heads of Colleges was read in the Commons, which occasioned much time and dispute because the clerk had put the name of Cambridge before that of Oxford. At length it was resolved with much odds that Oxford should be put first.

2nd March. THE DEATH OF OWEN.

Owen, the servant of Garnet, being very obstinate in denying that he had ever seen or heard of either Garnet or Oldcorne was yesterday for the second time questioned in the Tower. As he persisted in his obstinacy, his thumbs were tied together and he was suspended thereby from a beam. When the questions were again put to him, he confessed his knowledge of Garnet and his attendance upon him at Hendlip.

To-day, complaining of illness, the keeper brought a chair for him to use at his dinner, and with his food a blunt-pointed knife was brought for him to cut his meat. Hereupon Owen, finding fault with the coldness of his broth, besought the keeper to set it on the fire for him in an adjoining room. As soon as the man had left the room, Owen in a frightful manner cut open his own belly. When the keeper returned he saw the pale and ghostly countenance of his prisoner, and blood sprinkled upon the floor, and drawing aside the straw with which Owen had covered himself he perceived what he had done. He therefore ran to the Lieutenant of the Tower who was at his dinner. So the Lieutenant and his guests who were with him hastened to the place where Owen lay, who declared that he had committed this act upon himself entirely from the fear of severer torture than he had suffered yesterday. He died soon afterwards.

4th March. GARNET'S CONVERSATIONS OVERHEARD.

It now appeareth that Garnet knew of the Powder Plot more than he hath hitherto confessed, for being informed, as it were secretly by his keeper, that by opening a hidden door in his cell he could speak with Oldcorne who was in the cell adjoining, he hath divulged some things which he had otherwise denied. Their conversations were overheard by two worthy persons conveniently placed to that end. When the two priests were charged with these conversations before the commissioners they denied them. But Oldcorne at length confessed, and Garnet being shown Oldcorne's confession, and the testimony of those who had overheard them, did at length acknowledge the conferences and much more.

6th March. THE WRETCHED STATE OF IRELAND.

The Lord Deputy complaineth greatly of the want of money for the Irish service, and sees no remedy but that our men must break and fall upon the country next them. All things there are worse than in time of war, and a greater scarcity of money, the commanders never so poor. Most men are disheartened to labour in the service, and wish any employment to be discharged thence, where a fourth part of their payment being taken away in the coin, they would give half of the remains to have the other half. He is wearied of their complaints, for he can do nothing to satisfy them, and can no longer stay them from resorting to England. The principal recusants of Dublin remain very obstinate, though the meaner do in reasonable sort conform themselves in most parts of the towns.

9th March. SIR EDWARD CLEVE BEFORE THE COUNCIL.

Sir Edward Cleve was called before the Council for his contempt in assuming the order of knighthood and of St. Michael with a patent thereof from the French King. It was resolved that the general order of knighthood may be accepted as a general favour from any foreign Prince; but to take the Order of St. Michael, being an order whereby his duty of allegiance to the King is in part obliged to a foreign king is most unlawful and undutiful, especially if he take an oath which ties him to obey certain orders incident; and although Sir Edward took no oath, yet is he bound to observe the institutions of the Order. Therefore without the King's licence he may not assume it. He is therefore committed to prison to the Marshalsea of the King's House till he shall willingly and by writing resign his Order and Patent to the King.

10th March. 'A DISCOURSE OF CIVIL LIFE.'

Mr. Lodovick Bryskett hath sent to the press *A discourse of civil life: containing the ethic part of moral philosophy*, dedicated to my Lord of Salisbury, but written some years since to Lord Arthur Grey of Wilton. This book is in form of a dialogue or conversation that was held in Mr. Bryskett's cottage near Dublin between Dr. Long, Lord Primate of Armagh, Sir Robert Dillon, Mr. Dormer, the Queen's Solicitor, Captain Christopher Carleil, Captain Thomas Norris, Captains Warham, St. Leger, and Nicholas Dawtry, Mr. Edmund Spenser, and Thomas Smith, apothecary; whence it appeareth that Mr. Spenser, refusing at that time to show his *Faery Queen* to the company, turned aside their request by declaring that Mr. Bryskett had made a translation of the Ethic part of Moral philosophy out of Giraldi Cinthio; whereupon followeth the discourse.

12th March. 'NOBODY AND SOMEBODY.'

There is printing the play called *Nobody and Somebody* that hath been sundry times acted by the Queen's Majesty's servants

wherein is shown the history of the Prince Elidure that was for-
tunately three several times crowned King of England, together
with the continual pursuit of Nobody by Somebody.

THE CHARACTER OF NOBODY.

Come twenty poor men to his gate at once,
Nobody gives them money, meat and drink,
If they be naked clothes; then come poor soldiers,
Sick, maim'd, and shot, from any foreign wars,
Nobody takes them in, provides them harbour,
Maintains their ruin'd fortunes at his charge.
He gives to orphans and for widows builds
Alms-houses, spitals, and large hospitals,
And when it comes in question, who is apt
For such good deeds, 'tis answer'd *Nobody*.
Now *Nobody* hath entertained again
Long banished Hospitality, and at his board
A hundred lusty yeomen daily wait
Whose long backs bend with weighty chines of beef
And choice of cheer, whose fragments at his gate
Suffice the general poor of the whole shire.
Nobody's table's free for travellers,
His buttery and his cellar ope to all
That starve with drought or thirst upon the way.

17th March. 'THE WONDER OF WOMEN.'

The Wonder of Women, or the Tragedy of Sophonisba, by
Mr. John Marston is now printing, as it hath sundry times been
acted by the Children at the Blackfriars. This Sophonisba is a
princess of Carthage newly married to Massinissa, and the scene
opens upon their wedding night, but before they can enjoy each
other's love, Massinissa is called forth to march against Scipio
and Syphax. Hereupon the senators of Carthage, to win Syphax
to their part, send Sophonisba to him, but she will none of him.
He therefore seeks Erictho, a sorceress, by her art to bring him
to Sophonisba's bed, but when, as he supposes, he has lain with
her, he discovers it to be the witch herself. In the meantime
Massinissa, being now in league with Scipio, makes oath that he
will obey the Roman and returns to Sophonisba; but Scipio commands that she shall be delivered to the Romans, intending to

give her to Syphax. Hereupon, lest Massinissa be forced to break his vow, she takes poison, and Massinissa delivers her dead body.

20th March. JONSON'S NEW COMEDY.

The King's men have a new comedy at the Globe called *Volpone: or the Fox*, writ by Ben Jonson, who protesteth (against those who used to mock him for a tedious slow worker that can but write a play once a year) that this was the work of five weeks, without co-adjutor or journey man to aid him.

THE ARGUMENT.

Volpone, childless, rich, feigns sick, despairs,
Offers his state to hopes of several heirs,
Lies languishing: his parasite receives
Presents of all, assures, deludes; then weaves
Other cross plots, which ope themselves, are told.
New tricks for safety are sought; they thrive: when bold,
Each tempts the other again, and all are sold.

22nd March. AN ALARMING RUMOUR.

About half-past 6 of the clock this morning the report was suddenly spread through the Court and City that for certain news the King was slain at Woking. The Court being sore frighted as well the great lords as others, the Court gates were shut with double guard at all places; and in the City the Lord Mayor gave forthwith precepts unto the wards to levy trained soldiers who should repair to their London Captains. The Lieutenant of the Tower likewise drew the bridge, shut close his prisoners, charged divers pieces of great ordnance and stood prepared at all points, as the news grew more and more that not only the King was slain, but with him in his defence the Earl of Montgomery, Sir John Ramsay and Sir James Hay. Some said the treason was performed by English Jesuits, some by Scots in women's attire, others by Spaniards and French, most reports agreeing that the King was stabbed with an invenomed knife.

This rumour reached the Commons House of Parliament somewhat before 8 of the clock, so that the Commons were mightily perplexed. Some said, 'Let us rise and go hence for our better safety lest we be suddenly surprised,' but in brief it was agreed that they should sit still in their accustomed peaceable manner until the truth were known, lest their sudden rising should add more terror without. So they sent every half-quarter of an hour unto the Earl of Salisbury and others of the Council to be truly ascertained, and for almost two hours space they received news that the King was stabbed, smothered in his bed, or shot with a pistol as he was riding.

At length about 9 of the clock the Council, upon extraordinary expedition having true knowledge of his Majesty's safety, to quiet the people's distracted minds made proclamation that the King was in good and perfect health and that the people should contain themselves from assemblies or gathering together in arms or conventicles.

They sent also Sir Lewis Lewkenor, Master of the Ceremonies, to advertise the ambassadors of foreign Princes and to take order with the magistrates to see their houses and persons secured. At the news of the King's safety the Spanish Ambassador was almost ravished with sudden joy and gave Sir Lewis a very great chain of gold of a large value.

This afternoon the King himself came to London and about Knightsbridge was met by the Prince, the Council, the Speaker with his mace, and other lords and burgesses and thousands of the people flocking that way. The Lord Mayor and aldermen also came to Court, where the Recorder in all humble and hearty manner signified the inconceivable joy felt upon assurance of his Majesty's safety.

The rumour is now said to have been started first with the Constable of Kennington, who said that he had a warrant to warn men to be under arms.

23rd March (Sunday). THE GENERAL REJOICING.

The general rejoicings at the King's safety were again shown to-day by the people's acclamations as he went to the sermon, at which the King declared that he took these demonstrations more kindly than if they had won a battle for him; that a better king they might have, but a more loving and careful for their good they could not, and that these signs were the more welcome to him for that foreign ambassadors might see the vanity of those reports that were spread abroad in other countries of mislikes and distastes between him and his people.

24th March. THE KING'S ACCESSION DAY.

The tilting for the King's Accession Day was observed to be barren and brought forth nothing of great show or substance, most of the equipage being poor and penurious, excepting the Earls of Pembroke and Montgomery that was both rich and dainty. It was hard to tell who did best where scant any did well; Montgomery for a young beginner did extraordinary, but my Lord of Effingham did absolutely worst.

25th March. THE SUBSIDY.

After much debate for several days the Lower House has at last agreed upon the subsidy to be given to the King. The first payment of the first subsidy is to be made upon the 1st of August, the second upon the 1st of May; of the second subsidy, the first payment is to be November twelvemonth, the second payment May come two years. When the House divided upon this question, there voted with the Noes 113, with the Yeas 121.

28th March. THE TRIAL OF GARNET.

Henry Garnet, Superior of the Jesuits in England, was indicted for High Treason at the Guildhall before the Commissioners, who were Sir Leonard Halliday, Lord Mayor of London, the Earls of Nottingham, Suffolk, Worcester, Northampton, Salisbury, Sir John Popham, Lord Chief Justice, Sir Thomas Fleming, Lord Chief Baron of the Exchequer, Sir Christopher Yelverton, one of the Judges of the King's Bench, and several Aldermen of the City of London. The King himself was there privately and held it out all day besides many courtiers and ladies, amongst them the Lady Arabella, my Lady of Suffolk, Walsingham and others.

First the indictment was read wherein Garnet was charged that he with Catesby and Greenway had traitorously conspired on 9th June, 1605 to kill the King and the Prince, to raise sedition and cause a miserable slaughter amongst the King's subjects, to excite rebellion, to alter and subvert the government of the Kingdom and the true worship of God established in England, and to procure foreigners to invade the Realm and to levy war against the King. And further that on the same day he conspired that Catesby, and other traitors should blow up and utterly destroy with gunpowder the King, the Prince and the

288

Lords and Commons when assembled in the Parliament House. To this indictment Garnet pleaded not guilty. So the jury were called, being freemen of the City of London, but before they were sworn Garnet excepted to one of them, and the exception was allowed. Then the indictment was read over again; after which proclamation was made that if any person could inform against the prisoner, he should come forth and be heard.

Then Sir John Croke, the King's Sergeant-at-Law, opened the effect of the indictment, after which Sir Edward Coke, the Attorney-General, spake at some length. He began by giving satisfaction to those who had conjectured diversely of the cause of delay of proceeding against Garnet, showing that he hath been examined and interrogated twenty-three several times. Then entering into his speech he said that since he was dealing with the Superior of the Jesuits he would touch only such treasons as have been plotted and wrought by the Jesuits since the superiority of this man in England, whereof he might truly say, *et quorum pars magna fui*; and inasmuch as the prisoner was a grave and learned person, he would force his nature to deal mildly with him. Thence he ran over all the treasons of the Jesuits since the coming of Garnet into England, which was in July 1586, until the plot. He showed that in January 1604 Garnet took out a general pardon of all treasons (which pardon the King granted to all men at his first entrance into the Kingdom). In the March following Catesby, Winter and his crew resolved upon the Powder Plot, and they met with Fawkes and others and took on an oath of secrecy together. In June Greenway the Jesuit did consult with Garnet his Superior about divers treasonable matters, and in that conference inform him of the whole course of the Powder Treason at large, which (such was his politic and subtle dealing) he heard as if it were in confession. In this same month there was a great consultation between Garnet, Catesby and Francis Tresham concerning the strength of the Catholics in England to the end that Garnet might by letters send direct advertisement thereof to the Pope, for his Holiness would not be brought to show his inclination concerning any commotion or rising of the Catholic party until he should be informed that they had sufficient force to prevail. Meanwhile, in December 1604 the conspirators entered into the mine. In June

1605 Catesby, fearing lest some of his confederates, being touched with the horror of so damnable a fact, seeks from Garnet (as being the Superior of the Jesuits) his judgment and resolution in conscience, concerning the lawfulness of the fact, telling Garnet there would be stirs. Garnet seemed to dissuade him (but this was most plainly only a colour). Whereupon Catesby propounded unto him the case whether for the good and promotion of the Catholic cause against heretics (the necessity of time and occasion so requiring), it be lawful or not amongst many nocents to destroy and take away some innocents also? To this question Garnet advisedly answered that if the advantage was greater to the Catholic part, then doubtless it should be lawful. And this resolution of Garnet, the Superior of the Jesuits, was the strongest and only bond whereby Catesby afterwards kept and retained the traitors in that detestable confederacy.

Now in August doth Garnet write to Rome that commandment might come from his Holiness, or from Aquaviva, the General of the Jesuits, for the staying of all commotions of the Catholics here in England, intending by this to set the whole rest of the Catholic cause upon the Powder Plot, and in the meanwhile to lull us asleep in security in respect of their dissembled quietness and conformity; as also fearing that impediment might be offered to this main plot by reason of any suspicion of the stirring of the Papists, or of inquiry after them upon occasion of any petty commotions or broils. Garnet also, in a conference about the acquainting of the Pope with the Powder Treason, appointed Sir Edmund Baynham (a very desperate man and known as Captain of the Damned Crew) to carry the message. And by Baynham doth Garnet write letters in that behalf, as also for staying of commotions, well knowing that before his letters could be answered the Houses of Parliament (according to their designs) should have been blown up and the whole State overthrown.

Then, having spoken somewhat further of the Powder Plot, the Attorney spoke of Garnet himself, saying that he was a man of many names such as Garnet, Wally, Darcy, Roberts, Farmer, Philips, 'and,' quoth he, 'surely I have not commonly known and observed a true man that hath had so many false appellations. He is by country an Englishman, by birth a gentleman, by education a scholar of Westminster, and then of Oxford, for I never knew any priest of Cambridge arraigned; afterwards a corrector of the common law print with Master Tottel the printer, and now is to be corrected by the law. By nature he hath many gifts and endowments; by art he is learned, a good linguist; and by profession he is a Jesuit, and a Superior, as indeed he is superior to all his predecessors in devilish treason. He is a doctor of Jesuits, that is, to speak more plainly, a doctor of five D's, namely, of dissimulation, of deposing of Princes, of disposing of Kingdoms, of daunting and deterring of subjects, and of destruction.'

Next Master Attorney spoke of equivocation, saying that by the Treatise of Equivocation, seen and allowed by Garnet and by Blackwell the archpriest, it is maintained that it is lawful and justifiable to express one part of a man's mind and retain another. By this doctrine people are indeed taught not only lying but fearful and damnable blasphemy. And as example Mr. Attorney instanced Francis Tresham who at point of death protested on his salvation that he had not seen Garnet for sixteen years before, whereas Master Garnet himself and Mrs. Vaux and others directly confess that Garnet and Tresham hath within two years' space been very often together and also many times before.

When he had spoken somewhat further of doctrines of the Jesuits concerning the deposing of princes, he called for the confessions.

Then were the confessions read concerning Cullen's treason in 1594, and Patrick and Yorke's treasons in the same year, and of Squire's treason in 1598. Then followed the evidence of the Spanish treason from the confessions of Winter and Fawkes, and many extracts taken from the confessions of Garnet himself and of the other conspirators.

The reading being ended, Mr. Garnet, having licence of the Court to answer what he could for himself, said that he would divide all that had been objected into four parts, namely, 1st, Doctrine; 2ndly, Recusants; 3rdly, Jesuits; 4thly, himself in particular. Concerning equivocation he declared that if a man be brought before a lawful judge to be examined he must answer all things truly which that judge had cognizance to inquire of: but if he be examined before one who hath no authority to interrogate, or be asked concerning something which belongeth not to the cognizance of him who asketh, as what a man thinketh etc., he is not bound to answer, and may equivocate. To prove this opinion, quoth he, 'I may cite the practice of our Blessed Saviour, Who said that He knew not the day nor the hour in which the Son of Man should come; and yet no man who hath faith in Christ could even make a doubt that in His Godhead Our Saviour well knew when the Day of Judgment should be, though He did not know it so as to tell it to men.'

As for the Pope's authority over kings and princes, it was not his doctrine but the general doctrine of the Church; and as for the doctrine of Jesuits that kings excommunicated may be deposed, it is meant only to such kings as having once been Catholics have forsaken and fallen away from the See of Rome. He made great distinction between his Majesty, who had never fallen from the See of Rome, for he never belonged to it. Further, he said that Catholics in general did never like of this action of the powder, for it was prejudicial to them all; and it was a particular of his that when he knew of the action he did not disclose it; for he knew indeed that all quiet Catholics had ever a better opinion of the King than of the late Queen.

After he had spoken of recusancy, and of the Jesuits in Spain who had particularly denied upon their eternal salvation that they were in any way privy to the damnable treasons set forth by Master Attorney, he went on to speak of himself, praying the jury to be guided not by light and vain conjecturers, but by eye-witnesses and proofs. As for the things charged against him, most of them he directly denied, save that he had understood from Catesby that he had some great thing in hand for the good of Catholics, which he much misliked and dissuaded him; only he confessed that he did conceal it.

At this point both my Lord of Northampton and my Lord Salisbury asked him certain questions concerning his letters and commendations of Baynham and Fawkes; and when Garnet had answered, two witnesses were called who had overheard what passed between Garnet and Oldcorne (*alias* Hall), the Jesuit in the Tower, which were Mr. Forset, a man learned and a Justice of Peace, and Mr. Lockerson. Mr. Forset not being present was sent for, and in the meantime Mr. Lockerson was called.

Garnet thereupon acknowledged that he could not deny the substantial part of this testimony, and did admit that Greenway had indeed told him of the whole plot and the particulars thereof, with which he was very much distempered and could never speak quietly afterwards, and oftentimes prayed God that it should not take effect.

At which the Earl of Salisbury put him in remembrance that he had confessed to the Lords that he had said many masses and offered sacrifice to God that the plot might be prevented, unless it were for the good of the Catholic cause; and in no other fashion was the state beholden to him for his masses and oblations. And further he asked Garnet why he did not write to his Superior Aquaviva as well of this particular Powder Treason.

To which Garnet faintly answered that he might not disclose it to any because it was matter of secret confession. When further the Earl of Salisbury asked him did not Catesby as well as Greenway tell him of it, Garnet replied, 'That, my lord, I may not tell.'

Then the Earl of Salisbury desired leave of the Lords Commissioners that to satisfy the jury and the world he might use some speech concerning the proceeding of the State in this great cause, wherein he answered certain calumnies that have been uttered, particularly concerning the treatment of Garnet, who confessed before all that he hath been used as Christianly, as courteously, and as carefully as ever man could be. After which he showed how after the interlocution with Hall, Garnet had been called before the Lords and asked, not what he had said, but whether he and Hall had conference together, being desired not to equivocate. Yet he stiffly denied it upon his soul, reiterating it with so many detestable execrations that their hair stood upright. And afterwards Hall being called, at first denied but being examined apart, confessed it. Whereupon Garnet also confessed what he had so vehemently denied an hour before.

After some further disputation between them the Earl said, 'Master Garnet, give me but one argument that you were not consenting to it that can hold in any indifferent man's ear or sense, besides your bare negative.' Whereat Garnet was mute.

Then Mr. Attorney spake in answer to Garnet's words, and by the time he was ended Mr. Forset came in and was examined concerning the interlocution between Garnet and Hall. After this the Earl of Northampton made a long and laboured address. Then sundry other confessions were read concerning the equivocations of Tresham, and at last the Earl of Salisbury said, 'Mr. Garnet, is this all you have to say? If it be not, take your time; no man shall interrupt you.'

To which Garnet answered 'Yea, my lord.'

Mr. Attorney then humbly desired all the Lords Commissioners that if he had forgotten to speak of anything material their Lordships would be pleased to put him in mind of it; who was assured by my Lord of Salisbury that he had done very well, painfully and learnedly.

Then Mr. Attorney desired the jury might go together. So the jury went forth out of the court and within less than a quarter of an hour returned with a verdict of guilty. Whereupon Mr. Sergeant Croke prayed judgment. Then Mr. Waterhouse, the Clerk of the Crown, demanding what he could say for himself why judgment should not be given against him, Garnet made answer that he could say nothing, but referred himself to the mercy of the King and God Almighty.

Then the Lord Chief Justice, making a pithy preamble of all the apparent proofs and presumptions of his guiltiness, gave judgment that he should be hanged, drawn and quartered.

My Lord of Salisbury again demanded if Garnet would say anything else; to which he answered, 'No, my Lord; but I humbly desire your Lordships all to commend my life to the King's Majesty nevertheless. At his pleasure I shall be ready either to die or to live and do him service.'

And so the court rose, having sat from 8 of the clock in the morning until 7 at night.

30th March. GREAT WINDS.

Yesterday and to-day, the wind was extraordinary great and violent, causing great shipwreck.

1st April. GARNET'S DECLARATION IN THE TOWER.

Garnet doth affirm before the Lieutenant of the Tower that if any man hath or should undertake to kill his Majesty that he is not bound to confess it, though he be brought and examined before a lawful magistrate, unless there is proof to convict him.

Further, he hath written a declaration with his own hand concerning the obligation of the laws.

'One necessary condition,' quoth he, 'required in every law is that it be just; for, if this condition be wanting, that the law be unjust, then it is, *ipso facto*, void and of no force, neither hath it power to oblige any. And this is a maxim not only of divines, but of Aristotle and all philosophers. Hereupon ensueth that no power on earth can forbid or punish any action, which we are bound unto by the law of God, which is the true pattern of all justice; so that the laws against recusants, against receiving of priests, against mass, and other rites of Catholic religion, are to be esteemed as no laws by such as steadfastly believe these to be necessary observances of the true religion. Likewise Almighty God hath absolute right for to send preachers of his gospel to any place in the world; "*Euntes docete omnes gentes.*" So that the law against priests coming into the Realm sincerely to preach is no law; and those that are put to death by virtue of that decree are verily martyrs, because they die for the preaching of true religion. Being asked what I meant by "true treason," I answer, that is a true treason which is made treason by any just law; and that is no treason at all which is made treason by an unjust law.'

4th April. THE DEATH OF THE EARL OF DEVONSHIRE.

The Earl of Devonshire died late last night, soon and early for his years, but late enough for himself; and happy had he been if he had gone two or three years since, before the world was weary of him or that he had left scandal behind him. He was not long sick, but eight or ten days, and died of a burning fever and putrefaction of the lungs. He hath left his lady (for so she is now generally held to be) £1,500 a year, and most of his moveables, and of the five children that she fathered upon him at the parting of her former husband, 'tis said that he hath provided only for three, leaving his eldest son between £3,000 and £4,000 a year, and to a daughter £6,000 in money.

THE CHARACTER OF THE EARL OF DEVONSHIRE.

He was in stature tall, and of very comely proportion, his skin fair, and his hair (which was inclined to black) thin; his forehead was broad and high, and his eyes great, black and lovely. His apparel was commonly of white or black taffetas or satins, and he was so careful to keep his body warm that in the country and in the field he wore sometimes three waistcoats in winter and a thick ruff besides a russet scarf about his neck thrice folded. For his diet he fared plentifully and of the best, with the best wines which he drank plentifully but never in excess. He took tobacco abundantly. He was very neat, loving cleanliness both in diet and apparel, and so modest in the necessities of nature that he never used any liberty therein. His behaviour was courtly, grave, and exceeding comely, especially in actions of solemn pomps. In his nature he loved private retiredness, with good fare and some choice friends. He delighted in study, in gardens, a house richly furnished and delectable for rooms of retreat, in riding on a pad to take the air, in playing at shovel board, or at cards, in reading playbooks for recreation, and especially in fishing and fishponds, seldom using other exercises and those rightly as pastimes. He was very valiant, and wise. He much affected glory and honour, having a great desire to raise his house, which was greatly decayed, not so much by his progenitors' prodigality as by his father's obstinate addiction to the study and practice of alchemy, so that he was frugal in gathering and saving, which in his later days declined to vice. In his studies he was bookish, delighting much in divinity. He was a close concealer of secrets, and sparing in speech, but when drawn to it, eloquent. He never used swearing; slow to anger, but once provoked spake home. To his servants he was mild, seldom reproving them and never with ill words. He kept his word in public affairs inviolable, without which he could never have been trusted of the Irish. In battle he bravely adventured his person, more than a General ordinarily should. In short, this worthy Lord cured Ireland from the most desperate estate in which it ever had been, and brought it to the most absolute subjection in which it hath ever been since the first conquest thereof by our nation.

7th April. THE EARL OF LINCOLN'S FOUL ACTION.

Sir Robert Stapleton, having taken that house at Chelsea which lieth next to the Earl of Lincoln's place, now in his turn suffereth from my Lord's strange humours. For the Earl procured a jakes-farmer to take his dung boat, full of filthy dung, and to unlade it to the east and west of Sir Robert's house near to his two fountains so that be the wind east or west the household is incredibly annoyed with the stench thereof, and the well which serveth the house tainted with ill savours. My Lord himself departed for Lincolnshire before this was effected.

10th April. A Patent for Virginia.

The King hath granted a patent for the plantation of Virginia, being petitioned thereto especially by Sir Thomas Gates, Sir George Summer, Master Richard Hakluyt, Prebendary of Westminster, Edward Maria Wingfield, Ralegh Gilbert, esquires and other persons. The undertakers propose to divide themselves into two companies, the one consisting of certain knights, gentlemen, merchants and other adventurers from the City of London, the other company being from Bristol, Exeter and Plymouth. To the first company is assigned the coast between the 34th and 41st degrees and for the space of 50 miles to the west and south-west, and for 100 miles inland; and none other shall be permitted to plant or inhabit behind them without the consent of that Colony. And to the second Colony the like privileges between the 38th and 45th degrees of latitude; but neither colony to plant within 100 miles of the other. Each colony shall have a council of thirteen persons to rule and be ruled according to articles set down and confirmed under the Privy Seal.

The Great Wind.

From foreign parts the news is that the violent wind at the end of last month caused great wreck in Scotland, France, and the Low Countries. It blew down part of the Huguenot Church in Dieppe, and divers other churches in lower Belgia, and in Germany, also in all places villages, trees and windmills. It caused also the sea and divers rivers to overflow their bounds, drowning many people and much cattle. In Holland the town of Flushing was in danger of being overwhelmed. There had been nothing like it for nearly forty years. The water rose 7 feet. It was impossible to walk the streets; even the birds were blown into the water.

A Book on Beauty.

There is printed a little book called *Problems of Beauty and all human afflictions*, written in Italian by Thomas Buoni and translated into English by Mr. Samson Lennard, wherein are considered more than 120 problems, such as these: why is beauty especially apprehended by the sight?; why is beauty enjoyed less desired?; why do women which are not born fair attempt with artificial beauties to seem fair?; why is love so potent?; why do lovers delight in flowers?; why is the hatred of women without end or measure?; and many more.

12th April. AN ORDER FOR FLAGS UPON SHIPS.

To avoid certain contentions which have arisen about the bearing of their flags between his Majesty's subjects of South and North Britain travelling by seas, it is ordered that from henceforth all the subjects of this Isle shall bear in their main top the Red Cross (commonly called St. George's Cross) and the White Cross (commonly called St. Andrew's Cross) joined together to a form made by the Heralds; and in the fore top the subjects of South Britain shall wear the Red Cross only, and of North Britain the White Cross.

14th April. THE PARLIAMENT.

A Bill was read in the Lower House for the better discovering and repressing of popish recusants which is so long that it took one whole hour and a quarter in the reading, and filled twelve presses of parchment and a half. Upon the question, it was passed.

IRISH STIRS.

The Jesuits and seminaries in Ireland being now put to their shifts are busy contriving innovation, and of late pretend that a Bull is come from the Pope of Rome, commiserating with the Irish Catholics, and assuring them of the aid of great strengths of Romans, Germans, and Spaniards, with shipping and great store of arms. It is also rumoured that this summer, Henry, the second son of the Earl of Tyrone, who is now with the Archduke (to whom many loose men flock constantly), will come in command of 4,000 Irishmen who went to the King of Spain and the Archduke, and that there will be greater troubles and garboils than ever heretofore.

18th April. THE NORTH-WEST PASSAGE.

There is again much zeal in these days to discover a shorter passage to the East Indies by way of the north-west, across the North of America. Last year the King of Denmark sent out Captain James Hall, an Englishman, with sundry ships. They found indeed a mighty strong current setting north-north-west, but they could not progress farther by reason of the great banks and islands of ice. These ships set sail in May and returned in August, bringing back many reports of Greenland, and the savages who dwell there. In this company went Master John Knight, captain of a pinnace.

Now our merchants of the Muscovy Company and the East Indies Company have manned and victualled a bark of 40 tons called the *Hopewell* which they send out in the command of Master Knight to make a further attempt to discover the north-west passage.

24th April. THE WEST INDIAN VOYAGE.

This voyage to the West is chiefly fostered by those gentlemen who have hitherto lived by privateering and are now deprived of that dishonest profession by the peace. The ships are being fitted out, but the Spanish Ambassador does all he can to hinder, for his Master would keep our people from meddling with his trade in those parts.

1st May. GARNET'S EXECUTION POSTPONED.

Yesterday a high scaffold was set up in St. Paul's Churchyard for the execution of Garnet which was looked for to-day; but upon better advice it is put off until after to-morrow for fear of disorder among prentices and others in this day of misrule. The news of his death was sent to him three days ago by Dr. Abbot, which he could hardly be persuaded to believe, having conceived great hope of grace by some good words and promises he said were made him by the Spanish Ambassador's mediation, who he thought would have spoken to the King for him. He hath since often been visited and examined by Mr. Attorney, who finds him shifty and faltering in all his answers and it is looked he will equivocate at the gallows.

3rd May. THE EXECUTION OF GARNET.

Henry Garnet was drawn on a hurdle from the Tower to the scaffold in Paul's Churchyard, where the Recorder of London was present, as also the Dean of St. Paul's and the Dean of Winchester. When he had gone up the scaffold, the Deans exhorted him to a true and lively faith to Godward, a free and plain acknowledgment to the world of his offence; and if any treason lay in his knowledge, to unburden his conscience and show a sorrow and detestation of it. But Garnet was impatient of their persuasions and desired them not to trouble him.

Then the Recorder asked Garnet if he had anything to say unto the people before he died, for it was no time to dissemble and now his treasons were too manifest to be dissembled; therefore, if he would, the world should witness what at last he censured of himself, and of his fact; it should be for him to speak what he liked. But Garnet, unwilling to take the offer, said his voice was low, his strength gone, the people could not hear him, though he spake to them. Nevertheless to those about him he said that the intention was wicked, and the fact would have been cruel, and from his soul he should have abhorred it, had it effected.

Then followed certain disputations between Garnet and the Recorder and the Dean of Winchester concerning the proof of his guiltiness; but at length he confessed himself justly condemned. Hereupon the Recorder led him to the scaffold to make his confession public.

Then Garnet said, 'Good countrymen, I am come hither this blessed day of The Invention of the Holy Cross to end all my crosses in this life. The cause of my suffering is not unknown to you. I confess I have offended the King, and am sorry for it, so far as I was guilty; which was in concealing it, and for that I ask pardon of his Majesty. The treason intended against the King and State was bloody, myself should have detested it had it taken effect. And I am heartily sorry that any Catholics ever had so cruel a design.'

Then turning himself from the people to those about him he made an apology for Mistress Anne Vaux, saying, 'There is such an honourable gentlewoman who hath been much wronged in report, for it is suspected and said that I should be married to her, or worse. But I protest the contrary: she is a virtuous gentlewoman, and for me a perfect virgin.' For other matters he referred himself to his arraignment and his confessions, for, said he, 'Whatsoever is under my hand in any of my confessions is true.'

Then addressing himself to execution he kneeled at the ladder foot and asked if he might have time to pray, and how long. It was answered that he should limit himself; none should interrupt him. It appeared that he could not constantly pray, fear of death or hope of pardon even then so distracted him. For oft in these prayers he would break off, turn and look about him, and answer to what he overheard while he seemed to be praying. When he stood up, the Recorder finding in his behaviour as it were an expectation of pardon, wished him not to deceive himself, nor beguile his own soul, he was come to die, and he must die. He required him not to equivocate with his last breath; if he knew anything that might be danger to the King or State, he should now utter it.

Garnet replied that he did not now equivocate, and more than he had confessed he did not know.

Having ascended the ladder, he used these words, 'I commend me to all good Catholics, and I pray God preserve his Majesty, the Queen, and all their posterity, and my Lords of the Privy Council, to whom I remember my humble duties, and I am sorry that I did dissemble with them; but I did not think they had such proof against me, till it was showed me; but when that was proved, I held it more honour for me at that time to confess than before to have accused myself. And for my brother Green-way, I would the truth were known; for the false reports that are, make him more faulty than he is. I should not have charged him, but that I thought he had been safe. I pray God the Catholics may not fare the worse for my sake, and I exhort them all to take heed they enter not into any treasons, rebellions or insurrections against the King.' And with that he ended speaking and fell to praying. In the midst of these prayers the ladder was taken away, and, by the King's express command he hung till he was dead, before his body was quartered.

This Garnet has always been a desperate fellow. He was first in Winchester School where with some other scholars he con-spired to cut off his schoolmaster's right hand, but his design was discovered. Being prepositor of the School, he abused five or six of the handsomest youths therein. Hereupon his schoolmaster advised him silently to steal away rather than stand candidate for a repulse in his preferment to New College. So he fled to Rome and there being a Jesuit, was made Superior of the English Jesuits, and thence returned into England. He was fifty-one years old.

7th May. THE SHIPS FROM THE EAST INDIES RETURN.

The four ships sent out by the Company for trading in the East Indies left England in April 1604, and reached Bantam Road in Java on the 23rd December where they found six Holland ships and three or four pinnaces. They traded in the islands for some months, until March of last year, when the *Hector* and the *Susan* were sent home and set sail on the 4th March. The other two ships, being the *Dragon* and the *Ascension*, set sail from Bantam Road on the 6th October, and on the 27th December came to anchor in the Saldania Road, near the Cape called the Cape of Good Hope. Here they encountered the *Hector*, in sad case, for there were but ten men alive in her, out of sixty-three which had set out from Bantam, all the rest being dead. They had parted with the *Susan* three months before, and never saw her again. They came to anchor in the Downs on the 6th of this month of May. They bring with them some four of those that were left behind in Java at the first voyage, who have much to report of their dealings with the natives there, and with the Dutch.

THE FACTORY AT BANTAM IN JAVA.

When the first fleet departed for England in February 1603 there were left behind in Bantam a small company of English merchants, nine persons in all with Mr. William Starkey as chief commander, as well as thirteen with the pinnace, to establish a factory, to sell the goods left behind, and to gather commodities, especially pepper. Captain Lancaster also left fifty-six chests and parcels of goods in the pinnace, and two houses full of goods in the town, and other goods in the Dutch houses. They report that this town of Bantam is about 3 English miles in length and very populous. The houses of the Javans are altogether built of great canes, but at one end of the town is the China town, for the most part built of brick, every house square and flat overhead. In this part are built the houses of the English and Dutch, made of brick to guard against fire. The Javans are exceeding proud but extremely poor, for not one in a hundred will work, so that the Chineses, being frugal, suck away all their wealth from them. The ordinary weapon of the Javan is called a *crise*, it is almost two foot in length, the blade being waved and crooked to and fro, indenture like, and exceeding sharp and poisoned. The apparel of the better sort is a tuck on their heads, and about their loins a fair pintado, all the rest of their bodies naked. They are a dull and blockish people, whereby all strangers overreach them, and especially the Chinese, who are a very crafty people in trading, using all kinds of cozening and deceit.

The Javans of the poorer sort soon had a quarrel with our merchants, and as soon as the pinnace had departed tried to burn down the principal house with fiery darts and arrows; and all the time they remained there they lived constantly in great and perpetual terror of fire, which is so frequent that in three months' space the town near to them was burned down five times.

Not long after their arrival there came into the road nine sail of Hollanders whose General was named van Warwick, a man very kind to Englishmen because in former times Sir Richard Leveson had saved his life. Divers of these Dutchmen remained to trade, but there were many quarrels between them and our English, or such few as remained, for Mr. Starkey died in June 1603, and by April 1604 there were but ten men and a boy still living.

By that time they had built themselves a great house, which was nearly spoiled in strange manner. A Chinese born, but turned Javan, was their next neighbour, who kept a victualling house. He gathered to himself eight others, and they began to dig a mine from his own house to the English house, and in this way came up under the planks of the warehouse, which at first put them to a nonplus. At length one of them, being a smith by trade, said that he would work out the planks by fire. So they set up a candle and in this way burnt a hole through one of the boards, but the heat set alight to the mats of some of the packs, and the whole place was filled with smoke. With much ado and labour and help of some Chinese our few men saved their goods and put out the fire. By and by they examined the place, and there found a little round hole. So Mr. Edmund Scot, who was now chief of the English merchants, put down a long stick but could feel no ground. Then he took an axe, and very quickly wrenched up the plank, and under it found a way that the greatest chest or pack in the place might have gone down. So he called three of his men, and with weapons in their hands they went along the mine and so into the house where they found three, one of whom was a dweller in the house. Him they took, demanding of the Governor of the town that justice should be done on him. They used this man very cruelly with divers torments to make him confess, and likewise another who was taken the same day, and afterwards shot to death.

These few English in Bantam won a great reputation for themselves, for they never allowed any wrongs to be committed against them by any of the Javans, but they would punish it by death, wounding or beating. Moreover, few as they were they did not forget that they were English, for on the anniversary of the Queen's coronation (who was indeed dead at that time, albeit they did not know it) they suited themselves in new apparel of silk, and made themselves scarfs of white and red taffeta, being our country's colours; also they made a flag with the red cross in the middle. When the day came they set up their banner of St. George upon the top of their house, and with their drum and shot marched up and down within their grounds, being then but fourteen persons, wherefore they could but march single one after another, and so discharged their pieces and cast themselves into rings and esses, to the great admiration of the Governor and others who came to inquire the cause of their triumph.

At length just before Christmas the English ships came to anchor in the road, but in such a bad way that they hardly had fifty sound men in the four ships, and many died there.

9th May. 'THE BLACK YEAR.'

There is a little treatise by Master Anthony Nixon called *The Black Year*, occasioned chiefly by the late treacherous proceedings but mingling lighter matters with serious upon the abuses of these times, noting that all things we perceive to wax daily worse and worse, and to decrease in their virtue. The air is oftentimes corrupt, sometimes with untimely showers, some-times with unprofitable dryness: now with too much cold, now with extreme heat. The fruitfulness of the fields is not such as it hath been before time. Lords and great men bend their cogitations to the oppressing of their poor tenants, and by often fines and exactions, bring honest men to beggary, and by example of Pharaoh make slaves of their servants and subjects. Another great argument of this year's, or rather of the world's, corruption is that all good arts and learning are so contemned and little rewarded or respected. No longer do we see that advised judg-ment, nor that industry, nor those exercises in studies which have been. 'Every man,' quoth this author, 'hath his particular manner of parley, strives to speak in print, hunts after metaphors, coins phrases, and labours extremely that his words may smell of subtlety, elegancy and neat delivery in such affected sort that for the most he leaves nothing behind him but a scent of verbal pride and foolish affection.'

10*th May.* SIR FRANCIS BACON MARRIED.

Sir Francis Bacon was married to-day in Marylebone Church to a young wench, daughter of Sir John Packington. He was clad from top to toe in purple, and hath made himself and his wife such store of fine raiments of cloth of silver and gold that it draws deep into her portion.

14*th May.* THE LADY RUSSELL'S CLAMOROUS SPEECHES.

In the Star Chamber the Lady Russell complained against the Lord Admiral for riotously and forcibly entering the Castle of Donnington. The counsel for the Lord Admiral urged that the Castle and park being his and the plaintiff having but custody thereof it could be no riot, and that so great and honourable an Earl, Lord High Admiral of England, should be brought there as a delinquent they did leave to the consideration of the Court. The counsel for the plaintiff urged what they could against the defendants but as it seemed unwillingly. Then, as the day was far spent and the Lords of the Council were to attend the King after dinner, the Lord Chancellor moved that the plaintiffs should be read, and as the matter appeared doubtful, the Lady Russell interrupting them desired to be heard, and, after many denials by the Court, violently and with great audacity began a large discourse and would not by any means be stayed or interrupted but went on for the space of half an hour and more.

In her speech she did with much bitterness object that my Lord Admiral in the beginning of his answers had denied her to be Lady Dowager to the Lord Russell. The Lords severally would have stayed her and much distasted her proud speeches, but still she went on, though all the Court and presence murmured and made great noise, giving no ear to anything she said, her own counsel going from the bar also. Yet she went on without any change or anyway abashed at all in a very bold and strait manner without show of any distemperature or any loud speaking.

Hereupon the Lord Chancellor told her, 'Madam, you must give us leave; we have suffered you to wrong yourself, this court and our Master his service.' And the Earl of Northampton could not forbear but stayed her, saying that by the law of arms she was no Lady Dowager, nor are there none under the degree of an Earl's wife. Upon that she plucked him by the cloak and told him the law was otherwise before he was born. He, much misliking the usage, told her that such violent interruption of a Judge in delivering his sentence had never before been uttered, and bade her forbear and hear him; 'for,' said he, 'the Lord Russell your husband was a noble gentleman but ill beseeming you with so many fitting detractions to compare him to the Earl of Nottingham; and he died in his father's lifetime, so you could not be Lady Dowager, for your husband was never Earl.'

Then the Lord Chancellor and the rest of the Lords much condemned her for her words against the Lord Admiral, and her pride and wilfulness in the matter. The case is left adjourned.

20th May. JESUITS' TALES OF GARNET AND OLDCORNE.
The Jesuits spread abroad many absurd marvels and wonders concerning Garnet and Oldcorne, as that after Oldcorne had been drawn at Worcester his guts continued burning for sixteen days (being the number of years he laboured in England) nor could they be quenched. They declare also that at Hendlip, at the place where Garnet and Oldcorne last set their feet a new and unknown kind of grass grew up in the form of an imperial crown, which for a long while remained; also that immediately

after Garnet's execution a spring of oil suddenly burst forth at the western end of St. Paul's at the place where he died.

25th May. AN OFFENSIVE SERMON.

To-day Dr. Parker, precentor in the Cathedral at Lincoln, preached at Paul's Cross and spoke very indiscreetly of a piece of scripture wherein there is mention of the Parliament of Trees, and took occasion thereby to inveigh against the proceedings in the Lower House.

26th May. THE COMMONS' INDIGNATION.

There is great stir in Parliament because of the sermon preached yesterday by Dr. Parker. Some were for having him sent for by the Bishops; others that he should be degraded; others that he should be summoned before the House, but some doubted whether this might be since he is a member of Convocation. The Commons' complaint has been taken to the King by Sir Roger Ashton and the Recorder.

A PAPISTICAL PARRICIDE.

Some days since a young man by name Inigo Jeans of Padstow in Cornwall very barbarously slew his father. This Inigo, being at first somewhat reclaimed from popery, had of late relapsed Catholic again. Whereupon his father, whether fearing God or the law, would have restrained his son from going secretly to Mass, who was so enraged that he took up a club or beetle (wherewith they used to cleave wood) and struck his father violently on the head to the ground, and then doubting whether he had thoroughly despatched him, smote him with a bar of iron so that his back was broken and he died instantly. Then this Jeans fled to a chapel near Padstow and there hastily unclothing himself, with a blunt knife (adding all his force thereto) in two or three places gashed his own belly athwart so that his bowels were to be seen. All these things he confessed to the Sheriff, and also that on this very morning he had been secretly at Mass with seven men and eight women more. After two or three days' languishing he departed this life, seeming very sorrowful for the fact.

27th May. THE COMMONS AND THE PREACHER.

The King has called Dr. Parker before him and Mr. Recorder to charge him. The doctor excused himself saying that he meant only the Puritans that should defend deprived ministers. Yet the King has committed him prisoner to the Dean of Paul's; which gives much satisfaction to the House.

PARLIAMENT PROROGUED.

In the afternoon about 5 o'clock the Speaker with the Commons went up to the Upper House where he delivered his speech to the King, who answered it in several particulars, and amongst them showing what he had done in the case of Dr. Parker, for, said the King, howsoever he might clear himself of any ill-meaning, yet he had committed him rather to correct his indiscretion.

The Parliament is now prorogued until the 25th of November next.

A NOTE OF THE CHIEF STATUTES ENACTED IN THE LATE SESSION OF PARLIAMENT.

An Act for a public thanksgiving to Almighty God every year on the Fifth day of November.

An Act for the attainder of divers offenders in the late most barbarous, monstrous, detestable and damnable treasons.

An Act for the better discovering and repressing of popish recusants, whereby it is enacted that a popish recusant who will not attend divine service in Church or receive the Sacrament once a year shall forfeit for the first year £20, for the second £40, and thereafter £60 each year, of which one moiety shall be forfeited to the King and the other to him that shall sue for it. Further, an Oath of allegiance shall be tendered to recusants whereby they acknowledge King James as the lawful King of this Realm and that the Pope has no authority to depose the King nor to give licence to any of his subjects to bear arms against him; that they will bear true faith to his Majesty and will defend him against all conspiracies; that they abjure the damnable doctrine that Princes, excommunicate by the Pope, may be deposed or murdered by their subjects; that neither the Pope nor any other hath power to absolve them of this oath, renouncing all pardons and dispensations, and swearing without any equivocation or mental evasion or secret reservation whatsoever.

An Act to prevent and avoid dangers which may grow by

popish recusants, limiting their dwelling places and actions in divers ways.

An Act to reform the misdemeanours of Attorneys and Solicitors at law who charge their clients with unnecessary fees.

An Act for the rating or levying of the charges for conveying malefactors to jail.

An Act for the better preservation of sea-fish, whereby it is forbidden to take the spawn or fry with draw nets or nets of canvas in havens, harbours or creeks.

An Act against unlawful hunting and stealing of deer and conies, because there have been divers grounds enclosed for the preservation and maintenance of deer and conies, and there is an Act of force too against evil-disposed persons who chase and kill deer and conies, whereby many riots, manslaughters and mischiefs have been committed.

An Act to restrain abuses of players, whereby it is forbidden in any stage-play or show jestingly or profanely to speak or use the Holy Name of God, or of Christ Jesus or of the Holy Ghost or of the Trinity: and for every offence the fine shall be £10.

An Act for confirmation of the subsidies granted by the Clergy.

An Act for the grant of three entire subsidies and six fifteenths and tenths granted by the Temporality.

30th May.   A STRANGE CASE CONCERNING A CORPSE.

In the Star Chamber to-day complaint was made concerning certain ministers, two coroners and others by the widow of one Mr. Gawen. In August 1603 this Gawen, who was a stiff Papist, died and being a fat and corpulent man his wife made haste the next day to bury him. At one parish the minister refused, saying that he was excommunicate. So they went to another parish, and in the night-time some ten or twelve of his friends got into the church and buried him in the chancel, without minister, clerk or sexton, and locked the church door. Next day they rang the bells in the two parishes, and so disorderly that the constable, the tithing man, the minister and some forty of the parish doubting some fire or other disorder repaired to the Church, and could not be permitted to enter but got in by a little privy door. So after some words had passed between the parties, the constable and tithing man forcing them out of the chancel, the widow spat in the tithing man's face. Hereupon the constable put her in the stocks and thrust all the rest out of the church.

After this there was a bruit raised that Mr. Gawen was not dead but had been seen alive. Whereupon one Kennell, having an estate for Gawen's life, grew suspicious of his death, and in the night-time with his man went to the church, digged up one end of the grave and found his coffin, and so leaving the grave open, went his way. And within a few days afterwards, Kennell went to Sir James Mervyn, a Lieutenant and Justice of the Peace, asking that by reason of the many rumours the crowners might view the body.

So a jury was summoned, but the foreman of the jury, being fearful of the plague then raging, desired that he might lie in the ground somewhat longer. After fourteen days the jury again came together and crowner commanded the tithing man to dig up the grave and take out the body, which he utterly refused to do. Kennell therefore hired a man to do it, and the corpse was dragged into a meadow where there would be more air than in the churchyard. But none of the jury save one durst for the strong savour of the corpse come near. Kennell therefore caused one to open the shroud and gave evidence himself to the jury that there was a suspicious mark about his neck that he should be strangled. But the jury did acquit him, and found he died of a natural disease. So they all departed; the crowner gave charge to the parish and officers that they should bury the corpse, which they refused to do.

Then Kennell caused it to be drawn into the church porch and hid away the key of the church door and there let him lie divers days whereby all the parish were so annoyed that they durst not come to the church. But within a few days afterwards Kennell gave directions that he should be buried in the church-yard, but whereas for the most part all are buried east and west, he caused the grave to be made north and south; and some finding fault with it, he said 'As he was an overthwart neighbour while he lived, so he shall be buried overthwartly, and if you mislike it, I will have him dredged at a horse-tail and laid upon the downs.'

When the case had been heard, the other defendants were acquitted, but Kennell was much condemned to have proceeded in this business with great malice, so he is sentenced to a fine of £100 and imprisonment; and the other defendants in the case are allowed their costs. The Archbishop in his speech delivered that it is a secret practice of the Papists to wrap their dead bodies in two sheets, and in one of them they straw earth that they themselves have hallowed and so bury them they care not where, for they say they are thus buried in consecrated earth.

1st June. COMPLAINTS AGAINST THE SPANIARDS.

To-day, being Sunday, divers merchants and merchants' wives came to Court and made grievous complaint to the King, the one of their servants, the other of their husbands imprisoned and put to the galleys in Spain, and of much oppression and injustice done there to our nation, besides some particular contumely to the King personally; the like complaint was made to the Lords. It hath moved much and the Kingdom generally wishes this peace broken, but *Jacobus Pacificus*, 'tis thought, will scarce incline to that side. We are in daily expectation of the King of Denmark's arrival and the Queen's delivery, charges that we have little need of.

3rd June. THE LORDS STOURTON AND MORDAUNT IN THE STAR CHAMBER.

The Lords Stourton and Mordaunt were brought from the Tower to the Star Chamber before the Lord Chancellor and others of the Council and there charged that being Peers of the Realm and Barons of the High Court of Parliament, and summoned thereto by writ under the Great Seal, neither of them had made their appearance.

The Attorney informed against them, and showed how closely they were in league with the plotters who had agreed that they were to be spared. Moreover, their excuses for absenting themselves rather accused them. The Lord Stourton had declared that he had no money and was in debt, his wife delivered but two months before, and her father dead: besides the plague was increased in London. All these were hindrances, said he, why he could not come upon Tuesday;

yet they were no hindrance upon Friday, for then he came. The Lord Mordaunt's excuse was that being in London with Catesby in October he went down to look up his evidence for assart lands. He had all the summer to do it, said Mr. Attorney, and he kept continual company with all the great traitors.

By sentence of the Court they are fined, the Lord Mordaunt 10,000 marks, and the Lord Stourton 6,000 marks, and to remain imprisoned in the Tower during his Majesty's pleasure.

7th June. THE DEBTS OF THE UNITED PROVINCES.

Sir Noel Caron continually urgeth the necessities of the United Provinces, declaring that they cannot subsist unless his Majesty do help them by some secret and underhand assistance, either by some round sum of money, or that he will remit some three or four years' payment of their great debt, or that of the debt owed by the French King a third part should be paid to the States, a third to his Majesty, and third part remitted; which last proposal is made by M. de Beaumont. But the King is not willing to give so great a cause of jealousy and scandal to the King of Spain by breaking his peace with such a practising course.

10th June. A PROCLAMATION AGAINST PAPIST PRIESTS.

There is a new proclamation published of his Majesty's determination for avoiding of effusion of blood, to banish by the first day of August all Jesuits, seminaries, friars and any other priest whatsoever, regular or secular, made by authority of the Church of Rome. Any of them (Gerrard or Greenway only excepted) that shall resort to any port town and there declare himself to the magistrate or other officers that he is a priest and that he is there to take shipping for his passage, they shall suffer him quietly to depart, and shall see them shipped and sent away, and give them furtherance for their departure.

15th June. A TREATISE OF POLICY AND RELIGION.

Mr. Thomas Fitzherbert, that for many years hath been on exile abroad and is now turned Catholic priest hath written *The first part of Treatise concerning policy and religion,* wherein the infirmity of human wit is declared, with the necessity of

true religion for the perfection of policy; and by the way some
political matters are treated; divers principles of Macchiavel
confuted; and many advices given, tending no less to religious
piety than to true policy; with a confutation of the arguments
of atheists against the providence of God. This author left
England in 1582 and in 1598 was fellow with Edward Squire
who practised to poison Queen Elizabeth. Declareth in the
Epistle 'I perceive by such English books as I have chanced
to see, printed in England of late, that the English tongue is
much altered since I came thence, and therefore I may fear
that the language current in my time (which I am forced to use
because I never used nor learned other) may now seem no less
barbarous to some men than divers new words and phrases
seem to me.'

21st June. 'SIR PHILIP SIDNEY'S OURANIA.'

Mr. Nathaniel Baxter, that was formerly tutor to the
renowned Sir Philip Sidney, hath written a poem entitled
Sir Philip Sidney's Ourania, or Endimion's song and tragedy,
containing all philosophy, dedicated to the Lady Mary, Countess
of Pembroke, and other noble ladies.

MR. BAXTER'S NOTE OF EARTHQUAKES.

The earthquake is a simple meteor
Airy and uncompounded as before;
An airy vapour, closed in some den,
Or concave of the earth, remote from men,
Searching for an issue, and finding none,
Beateth up and down, seeking to be gone,
But all in vain, then being fast inclosed,
It shakes the earth in searching to be losed,
This is the cause of great Tellus trembling
(A man in shaking fever resembling):
What future events it doth prognosticate,
I will not presage, th'effect is intricate.
But if a small vapour be of that power
To shake the whole frame of the earth in one hour
How may proud man, full of infirmity,
Sustain the fury of the Deity?

His Praise of the Spaniel.

How may my pen these spaniels commend
Whose qualities are such as have no end?
If thou wilt seek a constant faithful friend
In life and death, thy body to defend
Walking and running by thy horse's side,
Scorning all dangers that may thee betide,
Being a faithful and true companion
In joy and woeful desolation,
Whom neither change, nor sad calamity,
Nor raging famine, or adversity,
Nor naked state, or pining poverty
Can make to shun or leave thy company;
Then take thy dog.

22nd June. THE QUEEN DELIVERED.

At 3 o'clock in the morning, the Queen gave birth to a daughter which is named Lady Sophia.

23rd June. THE EARL OF NORTHUMBERLAND.

The Lords have sat much in Council about my Lord of Northumberland, and to-day they were with him in the Tower but it is not known what passed, but only the common voice goes that the King would have him to the Star Chamber. My Lord's brother, Sir Allan Percy, being also convented before them is committed to the custody of the Lieutenant of the Tower: some say it is about the old matter of Percy, that he was not sworn when he was admitted pensioner; others for conveying letters to my Lord. Howsoever the matter is not thought to be great, for his lady is allowed to go to him.

THE LADY SOPHIA DEAD.

The infant daughter of the King and Queen lived but one day, and is now dead.

26th June. THE LADY SOPHIA BURIED.

To-day was the body of the infant Lady Sophia conveyed from Greenwich by a barge covered with black velvet, accompanied with three other barges, unto the Chapel Royal at Westminster, and there interred by Dr. Barlow, Lord Bishop of Rochester, in the presence of all the great Lords of the Council, with the Heralds and divers officers of the Court.

27th June. THE EARL OF NORTHUMBERLAND CONDEMNED IN THE STAR CHAMBER.

The Earl of Northumberland was to-day brought from the Tower by Sir William Waad, the Lieutenant, and Sir William Lane to the Star Chamber where a great scaffold was erected for the courtiers and other men of great account, with a side bar for the prisoner. He was charged with six offences, *videlicet*:

For endeavouring to be the head of the English Papists, and to procure them toleration;

For admitting and placing Thomas Percy to be one of the King's Gentlemen Pensioners without ministering unto him the Oath of Supremacy, knowing Percy to be a recusant;

That when he was commanded to keep his house upon discovery of the treason he wrote two letters to his friends in the North parts (supposing Percy to have fled thither) to have a care of his money and revenues, but utterly neglecting in those letters to take any order for the apprehension of Percy;

For presuming to write letters abroad after his restraint without leave of the King or the Council;

That being a Privy Councillor he had more care of his treasure than of the King and the State;

That his letters to the North parts were to give a watchword to Percy to further his escape, and besides that he had confessed that since his Majesty's reign he had conference concerning the King's nobility, and how long, and in what manner he would reign.

Sir Edward Coke, the Attorney-General, informed against him. He began with very great respect as towards the greatest person and cause ever brought into this Court. Then he divided the cause in four parts: first, the honour and order of the King's proceeding that this great offence was brought down to a small contempt; secondly, the offences he was charged withal; thirdly, the circumstances that aggravated the offences; fourthly, the great and many misfortunes.

In the beginning of the King's reign and at the end of the Queen's, the Earl of Northumberland became the head of the

Catholics and a friend to the Catholic cause, and he desired Catholics might depend on him. After the Pope had set forth two damnable bulls against the King, the Earl, knowing of them, sent this Percy into Scotland to ask for a toleration for the Catholics, with two letters and a message pretending the more easy entrance if he would give hopes of toleration; which were intolerable and not to be endured, for that an Englishman's heart grieves to see another kind of worship. Upon Percy's return out of Scotland the Earl of Northumberland told the Catholics that the King's commandment was that they should be eased of their persecutions, which the King himself *in verbo regis* says he never did promise or command. After this Percy and Catesby plotted their treason and yet soon after Percy was made a Pensioner; a fit man to put an axe into his hands to carry it over the King's head! And not only was he made a pensioner, he never took any oath.

Then Master Attorney enlarged upon the other matters of the charges at length and after his accustomed manner. It was concluded that he shall be fined £30,000, lose his place as a Privy Councillor and be deprived of all other offices, and to return to the Tower there to remain prisoner during his life.

30th June. STRANGE NEWS FROM VENICE.

Strange news is come from Venice of the coming wars of the Turks with the King of Hungary, who it is said shall have great succours from Christian princes; but strangest of all is of a great host of Hebrews, descended of nine and a half tribes that were driven beyond the mountain Cospe by Alexander the Great and long since lost; they are now about to bring two mighty armies to recover the Land of Promise, and the first is already arrived upon the limits of Turkey putting all to fire and sword. These people have for many generations been cut off by reason of the sea of sand, but now by the means of the new navigation that the Hollanders have made they have been taught the science of artillery, wherein they are marvellous apt; and they have learnt moreover the way through this sea of sand. These things are set forth in a little pamphlet together with the prophecy of one Caleb Shilock, a Jew, of great calamities to happen next year when the Moon is in the watery sign, and of a flood next May, the greatest since Noah's day.

3rd July. THE EARL OF NORTHUMBERLAND.

The Earl of Northumberland has written to the King complaining bitterly that Percy abused both his Majesty and himself. As for his own loyalty he protests with a very solemn oath that his heart is without spot or blemish, and prays that any neglect of duty or indiscretions and oversights may not overbalance the King's forgiveness.

4th July. 'THE NINE ENGLISH WORTHIES.'

Mr. Richard Fletcher hath penned a book, part prose, part verse, called *The nine English Worthies*, being the eight Kings that bore the name of Henry, with the Prince for the ninth, which is commended by verses written by sundry gentlemen.

9th July. A PLOT AGAINST THE KING.

Another suspected plot against the King is come to light. Some time since one Captain William Neuce, who had conceived great discontent against his Majesty for being now cashiered and left without any entertainment, came over from Brussels. About the same time one Thomaso Francheschi Jacques, brother to Colonel Jacques that was sometime page to the Lord Chancellor Hatton, came over in the company of a certain John Ball, an Irishman, and servant to the Spanish Ambassador. These three met often at Ball's chamber in the Ambassador's lodging and there a priest was brought who resolved Neuce that he may do anything against heretics because they are worse than Turks and Infidels. Hereupon Thomaso and Ball would set Neuce on to murder the King with a pistol while he is hunting at Royston. But it seems that the other two at length grew tired of Neuce, for last Sunday being at the Ambassador's they gave him a piece of sweetmeat called 'paste of Genoa.' Neuce ate of it, and suspecting nothing, put a piece of it in his handkerchief to carry to a child of his. Coming home, his wife and two other women of her neighbours also ate a little of it, but towards night Neuce himself fell a casting and spewing, his stomach swelling, and so did the women, all of them, in the judgment of physicians, having all the

317   L*

accidents of having eaten some poison. Next morning (these things having been made known to my Lord of Salisbury) Jacques was apprehended, when it was learnt that he had sent for horses to be gone; and the Spanish Ambassador was written unto that Ball might be forthcoming. But two days since the Ambassador came to the King and showed great unwillingness to deliver Ball. Hereupon grew some contestation, the King affirming that the Ambassador had done that his master would not approve him in. In fine, the Ambassador denied to deliver Ball, but if his Majesty would send and take him in his lodging he might; which was done in quiet manner. Thomaso, after examination and confronting with witnesses of his words, is committed to the Tower; Ball yet remains at the Sheriff's House in London.

10*th July*. THE FRENCH KING AND HIS MISTRESS.

From France the speech is that the King has sent away two ships laden with Irish beggars (that lingered about Paris) home to their country again, after he had clad and refreshed them, with commandment that no more come thence into his dominions.

The King is now said to be vehemently bent for entertaining the Marquise D'Entragues again, whom the Queen of all women fears as one that hath had very handsome children by the King, pretendeth a contract of marriage with him before the Queen, and in way of discourse is capable and sufficient above any woman in France; to which kind of delight with women he now bendeth himself, being not any more in case to emulate the prowess of Hercules. The Queen, hoping to divert him, sent another lady to him who began to play the preacher with him, and would persuade him to content himself with his Queen. The King answered that she was his daily bread, but he must have besides somewhat for collation. Therefore the Queen falls into great passions and weepings if she hear that either the King goes to the Marquise or she comes to Paris. Moreover, she grew into such sharp terms that she protested, rather than she would endure such indignities, she would return to Florence again; and received as quick an answer that for to bring her thither she should have the easiest coaches and litters of all France provided for her.

11*th July.* THE RETURN OF SIR EDWARD MICHELBORNE'S
  SHIPS.

Sir Edward Michelborne that set out for the East Indies
with Captain John Davis in the *Tiger*, a ship of 240 tons, with
a pinnace called the *Tiger's Whelp,* is returned to England. At
Bantam he missed the English fleet which was gone for England
three weeks before they came, but the English that remained
there as factors came aboard, very glad to see any of their own
countrymen in so foreign a place and withal told the general
that the company of the Hollanders' ships that were in the Road
had used very slanderous reports of him to the King of Bantam,
saying that the English were thieves and disordinate livers and
durst not come into the Road among them but kept two or
three leagues from thence for fear. These tidings so moved
Sir Edward that he sent the Hollanders word that if they did go
about either to brave or disgrace him or his countrymen, he
would sink them or sink by their sides.

They were in great danger from certain Japons that they
met sailing helpless in a junk laden with rice, that they understood to be men of war that had pillaged on the coast of China
and Camboia. These rogues, being desperate in fortunes and
helpless in their paltry junk ever to return to their country,
resolved to possess themselves of his ship, and upon mutual
courtesies with gifts and feastings some six and twenty came
aboard the *Tiger.* Then Sir Edward, somewhat mistrusting
them, willed Captain Davis in the morning to possess himself
of their weapons and to put the company before the mast and
to leave some guard on their weapons while they searched in
the rice. But Captain Davis, being beguiled by their humble-
ness did not possess himself of their weapons. At length upon
a watchword between the Japons in the junk and those in the
ship, they suddenly set upon Sir Edward's men, killing and
driving overboard all that were in the junk. Those that were
in the *Tiger*, sallied out of the cabin where they had been put
with such weapons as they had found. Sir Edward being left
on the deck leapt into the waist, where with the boatswain, the
carpenter and some few more, he kept them under the half deck.
At their first coming out of the cabin they met Captain Davis
coming out of the gunroom and thrust him out before them,

giving him six or seven wounds so mortal that he died as soon
as he came into the waist. It was near half an hour before they
could force the Japons back with their pikes into the cabin,
where for four hours more they resisted, often firing the bedding
and other stuffs. At length Sir Edward caused two demi-
culverins to be charged with crossbar shot, bullets and case
shot and bent close to the bulkhead and so discharged that it
left but one of them standing of two and twenty, their legs,
arms and bodies being strangely massacred by the shot.

Thereafter they fought a little with a Chinish ship, from
which they took some silks, giving twice as much in exchange;
but learning soon after from some Hollanders that the King
of Java would assault the English merchants in Bantam
because of the taking of the Chinish ship, whereby the King of
Bantam had lost his custom, Sir Edward thought that it would
be very dangerous for the English merchants if he remained
in those parts so determined to return home.

They came to anchor in Portsmouth Road two days ago.

13th July (Sunday). GENERAL NEWS.

My Lady of Northumberland to-day spoke with the King
as he went to the Chapel and had afterwards long conference
with the Earl of Salisbury, but the issue is not known, only she
was noted to part cheerfully from him. The late treason after
so hot pursuit is now come to a cold scent, and they can make
nothing of it. Yet Thomaso Francheschi, Jacques' brother,
after he was confronted yesterday with Neuce is sent to the
Tower where the rack may wring out his secret villainies, for
there is no hope to do any good to him by fair means, who in all
likelihood being sounded by Neuce (that was employed to wait
upon such fellows and learn out their plots) and discovering
him to be a false brother gave him the *bocado* and now denies
all as fast as he affirms, so that it should seem this ulcer was
opened before it was ripe.

At the Sessions this last week there were two Spanish cut-
purses condemned, the one to be pressed, the other hanged;
but they are both still reprieved, whereat our common people
repine and say our own cannot find such favour. One Francis
Dormer this day hanged himself upon shame that he was beastly

drunk the day before. Derrick the hangman (to the great rejoicing of all the boys in the town) was well whipped in Bridewell for burning a fellow in the hand with a cold iron.

There is a huge number of popish books lately taken, and a whole sackful of letters, but for the most part without inscriptions.

14th July. THE KING.

The King has gone to Oatlands and so forward to Farnham whereabout he means to tarry a fortnight unless the King of Denmark's coming call him back; from whom comes a pinnace of advice that he is near our coast, so that either he is landed or else it is doubted this wind that is come about full in his teeth may send him back the way that he came.

16th July. A MONSTROUS MURDER.

Yesterday the wife of one Richard Homewood of East Grinsted in Sussex most unnaturally murdered her own three children. She first cut their throats, and then threw them into a pit, and straightway cut her own throat, and leapt into the pit after them, herself being (as is generally supposed) with child. She was taken up and buried in a crossway according to law.

NEWS FROM BARTHOLEMEW FAIR.

There is a new rhyme printing how all the red and copper noses being gathered at Bartholemew Fair there comes a post to say that *Nos maximus omnium* is gone and dead, whereupon his friends are called to make ready to his funeral, and to the Mass following; and after all the noses come together to comfort *nose defunctus* his man, and draw up a supplication to the Gods, as followeth:

In most humble wise we beseech you and show
Unto your Godheads all in a row,
The Vintners remaining in all kind of places,
That whereas by maintaining of noses and faces:
There hath been great sale and utterance of wines
Besides beer and ale, and ipocras fine:
In every country region and nation,
Chiefly at Billingsgate at the Salvation,
At the Boar's Head, near London Stone.

The Swan at Dowgate, a tavern well known,
The Mitre in Cheap, and then the Bull Head,
And many like places that make noses red:
The Boar's Head in old Fish Street, Three Cranes in the
    Vintry,
And now of late St. Martins in the Sentry.
And Windmill in Lothbury, the Ship at the Exchange,
King's Head in New Fish Street where roysterers do range,
The Mermaid in Cornhill, Red Lion in the Strand,
Three Tuns Newgate Market, Old Fish Street at the Swan.
Of late (may it please you) for want of good order,
The colours are decayed in every good border:
By such as intrude and seem to oppress,
Forestalling country markets with wines that be less,
They are great dealers in uttrance of wine,
And are but ale stealers, and put water in their wine.
May it therefore please your godheads we may be friended
To have this disorder among them amended
And grant, we beseech you, of mercy and pity,
Your licence to our new Master Nose of this city,
To apprehend, arrest, and take in all places,
All manner of men having metal in their faces.
And that everyone arrested in this manner,
Shall carry a pot under the Vintners' banner.
That if any man denay,
Your licence to obey:
Then while his nose is hot,
We may ply him with the pot:
And banish him his ale,
And set his coat to sale,
Till he hath professed
Good fellowship with the rest.

17th July. THE KING OF DENMARK'S COMING.

This day the ship carrying his Majesty the King of Denmark
arrived and anchored at Gravesend, whither the King sent the
Duke of Lennox, the Earl of Rutland and other noblemen to
welcome him; but it was past 11 of the clock before they came
to Gravesend. The Lords were desirous to have gone aboard

the Admiral, but the Captain of the ship told them that they might not come aboard, for that the watch was set and the King asleep whom now they durst not wake, being so late.

18th *July*. THE MEETING OF THE TWO KINGS.

This morning the King with Prince Henry, the Duke of Lennox, the Lord Admiral, the Lord Chamberlain, the Earls of Rutland, Pembroke, Montgomery, and divers other noblemen came by barge from Greenwich to Gravesend; and as they from the ships descried the barges, they gave notice to their King, and the company was by the boatswain's whistles called up, each man in his livery making a gallant show and noise of trumpets after the sea manner. When the King of Denmark beheld them near his ship, he went to descend to entertain them; but perceiving the narrowness of the stairs would not permit two at once either to ascend or descend, he stayed in his ship, and with all princely courtesy entertained the nobility as they came aboard; and when the Kings met they embraced.

Then the King of Denmark led King James into the cabin, which is very beauteous, and placed him at the upper hand, giving him precedence all the while they were aboard. Both Kings dined in the cabin, and the Lords with others were very honourably feasted in another room. They rested awhile, and after supper, the tide serving, they went on board the King's barge, and with the noblemen of both courts were rowed to Greenwich palace. After they had rowed some small way, the Admiral discharged a thundering peal of ordnance which was taken up by the other ships, and so by the block house at Gravesend. At their landing great multitudes of people assembled, and thence in royal manner they entered the Court of Greenwich where King Christianus most joyfully met the Queen, his royal sister. The King is of a goodly person, of stature in no extremes, in face so like our Queen that he who hath seen the one may in fancy paint the other. He was apparelled in black cut out on cloth of silver, and about his hat wore a band of gold, wrought in form of a crown, and set with precious stones.

20th *July*. THE DANISH KING.

To-day being Sunday King James, with King Christianus,

accompanied with the nobility of both kingdoms went to the chapel where they heard a sermon by Dr. Barlow, now the Bishop of Rochester. All the way as they passed and returned there was a great multitude of people present, and the company was very sumptuous, with the Gentlemen Pensioners and the Guard in their rich coats. At dinner the Guard of King James were appointed to attend on the Gentleman Sewer and carried up the kingly viands, with plentiful wine and beer, all served in most honourable manner with noise and excellent music of drums and trumpets, which moved King Christianus to much delight.

21st July. THE DANISH KING.

The two Kings, accompanied with Prince Henry, and many honourable persons, most richly mounted, hunted in Greenwich Park in the morning and killed two bucks. In the afternoon they went to Eltham, where in the park they hunted with great pleasure and killed three bucks on horseback, being followed with many companies of people who endeavoured to keep up on foot. Towards sunset they returned to the Court, all the way pacing easily that the people might the better behold them.

24th July. THE KINGS ENTERTAINED BY THE EARL OF SALISBURY.

This morning about 11 of the clock the two Kings with the Prince came on board the barges and were rowed to Blackwall, where their coaches with their train attended their coming with an innumerable multitude of people; and at their landing the merchants' ships, anchored in the road, discharged their ordnance. Thence they set forward to Stratford and so to Theobalds, where my Lord of Salisbury entertaineth them. All the way there were so many people, some on foot, some on horseback and others in coaches that there was hardly way left for the royal company to pass them. As they came near to Theobalds, there was strewed in the highways abundance of leaves, coloured green, cut like oak leaves, and on each was written in large roman letters of gold 'WELCOME, WELCOME,' which device much pleased their Majesties. In the inner court as they entered there was a device of three Hours that spake verses of gratulation made by Ben Jonson, who also wrote certain epigrams in Latin which were hung on the walls.

28th *July*. THE KINGS AT THEOBALDS.

After dinner the two Kings left Theobalds, returning gracious thanks to my Lord of Salisbury for their cheer and pleasures and this night they came again to the Court at Greenwich. At Theobalds many delights were prepared for them in hunting in the parks and chases where they killed many deer. There was much feasting and carousal, and on the night of the great feast, by the device of the Earl of Salisbury and others, there was an entertainment made of Solomon and his Temple and the Queen of Sheba, which was a little dashed by the drunkenness both of those that would perform it and of the spectators. The lady that played the Queen of Sheba did carry up a rich present, and wine, cream, jelly and other matters; but forgetting the steps arising to the canopy, she overset her casket into the Danish King's lap and fell at his feet. There was much hurry and confusion; clothes and napkins were at hand to make all clean. Then his Majesty got up and would dance with the Queen of Sheba, but he fell down and was carried to an inner chamber and laid on a bed of state. Nevertheless the entertainment went forward, and next appeared Hope, Faith and Charity. Hope essayed to speak, but wine rendered her endeavours so feeble that she withdrew and hoped the King would excuse her brevity; Faith also left the Court in a staggering condition. Charity then came to the King and said somewhat, and then returned to the other two who were now spewing in the lower hall. Next came Victory in bright armour and presented a sword to the King who did not accept it, and after much lamentable utterance she was led away and laid to sleep on the outer steps of the anti-chamber. Next came Peace, but finding her passage hindered, with great wrath she lustily laid on the pates of those that opposed her with her olive branch.

Such things greatly astonish those courtiers who knew the good order, sobriety and discretion of the old Queen's time, so that in secret they say that the Danes have again conquered England, such is the beastliness, riot and excess at Court.

31st *July*. THE KINGS ENTERTAINED IN THE CITY.

About 2 of the clock this afternoon the Kings, accompanied

by the Prince, the Privy Council, and many of the nobility went on board the King's barges and were rowed to the Tower where they landed; and as soon as the train could be marshalled they set forward, being entertained by the Lord Mayor who delivered the Sword unto his Highness who graciously received it and then proceeded. First came the Marshals of the City with their men suited in yellow fustian, with ash-coloured hats, red bands and red scarves and each a tipstaff in his hand. Next came two trumpeters of King James, and the Knight Marshal and his followers in clay-colour cloaks, white doublets and green hose with white hats. Then followed the Messengers, and a Herald of Arms; and the King's Trumpeters, led by their Sergeant in a cloak of carnation velvet. Next came the King of Denmark's Drum, riding upon a horse, with two drums one on each side of his horse's neck, whereon he struck two little mallets of wood, a thing much admired by the common sort. There was also a troop of knights, very gallant, of whom many wore strange feathers which they called 'the birds of paradise,' and after them the Knights of the Bath; the Barons and nobility of England; the Lord Archbishop and the Bishop of London; then the Earl of Salisbury and other Earls of the Council and others amongst whom were placed the Lords and chiefest of the Denmark's King's nobility and Council. After them came the Earl of Nottingham, Lord High Admiral of England, who carried the Sword, and the Lord Mayor of London who carried a mace. Then followed Prince Henry, who was much applauded by the whole company.

After him came their two Majesties, both attired in plain suits but rich in jewels and their horses near alike, about whom marched divers of the Denmark Guard, suited in watchet coats and hose, soldier-like, laced with white and blue lace, wearing whitish hats, with blue bands, and carrying gilt halberts.

Behind them came the Earl of Worcester; then the Gentlemen Pensioners on horseback, with their feathers yellow and red, and their scarves very large, laced with fair gold lace at each end. They were followed by the King of Denmark's Guard, marching three and three; after whom came the King's Guard in their rich coats to the number of 180.

This train rode on from Tower Hill until they came to

Cheapside, and all the way stood the Companies of London in their livery gowns and hoods, for whom there were places double railed, hung with blue broadcloth, and adorned with the ancients of silk of each Hall. The windows and penthouses were richly decked with arras and other costly hangings. At the Great Conduit in Cheapside was made a very artificial arbour, garnished with all sorts of delightful fruits. In this arbour was placed secret music. At the Little Conduit there was erected a stately pageant such as for rare device and beauty hath been seldom seen, especially in so short a time accomplished, the work-men and plotters thereof having not twelve days' respite after their first warning. Here the Recorder of London presented the King of Denmark with a fair cup of gold. Then the pageant began to express the purpose there, which was, that Divine Con-cord, as sent from Heaven, descended in a cloud from the top unto the middle stage, and with a loud voice spake an excellent speech in Latin, purporting their hearty welcome and to the like effect; but such was the noise of the unruly multitude that the Kings heard but little of it.

Thence they proceeded till they came to Paul's Churchyard where at the school of the worshipful Company of Mercers, called Paul's School, other speeches were delivered. Then they rode on without stay to Fleet Conduit, which was likewise garnished, and on the top was placed secret music; and here also were presented with other speeches. When they came to St. Dunstan's Church they were presented with a noise of cornets. Thence they proceeded to Temple Bar where both Kings gave many thanks to the Lord Mayor and Citizens for their great charge and pains, and redelivered the Sword to the Lord Mayor. Then they went on to Somerset House where they rested, and which King James will henceforward have called Denmark House in honour of his brother-in-law.

This evening there were fireworks upon the water at Whitehall.

1st August. THE KING OF DENMARK.

This morning King Christianus and the Prince with others of both nations went to the Abbey of Westminster and into the Chapel Royal of Henry the Seventh to behold the monuments.

Against their coming the image of Queen Elizabeth and certain other images of the Kings and Queens were newly beautified, amended and adorned with royal vestures, but the King took most notice of St. Edward's Shrine.

After dinner the King, accompanied with the Lord Admiral, the Lord Chamberlain and others, came by coach unto Paul's Church, and into the quire and chapels. Then they ascended to the top of the steeple where the King took much delight to behold the situation of London; and when he had surveyed the City, he held his foot while Edward Soper, the keeper of the steeple, cut the length and breadth thereof in the lead. But amongst all other things he admired most when the noblemen accompanying him did report the being of a horse upon that place, coming up a way so dangerous and so high; which was done by Banks in 1601.

Thence the King took coach to the Royal Exchange, and on his way down Cheapside the goldsmiths, mercers and other rich trades set out their commodities for sale. At the Exchange he walked about on the pawn above, and in the merchants walks beneath, where was told him the manner of our merchants and the hours of their meetings, when from all countries there is daily news to be heard by one means or other; and how in this place they make great exchanges of their merchandise, make traffic to foreign countries, ship their men for service so that their greatest affairs are here twice every day effected.

Thence they proceeded by Cornhill, Gracechurch Street and Fenchurch Street to the Tower, where King James himself met his Highness, and in his own person conducted him to the Jewel House where the most rare jewels and beautiful plate were shown him, and likewise in the Wardrobe the richest robes, hangings, clothes of estate, and furniture were displayed. Then they passed on to the Office of the Ordnance, where he viewed the warlike provision of the great ordnance, which at an hour is ready for any service, over every piece being the ladles and sponges, and the traces and collars for the horses to draw them away; and after that to the armoury where all manner of arms are kept in readiness. Then King James led him up to the Mint, which they viewed, and thence to the lions. When their pleasures had been well delighted with these shows, the tide serving to shoot the bridge, they took their barges and were rowed to Whitehall.

2nd August. THE KING OF DENMARK.

Very early this morning the two Kings hunted in St. James's Park and there killed a buck. Then they passed on to Hyde Park where they hunted the rest of the forenoon, returning about dinner time. About 4 of the clock they took barge at the Privy Stairs and were rowed to Greenwich.

3rd August. THE QUEEN CHURCHED.

To-day being Sunday the Queen was churched, in the presence of the two Kings, when they heard a learned sermon.

4th August. TILTING AT COURT.

This afternoon the Queen, who has not hitherto been partaker of any of the sports, accompanied the two Kings and the Prince, attended by the nobility and courtiers, to see the tilting in which exercise both Kings showed their skill.

5th August. THANKSGIVING DAY AT COURT.

On this day, being the anniversary of his Majesty's deliverance from the treacherous practices of the Gowries, the morning was spent in thanksgiving, the preacher being Dr. Launcelot Andrewes, Bishop of Chichester, who preached in Latin upon Psalm cxliii ver. 10: *Qui das salutem regibus; qui redemisti Dauidum seruum tuum de gladio maligno*, wherein he spake of our King's escape from Gowry, this day six years ago. In the afternoon the bears and bulls were baited for a short while, and then the company repaired to the Tiltyard. The tilters were all in plain armour except King Christianus whose armour was sky-coloured, spangled with some gold; he wore in his helm a bunch of blue and white feathers, as also the rest of his company. He ran eight courses, four with my Lord of Effingham, both breaking three staves very gallantly but failing the fourth; the other courses he ran with the Earl of Arundel. Then followed the rest of the tilters who continued their sport until the sun set and forced them to give over. At this exercise Prince Henry showed himself in his armour, being gallantly mounted, and took his part.

A MOST CRUEL AND BLOODY MURDER.

Some four years since, one Anthony James and his wife, with their two children, a girl named Elizabeth aged 8 years and a boy aged 7, lived near Devonshey hundred in Essex. One night, the servants being away at the Fair, certain villains with a whore in their company brake into their house where they bound the two parents, and ransacked the house. Then, bethinking them that they could not be safe from pursuit and death, they stabbed the parents and buried their dead bodies in a wood, but the children they carried away to Bishop's Hatfield in Hertfordshire and bestowed them in an inn kept by the wife of one Dell. That night they took the boy into the yard and there, first stopping his mouth with cowdung that he might make no noise, they slit up his throat from ear to ear. Then with the aid of this Dell's son they carried the body of the boy and cast it into the bottomless pond, the whore leading the girl after them, with soothing words, until they came to a stile, when the whore wresting open the child's jaws, cut out her tongue even to the root. The next day they sold the child to a beggar for a piece of money and took their departure. But the beggar lost the child who thereafter strayed to Barnet and thence to London where a barber surgeon took pity on her and healed her wound. Thus for four years space the wench strayed about from place to place begging her food.

Now it happened that after three weeks the body of the little boy was discovered in the pond by some gentlemen hunting for wild fowl. Some suspicion lit upon this Annis Dell, but she resolutely denying the fact no charge was preferred against her save that she was commanded to attend at each assizes. At length the dumb wench came to Hatfield, and by chance to Dell's house where she made strange outcries, and would not be drawn thence, so that after much questioning (she answering by signs) she was shown her brother's coat which put her in a vehement passion. This wonder was much talked off in the country and the Justices thereupon took special note of it, and the town was charged with her care.

About a month before Christmas last as the girl was playing with the daughter of the goodwife with whom she sojourned, a cock hard by fell a-crowing, when the other girl mocked it, saying 'Cock a doodle do, Peggy hath lost her shoe,' and called to her, 'Bess, canst not then do so?' And straightway the wench did so. Hereupon the other child in great amazement ran home crying, 'The dumb girl Bess can speak! The dumb girl Bess can speak!' This wonder caused all the town to gather in flocks to meet her, but the bailiff and constables discreetly kept the hurly from her. Forthwith she began to answer to every question and to reveal the murders. The news was speedily carried to the Justices and they were very careful to sift her tale, even threatening her with what vengeance God would stir up for her in hell and plagues here upon earth if by her false testimony Dell's wife and son should be brought to death through her false testimony. Moreover, one of Sir Henry Butler's men to make further trial of her constancy altered himself in a vizard with horns like a devil and leapt out of a thicket at her, threatening that he would tear her in pieces if she belied George Dell and his mother. To which she answered, 'Good gaffer devil, do not hurt me: I speak nothing but truth, and what the thing within me instructeth me to speak.'

At length when the assizes were again held at Hertford, George Dell and his mother appeared, when the girl gave testimony against them, and sundry witnesses being called, the jury found them guilty and they were condemned to death on Saturday last and yesterday hanged.

TWO WITCHES HANGED.

At the same time there were executed one Joan Harrison and her daughter of Royston for damnable witchcraft. This woman, being long suspected of witchcraft, was apprehended; and her house being searched there was found in a chest all the bones due to the anatomy of a man and a woman, and hairs of all colours, and a parchment wherein was inscribed a heart with sundry branches thereto. Upon her examination the witch confessed that she had the power by these instruments to inflict pain or death with the aid of her spirits upon man or cattle. Amongst others she bewitched a country yeoman who had called her 'old hag' or some such name of reproof; to whom she made answer, 'I will say little to thee, but thou shalt feel more from me hereafter.' And scarce half an hour after the man felt such aches and

331

wracking of his limbs as if the Devil had set him on his tentors to make broadcloth of him. So the honest man persuaded a neighbour by the aid of his wife to entice the witch into his house, where being come she is well scratched, and the man recovered. Hereupon the witch had an action of battery against him and was awarded 5s. damage and the costs of her suit; but no sooner had the man paid the money than he again fell into his former passion, and languishing a while after died.

Some time after a certain young woman, washing clothes in an outer room next the street, cast out some rinsing water, and some drops fell on the witch's daughter that chanced to be passing by, who called out, 'Do you throw your water upon me, gossip? Before long I'll be revenged for it.' The young woman, thinking no more of it, went into the next room to hang up some clothes, when the wainscot cradle, wherein her child lay, was on the sudden thrown over, and shattered all to pieces, and the child overwhelmed under it and killed. These and a number more instances were inferred against the women at their trial.

6th August. THE KING OF DENMARK.

Early this morning the King of Denmark was invited to see a show of fencers in the Privy Gardens where it was a wonder to see how foolishly ambitious these fellows were, if they could, to have killed one another, for they would most willingly have taken the buttons off the foils; but the sport was interrupted by a great rain. The two Kings are now gone towards Windsor.

7th August. THE KING OF DENMARK ADMITTED TO THE ORDER.

To-day the two Kings came to Windsor, where was presented unto the King of Denmark the Knights of Windsor, being all goodly gentlemen, and such as served Queen Elizabeth in her wars, and for service done are preferred in their latter years to this place of rest, and called by the name of 'King James's Knights of Windsor.' These ancient gentlemen were habited in their robes of purple and scarlet, with the Garter and St. George's Cross upon them. Then the King of Denmark was installed Knight of the Garter, and in his robe of the Order did his obeisance at the altar.

10th August. THE KING OF DENMARK.

Yesterday the fleet of the King of Denmark who is now about to depart went down the river as far as Rochester, where he rested the night at the house of Sir Peter Buck, King James spending the night at the house of the Bishop. This morning, being Sunday, they came to the Cathedral Church and there heard a sermon in Latin by Dr. Parry, the Dean. The sermon being ended they were rowed aboard the *Elizabeth Jonas*, where a most sumptuous dinner was served. This ship was joined to the *White Bear* by a gallery or bridge of fir masts, railed in on either side, which floated upon the water; in the midst of this bridge was a great hoy, furnished with ovens for baked meats, and three fair ranges to roast with. Dinner being ended the Kings, accompanied with the Queen, the Prince and the nobility, took their barges and rowed on towards Chatham, where they saw all the ships. Then they were rowed to shore, where on a hill places were prepared for them. When they were seated, every ship in due course discharged her whole ordnance, one after the other, to the number of 2,300. In the evening the gunners of the navy showed very excellent fireworks.

11th August. THE KING OF DENMARK'S DEPARTURE.

About 10 of the clock this morning King James, Queen Anne, and Prince Henry with divers of the nobility went on board the King of Denmark's greatest ship, commonly called the Admiral, which was riding at anchor at Gravesend (a very gallant ship of high and narrow building, richly ornamented), and were royally feasted; and as they sat at banquet greeting each other with pledges of lasting health, the same was straightways made known by sound of drum and trumpet, and by the cannon beginning first in the Admiral, seconded by the English block-houses, then followed by the Vice-admiral and after her the other six Denmark ships, ending always in the smallest.

About 4 of the clock when the banquet was ended, King James began to take his leave to depart, but his royal Brother being loath would have had them stay till evening to see a rare invention; but when he saw the King and his train ready to depart, notwithstanding the brightness of the sun, he caused fire to be put to it. This device of wild fire was in pageant wise, between four round pillars upon a lighter framed, where the seven deadly sins in their lively characters sat chained, and over their head a fierce lion couchant holding with his teeth the loose end of the chain. From the lion's mouth did first pour forth the fire, and thence without any confusion or further aid descended into all parts, and for the space of more than a quarter of an hour the images sat burning until at last all were consumed.

At last their solemn farewells being ended, King James with the Queen, the Prince and his train, went on board their barges and returned to Court, King James saying at his departure that never man was to him so welcome as the King of Denmark; nor ever should any be, till he came again.

The gifts which our King bestowed upon the King of Denmark were a sword and hanger valued at £17,000 and a cup of £5,000; and to his Council plate of the value of £2,000; and to his Gentlemen chains of gold to the same value; and £1,000 in money to the inferior Danes. The King of Denmark for his part hath not been inferior in gifts, for he hath given in Court 30,000 dollars, and to every one of the King's and Queen's Bed-chamber jewels of great value. On the Queen he hath bestowed his picture richly set; and on the Prince his Vice-admiral and best fighting ship, worth with all its furniture not less than £25,000, and a rapier and hanger valued at 20,000 marks.

At his coming the King of Denmark appointed a Marshal, with divers officers to keep order amongst his people to prevent breeding of quarrels, and especially the vice of drunkenness; such as were found drunk were brought to a house appointed for their prison where their thumbs were chained together and nailed by the chain to a post, and there they remained till some suit was made for their delivery, which kept them in such awe that after the first week seldom any were seen out of order. So the King of Denmark hath departed, leaving behind him a general commendation of his virtues. For although sundry have thought it dangerous that Princes should see each other, yet in the meeting of such Kings what peril could the most politic judgment foresee? They are not jealous of one another's estate or worth, each of them wishing double happiness to his Brother. Their Kingdoms lay not together, whereby they might be instigated by avarice or ambition. They met brothers; and depart more than brother, as friends.

Sir Robert Mansell, with the *Vanguard* and the *Moon*, is appointed to attend the King upon his way homeward.

16th August. THE KING OF DENMARK'S FOOTPRINT.

A few days since Soper, the keeper of Paul's steeple, made the King of Denmark's character in gilded copper and fixed it in the print of the King's foot cut in the leads of the steeple, but some rusty minds of this iron age thinking all gold that glisters with violent instruments have attempted to steal it.

22nd August. A CONFERENCE WITH THE SPANISH AMBASSADOR.

The King and the Council have lately debated the many complaints received from Spain, and because it did not appear certain whether these injuries spring out of an intention in that State to break the amity with us, or whether from the distractions amongst themselves, aggravated by misreports of the Ambassador here. The King therefore thinking it best beseeming in honour and justice first to draw the Ambassador to an orderly conference wherein our grievances might particularly be deducted, and if he could show just reason for his complaints then to give him satisfaction. To this conference therefore the Spanish King's Ambassador was this day summoned, together with the Archduke's Ambassador. Hereupon the Earl of Salisbury having used a short speech, which he caused to be written in Spanish, the Ambassador replied that he came hither to receive complaints, but not to make any until he had heard from Spain. To which it was answered that as the main grievances had principally to do with himself, the Council were ready either to give him satisfaction, or if not, that by seeing his error he might countermand his former acts and so be more able to do good offices in Spain. After some time spent in disputing, at length he entreated that, as he came not prepared to debate those matters, he might first receive the complaints of the Council and then at another meeting propound his own. So the Council proceeded to lay before him the complaints, showing the general points in which the Spaniards have broken the Treaty, and then the particular, in which for many things the Ambassador blamed his Master's ministers.

As for the matter of Ball, since the parties live that were suspected to be poisoned, and because from crafty knaves discoveries of their own treasons cannot be drawn but by such means as are used in such cases (which would breed an opinion that the Council wished to extract something to the scandal of the Ambassador), it is concluded that Ball shall be redelivered to him, unless he stand so much upon his pride as to refuse him.

THE GREAT TURK'S LETTERS.

There is printing a copy, taken from the French, of letters sent by the Great Turk to the Pope and Rodolphus, King of Hungary, wherein all manner of evil and mischief is denounced upon Rodolphus for taking the name of a king, and the Pope bidden to receive his commands, for, quoth he, 'by the consent of the whole earth, by the will of the high God of Heaven and of the great prophet Mahomet, I am the only Monarch and sole Prince under heaven in the shape of man, by similitude and likelihood according to the celestial form and shape.'

The Great Turk's style: 'Annet Harioson by the Grace of the High God Most wellbeloved in Heaven, descended of the Line of the great Prophet Mahomet; Champion of Babylon; God on the Earth; Baron of Turkey; Lord of the country of India, even unto the Earthly Paradise; Conqueror of Constantinople, and of Greece; Governor of the High and Lower Seas; Commander of Hungary and the future Conqueror of Christendom.'

14th September. THE EARL OF NORTHUMBERLAND AND THE KING.

The Earl of Northumberland has again written to the King praying for some mitigation of his fine which is the greatest ever laid on a subject in this Realm; for his estate is less than the world supposes, and his debts greater, and there is a company of little ones to be provided for. Howsoever, saith he, it hath pleased the Lords to censure him, he appeals to his Majesty, a higher Judge, who knows more than they in this case.

15th September. THE COUNTESS OF NORTHUMBERLAND AND LORD SALISBURY.

The Countess of Northumberland that in former times inveighed so bitterly against her Lord is now turned his advocate

336

so lustily, that the Earl of Salisbury refuses again to see her, and the more so since she told him to his face that he is one that useth to devise causes and colours and tricks to procure favour and the contrary wherever he listeth. This zeal does more harm than benefit to her cause, insomuch that my Lord hath written to the Earl of Northumberland complaining of her usage of him.

19th September. GARNET'S MIRACULOUS STRAW.

There is much talk of a miracle which the Catholics declare to have been caused by Garnet's working. At the time of his condemnation a certain John Wilkinson, living at St. Omers, posted over to England that he might obtain some relic. He came very early to the place of execution, and stayed till all was ended and the people had departed. Then it was his good fortune to obtain a straw with the ear at the end of it sprinkled with some drops of Garnet's blood. With this treasure he departed, and entrusted it to the care of the wife of one Hugh Griffith, a tailor and a zealot of that persuasion who provided a crystal case for the more careful keeping of the relic. Lately upon careful inspection of the straw, it was declared that upon the outside of the leaf which enclosed a grain appears a face in little which many affirm to be an exact portraiture of Garnet.

22nd September. THE LORD DEPUTY'S JOURNEY.

During August and September the Lord Deputy of Ireland made a journey through the counties of Monaghan, Fermanagh, and the Cavan. He findeth the people very poor, and unacquainted with the laws of good government, having been long subject to oppression and tyranny, as they shall ever be, unless some men of more civility and understanding be sent among them to instruct and defend them; for it is death to their great Lords that their tenants and followers should know or understand more than brute beasts, for their greatest profit in times of peace, and for opposition and defence in times of rebellion ariseth from the ignorance of the baser sort.

In Fermanagh the Deputy hath commanded that at Lisgool a quarter sessions shall be held, and a weekly market, hoping that the town shall increase there, and that this peace will beget civility and bring forth plenty. Urgeth that some charge shall be spent in planting towns, forts, and castles in places of advantage, for howsoever untuneable that string, yet it is good husbandry for the King to spend a pound now to save a hundred; for this people, having entered into rebellious courses, never subject themselves out of any true feeling of duty to their Prince, but are brought thereto by famine and necessity; whereby the country is long after poor and miserable, when small forces may carry sundry businesses to good ends. But they no sooner increase in store of corn and cattle, but forthwith they become proud and contemptuous.

24th September. THE RETURN OF THE 'HOPEWELL.'

The bark *Hopewell* which set forth last April for the discovery of the north-west passage is returned, but in poor case, for they have lost Captain Knight, their master, and three of their company. They reached the northernmost end of the land of America on the 19th June, in the latitude 56 degrees and 48 minutes, their compass showing a variation of 25 degrees to the west, and all the coast there broken land or islands. Here the weather continued very rough and stormy, and the ice very dangerous, for the ship was full of leaks so that they were forced to go aground to save their clothes, furniture and victuals. Then the master, taking five of his company, determined to go over in the boat to a great island, not above a mile from the ship, to see if he could find any harbour or cove. He left two in the boat, but they never saw him nor the other three men, and supposed that they were slain by the savages, who afterwards assaulted the remainder of the company, being but ten men and a great dog, of which the savages were greatly afraid. At length by the skill of the carpenter, after great difficulty they sailed their leaking bark to Newfoundland and here found succour. They arrived safely in Dartmouth four days ago.

25th September. THE PRINCE OF VAUDMONT IN LONDON.

Francis, Prince of Vaudmont, arrived in London two days ago with seven Earls, ten Barons, forty gentlemen of quality, all very brave and comely in their apparel and six-score common persons. To-day they went by coach to Hampton Court, where the King entertains them.

28th September. THE SERMON AT HAMPTON COURT.

This Sunday, Dr. Launcelot Andrewes, Bishop of Chichester, preached before the King at Hampton Court upon Numbers x. ver. 1–2, concerning the right and power of calling assemblies, concluding that it is of the Prince.

1st October. THE DECAYED STATE OF THE SOLDIERS IN IRELAND.

The state of the soldiers in Ireland is said to be very miserable. They want clothes, by reason of their want of pay which of late hath been reduced, and if they continue in such a sorry state as they now are (having had no means to repair their last winter's suit of apparel) they will become a scorn and occasion of laughter to the people, rather than a bridle to restrain them. Moreover, if for want of sufficient means the soldiers shall be forced to plead 'need has no law,' then will follow robbing and murder, discontentment in the country and revenge, and encouragement to secret practisers.

2nd October. SIR ROBERT DRURY'S PASSPORT.

Sir Robert Drury of late went to Spa, and on his way back passed through Flanders by way of Antwerp and so to Lillo, where being arrived without the States' passport, the Governor of the Fort sent him fair and mannerly to Middleburgh to the States, who have brought him before them and very dapperly searched his trunks and his papers, and well and truly examined him, whereat he fretteth not a little, to the no small pleasure of some Englishmen there to whom it is good mirth to hear him rail.

5th October. THE YOUNG LORD CRANBORNE.

It is much noted that the young Lord Cranborne (my Lord of Salisbury's son), having one Will Lytton as his mignon is allowed to go a long hunting progress into Stafford, Lancashire and elsewhere, his father half *nolens volens* being fain to furnish him with new clothes, two men to attend him, two geldings for his own saddle and all things else answerable. Yet it is thought strange so wise a father should so far humour his son, being yet a child, as to let him run these wild courses, and to have all his will. But some make answer that he means to give him his fill, and when he hath

339

taken a surfeit of these pleasures to recall him to better matters, as though it were not ordinary seen that men fall from one vanity to another.

6th October. 'THE SEVEN DEADLY SINS OF LONDON.'

Dekker hath written a book called *The Seven Deadly Sins of London*, by which, saith he, the City is become the scorn and contempt of nations. These be Politic Bankruptism: Lying: Candlelight (in whose time many sins are committed): Sloth (whose attendants are anglers, dumb ministers, players, exchange wenches, gamesters, pandars, whores and fiddlers): Apishness (whereby many a young gallant apes his fashions from every nation, so that his codpiece is in Denmark; the collar of his doublet and the belly in France; the wing and narrow sleeve in Italy; the shirt waist hangs over a Dutch butcher's stall in Utrecht; his huge slops speaks Spanish; Polonia gives him the boots; the block for his head alters faster than the feltmaker can fit him, and therefore in scorn are we called block heads): Shaving (not that of barbers but by short weights, shaving of fatherless children by executors, of poor clients by attorney's clerks, and of prisoners by extortion): and Cruelty (whereby young virgins are forced into marriage with old men, and young prentices turned out to starve when their seven years be out, and a decent grave denied even to the dead in time of plague).

10th October. THE MIRACULOUS STRAW.

Certain witnesses of the alleged miraculous portrait of Garnet the Jesuit were of late examined before the Archbishop of Canterbury, whereby it appears that the face is not so exact that it might justly entitle Heaven to the workmanship thereof. One witness declareth that a good artisan might have drawn one more curiously and the tailor himself declared that it was no more like Garnet than any other man with a beard, and that it was so small none could affirm it to resemble him, nor was there any glory or streaming rays about it as some report.

17th October. 'THE MOUSE-TRAP.'

There is a book of a hundred epigrams by one H. P. called *The Mouse-Trap*, for, saith the author, he aimeth but at the silly mouse and not any greater or more venomous vermin. Two epigrams from the same:

340

On Tobacco.

The humour of *tobacco* (and the rest)
    Wherein our gallants took their chief delight
Is daily had, methinks, in less request,
    And will, I fear, in time be worn out quite.
For now each peasant puffs it through his nose,
As well as he that's clad in velvet hose.

On Ben Jonson's New Play.

Magus would needs forsooth this other day,
Upon an idle humour see a play.
When asking him at door, that held the box,
'What might you call the play'? Quoth he '*The Fox.*'
In goes my gen'man (who could judge of wit),
And being asked how he liked it,
Said all was ill, both Fox and him that play'd it;
But was not he, think you, a Goose that said it?

22nd October. An Unfortunate Astrologer.

From Venice it is reported that of late a certain poor old man,
by profession an astrologer, came panting to the house of a principal senator denouncing unto him the impending destruction of
the State which he had foreseen by his art, and the thing, he
declared, was a practice of gunpowder laid in a room right under
the hall of the Great Council. Search being made there was
found 16 or 20 lbs. of gunpowder laid as the man related. But
the old man was not rewarded, as he had expected, but instead
put to the torture of the cord for maintaining that he had discovered the fact by his art, but is now released still protesting
that he foresaw it by the stars; whereas it is thought very prob-
able that he conveyed the powder thither himself with hope of
getting in time of jealousy, and after the like example among us,
some better recompense.

23rd October. The Art of Drawing and Painting.

There is a book entered for printing by Mr. Henry Peacham
treating of the art of drawing with the pen and limning in water
colours, with exact instructions for the making of colours and
painting upon glass. Noteth, amongst sundry absurdities to be

condemned, the accident of time, as when the proprieties of ancient times are fashioned and attributed to ours, or ours to theirs; as at an inn he found painted Bethulia besieged by Holophernes, where the painter, as if he had been at Ostend, made his east and west batteries with great ordnance and small shot playing from the walls, when that ordnance was not invented in 2,000 years after.

28th October. THE FRENCH KING'S CHILDREN BAPTIZED.

From Paris comes news that the three legitimate children of the French King are at last baptized with much pomp, being Lewis, the Dolphin, now a child of five years, and his two younger sisters, who are christened Christine and Elizabeth.

29th October. THE CITY PAGEANT.

This day was a pageant entitled *The Triumphs of Reunited Britannia* performed at the cost and charges of the Company of the Merchant Taylors in honour of Sir Leonard Halliday to solemnize his entrance as Lord Mayor of London, devised by Mr. Anthony Munday. On a mount triangular was seated a nymph portraying Britannia, with sundry others in representation of Brute's divided Kingdoms Loegria, Cambria and Albania and others, all being presented by several children who delivered sundry poetical speeches.

3rd November. 'CHOICE, CHANCE AND CHANGE.'

There is a book printing called *Choice, chance and change; or, Conceits in their colours*, in form of a dialogue between Arnofilo and Tidero of the country manners of these days, with sundry verses to the end of it, as of a Cunning Tit:

> She that looks fifteen thousand ways at once,
>   Makes twenty faces ere she dress her head,
>   Studies for words to serve her for the nonce,
>   With idle tricks to bring a fool to bed:
>
> Turns up the white of an ill-favoured eye,
>   Treads on her toes because her heels are sore,
>   Splays out her foot, and holds her head awry
>   And bears her placket far enough before.

Speaks all in print, and reads with a strange grace,
Writes like a scrivener, like a fiddler sing,
Sits fourteen hours a painting of her face,
And tries the use of many a secret thing:
    Of such a minx what memory will pass?
    A cunning ape will cosen many an ass.

7th November. THE LADY RUSSELL'S CASE.

The case between the Lady Russell and the Lord Admiral was this day concluded in the Star Chamber and after learned speeches by the Judges the defendants were all acquitted with costs against the plaintiff.

8th November. A DRUNKEN FROLIC.

Last night five young gentlemen, by name Welby, Vaux, Gosnall, Fitch, and Loss, supping together in Holborn, did resolve to do something that may be spoken of when they are dead. Thereupon late in the night after supper they took a boat over to Lambeth Marsh to the Swan, where one Davis dwelleth, a lewd fellow and a very lewd house; and here they call for drink and a wench; but being denied they brake down the windows of the house and of ten or twelve houses more, insomuch that the constable with the watch set upon them and took them, but beat down some of them to the ground before they could take them. This morning they were carried to the Lord Chief Justice who, upon examination, hath committed them to the King's Bench prison.

10th November. GENERAL NEWS.

The King has gone to Richmond. The City has received £10,000 in part payment of £60,000 lent to the late Queen upon mortgage of land, and are to have £20,000 more the next term, and the rest at convenient days. Though money go low in the Exchequer yet they say the King hath undertaken to pay the debts of the Earl of Montgomery, the Lord Hay, and the Lord of Haddington which arise to no small rate.

15th November. A MURDER TWENTY-FIVE YEARS CON-
    CEALED.

There is lately come to light a murder performed twenty-five years since by one Thomas Cash upon his wife, and but now revealed. This Cash, by profession a tailor and feather-bed driver, then dwelling at Howlton in the Moor in Lincolnshire, was suspected by his wife of familiarity with one Newton's wife. Cash's wife, what with the discontent of her mind and the disquiet of her mind, fell into a lingering sickness which made her very troublesome not only to her servant, called Anne Potts, but to her husband also, insomuch that they would gladly be rid of her. Whereupon one day Cash in his right hand grasped his wife by the throat and having a napkin in his left hand stopped her mouth so that in a short space she was bereaved of all breath. Then he called Anne Potts, and together they made great show of sorrow and summoned the neighbours, who came in and used the best words they could to dissuade Cash from the extreme grief that he seemed to take for her death. The next day the woman was buried, and none suspected but that she died a natural death. Shortly afterwards the aforesaid Newton also died, and then this Thomas Cash, within the space of one half-year after the making away of his wife, was married to the widow. Hereby the hope that Anne Potts had of being married to her master was quite dashed and she in a spleen would needs leave his service, yet she durst not reveal what had passed because she had run herself so deep into the danger of the law by concealing the fact.

Since that time Cash hath lived at Long Oarsby and Middle Rayson, and his second wife dying after he had been married to her fourteen years, he married again and by his present wife (to whom he hath been married nine years) he hath had two children.

The manner in which the murder was revealed was that Anne Potts, who was now resident in the parish of St. Leonards in Shoreditch, of late fell sick unto death and confessed all to the minister before she died. Hereupon order is sent down for the apprehending of Cash, who is brought before Sir William Wray and one Master Robert Turret and straightway confesseth all. He now remaineth in Lincoln Castle till the next assizes.

18th November. THE THIRD SESSION OF THE PARLIAMENT.

The Parliament assembled for the third session, and in the afternoon the Speaker, with the Commons, was sent for to attend his Majesty. After the Lord Chancellor had spoken touching the King's presence at that time (not being usual at the beginning only of a new session) and of the grievances presented by the Parliament in the last session, the King himself made a speech.

He spoke first of the great deliverance about twelve months since from the treason intended against them all. As for their grievances, they were collected with more industry than dutiful diligence, and yet the form in which they were presented was so full of discretion and moderation that he was loath his answer should smell of the spirit of Rehoboam. But, saith he, there is in Parliament, as there is in all multitudes, diversities of spirits, as there were amongst the very apostles themselves; and that some were more popular than profitable either for that Council or for the Commonwealth; and that there were some tribunes of the people whose mouths could not be stopped either from the matters of the Puritans or of the purveyance. But for himself he would never make a separation of the people's will and the wish of the King. After which he spake of the grievance of purveyance.

But, he went on, the weightiest matter of all is this of the Union, wherein he answered the two main objections; of which the first was there was no necessity of a Union; which, he replied, was indeed necessary to the firm continuance of the union and marriage of the two Kingdoms. The second was a scornful objection; that Scotland was not so rich or so wealthy or so potent a Kingdom; to which he answered that if the greatness of England was so great, what decrease could it sustain by such a participation. But some were so suspicious that they dare not trust the present times nor the present King with this Union, because he was a partial King; for he had his birth, education, acquaintance and familiarity during the first part of his age there. But this was to do him wrong, for the so miraculous applause he received by the general voice of all this nation had prevailed as much, and had as great a part of his heart, as the place of his birth. Further, said he, that if this proposal for Union failed, it would be imputed either to his folly to propose it or their obstinacy to refuse it. And thus with sundry other weighty arguments, he concluded.

20th November. CAPTAIN LOVELACE'S MISFORTUNE.

Captain Lovelace, the son of Sir William Lovelace, who is of the English garrison in Flushing, by misfortune killed an English woman for which he is in great danger of condemnation. It appears that she was a light woman, at whose house Captain Lovelace's Lieutenant and some soldiers had lain, and there was owing 14s. which the Lieutenant said that his Captain should pay. The woman came clamorously into the street demanding her money, and offering to put off the Captain's cloak. He drew his dagger, meaning to prick her in the fingers to make her loose her hold, but struck her in the belly whereof she died suddenly. Had not Sir William Browne, the Deputy Governor for my Lord Lisle, persuaded the townsfolk to stay their sentence, he would have been executed the next day and after the fashion of the country buried with her he killed; and the matter is still doubtful.

29th November. A COMMITTEE TO CONSIDER THE UNION.

It was resolved in the Lower House that a committee should be appointed to treat every afternoon of the articles and to report next day what they had done; which committee is to be of all the Commissioners, all burgesses of Port Towns, all knights and burgesses of Cumberland, Northumberland, and Westmorland, and the Bishopric of Durham; and all the House to be present and have free speech.

THE RIOTOUS YOUNG GENTLEMEN.

The five young gentlemen that were imprisoned in the King's Bench three weeks ago were to-day before the Star Chamber, and their offence is generally condemned as great and base, ill beseeming gentlemen as most of them are reputed to be both in name and blood; and for example's sake they are punished, Welby, Vaux and Gosnall being fined £50 apiece, Fitch and Loss £20 apiece and imprisonment. 'This drunkenness,' quoth the Lord Chancellor, 'is *voluntarius demon*, it carries a legion with him.'

30th November. JOHN LYLY DEAD.

Master John Lyly is dead at the age of 52 years and was this day buried in churchyard of St. Bartholomew the Less. He it was

346

that in his younger years penned that witty book of *Euphues* and *Euphues and his England* which was so much in request at Queen Elizabeth's court that nobody was at all regarded who could not parley Euphuism, though that fashion is long since fallen into disuse. He made also divers conceited comedies for the Children of Paul's which in their time were crowned with the applause of gentle spectators.

4th December. MR. HALL'S BOOK OF MEDITATIONS.

Mr. Joseph Hall (that formerly set a fashion for satires but is since turned churchman and now vicar of Halstead in Suffolk) hath written this year certain little books entitled *Meditations and vows divine and moral*, gathered into centuries; also another, of tranquillity of mind entitled *Heaven upon Earth* which is eagerly read.

ON OSTENTATION AND LEARNING

I have seldom seen much ostentation and much learning met together. The sun, rising and declining, makes long shadows: at midday when he is highest none at all. Besides, that skill when it is too much shown loseth grace; as fresh coloured wares, if they be often opened, lose their brightness, and are soiled with much handling. I had rather applaud myself for having much that I show not, than that others should applaud me for showing more than I have.

5th December. INSOLENCIES OF THE STATES' SHIPS.

Many insupportable insolencies are reported of the States' men-of-war these days. Of late a poor merchant of Southampton, by name Edward Barlow, coming from Rouen with a bark of his called the *Gift of Hampton* and entering within St. Helen's Point, within the Isle of Wight, was boarded by a Dutch ship, whereof the Captain was one Hendrik Willemson, who took out of her all the goods with the merchant's chest and apparel, to the quantity of 4,000 ells of canvas, and to the value of £350; and, which makes the fault worse, this Captain was but a few days before at Portsmouth relieved with powder, victual and other necessities by the States' men-of-war that lie in wait there for a Dunkirker.

16th December. A BILL AGAINST DIVORCE REJECTED.

In Parliament to-day a Bill to prevent causeless divorce and separation of man and wife, and to continue the right of lawful marriage was read but rejected.

17th December. THE PARLIAMENT ADJOURNED.

A message was brought into the Commons from the Lords that his Majesty, considering the great travail of the committees employed in the matters of the Union, and the solemn Feast of Christmas approaching, it was fit that gentlemen repair into their several counties to solace themselves, comfort their neighbours, and perform other duties in their several places. The Parliament is therefore adjourned until the 10th of February.

19th December. THE PLANTATION OF VIRGINIA.

This day the fleet for the plantation of Virginia set sail from Blackwall, being three ships, one of 100 tons, one of 40, and a pinnace of 20. The transportation is committed to Captain Christopher Newport, but their orders for government together with the names of those who are appointed to be the first Council are put in a box not to be opened until they shall have reached Virginia. The principal persons that go in this voyage are Master Edward Maria Wingfield, Captain Bartholomew Gosnold, Captain John Smith, Captain John Ratcliffe, Captain John Martin, Captain George Kendall, Master Robert Hunt, Preacher, Master George Percy, Captain Gabriel Archer. As well there go twenty-eight gentlemen, four carpenters, a blacksmith, a sailor, a barber, two bricklayers, a mason, a tailor, a drummer, a surgeon, twelve labourers, four boys, and others making in all 105 persons.

They are instructed, before landing their victuals, to let Captain Newport discover how far the river may be navigable that they may make choice of the strongest and most wholesome place, and avoid many removes which will lose time and spoil the victuals and casks; and the farther up the river the better. They must take great care of the naturals, neither to offend them, nor to trust them lest they be surprised; if they hire guides let them be well looked to, and let those who go out as discoverers take a compass with them and write down how far they go upon every point of the compass; and how weary soever the soldiers be, let them never trust the country people with the carriage of their weapons. They shall not allow the mariners

that go for wages to mar their trade for a little private gain.
The carpenters and other workmen shall first build the store-
house and other public rooms before any house is set up for
private persons.   Moreover, they shall send back by Captain
Newport a perfect relation of all things, but not to allow anyone
to write any letter that may discourage others.

21st December.   THE KING AT WARE.

This week the King lay two or three days at an inn at Ware
with his hawks, but was so little pleased either with the sport
or the weather that it is hoped he will take no great liking to the
place.

26th December.   A PLAY OF KING LEAR.

This night at the Court at Whitehall before his Majesty the
King's Men played a tragedy called the *True Chronicle History
of the Life and death of King Lear and his three daughters*,
together with the unfortunate life of Edgar, son and heir to the
Earl of Gloucester, and his sullen and assumed humour of Tom
of Bedlam written by Shakespeare.   This is that old story of
King Lear from the Chronicle, but with certain differences, for
whereas Holinshed and all other writers do declare that Lear
was restored to his kingdom by Cordelia his true and loyal
daughter, yet in this play Cordelia is hanged by order of the
bastard son of the Earl of Gloucester, and Lear dies of grief and
old age.

The History of Great Britanny.

The History of Great Britanny, declaring the success of times and affairs in this Island, from the Roman's first entrance until the reign of Egbert, the West Saxon Prince, who reduced the several principalities of the Saxons and the English into a monarchy, and changed the name of Britanny into England.

The Maps of Ortelius.

A new and great edition of that famous work *Theatrum orbis terrarum*, set forth by that excellent geographer Abraham Ortelius, is printed by Mr. John Norton, printer to the King's Majesty in Hebrew, Greek and Latin, wherein the whole world is described and lively set forth in maps.

'Eliosto Libidinoso'

An euphuistic tale entitled *Eliosto libidinoso* intermixed with sundry madrigals and roundelays by Mr. John Hind, describing how the King Amasias had to wife Philoclea who begat him Eliosto, a boy of surpassing beauty. But Philoclea being thrown from her horse in the chase died, and after a time Amasias took to wife Cleadora. Now Amasias, being a man of disordered and wanton affections, neglected his wife Cleadora who in her distress cast her eyes upon Eliosto; and he enflamed by love yielded to desire. When these things were brought to Amasias he cast them to prison and caused them to be executed for their incest.

A Discourse of the East Indies.

Master Edmund Scot that for the space of three years and a half was resident at Bantam in the East Indies hath written *An exact discourse* of the subtleties, fashions, policies, religion and ceremonies of the East Indians, as well Chinese as Javans; together with the manner of trading used both by our English and by the Hollanders; also what happened to the English nation at Bantam while he was there; to which is added a brief description of Java Major. Noteth of the Dutchmen trading in those parts that though they were mortal enemies in their trade, yet in all other matters our Englishmen were their friends, and they would have lived and died one for the other.

'PARASITASTER.'

Master John Marston's comedy of *Parasitaster, or the fawn*, formerly presented by the Children of the Queen's Revels at the Blackfriars and lately at Paul's, the argument whereof is how the Duke Hercules, failing to persuade his son Tiberius to marriage, sends him as his ambassador to woo Dulcimel on his behalf, she being daughter to the foolish Duke of Urbin; and to see the event the Duke Hercules himself followeth disguised as Faunus, a plain-spoken courtier. Hereupon the Lady Dulcimel, herself falling in love with Tiberio, conveys her love through her foolish father, so that Tiberio, by this means now enkindled with love, climbs to her window, is married to her and enjoys her. Showeth also the follies of the courtiers at Gonzago's court, who at the end are all arraigned at a Court of Love.

This comedy was twice printed this year, the first printing being full of errors by reason of the author's absence. Noteth in the epistle to the Equal Reader how powerfully he hath been enticed with the delights of poetry, and most fortunate in his stage-pleasings, which delights he hath over vehemently pursued. 'Comedies,' saith he, 'are writ to be spoken, not read; remember the life of such things consisteth in action.'

'DOOMSDAY BOOK.'

A pious work by Dr. Samuel Gardiner, called *Doomsday Book*, being an alarum for atheists, a watchword for worldlings, and a caveat for Christians; which argument, saith he, is thrust upon him by the security and iniquity of these times; for having been four-and-forty years surfeited with peace and plenty, we have not only forgotten but as it were set our faces against piety. Wherefore it is high time to put the world in mind of those lying vanities which enchant the soul by placing before their eyes the day of doom, which must certainly come, and shortly come, which shall give to everyone according to his works.

ADDENDA AND CORRIGENDA

30th May, 1603. A DEFENCE OF RHYME.

Only one of the editions (S.T.C. 6259) of *A panegyric congratulatory* contains *A Defence of Rhyme*.

14th June, 1603. IRISH NEWS.

The source for this entry is *S.P. Ireland*, p. 61. Letter from Sir George Carey to Privy Council, dated 4th June.

28th April, 1605. A CUCKOO IN PAUL'S.

Dr. S. H. Atkins points out that this cuckoo was a malicious mocker. Dr. John Milward was one of the chief characters in a lively scandal which was dramatised in the lost comedy of *The Old Joiner of Aldgate*. He had married with more haste than legality a young woman named Agnes Howe. In 1603 Sir Julius Caesar declared the marriage null and void, but the decision was reversed in the Star Chamber in 1604. The case was complex and celebrated; the whole scurrilous story is rescued from oblivion in Professor C. J. Sisson's *Lost Plays of Shakespeare's Age*.

5th February, 1606. 'THE ISLE OF GULLS.'

There is a modern edition in the Shakespeare Association Facsimiles, No. 12, edited by G. B. Harrison.

29th October, 1606. THE CITY PAGEANT.

This entry should be dated 29th October, 1605.

ABBREVIATIONS

The following abbreviations have been used for sources frequently cited:

A.P.C. *Acts of the Privy Council*, edited by J. R. Dasent, 1900, etc.

BIRCH'S JAMES I. *The Court and Times of James the First*. Edited from the Collections of T. Birch by the Author of *Memoirs of Sophia Dorothea*, 2 vols., 1848.

BOWYER. *The Parliamentary Diary of Robert Bowyer*, 1606–7, edited by D. H. Willson, 1931.

BRADLEY. *Life of the Lady Arabella Stuart*, by E. I. Bradley, 2 vols., 1889.

C. J. *The Journals of the House of Commons from November the 8th 1547 . . . to March the 2nd 1628* [vol. i].

C.S.P. VENETIAN. *Calendar of State Papers and Manuscripts existing in the Archives and Collections of Venice*, vol. x, 1603–7, 1900.

CHAMBERLAIN'S LETTERS. *The Letters of John Chamberlain*, edited by N. E. McClure, 2 vols., 1939. The letters quoted all come from the first volume.

DE FONBLANQUE. *Annals of the House of Percy*, by E. B. De Fonblanque, 2 vols., 1887.

I ELIZ. JOURNAL, II ELIZ. JOURNAL, III ELIZ. JOURNAL. *An Elizabethan Journal . . . 1591–1594* (1928); *A Second Elizabethan Journal . . . 1595–1598* (1931); *A Last Elizabethan . . . 1599–1603* (1933); by G. B. Harrison. [Reprinted 3 vols. in one, 1938.]

ELIZ. STAGE. *The Elizabethan Stage*, by E. K. Chambers, 4 vols., 1923.

FOLEY. *Records of the English Province of the Society of Jesus*. By Henry Foley, S. J., 1877, etc.

GAWDY LETTERS. *Letters of Philip Gawdy*, edited by I. H. Jeayes, 1906.

HAWARDE. *Les Reportes del Cases in Camera Stellata*, 1593–1609. By William Hawarde. Edited by W. P. Baildon, 1894.

HOWELL'S STATE TRIALS. *Cobbett's Complete Collection of State Trials . . .* vol. ii, 1603–1627. Compiled by T. B. Howell, 1809.

JARDINE. *Criminal Trials*. By D. Jardine, 1832.

L.J. *Journals of the House of Lords beginning Anno Vicesimo Elizabethæ Reginæ* [vol. ii].

LODGE'S ILLUSTRATIONS. *Illustrations of British History . . .* By E. Lodge, 3 vols., 1838.

MANNINGHAM'S DIARY. *Diary of John Manningham, 1602–1603*. Edited by J. Bruce, 1868.

MORYSON. *An Itinerary containing his ten years travel*. Written by Fynes Moryson, Gent. References are to the MacLehose edition of 1907.

NUGÆ ANTIQUÆ. *Nugæ Antiquæ: being a miscellaneous collection of original papers* . . . by Sir John Harington, etc. Edited by T. Park, 2 vols., 1804.

PENSHURST PAPERS. *Papers of Lord De Lisle and Dudley at Penshurst Place.* Historical Manuscripts Commission.

PROCLAMATIONS. A collection of original proclamations in the British Museum [506 h. 10].

PROGRESSES. *The Progresses, processions and magnificent festivities of King James the First* . . . By J. Nichols, 4 vols., 1828. This magnificent collection is the most important source for the pageantry (and much else) of the reign. Nichols collected his materials widely, and reprints entire many of the contemporary news pamphlets, especially those describing state affairs.

PURCHAS. *Hakluytus Posthumus or Purchas His Pilgrims*. By Samuel Purchas, B.D., 1625. References to the MacLehose edition, 1906.

S.P. IRELAND. *State Papers Ireland* preserved in the Public Record Office; abstracted in the *Calendar of State Papers relating to Ireland*, edited by E. G. Atkinson, 1893.

S.R. *A Transcript of the Register of the Company of Stationers of London, 1554–1640.* Edited by E. Arber, 5 vols., 1875–1894.

S.T.C. *A Short title catalogue of books printed in England, Scotland and Ireland, and of books printed abroad, 1475–1640.* Compiled by A. W. Pollard and G. R. Redgrave, 1926.

SIDNEY PAPERS. *Letters and Memorials of State* . . . *from the originals at Penshurst Place*, etc. By Arthur Collins, 2 vols., 1746.

STOW. *ANNALES, or a General Chronicle of England.* Begun by John Stow. Continued and augmented with matters foreign and domestic, ancient and modern, until the end of this year 1631. By Edmund Howes, gent. John Stow died in April 1605. The *Annals* for these years though full are not always to be trusted for an accurate date.

STRYPE'S WHITGIFT. *The Life and Acts of John Whitgift* . . . By John Strype, 1718 and 3 vols., 1822.

WILBRAHAM'S JOURNAL. *The Journal of Sir Roger Wilbraham* . . . Edited by H. S. Scott. Camden Miscellany, vol. x, 1902.

WILSON. *The Plague in Shakespeare's London*. By F. P. Wilson, 1927.

WINWOOD'S MEMORIALS. *Memorials of affairs of State* . . . *Collected chiefly from the original papers of the Right Honourable Sir Ralph Winwood, Bt. Sometime one of the Principal Secretaries of State* . . . By Edmund Sawyer, 3 vols., 1725.

NOTES

1603

24th March. THE DEATH OF QUEEN ELIZABETH. Stow, p. 812.

THE ACCESSION OF KING JAMES. *Proclamations*, 1.; Manningham's *Diary*, p. 147; Wilbraham's *Journal*, p. 57; *Salisbury Papers*, xv. 25; Stow, p. 813; *Sloan MSS.* 718, f. 34.
'This peaceable coming in of the King was unexpected of all sorts of people' noted Lady Anne Clifford in her diary.

26th March. THE CORPSE OF QUEEN ELIZABETH. Chamberlain's *Letters*, p. 190; *Sloan MSS.* 718, f. 36v.

THE QUEEN'S DEATH. Chamberlain's *Letters*, pp. 188–90. *Lady South-well's MSS.* quoted in Agnes Strickland's *Life of Queen Elizabeth*, Every-man Edition, p. 700.

27th March. THE PAUL'S CROSS SERMON. Strype's *Whitgift*, ch. xxxix.

THE CORPSE OF QUEEN ELIZABETH. *Lady Southwell's MSS.* as above, p. 705.

28th March. THE NEW KING WELL RECEIVED. *Salisbury Papers*, xv. 4, 10 etc. The relief was general and very genuine, for the prospect of a dis-puted succession had caused the utmost alarm: see *III Eliz. Journal*, p. 326.

30th March. BERWICK LANDED OVER. Stow, p. 818.

31st March. SIR ROBERT CAREY'S RIDE. *Memoirs of Robert Carey*, Edited by G. H. Powell, 1905, p. 77; *Salisbury Papers*, xvii. 620; *Fuller's Church History*, Book x.

HESITATIONS AT YORK. Stow, p. 818.

THE KING'S LETTER TO THE LORD MAYOR. *Proclamations*, 2; Manningham's *Diary*, p. 156.

1st April. THE GENTLEMEN PENSIONERS. *Progresses* i. *125. Lord Huns-don died on 6th September 1603, and was succeeded as Captain of the Pensioners by the Earl of Northumberland.

2nd April. THE DEAD QUEEN. *C.S.P. Venetian*, p. 2.

3rd April. THE KING'S BOOKS PRINTED IN ENGLAND. *S.R.*, iii. 231; *S.T.C.*, 14350–4, 14365, 14410. Βασιλικὸν δῶρον was entered in the Register on 28th March and on sale on the 30th. *S.T.C.* notes five English editions in 1603. It is a sensible book, one of several books of advice for the young.

5th April. A PROCLAMATION CONCERNING OFFICERS OF THE STATE. *Proclamations*, 3.

6th April. TROUBLES ON THE BORDERS. Stow, p. 819.

7th April. A JAR AT COURT. Manningham's *Diary*, p. 160.

A BELATED ANSWER TO DOLEMAN'S 'CONFERENCE.' *S.R.*, iii. 231, *S.T.C.*, 12988. For the troubles over John Hayward's *Henry the Fourth*, see *III Eliz. Journal* (index). There was no hint in the many examinations taken in 1600–1 that the book had anything to do with the succession. It was suspected that Hayward was making propaganda for any claims that might be put forward by the Earl of Essex.

8th April. THE WAR IN THE LOW COUNTRIES. *Salisbury Papers*, xv. 38.

10th April. COURT NEWS. Chamberlain's *Letters*, pp. 192–4.

A FOOLISH RHYME. Manningham's *Diary*, p. 168.

A VOYAGE SET OUT FROM THE CITY OF BRISTOL. Purchas, xviii. 322–3. See later 3rd October 1603.

11th April. THE KING'S JOURNEY BEGUN. *Progresses*, i. 60–9. From *The True Narration of the Entertainment of his Royal Majesty* [*S.T.C.*, 14433].

12th April. THE SUBMISSION OF TYRONE. *S.P. Ireland*, pp. 13, 21. The submission was made on 8th April; the news reached London on the 12th (Chamberlain's *Letters*, p. 193). The time taken for news and travellers to reach London from Dublin varied greatly according to the wind. When Essex left his command in Dublin in September 1599, he reached London in four days; but sometimes letters took several weeks.

14th April. A SERMON AGAINST WOMEN. Manningham's *Diary*, p. 172.

16th April. THE SECRETARY GOES TO SEE THE KING. *Salisbury Papers*, xv. 49–50.

20th April. THE STATES WANT VOLUNTEERS. *Salisbury Papers*, xv. 47. Letter dated 14th April.

21st April. SIR ROBERT CECIL AT YORK. *Salisbury Papers*, xv. 52. Cecil reached York from Huntingdon in one day's travel by coach: he must have been very weary. This was the first meeting of King and Secretary, though they had corresponded in secret for several years.

22nd April. THE ORDER OF THE GARTER. *Progresses*, i. 194.

23rd April. THE KING'S JOURNEY. *Progresses*, i. 68–83.

25th April. NEW COUNCILLORS. *A.P.C.*, xxxii. 495.

THE KING HANGETH A THIEF. *Progresses*, i. 85–93. Sir John Harington commented upon this incident: 'I hear our new King hath hanged one man before he was tried: 'tis strangely done; now if the wind bloweth there, why may not a man be tried before he hath offended?'

26th April. THE MAUNDY. Stow, p. 819.

THE KING'S JOURNEY. *Progresses*, i. 93–4.

27th April. GOWRY'S BROTHERS SOUGHT. Stow, p. 819. *C.S.P. Venetian*, p. 26. The Venetian Secretary in London is responsible for the scandal.

28th April. THE FUNERALS OF QUEEN ELIZABETH. *Sloan MSS.* 718, f. 37; *Gawdy Letters*, p. 128; H. Petowe, *Elizabetha quasi vivens* (*S.T.C.*, 19804).

29*th April.* A POETICAL FLOOD. Nichols in *Progresses,* i. gives the titles of 33, and reprints a number.

30*th April.* THE KING'S JOURNEY. *Progresses,* i. 96–101; *Gawdy Letters,* p. 128.

A SCOTS SAYING. Arthur Wilson, *The History of Great Britain, being the Life and Reign of King James the First,* 1653, p. 3.

AN EXPLOSION OF POWDER. Stow, p. 819.

1*st May.* THE HUMBLE PETITION OF THE THOUSAND MINISTERS. Fuller (*Church History,* Book X, Section I, § 24) says that it was intended to be delivered to Parliament. S. R. Gardiner states that it was delivered to the King on his way to London. An answer of the University of Cambridge was made on 11th June.

2*nd May.* THE QUEEN'S JOURNEY. Stow, p. 823.

3*rd May.* THE KING AT THEOBALD'S. *Progresses,* i. 107–10.

4*th May.* THE KING. *Progresses,* i. 138.

THE KING AND THE PRIVY COUNCIL. *A.P.C.,* xxxii. 497.

5*th May.* THE STATE OF IRELAND. *S.P. Ireland,* pp. 24–6. Letter dated 25th April.

7*th May.* THE KING COMES TO LONDON. *Progresses,* i. 113–14, 139–40.

THE KING'S PROCLAMATION. *Proclamations,* 8.

HUNTING NEAR LONDON. *A.P.C.,* xxxii. 511.

8*th May.* SIR WALTER RALEGH DISMISSED FROM HIS POST. *A.P.C.,* xxxii. 498.

11*th May.* THE KING COMES TO THE TOWER. *Progresses,* i. 118–19; *C.S.P. Venetian,* p. 32.

13*th May.* THE SECRETARY PROMOTED. *Progresses,* i. 120, 154. *C.S.P. Venetian,* p. 33.

15*th May.* THE TROUBLES IN IRELAND. *S.P. Ireland.* pp. 22–4. Moryson, iii. 328–30.

18*th May.* THE NEW QUEEN. *C.S.P. Venetian,* p. 40.

A NEW CHANCELLOR OF THE EXCHEQUER. *Salisbury Papers,* xv. 94.

19*th May.* THE KING'S NEW PLAYERS. *Malone Society's Collections,* i. 264.

20*th May.* DIFFICULTIES ABOUT THE CORONATION. *C.S.P. Venetian,* p. 43.

22*nd May.* THE LORD DEPUTY AT CORK. Moryson, iii. 332–3.

25*th May.* 'SEJANUS.' *S.T.C.,* 14782. The Oxford Jonson, edited by C. H. Herford and Percy Simpson, i. 36–8; ii. 3–4; iv. 372–486. In the 1616 folio edition of his plays, Jonson noted that *Sejanus* was 'Acted, in the yeare 1603, by the K. MAIESTIES SERVANTS.' Further, the complimentary verses of 'Ev. B' show that it was acted at the Globe. If Jonson's statement is correct (and he was usually precise) the play was acted either at the end of May 1603 or between February and 25th March 1603–4. The earlier date is likelier. The Chamberlain's men became 'the King's Majesty's Servants' on 19th May and on the 26th May plague deaths rose to 30 a week when the playhouses were automatically shut. Jonson had retired from playwriting in the autumn of 1601 after his defeat in the Stage War, declaring that

'Since the Comic Muse
Hath prov'd so ominous to me, I will try
If Tragedy have a more kind aspect.

At the death of Queen Elizabeth he would thus appear to have swallowed his pride hurriedly, reconciled himself with the players (who were now officially royal servants), and joined early in the rush for favours under the new King. The failure of *Sejanus* was not surprising. Jonson had made himself very unpopular in the Stage War, and this classical tragedy with its minute, pedantic insistence on accuracy of detail was not likely to appeal to a hearty and hostile audience. Nor would it please Authority. A play on the theme of a royal favourite who fell disastrously had an obvious significance only two years after Essex's death. Indeed contemporaries saw a parallel in the story of Essex and of Sejanus. In a copy of Greneway's translation of *The Annals of Tacitus* (1598) which belonged to the late Sir Israel Gollancz, a contemporary hand had noted opposite the fall of Sejanus the words 'The Earl of Essex.' Not long afterward (see p. 179) Daniel was also in trouble for a similar offence caused by *Philotas*.

26th May, THE PLAGUE IN LONDON. Wilson, p. 87.

30th May. A DEFENCE OF RHYME. *S.R.*, iii. 235; *S.T.C.*, 6258–9. There were two issues; one opulently printed in folio for the noble reader.

31st May. A MASTER OF CEREMONIES APPOINTED. Stow, p. 824.

2nd June. THE KING. *C.S.P. Venetian*, p. 46. *Diary of Lady Anne Clifford*, edited by V. Sackville-West, 1923, p. 5.

6th June. VALENTINE THOMAS EXECUTED. Stow, p. 825. A belated and vindictive punishment: see *II Eliz. Journal*, pp. 279, 325.

THE LORD MOUNTJOY'S RETURN. *Salisbury Papers*, xv. 123; Moryson, iii. 334–6; *C.S.P. Venetian*, p. 53.

THE CHARGES OF THE IRISH WARS. Moryson, iii. 341–2. The Queen's annual income was about £300,000. The Irish wars were thus an intolerable burden for even a victory brought neither spoils nor profit.

THE FRENCH AMBASSADOR. *C.S.P. Venetian*, p. 54.

7th June. SIR WALTER RALEGH AND DURHAM HOUSE. *Egerton Papers*, pp. 376, 381.

8th June. A PROCLAMATION FOR THE EARL OF TYRONE. *Proclamations*, 13.

THE AMBASSADOR FROM FRANCE IN LONDON. Stow, p. 825. *Salisbury Papers*, xv. 125.

ESSEX'S APOLOGY TO BE PRINTED. *S.R.*, iii. 236; *S.T.C.*, 6788; *S.T.C.*, 21432. See *II Eliz. Journal* p. 281, and 86; *III Eliz. Journal* 86 and vi.

9th June. THE ARREST OF PATRICK RUTHVEN. *Salisbury Papers*, xv. 127–8.

10th June. A BOOK CALLED 'THE AMBASSADOR.' *S.R.*, iii. 237; *S.T.C.*, 13848. A nicely printed little volume designed for the pockets of distinguished persons.

11th June. THE UNIVERSITY OF CAMBRIDGE AND THE PURITAN DOC-TRINES. Strype's *Whitgift*, Bk. iv, Ch. iv.

12th June. THE FRENCH AMBASSADOR RECEIVED IN AUDIENCE. Sully's *Memoirs*, iii. 121–3. [*Memoirs of Maximilian de Bethune, Duke of Sully.* Translated from the French by the Author of the Female Quixote, 1757, 5 vols.]

15th June. COURT NEWS. Lodge's *Illustrations*, iii. 10. *Progresses*, i. 161–2.

18th June. A CITIZEN SLAIN BY THE FRENCHMEN. Sully's *Memoirs*, iii. 102.

22nd June. COURT NEWS. *Progresses*, i. 188.

THE GALLANTRY OF LORD CECIL'S LITTLE SON. *Salisbury Papers*, xv. 143.

23rd June. PIRACY TO BE REPRESSED. *Proclamations*, 15.

25th June. THE FRENCH AMBASSADOR'S DEPARTURE. Sully's *Memoirs*, iii. 187; *Salisbury Papers*, xv. 152.

THE QUEEN AT ALTHORP. *Progresses*, i. 176–189. Ben Jonson's *Particular Entertainment.*

27th June. THE KING MEETS THE QUEEN. *Progresses*, i. 189. *Diary of Lady Anne Clifford. C.S.P. Venetian*, p. 63.

28th June. THE EARL OF MAR. *Progresses*, i. 190.

TROUBLES AT PLYMOUTH. *Salisbury Papers*, xv. 151.

AN EMBASSAGE TO DENMARK. Stow, p. 825.

30th June. M. DE ROSNY'S SPLEEN. *Salisbury Papers*, xv. 152.

THE PLAGUE. Wilson, p. 90.

1st July. THE EARL OF SOUTHAMPTON AND THE LORD GREY. *Progresses*, i. 197–8. This quarrel was of long standing and first began in Essex's Irish wars; see *III Eliz. Journal*, pp. 23, 139.

2nd July. THE FEAST OF ST. GEORGE. *Progresses*, i. 193–5.

3rd July. A CONSPIRACY SUSPECTED. *Progresses*, i. 198. This conspiracy was a sequel to the Catholic Controversy of 1599–1603, which was an event of far greater importance than would appear from the scant notice taken of it by modern historians of the period. Watson, Clarke and Copley had taken considerable part in the pamphlet war of the Seculars against the Jesuits, being actively encouraged by Dr. Bancroft, Bishop of London. The Seculars had hoped that in return for loyalty to the Crown they would be granted some freedom of worship. They now found themselves deluded on all sides, and foolishly thought of making common cause with other malcontents. See *III Eliz. Journal*: index 'Catholic Controversy', and *Jacobean Journal*, pp. 47, 52.

5th July. A GREAT DROUGHT. *Diary of Walter Yonge*, edited by G. Roberts. Camden Society, 1848, p. 1.

7th July. SIR JOHN FORTESCUE'S COMPLAINT. *Salisbury Papers*, xv. 171.

10th July. A SECRET PRESS TAKEN. *Salisbury Papers*, xv. 181.

11th July. THE CORONATION CURTAILED. *Proclamations*, 19, 21.

12th July. THE STATE OF IRELAND. *S.P. Ireland,* pp. 66–7. Letters dated 2nd July.

14th July. SIR WALTER RALEGH AND OTHERS ARRESTED. Richard Smith's *Diary* (a MS. in the British Museum. *Sloan,* 414).

THE KING'S DELIVERANCE TO BE REMEMBERED. Strype's *Whitgift,* bk. iv. ch. xxx. For the conspiracy see *III Eliz. Journal,* pp. 104–9.

UNRULY NEGLECT OF PLAGUE ORDERS. *Salisbury Papers,* xv. 189.

15th July. THE CHARACTERS OF KING JAMES AND QUEEN ELIZABETH COMPARED. Wilbraham's *Journal,* pp. 58–60. This entry is abstracted from a longer comparison made by Wilbraham three months after the King's arrival 'according to the means of my apprehension without flattery.' It is a valuable comment on the impression created in the mind of an intelligent official by the new King. There is no suggestion here or in any other contemporary which I have encountered that the King was at this time in any way physically contemptible to Englishmen.

16th July. CONSPIRATORS TO BE APPREHENDED. *Proclamations,* 22.

17th July. FORTY-POUND LANDHOLDERS TO BE KNIGHTED. *Progresses,* i. 203. Rymer's *Foedera,* xvi. 530.

19th July. A NEW GREAT SEAL. Wilbraham's *Journal,* pp. 60–1.

20th July. SIR WALTER RALEGH TRIES TO KILL HIMSELF. *The Life of Sir Walter Ralegh,* by Edward Edwards, 1868, i. 375. *C.S.P. Venetian,* pp. 70, 82.

21st July. NEW PEERS CREATED. *Progresses,* i. 204–5.

THE PLAGUE. Wilson, p. 90.

22nd July. THE BASE MONEY IN IRELAND. *S.P. Ireland,* p. 70. Letter dated 12th July.

24th July. MORE KNIGHTS MADE. *Progresses,* i. 205–26. Stow, p. 827.

25th July. THE CORONATION OF THE KING AND QUEEN. *Progresses,* i. 229–34; Wilbraham's *Journal,* p. 61; Stow, p. 827.

A SCOTS PROPHECY FULFILLED. Arthur Wilson, p. 5.

26th July. THE RECORDER OF CORK ACQUITTED. *S.P.I.,* pp. 119–22, 227.

27th July. SIR WALTER RALEGH. *Salisbury Papers,* xv. 212.

28th July. THE PLAGUE. Wilson, p. 90.

31st July. DR. THOMAS LODGE. From the *Epistle to the Reader* in *S.T.C.,* 16676 (see p. 58).

1st August. SUITORS ORDERED TO AVOID THE COURT. Stow, p. 828.

4th August. THE LATE CONSPIRACY. Birch's *James I,* pp. 9–13.

THE PLAGUE. Wilson, p. 93.

5th August. A DAY OF THANKSGIVING. Stow, p. 828. See 14 July ante.

TROUBLE IN THE LOW COUNTRIES. *Sidney Papers,* ii. 277, 275.

6th August. THE EARL OF RUTLAND'S EMBASSAGE. Stow, p. 825.

A DEPUTATION FROM IRELAND. *C.S.P. Venetian,* p. 83.

7th August. THE NEW KNIGHTS. *Gawdy Letters*, p. 135.

8th August. FAIRS PUT OFF. *Proclamations*, 44.

9th August. A STRANGE COACH. From *The meeting of Gallants* in *Dekker's Plague Pamphlets.* Edited by F. P. Wilson, 1925, p. 117.

10th August. MASTER RALPH WINWOOD SENT TO THE STATES. Winwood's *Memorials*, ii. 1–3.

    PRAYERS FOR THE PLAGUE. Stow, p. 828.

    THE LADY ARABELLA. *C.S.P. Venetian*, p. 82.

12th August. THE CITY MARSHAL RESISTED. *Salisbury Papers*, xv. 266.

15th August. CLARKE ARRESTED. *Salisbury Papers*, xv. 230.

17th August. A PALL FOR THE QUEEN'S MOTHER. Stow, p. 828.

18th August. THE PLAGUE STILL INCREASING. Wilson, p. 93.

    TYRONE'S FEARS. *C.S.P. Venetian*, p. 87.

19th August. DR. LODGE'S TREATISE OF THE PLAGUE. *S.T.C.*, 16676; dated in the Epistle. A sensible, practical book.

23rd August. COURT NEWS. Bradley, ii. 181.

25th August. THE PLAGUE DEATHS. Wilson, p. 93.

31st August. DOGS KILLED. *Progresses*, i. 228. It was not realized that the bubonic plague was carried by the rat-flea. Dogs were considered in some way to be carriers. In the elaborate orders first put in force during the epidemic of 1592 there is a long clause dealing with dogs. Householders were commanded to keep their dogs in, and not to allow them to be taken out except 'in slip or line.' The common huntsman was charged to kill every dog found loose, and to bury it at least 4 feet deep. Further, any dog offending the neighbours with its howling or noise was to be killed. [See *Present Remedies against the Plague*, edited by W. P. Barrett, Shakespeare Association Facsimiles, No. 7, p. xi]. This wholesale killing of dogs benefited only the rats. See *I Eliz. Journal*, p. 168.

1st September. THE PLAGUE STILL INCREASING. Wilson, p. 93.

5th September. A BOOK AGAINST THE RELIGION. *S.T.C.*, 14912. This book contains 733 pages in addition to 46 pages of Epistles. A second edition came out in 1605.

6th September. THE ARRIVAL OF THE SPANISH AMBASSADOR. *Salisbury Papers*, xv. 245.

10th September. BEN JONSON'S SON. Jonson's *Epigrams*, xlv. and *Conversations with Drummond*, Section xiii. Exact date unknown.

11th September. COURT NEWS. Lodge's *Illustrations*, iii. 19. See also 1606.

    THE RETURN OF THE SHIPS FROM THE EAST INDIA VOYAGE. Purchas, ii. 392–437. See also *III Eliz. Journal*, pp. 121, 132, 151, 177.

15th September. THE PLAGUE DEATHS. Wilson, p. 93.

16th September. FOREIGN AMBASSADORS. Lodge's *Illustrations*, iii. 24, 25.

17th September. COURT NEWS. Lodge's *Illustrations*, iii. 30.

    NEW COIN FOR IRELAND. *S.P. Ireland*, p. 87. Letter from Woodstock of this date. For the debasing of the Irish coinage, see *III Eliz. Journal*, 141, 181, 183, 202, 282.

THE INCREASE OF VAGABONDS. *Proclamations*, 27.

24th September. COURT NEWS. *Progresses*, i. 258, 273, 274. The Lord Admiral was a doughty ancient; he died in 1624 at the age of 88.

25th September. AN INHUMAN REPORT FROM HERTFORD. From *The Meeting of Gallants*, in *Dekker's Plague Pamphlets* edited by F. P. Wilson, 1925, p. 132. Approximate date.

29th September. THE PLAGUE DECREASING. Wilson, p. 93.

30th September. THE VOYAGE TO VIRGINIA. Purchas, xviii. 329–35.

2nd October. THE BRISTOL MERCHANTS' VENTURE. Purchas, xviii. 322–9. See 10th April 1603.

3rd October. A COMPLAINT OF THE COUNT AREMBERG. Winwood's *Memorials*, ii. 7.

5th October. THE SPANISH AMBASSADOR. Winwood's *Memorials*, ii. 7.

8th October. MONEY FOR GENEVA. Strype's *Whitgift*, bk. x, ch. xxx. Whitgift passed the order on to the Bishops on 26th October with the necessary note that 'there be no deductions of charges made by any of their officers or apparitors out of any of these collections.'

THE GARTER FOR THE DUKE OF WIRTENBERG. Stow, p. 828. This Duke's endeavours to obtain the coveted Order began in 1592 when he visited England and caused some amusement. See *I Eliz. Journal*, pp. 151–9, *II Eliz. Journal*, pp. 22, 184.

9th October. COURT NEWS. Lodge's *Illustrations*, iii. 52.

THE SERMON IN PAUL's. *S.T.C.*, 13703; dated in Epistle 31st October. Approximate date.

13th October. THE PLAGUE DEATHS. Wilson, p. 105.

A TREATISE OF THE PLAGUE. *S.T.C.*, 1338. Dated 13th October in the Epistle which notes that from 7th May to 13th October in this one parish 2,640 had died, and that attendance at the Friday lecture had been as good as in the winter nights.

15th October. THE MARQUIS SPINOLA. *Penshurst Papers*, iii. 68.

17th October. COURT NEWS. Lodge's *Illustrations*, iii. 56.

21st October. THE NEW MONEYS PROCLAIMED IN IRELAND. *S.P. Ireland*, p. 93. See *ante* 17th September.

27th October. THE PLAGUE GREATLY DIMINISHED. Wilson, p. 105.

29th October. A STRANGE MIRACLE IN POICTIERS. *S.R.*, iii. 245; *S.T.C.*, 5326. Translated from the French by Anthony Munday, with a dedicatory sonnet by Dekker. There is some wonderful medical comment in this book.

1st November. RECUSANCY IN THE NORTH. *Salisbury Papers*, xv. 278, 283.

10th November. 'HAMLET' PRINTED. *S.T.C.*, 22275. The exact date of publication is unknown, but it was after 19th May and before the end of the year.

12th November. THE PRISONERS AT WINCHESTER. Stow, pp. 828–9.

15th November. THE ARRAIGNMENT OF THE CONSPIRATORS. Howell's *State Trials*, ii. 61; *Loseley MSS.*, edited by A. T. Kempe, 1835, p. 376. As often in State trials, the accused were judged by their intended victims.

17th November. THE TRIAL OF SIR WALTER RALEGH. Howell's *State Trials*, ii. 1–55; Birch's *James I*, pp. 20–1.

18th November. THE LORD COBHAM CONDEMNED. Howell's *State Trials*, ii. 47.

19th November. LORD GREY'S TRIAL. As above.

23rd November. A SAYING ABOUT RALEGH'S TRIAL. *Gawdy Letters*, p. 142.

24th November. THE PLAGUE DEATHS. Wilson, p. 106.

27th November. COURT NEWS. Birch's *James I*, i. 26.

29th November. WATSON AND CLARKE EXECUTED. Stow, p. 831; Howell's *State Trials*, ii. 51.

3rd December. THE IRISH MONEYS. *S.P. Ireland*, p. 113.

5th December. BROOKE EXECUTED. Stow, p. 831; Howell's *State Trials*, ii. 51, 55.

A BOOK FORBIDDEN. *S.R.*, iii. 249; *S.T.C.*, 20170. The book is somewhat cryptic, but otherwise seems harmless and is dull.

THE WONDERFUL YEAR AND A DESCRIPTION OF THE PLAGUE. *S.R.* ii. 837; *S.T.C.*, 6534. *The Wonderful Year* came out in the autumn. On 5th December, Ling, Smithwick and Browne were fined 10s. each for printing it without authority. The two former paid their fines on 7th April 1605.

6th December. LORD COBHAM AND RALEGH. Howell's *State Trials*, ii. 51.

THE KING'S PLAYERS SENT FOR. *Eliz. Stage*, iv. 168.

8th December. COURT NEWS. Bradley, ii. 190.

9th December. THE KING'S GREAT CLEMENCY. Howell's *State Trials*, ii. 52–5.

'To walk with Prince Arthur'—because the Great Hall of Winchester Castle was supposed to be the meeting-place of the Knights of the Round Table. The ancient Round Table, inscribed with the names of King Arthur's Knights, is still hung on the wall.

10th December. THE KING'S CLEMENCY. Stow, pp. 831–3; Howell's *State Trials*, ii. 52–5.

THE KING'S LETTER TO THE SHERIFF OF HAMPSHIRE WRITTEN WITH HIS OWN HAND. Stow, p. 833. The King's letter (and spelling) caused much interest; it is reproduced *literatim* both by Stow and by Speed and elsewhere.

15th December. THE PLOTTERS. Stow, p. 833.

18th December. PREPARATION AT COURT. Bradley, ii. 190, 195.

22nd December. THE PLAGUE. Wilson, p. 114.

28th December. COURT NEWS. Lodge's *Illustrations*.

24th December. NEWS FROM GRAVESEND. *S.T.C.*, 12199. Printed according to the Epistle at Christmas time. F. P. Wilson includes it in his edition of *Dekker's Plague Pamphlets*.

26th December. THE PRINCE'S PLAYERS. *Eliz. Stage*, ii. 186. Approximate date.

OTHER BOOKS PRINTED THIS YEAR 1603

A Book for Gardeners. *S.T.C.*, 11571. An early example of a seeds-man's catalogue, with cultural notes. The following prices are of interest:
Carrots, large, seed, 2s. a wax pound.
        vegetable, 2d. a stone of 10 wax weights.
                3d. a stone preserved in snow, January–March.
Carrots, small, 1d. for 5 wax pounds.
Cabbage seed, 4d. per oz. ('the which seeds are hardly sold in this country of Salop for being devoured with birds').
Cabbage, vegetable large, 2d. for 2 wax pounds.
Turnip, seed, 12d. a pound.
      vegetable, 2d. a stone.
Beans (broad), seed, 2d. a quart.
        green, 1d. a quart.
Artichokes, $\frac{1}{3}$d. to 1d., according to size.
Porrets (in the text) are young leeks or onions.

The Bachelor's Banquet. *S.T.C.*, 6476. This book was formerly attributed on slender evidence to Dekker. F. P. Wilson in his edition shows that it was a free translation of *Les Quinze Joyes de marriage*, and is probably a renaming of the book banned in 1599 (see *III Eliz. Journal*, p. 21). He suggests that the translator was Robert Allot. Several other books banned in the late reign appeared this year (see p. 36).

Microcosmos. *S.T.C.*, 6333.

Montaigne's Essays. *S.T.C.*, 18041. The *Essays* were first entered to Aggas on 20th December, 1595, and to Blount on 3rd June, 1600; they were first printed in 1603.

The Siege of Ostend. *S.T.C.*, 18895. The book was entered on 20th September—an example of entry used to stake a claim in a piece of exciting news; it could not have been finished by this date.

4th January. THE CONFERENCE AT HAMPTON COURT. Strype's *Whitgift*, bk. iv. no. xlv. appendix.

5th January. THE KING AND SIR JOHN HARINGTON. *Nugæ Antiquæ*, i. 367; from a letter written by Harington to Sir Amyas Paulet. The date of this famous interview is uncertain. Park finding the letter dated 'January 1604' altered it to 'Jan. 1606–7'—'because Lord Harington of Exton who is spoken of as lately honoured was created a baron, November 18, 1606.' Park was wrong; the correct date was 21st July, 1603. Nichols gives the date 'Jan. 1604–5'; N. E. McClure in *The Letters and Epigrams of Sir John Harington*, p. 109, dates the letter '? December 1603.' The date 5th January, 1604, is probably not far out. Harington presumably came up to Court for Christmas.

11th January. A PROCLAMATION CONCERNING THE PARLIAMENT. *Proclamations*, 33.

14th January. THE CONFERENCE AT HAMPTON COURT. Fuller's *Church History*, bk. x. Section I, § 20.

THE DOWNFALL OF POPERY. *S.T.C.*, 1817. Dated 14th January, 1603–4 in the Epistle Dedicatory. The book went into three editions in 1604–5. The second edition was entered on 18th March.

15th January. A LEWD RHYME ON LORD CECIL. *Salisbury Papers*, xvi. 15.

16th January. THE SECOND DAY'S CONFERENCE ABOUT RELIGIOUS MATTERS. As for 14th January.

18th January. THE CONFERENCE CONCLUDED. As for 14th January.

20th January. THE CENSURE OF THE CONFERENCE. As for 14th January.

25th January. PURITAN REPORTS OF THE LATE CONFERENCE. Appended to Dr. William Barlowe's account of the Conference. See p. 138.

30th January. A MOTHER'S BOOKS. *S.R.*, iii. 251; *S.T.C.*, 12407. The lady was Catholic. Not much is known of her but her book went into at least four editions. In the epistle she says that she has been brought to languishing consumption by 'my mother's undeserved wrath so violent.'

31st January. THINGS TO BE REFORMED IN THE CHURCH. Strype's *Whitgift*, bk iv. ch. xxxi.

1st February. THE MEETING OF GALLANTS AT AN ORDINARY. *S.T.C.*, 17781. Assigned to Dekker by F. P. Wilson in *Dekker's Plague Pamphlets*, 1925. From internal evidence the pamphlet was written about this time.

2nd February. COURT NEWS. Lodge's *Illustrations*, iii. 86.

4th February. THE CHILDREN OF THE CHAPEL. *Malone Society's Collections*, i. 267; *Eliz. Stage*, ii. 49.

8th February. THE KING'S PLAYERS. *Eliz. Stage*, iv. 160.

12th February. TWO TREATISES OF TRADE. *S.R.*, iii. 252; *S.T.C.*, 17929, 17932.

15th February. THE TRANSLATION OF THE BIBLE. Strype's *Whitgift* bk. iv. ch. xxxiii. Approximate date.

22nd February. A PROCLAMATION AGAINST PAPIST PRIESTS. *Proclamations*, 34.

26th February. THE ARCHBISHOP TAKEN SICK. Strype's *Whitgift* bk. iv. ch. xxxii.

28th February. THE KING VISITS THE ARCHBISHOP. As for 26th February.

29th February. THE DEATH OF THE ARCHBISHOP. As for 26th February. Stow, p. 835.

10th March. AN EXCESS OF LAW STUDENTS. *Salisbury Papers*, xvi. 38.

12th March. THE COURT AT THE TOWER. *Progresses*, i. 319; *S.T.C.*, 13899.

A LION BAITED. Stow, p. 935.

15th March. THE TRIUMPHAL PROGRESS THROUGH LONDON. Stow, p. 836; *Progresses* i. 324–423, where the very elaborate shows and speeches are fully detailed and various contemporary pamphlets reprinted. Dekker, Jonson, Middleton, Drayton and others had a hand in this extravagant pageantry, while Shakespeare and his fellow-actors of the King's Company walked in the procession for which they received 4½ yards of red cloth for their liveries as grooms of the chamber. The designs of the Triumphal Arches were published in 1604 by Stephen Harrison [*S.T.C.*, 12863]; to this volume Dekker and Webster contributed commendatory verses. It is the first surviving piece of Webster's writing.

19th March. THE ASSEMBLING OF PARLIAMENT. *Lords Journals*, ii. 264; *C.J.* i. 140; *S.T.C.*, 14390.

AN INSOLENT YEOMAN. *C.J.*, i. 141.

1st March. A VOYAGE FOR THE PLANTATION OF VIRGINIA. Purchas, xvi., 309.

22nd March. THE PRINCE'S SHIP. *Progresses*, i. 425.

THE KING'S SPEECH REPEATED and CASES OF PRIVILEGE. *C.J.*, i. 142 and 149.

Seeing that Sir John Fortescue was a Privy Councillor his rejection in favour of Sir Francis Goodwin was a snub to that august body.

A BOOK AGAINST ENCLOSURES. *S.R.*, iii. 256; *S.T.C.*, 24280.

23rd March. THE PARLIAMENT. *C.J.*, i. 150.

24th March. TILTING AT WHITEHALL. Foley, i. 60.

DISORDERLY PAGES, *C.J.*, i. 152.

26th March. THE PARLIAMENT. *C.J.*, i. 152, 154.

27th March. THE FUNERALS OF DR. WHITGIFT. Strype's *Whitgift*, bk. iv. ch. xxxii; *S.T.C.*, 20574; Hawarde, p. 222.

THE PARLIAMENT. *C.J.*, i. 154–7.

A VIEW OF FRANCE. *S.R.*, iii. 257; *S.T.C.*, 6202. The date of composition can be deduced from the remark on Sig. 42v ' this last yere 97.' A very lively book, full of little touches of keen observance and comparison; reprinted in *The Shakespeare Association Facsimiles*, edited by W. P Barrett.

28*th March.* THE PARLIAMENT. *C.J.*, i. 156–7.

29*th March.* THE PARLIAMENT. *C.J.*, i. 157–8; Foley, i. 60.

30*th March.* THE CASE OF SIR FRANCIS GOODWIN. *C.J.*, i. 159.

31*st March.* RECUSANCY IN THE NORTH. *Salisbury Papers*, xvi. 44.

1*st April.* THE FRENCH AMBASSADOR AND THE CATHOLICS. Foley, i. 60, 61; *S.T.C.*, 5557.

2*nd April.* THE CASE OF SIR FRANCIS GOODWIN. *C.J.*, i. 161. For another example of an election see *II Eliz. Journal*, 209.

A NOTABLE CONTEMPT. *Salisbury Papers*, xvi. 50. The King's neglect of public business was already causing serious inconvenience.

FOUR PARADOXES OF WAR. *S.R.*, iii. 258; *S.T.C.*, 6872.

3*rd April.* THE PARLIAMENT and THE COMMONS' ANSWER TO THE KING. *C.J.*, i. 162–4.

5*th April.* A SECOND VOYAGE TO THE EAST INDIES. Purchas, ii. 496.

THE KING'S ANSWER TO THE COMMONS. *C.J.*, i. 166.

6*th April.* COURT NEWS. *Gawdy Letters*, p. 144. Churchyard the poet had long been one of the lighter sides of Court Life, ready on any occasion to produce a bad copy of topical verse. He was aged about 84.

THE SERMON AT COURT. *S.T.C.*, 597.

9*th April.* THE QUEEN'S DELIVERY. Stow, p. 862.

11*th April.* THE CASE OF SIR F. GOODWIN. *C.J.*, i. 168.

13*th April.* THE KING AND THE SPEAKER. *C.J.*, i. 170.

18*th April.* THE UNION OF THE TWO KINGDOMS. *C.J.*, i. 176–7.

19*th April.* THE UNION DEBATED. *C.J.*, i. 179.

20*th April.* The UNION. *C.J.*, i. 179.

21*st April.* THE UNION. *C.J.*, i. 180.

25*th April.* AN ANSWER TO THE PURITANS. *S.R.*, iii. 259 ; *S.T.C.*, 5882. The book was to have been dedicated to Archbishop Whitgift, but as he died between writing and publication, the intended dedication was added as an appendix. For *The Plea of the Innocent*, see *III Eliz. Journal*, p. 268.

26*th April.* THE UNION. *C.J.*, i. 186.

27*th April.* THE UNION. *C.J.*, i. 187. Most of the objections are petty, pedantical or merely due to nationalistic pride.

A PETITION AGAINST PURVEYORS. *C.J.*, i. 190.

30*th April.* MASTER WILLIAM ALEXANDER'S WORKS. *S.R.*, iii. 260; *S.T.C.*, 337, 343, 346.

1*st May.* AN APOLOGY OF THE ROMAN CHURCH. *S.T.C.*, 3604; dated 1st April in the Advertisement.

THE KING'S LETTER ON THE UNION. *C.J.*, i. 193.

A MASQUE AT HIGHGATE. *Progresses*, i. 431; Ben Jonson's *The Penates.*

2nd May. THE HOUSE OF COMMONS. *C.J.*, i. 197.

4th May. THE CASE OF SIR THOMAS SHIRLEY. *C.J.*, i. 198.

7th May. THE CASE OF SIR THOMAS SHIRLEY. *C.J.*, i. 200.

9th May. SIR THOMAS SHIRLEY. *C.J.*, i. 204–5.

10th May. THE CONSTABLE OF CASTILE AND THE JEWELLERS OF ANTWERP. *Salisbury Papers*, xvi. 85.

11th May. THE WARDEN OF THE FLEET. *C.J.*, i. 207.

12th May. THE REPORT OF THE CONFERENCE AT HAMPTON COURT. *Salisbury Papers*, xvi. 95.

14th May. THE WARDEN OF THE FLEET. *C.J.*, i. 209.

15th May. SIR THOMAS SHIRLEY RELEASED. *C.J.*, i. 210–11.

16th May. THE PRISONERS IN THE TOWER. *C.J.*, i. 211.

18th May. SIR FRANCIS BACON'S APOLOGY. *S.R.*, iii. 261; *S.T.C.*, 1111. Two editions came out in 1604 and two in 1605.

19th May. THE WARDEN OF THE FLEET RELEASED. *C.J.*, i. 214.

21st May. THE BILLS FOR FREE TRADE. *C.J.*, i. 218–20. Sandys' report is a most illuminating commentary on current economic theory and practice.

A DIALOGUE ON WAR. *S.R.*, iii. 262; *S.T.C.*, 21001. An interesting dialogue and a valuable comment on the military profession. Captain Pill would have heartily endorsed Iago's irritation at Cassio's promotion.

26th May. A COMPLAINT AGAINST THE BISHOP OF BRISTOL. *C.J.*, i. 226.

1st June. THE SIEGE OF OSTEND. *Penshurst Papers*, iii. 114; *Sidney Papers*, ii. 290–1.

4th June. THE TREATY OF PEACE. Winwood's *Memorials*, ii. 22.

5th June. THE KING SENDS A MESSAGE TO THE HOUSE. *C.J.*, i. 232.

6th June. THE BILLS FOR FREE TRADE PASSED. *C.J.*, i. 233. The Bills were subsequently rejected by the Lords.

8th June. DR. DEE'S COMPLAINTS. *S.T.C.*, 6465–6.

9th June. A MURDER IN LINCOLNSHIRE. *S.T.C.*, 4768. Dilworth was subsequently tried in August at Lincoln and hanged at Bourne.

10th June. SIR THOMAS SMITH GIVEN AUDIENCE. *S.T.C.*, 22869. This is the Sheriff Smith who was in trouble over the Essex rising. His journey to Russia was much talked of.

THE PASSIONATE SHEPHERD. *S.R.*, iii. 264; *S.T.C.*, 3682. Breton is a poetical survivor from the days of Philip Sidney. The poems which he calls 'sonnets' are not written in decasyllabics, and only two are in fourteen lines.

12th June. SIR THOMAS SMITH SETS FORTH FOR RUSSIA. Stow, 844.

15th June. A POEM ABOUT THE EARL OF ESSEX. *S.T.C.*, 20339. *S.T.C.*, is mistaken in identifying this poem with one entered on 27th March. It is an answer to Bacon's *Apology*, and very outspoken in its criticism of Bacon and Essex's enemies, dedicated to the Earls of Southampton and Devon, and Lord Knollys.

20th June. THE HARD CASE OF MR. RICHARD HAWKINS. *Salisbury Papers,* xvi. 144.

22nd June. THE CASE OF SIR ROBERT DUDLEY. Hawarde, p. 169. See pp. 200, 202, 203, and note on 1st May, 1605.

25th June. AN ALARM AT COURT. *C.S.P. Venetian,* pp. 165, 168.

26th June. THE DEATH OF THE EARL OF OXFORD. *D.N.B.*; Stow, p. 868; *Salisbury Papers,* xvi. 258, 397 [a letter of King James to Cecil commenting on a petition for a pension from Lord Sheffield to whom he is willing to grant £1,000 and no more—'Great Oxford when his estate was whole ruined got no more of the Queen']. For the scandals, *Aubrey's Brief Lives,* edited by Andrew Clarke, 1898, ii. 270; Aubrey is not necessarily reliable, but the story is well known.

27th June. A LOYAL SUBJECT'S LOOKING-GLASS. *S.R.,* iii. 265. *S.T.C.* 25760. An interesting indication of social unrest.

29th June. THE KING HURT BY A HORSE. *C.J.,* i. 247, 248.

COMMISSIONERS FROM THE HANSE TOWNS. *Salisbury Papers,* xvi. 156, 297. See *II Eliz. Journals,* 249, 251. See later 12th August and 23rd September.

30th June. THE LORD COBHAM. *Salisbury Papers,* xvi. 157.

5th July. MARSTON'S MALCONTENT. *S.R.,* iii. 268; *S.T.C.,* 17479–81. This is Marston's maturest and most popular play: three editions came out this year. It was entered as *The Malecontent: Tragiecomedia.*

6th July. COPLEY SENT INTO EXILE. *Salisbury Papers,* xvi. 165.

7th July. PARLIAMENT PROROGUED. Stow, p. 844.

A NOTE ON THE CHIEF STATUTES ENACTED IN THE PARLIAMENT. *Statutes of the Realm: Anno I Jacobi Regis.*

8th July. THE DUKE CHARLES. *Salisbury Papers,* xvi. 163.

10th July. THE EARL OF LINCOLN'S HIGH-HANDED ACTION. From *Lodowick Bryskett and his Family,* by Deborah Jones (in *Thomas Lodge and other Elizabethans,* by C. J. Sisson), p. 266.

16th July. THE FRENCH KING'S MIRACULOUS ESCAPE. *The Fugger News Letters,* edited by v. von Klarwill, 1924, p. 246. This yarn comes from Venice via Lyons.

22nd July. THE TRANSLATION OF THE BIBLE. Strype's *Whitgift,* bk. iv. ch. xxxiii.

23rd July. THE SIEGE OF OSTEND. *Sidney Papers,* ii. 300–1.

25th July. DUTCH CRUELTY. *C.S.P. Venetian,* p. 172.

30th July. THE PRISONERS IN THE TOWER. *Salisbury Papers,* xvi. 137.

1st August. THE SPANISH COMMISSIONERS. Stow, p. 845.

3rd August. GREAT RAIN. Stow, p. 844.

5th August. A LIONESS WHELPS. Stow, p. 844.

7th August. THE LIONESS'S WHELP. *Salisbury Papers,* xvi. 207–8. The behaviour of the lioness on this and subsequent occasions caused the greatest interest and much correspondence.

8th August. THE CONSTABLE AT DOVER. *Salisbury Papers,* xvi. 203, 208.

10th August. THE COMMISSIONERS FOR THE PEACE. Stow, p. 845; *Eliz. Stage,* ii. 211.

12th August. THE COMMISSIONERS FOR THE HANSE TOWNS. *Salisbury Papers,* xvi. 225; Wilbraham's *Journal,* pp. 67–8; see 29th June and 23rd September.

13th August. THE ARCHBISHOP OF YORK'S LETTER TO LORD CECIL. *Salisbury Papers,* xvi. 220.

14th August. SUNDRY ACCIDENTS. Chamberlain's *Letters,* i. 197. Turner was careless or unfortunate. On 7th February, 1603, he had killed another fencer by a thrust in the eye (see *III Eliz. Journal,* p. 145). In May, 1612, he was shot dead by one of Lord Sanquhar's Scottish followers in revenge for the lost eye; the murderer was subsequently hanged (Chamberlain's *Letters,* i. 348, 362).

19th August. THE PEACE SWORN and THE ARTICLES OF PEACE. Stow, pp. 845–55, where the Treaty is printed in full; it contains in all 34 clauses.

20th August. LORD CECIL PROMOTED. Stow, p. 856.

24th August. JESUITS TO BE BANISHED FROM MÜNSTER. *S.P. Ireland,* pp. 190–1.

26th August. THE SPANISH AMBASSADOR DEPARTS. Stow, p. 846.

29th August. THE ILL-FEELING OF THE STATES. *Salisbury Papers,* xvi. 270–1. Letters from Flushing, dated 23rd.

4th September. THE TREATY AND THE STATES. Winwood's *Memorials,* ii. 29–30.

7th September. OSTEND. *Penshurst Papers,* ii. 131.

12th September. THE PLANTATION OF GUIANA. Purchas, xvi. 309–23.

17th September. OSTEND TAKEN. Winwood's *Memorials,* ii. 29.

21st September. THE KING VISITS ETON. *Progresses,* i. 457.

23rd September. THE COMMISSIONERS FOR THE HANSE TOWNS. *Salisbury Papers,* xvi. 316, 317; Wilbraham's *Journal,* p. 68; Stow's *Survey of London,* edited by C. L. Kingsford, i. 232; *II Eliz. Journal,* p. 249. See 12th August and 29th June.

25th September. A COLOUR NAMED AFTER THE ARCHDUCHESS ISABELLA. I do not know a source for this famous yarn earlier than D'Israeli's *Curiosities of Literature,* but it would be a pity to omit it! The *Oxford English Dictionary* however denies the origin, and Miss M. C. Linthicum (in *Costume in Elizabethan Drama*) claims that *Isabella* was used for yellow, and as early as 1593. The story is thus not authentic, but not necessarily not genuine; the protesting reader can delete it.

30th September. COURT NEWS. Winwood's *Memorials,* ii. 32–3.

2nd October. A BOOK OF PASCALE TRANSLATED. *S.T.C.,* 19446, dated in the epistle to the Reader. Though not exciting, the book reflects the growing feeling of discontent.

3rd October. COURT NEWS. *Progresses,* i. 457–8.

8th October. THE DUKE CHARLES. *Progresses,* i. 459–60; Carey's *Memoirs.*

10th October. A COUNTERBLAST TO TOBACCO. *S.T.C.,* 14363. The date of the book's appearance is uncertain, but perhaps timed for the tax imposed on 17th October.

15th October. A NEW LORD DEPUTY FOR IRELAND. *S.P. Ireland,* pp. 204–5.

ENGLISH SHIPS NOT TO BE SOLD. *Proclamations,* 43.

16th October. A BETROTHAL AT COURT. Lodge's *Illustrations,* iii. 100. Marriages, especially in noble families, were seldom arranged in this direct way between the parties chiefly concerned.

17th October. A TAX ON TOBACCO. Rymer's *Foedera,* 1715, xvi. 601.

23rd October. COMPLAINTS AGAINST THE STATES. Winwood's *Memorials,* ii. 33, 34.

24th October. THE KING'S NEW STYLE. Stow, p. 856.

28th October. THE SERMON AT COURT. *S.R.,* iii. 276. *S.T.C.,* 12059, Entered 26th November.

30th October. A TAX ON PLAYS PROPOSED. *Salisbury Papers,* xvi. 339.

1st November. THE MOOR OF VENICE. *Eliz. Stage,* iv. 171.

7th November. THE KING'S HOUND. Lodge's *Illustrations,* iii. 108.

10th November. THE ORDER FOR THE NEW TRANSLATION OF THE BIBLE and THE RULES TO BE OBSERVED. Printed in the Introduction by A. W. Pollard, to the Facsimile of the Authorized version of 1611 published in 1911, pp. 27–30.

MASTER CAMDEN'S 'REMAINS.' *S.R.,* iii. 275; *S.T.C.,* 4521.

14th November. THE DUKE OF HOLST IN LONDON. Lodge's *Illustrations,* iii. 106.

26th November. COURT NEWS. *Salisbury Papers,* xvi. 366.

30th November. THE TRUE COPY OF HAMLET PRINTED. *S.T.C.,* 22276. As some of the few copies of this quarto are dated 1604 and others 1605, presumably it appeared towards the end of the year.

5th December. COURT NEWS. Lodge's *Illustrations,* iii. 247, 240.

8th December. AGREEMENT CONCERNING THE UNION. Winwood's *Memorials,* ii. 37–8.

DISAPPOINTMENTS OF THE PEACE. Winwood's *Memorials,* ii. 38.

10th December. BORDER FEUDS. *Salisbury Papers,* xvi. 376. Letter from Berwick dated 4th December.

11th December. A QUARREL AT COURT. *Salisbury Papers,* xvi. 391.

12th December. COURT NEWS. Winwood's *Memorials,* ii. 36.

13th December. COURT NEWS. Chamberlain's *Letters,* i. 198; Winwood's *Memorials,* ii. 39–40. Lady Elizabeth Hatton (née Cecil) had married Sir Edward Coke, the Attorney-General, in 1598, and her scandalous treatment of him provided gossips with never ending delight.

17th December. THE COUNCIL'S PROTEST TO THE KING. *Salisbury Papers*, xvi. 388.

18th December. A PLAY OF THE GOWRY CONSPIRACY. Chamberlain's *Letters*, p. 199.

20th December. 'WESTWARD HO.' *Eliz. Stage*, iii. 295.

21st December. THE FRENCH KING'S MISTRESS. Winwood's *Memorials*, ii. 42. See *III Eliz. Journal*, pp. 81–2.

23rd December. PAPISTS IN THE NORTH. Strype's *Whitgift*, Appendix, bk. iv. no. 1; Winwood's *Memorials*, ii. 40. Cecil replied pompously refuting the criticism and complaining that the Archbishop has 'so indiscreet clerks as they are like to make my letters as common as they have made your own.' [Strype's *Annals* Appendix, no. ccxc].

24th December. PARLIAMENT AGAIN PROROGUED. *Proclamations*, 47; Winwood's *Memorials*, ii. 45.

THE BISHOP OF LONDON INSTALLED. Stow, p. 856.

28th December. A MARRIAGE AT COURT. Winwood's *Memorials*, ii. 43.

30th December. A DISORDER IN DUBLIN. *S.P. Ireland*, pp. 214–15.

31st December. THE YEAR'S MORTALITY IN LONDON. Stow, p. 857.

OTHER BOOKS PRINTED IN THE YEAR 1604

A DISCOURSE OF CLIMACTERICAL YEARS. *S.T.C.*, 26040. Queen Elizabeth's climacterical periods were much noted, and her death in her 70th year confirmed the belief. See *II Eliz. Journal*, p. 86.

THE UNMASKING OF A FEMALE MACHIAVEL. *S.T.C.*, 584. The poem is obviously personal, but in spite of Rowland's backing, somewhat dull. Except for drama, the period covered by this *Jacobean Journal* was lean in works of literary art.

GRIMELLO'S FORTUNES. *S.T.C.*, 3657. By Nicholas Breton.

A BOOK OF JESTS. *S.T.C.*, 19451. The collection is up to the usual standard of merry tales.

AN APOLOGY OF THE BROWNISTS. *S.T.C.*, 238.

TWO TREATISES BY WILLIAM BRADSHAW THE PURITAN. *S.T.C.*, 3528, 3526. Bradshaw differs conspicuously from his theological contemporaries. His arguments are based on sound common sense, and dispense with a multitude of references, and authorities, theological jargon and other scholarly lumber. See also p. 259.

2nd January. HOLIDAYS AT COURT. Winwood, ii. 43. Nichols in his *Progresses of Queen Elizabeth* records the presents exchanged at the New Year festivities. In later years under King James the practice was resumed at Court.

4th January. NEW KNIGHTS OF THE BATH. Stow, p. 856.

MASTER SAMUEL DANIEL IN TROUBLE. *Eliz. Stage,* iii. 275–6; *Apology to Philotas*; S.R., iii. 277; *Salisbury Papers,* xviii. 185. The play was entered on 29th November, 1604, but the letter to Cecil is endorsed 1605. It petitions 'my Lord of Northumberland and you (seeing the time will yield me no comfort, and that my studies, my faculties, are unnecessary compliments of the season) to bestow some small *viaticum* to carry me from the world.' It seems clear also from the letter that the offence was caused chiefly by the publication of the book, which probably appeared about the same time as the performance. The incident may therefore be dated Christmas, 1604–5.

5th January. THE KNIGHTS OF THE BATH. Stow, p. 856.

6th January. SOLEMNITIES AT COURT. Winwood's *Memorials,* ii. 43; Ben Jonson's *Masque of Blackness.* The original designs for the masque are in the collection of the Duke of Devonshire at Chatsworth. Many are reproduced in *Designs by Inigo Jones for Masques and Plays at Court,* Malone Society, 1924.

9th January. THE PLAYERS AT COURT. *Eliz. Stage,* iv. 171–2.

RELUCTANCY AT CAMBRIDGE. *Salisbury Papers,* xvii. 9.

10th January. COURT NEWS. Chamberlain's *Letters* i. 201; the letter is dated the 26th but the news is mostly a fortnight old.

11th January. A TREATISE OF SPECTRES. S.R., iii. 279. S.T.C., 15448.

14th January. 'THE POOR MAN'S PASSIONS.' S.R., iii. 280; *S.T.C.,* 25093. Although second-rate, this poem is worth the attention of editors of texts for the number of half-echoes.

16th January. THE KING AND THE BISHOP OF PETERBOROUGH. *Salisbury Papers,* xvii. 15.

THE LEVANT MERCHANTS AND THE KING. *Salisbury Papers,* xvii. 16.

20th January. THE KING AND A PROPHET. *Salisbury Papers,* xvii. 23, 33.

26th January. THE PROPHECIES IN HUNTINGDON. *Salisbury Papers,* xvii. 36.

28th January. MR. EGERTON THE PREACHER. Manningham's *Diary,* pp. 74, 101; *Salisbury Papers,* xvii. 38.

10th February. THE KING AND THE PAPISTS. Chamberlain's *Letters,* i. 204.

12th February. 'THE MERCHANT OF VENICE.' *Eliz. Stage,* iv. 172.

13th February. THE LORD CHANCELLOR'S CHARGE. Hawarde, p. 186.

16th February. PURITANS SUPPRESSED. Chamberlain's *Letters,* i. 203–4. Winwood's *Memorials,* ii. 48.

23rd February. A SAUCY MINISTER. *Salisbury Papers,* xvii. 65.

25th February. THE KING AND THE ARCHBISHOP OF YORK. Lodge's *Illustrations,* iii. 131.

1st March. A PROCLAMATION TO RECALL MARINERS FROM FOREIGN SERVICE. *Proclamations,* 51.

A PROCLAMATION FOR BUILDINGS IN AND ABOUT LONDON. *Proclamations,* 52.

3rd March. THE KING'S HEALTH. Lodge's *Illustrations,* iii. 137.

6th March. THE PURITAN BYWATER. *Salisbury Papers,* xvii. 85, 108.

10th March. COURT NEWS: MANY ROBBERIES. Winwood's *Memorials,* ii. 50, 52.

12th March. ANOTHER LION'S WHELP. Stow, p. 857.

21st March. THE DEPARTURE OF THE LORD ADMIRAL FOR SPAIN. S.T.C., 24268.

A BOOK ABOUT THE ENGLISH NATION. S.R., iii. 285; S.T.C., 21361. Printed in Amsterdam and dated 7th February, 1605, *stili novo;* entered S.R. 21st March. For affectation in talk, see also Nixon's *Black Year* (p. 304), and Lodge's *Wit's Misery (II Eliz. Journal,* p. 150).

23rd March. A LIBEL AGAINST THE LATE ARCHBISHOP. Hawarde, p. 223.

25th March. A CHARITABLE ACT. Stow, p. 862. Approximate date. The handbell is still shown in the Church.

26th March. THE EMBASSY FOR SPAIN. S.T.C., 24268.

28th March. COURT NEWS, and THE IMPUDENCY OF THE PLAYERS. Winwood's *Memorials,* ii. 54.

31st March. THE POPE DEAD. Stow, p. 862. *Penshurst Papers,* ii. 156.

4th April. THE HOLLANDERS' DISCONTENT. Winwood's *Memorials,* ii. 55. Letter dated 31st March; for the proclamation see 1st March.

6th April. COURT NEWS. Winwood's *Memorials,* ii. 56, 57. This Master William Herrick was Robert Herrick's prudent and rich uncle and guardian, to whom he was apprenticed some 18 months later. The poet's father had died by violence in 1592: *I Eliz. Journal,* 180.

THE EMBASSY FOR SPAIN. S.T.C., 24268.

8th April. THE DEATH OF JOHN STOW. Stow, p. 811. Stow's most worthy and painstaking efforts were not universally appreciated by his contemporaries. The most slashing attack on antiquaries and chroniclers in general—' that write of nothing but of Mayors and Sheriffs and the dear year and the great Frost'—was in Nashe's *Piers Penniless.*

'More than ten Holinsheds or Halls or Stows,
Of trivial household trash he knows——'

sneers Donne of his unendurable informer. After his death the *Annals* were continued by Edward Howes, who was less accurate but not less voluminous.

13th April. A STRANGE CASE OF A SLEEPING PREACHER. *Salisbury Papers*, xvii. 136.

TROUBLE AT CAMBRIDGE. *Salisbury Papers*, xvii. 137.

14th April. A SUPPLY SHIP FOR GUIANA. Purchas, xvi. 324.

15th April. THE SPANISH AMBASSADOR INSULTED. Lodge's *Illustrations*, iii. 147.

19th April. THE EMBASSAGE TO THE ARCHDUKE. Stow, p. 861.

A DEPUTY PURVEYOR'S MISCONDUCT. Hawarde, p. 193.

MEASURES AGAINST RECUSANTS IN THE NORTH. *Salisbury Papers*, xvii. 143–4.

20th April. THE DEATH OF THE POPE. Stow, p. 862; *Penshurst Papers*, ii. 156.

23rd April. THE GARTER FEAST. Stow, p. 863.

27th April. THE SLEEPING PREACHER. Lodge's *Illustrations*, iii. 153.

28th April. A CUCKOO IN PAUL'S. Chamberlain's *Letters*, i. 206.

29th April. THE SLEEPING PREACHER'S CONFESSIONS. Lodge's *Illustrations*, iii. 157.

1st May. SIR ROBERT DUDLEY'S CASE. Hawarde, p. 198. The editor of *Salisbury Papers*, vol. xvii. p. 142, gives the following note on this very famous case: 'The proceedings connected with the legitimacy claim of Robert Dudley, son of Leciester, and Lady Sheffield Douglas were as follows: (1) 20 May 1603 a commission for the examination of witnesses was procured from the Court of Audience of Canterbury. This was executed *ex parte* and quietly at Stoneleigh, the seat of Sir Thomas Leigh, Dudley's father-in-law. (2) 27th Sept. 1603, collusive proceedings were taken in the Consistory Court of Lichfield. (3) 10 Oct. 1603 the Privy Council issued a mandate to quash these proceedings and to compel the claimant to begin afresh in one of the higher Ecclesiastical Courts. (4) 10 Feb. 1603–4 Leicester's widow filed a bill in the Star Chamber against Dudley *et al.* for conspiracy and defamation. (5) The judgment of the Star Chamber was delivered on 10th May 1605 after an examination of over 150 witnesses. Dudley's chief witnesses were fined and declared for ever suspect as witnesses and fines were inflicted on Sir William Leighton and the Judge of the Consistory Court of Lichfield. The judgment thus pronounced bore only upon the prior proceedings. It did not touch the legitimacy claim itself save by implication. But Dudley abandoned all further proceedings. Copies of all the depositions &c. are . . . at Penshurst and . . . Longleat.' See later, pp. 202, 203. A 'knight of the post' was a professional perjurer.

4th May. NEW PEERS CREATED. Stow, p. 863; Winwood's *Memorials*, ii. 59.

5th May. THE LADY MARY CHRISTENED. Stow, p. 863. A 'voidy' is a tray.

6th May. RECUSANTS IN THE NORTH. *Salisbury Papers*, xvii. 192–4.

8th May. SIR ROBERT DUDLEY'S CASE. Hawarde, p. 205.

A Play of King Leir. *S.R.*, iii. 289. For Shakespeare's *Lear*, see p. 349.

10*th May.* Sir Robert Dudley's Case Concluded. Hawarde, p. 209. See also pp. 208, 211, 213, 234.

14*th May.* The Archbishop's Libeller Punished. Hawarde, p. 222. Salisbury in his speech commenting on some of the words of the libel, (see p. 122), and especially 'Old Virgin's Spectacle,' said that it was no vice to be an old virgin and wear spectacles, from which it would appear that Queen Elizabeth wore them. Pickering afterwards denied some of the charges and claimed to have rendered the King considerable service at his coming in: see page 6 and *Salisbury Papers*, xvii. 620–1.

15*th May.* A Project for Virginia. Purchas, xviii. 298; *The General History of Virginia, &c.* in *The Travels and Works of Captain John Smith*, edited by E. Arber and A. G. Bradley, ii. 384. This is no definite date for this entry, but in the *General History* it is noted that it was a year before the patent was granted [see 10th April, 1606]. The project was evidently attracting considerable notice during 1605 as can be seen from the contemptuous guying of would-be colonists in *Eastward Ho* [see p. 230], and the remarks of Sir Arthur Chichester p. 236.

19*th May.* The Queen Churched. Stow, p. 864.

20*th May.* The Earl of Hertford Returns. Stow, p. 861–2; *Salisbury Papers*, xvii. 172–4.

23*rd May.* A Commotion of the Papists in Herefordshire. *S.T.C.*, 25232. A printed account dated 29th June and entered 16th July.

1*st June.* The Duke Ulric Departs. Stow, p. 864.

3*rd June.* The King and the Lions. Stow, p. 865.

5*th June.* A New Pope Chosen. Stow, p. 862.

7*th June.* Sir Robert Dudley's Case. Lodge's *Illustrations*, iii. 163.

English Pirates. *Salisbury Papers*, xvii. 243.

8*th June.* The Soul's Immortal Crown, *S.R.* iii. 292; *S.T.C.* 3701.

9*th June.* The King and the Late Riots. *Salisbury Papers*, xvii. 254.

The French King's Escape. Quoted in *The Court of King James I.* By Dr. Godfrey Goodman. Edited by J. S. Brewer, 1839, ii. 98.

15*th June.* The Case of Thomas Douglas. Stow, p. 865.

20*th June.* The Lord Chancellor's Charge in the Star Chamber. *S.T.C.*, 25232.

26*th June.* The Dutch Courtesan. *S.R.*, iii. 293. *S.T.C.*, 17475.

27*th June.* Thomas Douglas Quartered. Stow, p. 865.

28*th June.* A Fierce Affray at Dover. Winwood's *Memorials*, ii. 81, 82.

1*st July.* An Ambassador from the Emperor. Stow, p. 870.

Sir Robert Dudley. J. T. Leader, *Life of Sir Robert Dudley*, 1895, pp. 46–50; *D.N.B.*; *Salisbury Papers*, xvii. 297–8. The lady was a granddaughter of the Lord Admiral.

4*th July.* A Proclamation Against Toleration in Ireland, *S.P. Ireland*, pp. 301–3.

6th July. A BRAWL AT FLUSHING. *Penshurst Papers*, iii. 173–4.

7th July. A GREAT CONTEMPT OF SCOTTISH MINISTERS. Stow, p. 870.

8th July. THE LORD ADMIRAL'S RETURN. *S.T.C.*, 24268.

11th July. THE EARL OF NOTTINGHAM'S RETURN and AN ACCOUNT OF THE EMBASSY TO SPAIN. *S.T.C.*, 24268. This account is taken mainly from the official description written by Robert Tresswell, Somerset Herald, and 'published by authority.' It was entered on 27th July. To Tresswell's great annoyance another member of the party anticipated him with a rival account, entered on 12th July, which he condemns as full 'of many false and erroneous observations.' The second account [*S.T.C.*, 13857] is called *The Royal Entertainment of the Right Honourable the Earl of Nottingham*; it is less detailed for the most part, but sometimes gives better or supplementary descriptions of some of the entertainments.

13th July. THE EMPEROR'S AMBASSADOR GIVEN AUDIENCE. Stow, p. 870.

16th July. THE PRINCE LODOVIC. Stow, p. 870.

THE COMMOTION AT HEREFORD. *S.R.*, iii. 296. *S.T.C.* 25232. This news pamphlet is in form of a letter dated 3rd August, though entered 16th July. The Earl wrote to Salisbury from Raglan on 5th July.

20th July. AN EXPLORATION OF VIRGINIA. Purchas, xviii. 335.

25th July. THE ARCHPRIEST'S COMMAND TO CATHOLICS. Tierney's Dodd, iv. Appendix, xix. For the Archpriest Blackwell see *III Eliz. Journal, passim.*

28th July. PARLIAMENT AGAIN PROROGUED. Proclamations, 54.

5th August. THE PAUL'S CROSS SERMON. *S.T.C.*, 25232.

JONSON'S 'SEJANUS' PRINTED. *S.R.*, iii. 273, 297; *S.T.C.*, 14782; the Oxford Jonson, iv. 329.

6th August. A SCHOOLMASTER STABBED. Lodge's *Illustrations*, iii. 170.

9th August. STRANGE CRUELTY. Stow, p. 87.

10th August. THE DESPERATE ACTIONS OF SIR JOHN FITZ. *S.R.*, iii. 298, 299, 300. *S.T.C.*, 10930. From a pamphlet called *The Bloody Book*, entered expeditiously on 12th August, and illustrated with woodcuts in two colours, the victims being generously ensanguined. There are two editions of the pamphlet, one in roman, one in black letter: and two ballads were entered.

12th August. MISTRESS SOUTHWELL. *Salisbury Papers*, xxiii. 366.

19th August. SIR WILLIAM WAAD MADE LIEUTENANT OF THE TOWER. *Salisbury Papers*, xvii. 373, 377.

24th August. THE TOWER DITCH. *Salisbury Papers*, xvii. 387, 402.

THE KING'S PROGRESS. *Progresses*, i. 530.

27th August. THE KING'S VISIT TO OXFORD. *Progresses*, i. 530–62.

28th August. THE KING AT OXFORD. *Progresses*, i. 548–50, 533, 535, 550.

THE SPANISH AMBASSADOR'S PASSAGE. *Salisbury Papers*, xvii. 420–1, 394–5, 397.

29th August. THE KING AT OXFORD. *Progresses*, i. 550–3, 534.

30th August. THE KING'S VISIT TO OXFORD. *Progresses*, i. 553–60.

31st August. AN AMBASSADOR FROM DENMARK. Stow, p. 871.

4th September. A PLAY CALLED 'EASTWARD HO.' See note on 15th September.

9th September. LORD ARUNDEL'S GREAT CONTEMPT. *Salisbury Papers*, xvii. 411–12, 415–16, 421–2. The affair caused a great sensation, and references to it are to be found in most collections.

15th September. THE AUTHORS OF 'EASTWARD HO' IMPRISONED. *Eliz. Stage*, iii. 254; F. E. Schelling's edition of the play in the Belles Lettres Series, introduction and pp. 158–64. Chambers is of opinion that it was the publication rather than the performance which caused the trouble; and it may be that—not for the first time—something was added to the printed text 'more than hath been publicly spoken or acted.' The play was entered on 4th September. The first edition exists with and without the offending passage about the Scots (p. 230); another, reset, edition was also published in 1605.

18th September. THE LORD LISLE'S MISUNDERSTANDING. *C.S.P. Venetian*, p. 271.

20th September. SIR THOMAS SMITH'S VOYAGE INTO RUSSIA. Stow, p. 371; *S.R.*, iii. 302; *S.T.C.*, 22869. From an anonymous pamphlet entered 27th September, in part taken from the diary or notes of one of the party, the rest written up in the windy literary manner fashionable at this time. In the preface the writer notes the interest taken in the voyage and adds: 'But I taking the truth from the mouths of divers gentlemen that went in the journey, and having some good notes bestowed on me in writing, wrought them into this body, because neither those should be abused with false reports, nor the voyage receive slander. I have done this without consent either of Sir Thomas himself or of those gentleman my friends that delivered it unto me.'

24th September. A SPANISH FOOL. *Salisbury Papers*, xvii. 431.

27th September. DOGS FOR THE KING'S USE. *Proclamations*, 56.

WITS PILGRIMAGE. *S.R.*, iii. 302; *S.T.C.*, 6344. This is the first considerable collection of sonnets for some years; they are of mediocre quality.

28th September. THE KING OF DENMARK'S AMBASSADOR. Stow, p. 871. See 31st August.

29th September. THE ARCHBISHOP MADE A COUNCILLOR. Stow, p. 871.

A STRANGE PRESENT. *Progresses*, i. 577.

1st October. A STRANGE MIRACLE AT DORT. *S.T.C.*, 14668; date uncertain (and perhaps immaterial).

5th October. SIR ROBERT DUDLEY AND HIS MISTRESS. As for 1st July, p. 49.

10th October. THE KING AND AN IMPOSTOR. *Salisbury Papers*, xvii. 450.

12th October. GENERAL NEWS. Chamberlain's *Letters*, i. 209.

THE STATE OF IRELAND. *S.P. Ireland*, pp. 326–6.

16th October. A PURVEYOR SENTENCED. Chamberlain's *Letters*, i. 211.

20th October. THE KING AND THE QUEEN ENTERTAINED BY SIR WILLIAM POPE. *Progresses,* i. 528–9.

21st October. THE EARL OF CUMBERLAND DYING. *Salisbury Papers,* xvii. He died on the 30th. For some of his exploits see the *Eliz. Journals* [*Index,* 'Clifford, George.']

22nd October. MEANS OF CURTAILING THE KING'S EXPENSES. *Salisbury Papers,* xvii. 463.

23rd October. THE PRIVILEGES OF COUNTESSES, Hawarde, p. 237.

24th October. GENERAL NEWS. Chamberlain's *Letters,* i. 211–12. The rumour about Michelbourne was false; see 11th July, 1606.

29th October. INDIGNATION AT PURVEYORS. *C.S.P. Venetian,* p. 285.

1st November. DANGEROUS RUMOURS. Stow, pp. 876, 877, 880.

THE FRENCH AMBASSADOR. Chamberlain's *Letters,* i. 214; Birch's *James I,* p. 34.

3rd November. THE ADVANCEMENT OF LEARNING. *S.R.,* iii, 128, 129, *S.T.C.,* 1164. The book was entered in two parts on 19th August and 19th September; it appeared between 24th October and 7th November when Chamberlain mentions its appearance [i. 214].

5th November. A MOST HORRIBLE CONSPIRACY DISCOVERED. Stow; pp. 876–80; Jardine; *The Works of King James I,* etc.

6th November. THE POWDER PLOT. Birch's *James I,* p. 37. From a letter of Sir Edward Hoby, which being in diary form, shows how the news came through.

7th November. THE EARL OF NORTHUMBERLAND. As for preceding entry.

9th November. THE KING PROROGUES THE PARLIAMENT. *C.J.,* i. 257; *L.J.,* ii. 357; *S.T.C.,* 14392.

GUNPOWDER PLOT. Chamberlain's *Letters,* i. 213. The long account which Chamberlain gives shows the accuracy of his information and the shrewdness of his judgment.

THE ARCHPRIEST'S LETTER TO CATHOLICS. Tierney's Dodd, iv. Appendix, xix.

NEWS FROM IRELAND; *S.P. Ireland,* p. 340. Letter dated 29th October.

FAWKES' SULLENNESS. Jardine, p. 108.

10th November. THE SERMON AT PAUL'S CROSS. *S.R.,* iii. 307; *S.T.C.,* 1455; entered 11th December. The 'Preacher's Friend' in a preface to the Reader apologizes for the shortcomings of the discourse: 'the *dreadfulness* of the *danger,* the *fresh escape* whereof could not but leave an impression of horror in the Preacher's mind (able to have confounded his *Memory*) who should have been one of the hoisted number.' It is difficult to imagine the universal horror which the plot caused, due partly to the realization of so many that they had themselves so narrowly escaped. Had it succeeded, it would have destroyed at one clap the whole executive of Government. Barlow had previously preached the official Paul's Cross sermon after Essex's execution; see *III Eliz. Journal,* 167.

10th November. THE PLOTTERS TAKEN OR SLAIN. Jardine, pp. 78–89.

11th November. THE EARL OF NORTHUMBERLAND. De Fonblanque, ii. 259, 278.

12th November. MR. FRANCIS TRESHAM ARRESTED. Jardine, p. 97.

13th November. A CASE OF ENCLOSURES. Hawarde, p. 247.

16th November. THE PORTS RE-OPENED. *Salisbury Papers*, xvii. 492.

20th November. A DISCOURSE OF BODIES NATURAL AND POLITIC. *S.R.*, iii. 305; *S.T.C.*, 11188.

21st November. THE LADY RICH DIVORCED. *Gawdy Letters*, p. 164; the letter is dated 26th November [Tuesday] and notes that the divorce was 'upon Friday was sevennight.' Most authorities, basing their views on Peter Heylyn's Life of Archbishop Laud, assume that the divorce was made in 1602 or 1603. See note on 27th December.

22nd November. A SORCERER SENTENCED. Hawarde, p. 249.

25th November. A RIOT IN SOUTHWARK. *Salisbury Papers*, xvii. 511.

27th November. NOBLEMEN SENT TO THE TOWER. Stow, p. 881; De Fonblanque, ii. 272; Birch's *Historical View*, pp. 242–6.

28th November. THE ARCHPRIEST'S SECOND LETTER TO THE CATHOLICS. *Salisbury Papers*, xvii. 518.

5th December. THE PILGRIMAGE OF MAN. *S.R.*, iii. 307; *S.T.C.*, 19919. A curious little book, conventional, homely, and yet with occasional flashes.

THE ROMISH DOCTRINE IN THE CASE OF CONSPIRACY AND REBELLION. *S.R.*, iii. 306; *S.T.C.*, 18184: one of the first of the crop of anti-Catholic pamphlets after the Plot.

9th December. THE DOUBLE P.P. *S.R.*, iii. 307; *S.T.C.*, 6498, by Dekker.

12th December. MY LORD NORTHUMBERLAND. *C.S.P. Venetian*, p. 305.

15th December. RELIGION IN IRELAND. *S.P. Ireland*, pp. 343, 143, 355–6, from various letters, the last dated 5th December.

18th December. BODIN'S COMMONWEALTH. *S.R.*, iii. 224; *S.T.C.*, 3193. Entered 8th January, 1603; Epistle dated 18th December, 1605; book dated 1606.

19th December. A PETITION FROM THE RECUSANTS IN THE PALE. *S.P. Ireland*, pp. 358–72. Received in England, 19th.

21st December. THE LORD MAYOR AND THE TOWER. *Salisbury Papers*, xvii. 558.

23rd December. A POWDER PLOTTER DEAD. Jardine, p. 101–2; Stow, p. 881.

27th December. MY LORD OF DEVONSHIRE'S ILL-ADVISED MARRIAGE. *D.N.B.*; *Lives and Letters of the Earls of Essex*, by W. B. Devereux, ii. 213–15; *Memoirs of the Reign of Queen Elizabeth*, by Thomas Birch, ii. 191–2; *Cyprianus Anglicanus* (or the Life of Archbishop Laud) by P. Heylyn, 1671, pp. 52–4, etc. William Laud, afterwards Archbishop and martyr, records in his diary that he was appointed chaplain on 3rd September, 1603. Under 26th December, 1605, he noted, 'My cross about the Earl of Devon's marriage' (*Works*, iii. 132). He was so greatly distressed by his part in the marriage (for he felt that he had sacrificed principle to ambition) that he ever afterwards regarded St. Stephen's Day as a day of penance, for which he composed a special private prayer. It is a curious comment on conventional morality that this marriage should have caused such scandal, for though the relations between the Earl of Devonshire and Lady Rich were notorious, yet they were everywhere received with high favour. Only in the time of Essex's disgrace Queen Elizabeth had expressed disapproval of his sister's adulteries; but then Penelope Devereux was one of the few women who was not afraid of the old Queen.

OTHER BOOKS PRINTED THIS YEAR 1605

SIR THOMAS BODLEY'S LIBRARY. *S.T.C.*, 14449.

THE HONOUR OF VALOUR. *S.T.C.*, 3660.

THE LONDON PRODIGAL. *S.T.C.*, 22333. It is not known why Nathaniel Butter, the printer, claimed this very poor play as 'By William Shakespeare' unless to cozen the public.

NEWS FROM HELL. *S.T.C.*, 6514. Written in imitation of Nashe's style and abounding in those little topical touches so useful to editors and dictionary makers.

THE OPINION OF THE PURITANS. *S.T.C.*, 3516. Another of Bradshaw's books [see p. 177 and note]; a sane and most important statement of the Puritan case against the Established Church.

TWO BOOKS ABOUT RATSEY THE HIGHWAYMAN. *S.T.C.*, 20753, 20753a; reprinted in the *Shakespeare Association Facsimiles*, No. 10, with an Introduction by S. H. Atkins.

3rd January. THE DEVIL OF THE VAULT. *S.R.*, iii. 308; *S.T.C.*, 12568. Guy Faux was nicknamed 'The Devil of the Vault.'

4th January. A PRESENT FROM THE KING OF SPAIN. Stow, p. 881.

5th January. THE MARRIAGE OF THE EARL OF ESSEX AND MISTRESS FRANCES HOWARD. Birch's *James I*, pp. 42–3. The bridegroom was born on 11th January, 1591; the bride was younger. This was the first scene in the grim grotesque tragedy that led to the ruin of the Earl of Somerset and Frances Howard.

6th January. THE BARRIERS AT COURT. *Progresses*, ii. 24–32; Jonson's Works.

10th January. TWO PLOTTERS TAKEN. Jardine, p. 89.

18th January. THE ESCAPE OF GREENWAY. Jardine, p. 196.

21st January. THE PARLIAMENT CONTINUED. *C.J.*, i. 257.

23rd January. A BILL FOR A THANKSGIVING. *C.J.*, i. 258.

THE SEARCH FOR THE JESUITS. Jardine, p. 203.

24th January. EXTRAORDINARY PUNISHMENTS PROPOSED. *C.J.*, i. 259.

THE COUNCIL'S ADVICE TO THE LORD DEPUTY. *S.P. Ireland*, pp. 389–90.

25th January. TWO JESUITS TAKEN AT HENDLIP. Jardine, p. 205.

A BOOK OF FAULTS. *S.R.*, iii. 312; *S.T.C.*, 20983.

26th January. GREAT FISHES IN THE THAMES. Stow, p. 881. The porpoise was taken on the 19th.

27st January. THE POWDER PLOTTERS ARRAIGNED. Jardine, pp. 115–181.

28th January. SLANDERS ON THE EARL OF SALISBURY. *S.T.C.*, 4895. Winwood's *Memorials*, ii. 192.

29th January. THE ABUSE OF PURVEYORS. Bowyer, pp. 10–11.

30th January. THE ARCHDUKE'S UNFRIENDLY ACTION. Winwood's *Memorials*, ii. 189.

FOUR OF THE PLOTTERS EXECUTED. *S.T.C.*, 784; Jardine, p. 181.

GARNET THE JESUIT AND OLDCORNE APPREHENDED. Jardine, p. 206.

31st January. THE OTHER PLOTTERS EXECUTED AT WESTMINSTER. As for 30th January; Hawarde, p. 257.

2nd February. CERTAIN SURVIVORS FROM THE GUIANA VOYAGE RETURN. Purchas, xvi. 324–37.

3rd February. 'FOUR BOOKS OF OFFICES.' *S.R.*, iii. 313; *S.T.C.*, 1468. Master Barnes after the very varied adventures recorded in *II Eliz. Journal* (pp. 42–3, 271, 279, 290) and more fully in *Thomas Lodge and Some Elizabethans*, edited by C. J. Sisson, 1933 (II. Barnabe Barnes by Mark Eccles), now desired to play Machiavelli, the sage councillor, to his new king: he was again unsuccessful.

5th February. THE ISLE OF GULLS. *S.T.C.*, 6412; Birch's *James I*, i. 60–1.

6th February. RECUSANTS' CHILDREN. *C.J.*, i. 264.

9th February. SEDITIOUS BOOKS PRINTED ABROAD. Winwood's *Memorials*, ii. 195.

10th February. A SUBSIDY PROPOSED. *C.J.*, i. 265.

A STRANGE ACCIDENT. Birch's *James I*, i. 44–5.

FEARS OF THE TURKEY MERCHANTS. Birch's *James I*, i. 59: 45.

11th February. THE KING'S THANKS. *C.J.*, i. 266.

STRANGE NEWS FROM CARLSTADT. *S.T.C.*, 4658. Dated in the Epistle. The pamphlet was translated from the High Dutch and sponsored by Edward Gresham, an almanack maker. The obvious parallels between the pamphlet and the well-known passage in *Lear* (I. ii. 115) were demonstrated in the *Times Literary Supplement*, 30th November, 1933, and 'The Background to *King Lear*,' 28th December, 1935.

12th February. A COMMITTEE OF BOTH HOUSES. Bowyer, pp. 38–45.

THE JESUITS BROUGHT TO LONDON. Jardine, p. 208.

13th February. THE LORD CHANCELLOR'S CHARGE. Hawarde, p. 263.

14th February. GARNET SENT TO THE TOWER. Jardine, p. 210.

17th February. THE PARLIAMENT. *C.J.*, i. 269.

23rd February. THE IRISH RECUSANTS. *S.P. Ireland*, pp. 401–2. Letter dated c. 13th February.

26th February. THE PRECEDENCE OF OXFORD. *C.J.*, i. 275. The comparative antiquity of the two ancient Universities occasioned much hard lying on either side; see *III Eliz. Journal*, p. 129.

2nd March. THE DEATH OF OWEN. Jardine, p. 214.

4th March. GARNET'S CONVERSATIONS OVERHEARD. Jardine, pp. 215–226.

6th March. THE WRETCHED STATE OF IRELAND. *S.P. Ireland*, pp. 406–7.

9th March. SIR EDWARD CLEVE BEFORE THE COUNCIL. Wilbraham's *Journal*, p. 78.

10th March. A DISCOURSE OF CIVIL LIFE. *S.R.*, iii. 316; *S.T.C.*, 3958–9.

12th March. NOBODY AND SOMEBODY. *S.R.*, iii. 316. *S.T.C.*, 18597. The character of 'Nobody' as a sympathetic person is quite cleverly sustained. He is illustrated in the woodcut as described on p. 41.

17th March. 'THE WONDER OF WOMEN.' *S.R.*, iii. 316; *S.T.C.*, 17488.

20th March. JONSON'S NEW COMEDY. *S.T.C.*, 14783. The Oxford Jonson, vol. ii. 49. A clear reference to the porpoise and the whale (see p. 267), Parrot's epigram (see p. 341), and Jonson's remark in the Folio that 'This comedy was first acted in the year 1605' show that it was played between the end of January and the 25th March, 1605–6.

22nd March. AN ALARMING RUMOUR. Stow, p. 882; Chamberlain's *Letters*, i. 223. There are many mentions of this sensational affair. Cynics whispered that the rumour was manufactured to ease any difficulties over the granting of the subsidies; but it is doubtful whether the art of propaganda, though well understood, had been developed so elaborately.

23rd March. THE GENERAL REJOICING. Chamberlain's *Letters*, i. 223; *C.J.*, i. 288.

24th March. THE KING'S ACCESSION DAY. Chamberlain's *Letters*, i. 217–18.

25th March. THE SUBSIDY. *C.J.*, i. 289.

28th March. THE TRIAL OF GARNET. Jardine, pp. 238–311, Chamberlain's *Letters*, i. 220–2.

30th March. GREAT WINDS. Stow, p. 883.

1st April. GARNET'S DECLARATION IN THE TOWER. Jardine, pp. 319, 317.

4th April. THE DEATH OF THE EARL OF DEVONSHIRE. Chamberlain's *Letters*, i. 226.

THE CHARACTER OF THE EARL OF DEVONSHIRE. Moryson, ii. 260–71, iii. 337.

7th April. THE EARL OF LINCOLN'S FOUL ACTION. As for 10th July, 1604, p. 267.

10th April. A PATENT FOR VIRGINIA. Purchas, xviii. 399–403.

THE GREAT WIND. Stow, p. 883. See *ante* 30th March. *Penshurst Papers*, iii. 256.

A BOOK ON BEAUTY. *S.R.*, iii. 315; *S.T.C.*, 4103. Entered 1st March; dated 10th April in the Epistle. The book is more interesting for the problems themselves than for their solutions.

12th April. AN ORDER FOR FLAGS UPON SHIPS. *Proclamations*, 63.

14th April. THE PARLIAMENT. *C.J.*, i. 298.

IRISH STIRS. *S.P. Ireland*, p. 438. Letters dated 29th March and 4th April.

18th April. THE NORTH-WEST PASSAGE. Purchas, xiv. 353.

24th April. THE WEST INDIAN VOYAGE. *C.S.P. Venetian*, 341, 344.

1st May. GARNET'S EXECUTION POSTPONED. Jardine, p. 334.

3rd May. THE EXECUTION OF GARNET. *S.T.C.*, 11618. Jardine, pp. 337–44. Fuller's *Church History*, bk. x.

7th May. THE SHIPS FROM THE EAST INDIES RETURN. Purchas, ii. 496–502. The profits of the Adventurers in the first two voyages of the East India Company came to about 95 per cent. on the original outlay.

THE FACTORY AT BANTAM IN JAVA. Purchas, ii. 438–96.

9th May. 'THE BLACK YEAR.' *S.R.*, iii. 321; *S.T.C.*, 18582. Another example of the peculiar gloom of this year. Nixon's comment on verbal affectation is what critics in their jargon call 'some aspects of the meta-physical movement.'

10*th May.* SIR FRANCIS BACON MARRIED. Spedding's *Bacon*, iii. 291.

14*th May.* THE LADY RUSSELL'S CLAMOROUS SPEECHES. Haywarde, p. 271.

20*th May.* JESUITS' TALES OF GARNET AND OLDCORNE. Jardine, p. 345.

25*th May.* AN OFFENSIVE SERMON. *Salisbury Papers*, xvii. 224.

26*th May.* THE COMMONS' INDIGNATION. *C.J.*, i. 313; *Salisbury Papers*, xvii. 224.

A PAPISTICAL PARRICIDE. *S.R.*, iii. 322; *S.T.C.*, 5441.

27*th May.* THE COMMONS AND THE PREACHER and PARLIAMENT PROROGUED. *C.J.*, i. 314; *Salisbury Papers*, xvii. 224.

A NOTE OF THE CHIEF STATUTES ENACTED IN THE LATE SESSION OF PARLIAMENT. *Statutes of the Realm, Anno III Jacobi Regis.*

30*th May.* A STRANGE CASE CONCERNING A CORPSE. Hawarde, p. 282.

1*st June.* COMPLAINTS AGAINST THE SPANIARDS. Winwood's *Memorials*, ii. 217.

3*rd June.* THE LORDS STOURTON AND MORDAUNT IN THE STAR CHAMBER. Stow, p. 883; Hawarde, pp. 287–92.

7*th June.* THE DEBTS OF THE UNITED PROVINCES. Winwood's *Memorials*, ii. 217.

10*th June.* A PROCLAMATION AGAINST PAPIST PRIESTS. *Proclamations*, 65.

15*th June.* A TREATISE OF POLICY AND RELIGION. *S.T.C.*, 11017. Printed at Douay; dated 31st October, 1605, in the Epistle; imprimatur dated 10th April. Approximate date of English circulation.

21*st June.* 'SIR PHILIP SIDNEY'S OURANIA.' *S.R.*, iii. 329; *S.T.C.*, 1598. A rare book, little known, but full of curiosities. This brief survey of all knowledge is set in the framework of a pastoral story.

22*nd June.* THE QUEEN DELIVERED. Stow, p. 883.

23*rd June.* THE EARL OF NORTHUMBERLAND. Chamberlain's *Letters*, i. 228.

THE LADY SOPHIA DEAD. Stow, p. 883.

26*th June.* THE LADY SOPHIA BURIED. Stow, p. 883.

27*th June.* THE EARL OF NORTHUMBERLAND CONDEMNED IN THE STAR CHAMBER. Stow, p. 884; Hawarde, pp. 292–9. This was Coke's last appearance as public prosecutor. Three days later he was elevated to be Lord Chief Justice of the Common Pleas. Northumberland remained a prisoner till 1621. He was hardly treated, but not well loved by the Salisbury clique. He was supremely conscious of the merits of the old nobility, and of the shortcomings of the new, haughty, quick-tempered, very frank in expressing his opinions, and handicapped by deafness. Though most of the charges were unimportant, the neglect to tender the oath to Percy was serious, for at this time every official from the scavenger upwards took an oath on entering office. Neglect of duty was thus an offence against God as well as man. The tendering of the oath was, however, a matter of administrative routine for which the Lieutenant was responsible. For the Gentlemen Pensioners, see p. 7.

30th June. STRANGE NEWS FROM VENICE. *S.T.C.,* 24585. Dated Venice 1st June. This year was full of terrors.

3rd July. THE EARL OF NORTHUMBERLAND. De Fonblanque, ii. 280–2.

4th July. 'THE NINE ENGLISH WORTHIES.' *S.R.,* iii. 315; *S.T.C.,* 11087. Entered 5th February; dated 4th July in the Epistle. Each Worthy is given his portrait; there is some attempt to give a likeness to Prince Henry and Henry VIII, but the others are entirely imaginary. A sycophant work.

9th July. A PLOT AGAINST THE KING. Winwood's *Memorials,* ii. 246.

10th July. THE FRENCH KING AND HIS MISTRESS. Chamberlain's *Letters,* i. 231; see *ante* p. 172.

11th July. THE RETURN OF SIR EDWARD MICHELBORNE'S SHIPS. Purchas, ii. 347. Captain Davis was pilot in the first East Indian voyage; see p. 60.

13th July (Sunday). GENERAL NEWS. Chamberlain's *Letters,* i. 231.

14th July. THE KING. Chamberlain's *Letters,* i. 230.

16th July. A MONSTROUS MURDER. Stow, p. 884.

NEWS FROM BARTHOLOMEW FAIR. *S.R.,* iii. 326; *S.T.C.,* 2526. Although not very amusing, this poem is interesting as a very rare example of Skeltonic verse in the seventeenth century. The list of the ale-houses is worth recording.

17th July. THE KING OF DENMARK'S COMING. Stow, p. 885.

18th July. THE MEETING OF THE TWO KINGS. *Progresses,* ii. 53.

20th July. THE DANISH KING. The account of the Danish King's visit is given in the full and elaborate news pamphlets of Henry Roberts, *The most royal and honourable entertainment of . . . King Christian the Fourth* and *England's Farewell to Christian the Fourth* [*S.T.C.,* 21085 and 21079]. Both are fully reprinted in *Progresses* ii. 54–85. Further details are given in Stow, pp. 885–88. [References to Stow are sometimes complicated by the casual pagination. Here the pages are numbered successively 884, 885, 889, 888, 889, 890, 890, 891, 891, 892, 893, 894, 895, 898, 897, 890, 900, 901, 991 etc.].

21st July. THE DANISH KING. As for 20th July.

24th July. THE KINGS ENTERTAINED BY THE EARL OF SALISBURY. As for 20th July.

28th July. THE KINGS AT THEOBALD'S. *Nugae Antiquae,* i. 348.

31st July. THE KINGS ENTERTAINED IN THE CITY. As for 20th July.

1st August. THE KING OF DENMARK. As for 20th July.

2nd August. THE KING OF DENMARK. As for 20th July.

3rd August. THE QUEEN CHURCHED. As for 20th July.

4th August. TILTING AT COURT. As for 20th July.

5th August. THANKSGIVING DAY AT COURT. As for 20th July.

A Most Cruel and Bloody Murder. *S.R.*, iii. 143; *S.T.C.*, 6552, 6553.

Two Witches Hanged. *S.T.C.*, 6552.

6th August. The King of Denmark. As for 20th July.

7th August. The King of Denmark Admitted to the Order. As for 20th July.

10th August. The King of Denmark. As for 20th July.

11th August. The King of Denmark's Departure. As for 20th July.

16th August. The King of Denmark's Footprint, Stow, p. 889

22nd August. A Conference with the Spanish Ambassador. Winwood's *Memorials*, ii. 249.

The Great Turk's Letters. *S.R.*, iii. 328; *S.T.C.*, 207.

14th September. The Earl of Northumberland and the King. De Fonblanque, ii. 283.

15th September. The Countess of Northumberland and Lord Salisbury. De Fonblanque, ii. 293–4.

19th September. Garnet's Miraculous Straw. Fuller's *Church History*, x.; Jardine, pp. 345–54.

22nd September. The Lord Deputy's Journey. *S.P. Ireland*, pp. 558–66. Letter dated 12th September.

24th September. The Return of the 'Hopewell.' Purchas, xiv. 353–65.

25th September. The Prince of Vaudmont in London. Stow, p. 888.

28th September. The Sermon at Hampton Court. *S.T.C.*, 615.

1st October. The Decayed State of the Soldiers in Ireland. *S.P. Ireland*, pp. 576–83. Letter dated 21st September.

2nd October. Sir Robert Drury's Passport. *Penshurst Papers*, iii. 205.

5th October. The Young Lord Cranborne. Chamberlain's *Letters*, i. 232.

6th October. 'The Seven Deadly Sins of London.' *S.R.*, iii. 330; *S.T.C.*, 6522.

10th October. The Miraculous Straw. Fuller's *Church History*, bk. x.; see p. 337; Jardine, pp. 345–54.

17th October. 'The Mouse-Trap.' *S.R.*, iii. 331; *S.T.C.*, 19334.

22nd October. An Unfortunate Astrologer. *Life and Letters of Sir Henry Wotton*. Edited by L. Pearsall Smith, 1907, i. 364. From Venice, 22nd Sept., N.S.

23rd October. The Art of Drawing and Painting. *S.R.*, iii. 331; *S.T.C.*, 19500. This is the first instance that I have met of a sense of historical accuracy in art, though Ben Jonson in *Sejanus* had been most particular to get the details of his Roman ceremonial correct.

28th October. The French King's Children Baptize'd. Stow, p. 809.

29th October. The City Pageant. *S.T.C.*, 18279.

3rd November. 'Choice, Chance and Change.' *S.R.*, iii. 331; *S.T.C.*, 5142. A good example of a type of verbal wit that had now grown musty.

7th November. THE LADY RUSSELL'S CASE. Hawarde, pp. 278, 309. See also p. 305.

8th November. A DRUNKEN FROLIC. Hawarde, p. 315.

10th November. GENERAL NEWS. Chamberlain's *Letters*, i. 238.

15th November. A MURDER TWENTY-FIVE YEARS CONCEALED. *S.T.C.*, 4768.

18th November. THE THIRD SESSION OF THE PARLIAMENT. *C.J.*, i. 314–5.

20th November. CAPTAIN LOVELACE'S MISFORTUNE. *Penshurst Papers*, ii. 329–30.

29th November. A COMMITTEE TO CONSIDER THE UNION. Bowyer, 158–9.

THE RIOTOUS YOUNG GENTLEMEN. Hawarde, p. 316.

30th November. JOHN LYLY DEAD. *The Works of John Lyly*, edited by R. Warwick Bond, i. 76; iii. 2.

4th December. MR. HALL'S BOOK OF MEDITATIONS. *S.T.C.*, 12679–84, 12666–70. Both works were very popular and went into at least five editions.

5th December. INSOLENCIES OF THE STATES' SHIPS. Winwood's *Memorials*, i. 277.

16th December. A BILL AGAINST DIVORCE REJECTED. Bowyer, p. 208.

17th December. THE PARLIAMENT ADJOURNED. *C.J.*, i. 331.

19th December. THE PLANTATION OF VIRGINIA. *Travels and Works of John Smith*, edited by E. Arber and A. G. Bradley, ii. 384; i. 93; i. xxxiii; Purchas, xviii. 403.

21st December. THE KING AT WARE. Chamberlain's *Letters*, i. 240.

26th December. A PLAY OF KING LEAR. *Eliz. Stage*, iv. 366. For the many topicalities in *King Lear* which was almost certainly written in the spring of this year, see *Lear* in the *Penguin Shakespeare*, and *The Background to King Lear*, Times Literary Supplement, 28th December 1935.

OTHER BOOKS PRINTED THIS YEAR 1606

THE HISTORY OF GREAT BRITANNY. *S.T.C.*, 5348. Assigned to John Clapham. A sane work, free from the romantic pre-history of Geoffrey of Monmouth.

THE MAPS OF ORTELIUS. *S.T.C.*, 18855. A magnificent tome.

ELIOSTO LIBIDINOSO. *S.T.C.*, 13509. A late survival of genuine euphuistic romance.

A DISCOURSE OF THE EAST INDIES. *S.T.C.*, 22061.

PARASITASTER. *S.R.*, iii. 316. *S.T.C.*, 17483.

DOOMSDAY BOOK. *S.T.C.*, 11576.

INDEX